THE INTERIOR CASTLE

ST. TERESA OF AVILA

STUDY EDITION

THE INTERIOR CASTLE

ST. TERESA OF AVILA

TRANSLATED BY

KIERAN KAVANAUGH, O.C.D.
AND OTILIO RODRIGUEZ, O.C.D.

STUDY EDITION
SECOND EDITION

PREPARED BY KIERAN KAVANAUGH, O.C.D.

ICS Publications
Institute of Carmelite Studies
Washington, D.C.

ICS Publications
2131 Lincoln Road NE
Washington, DC 20002-1199

www.icspublications.org

Cover design by Rose Design
Book design and typesetting by Rose Design

Produced and printed in the United States of America

This edition:
pbk: 978-1-939272-80-5
ebook: 978-1-939272-49-2

The Library of Congress has catalogued the first edition as follows:

Teresa, of Avila, Saint, 1515-1582.
    [Moradas. English]
The interior castle / St. Teresa of Avila ; translated by Kieran Kavanaugh and
Otilio Rodriguez. -- Study ed. / prepared by Kieran Kavanaugh and Carol Lisi.
    p. cm.
Includes bibliographical references and index.
ISBN 978-0-935216-80-6
    1. Spiritual life--Catholic Church--Early works to 1800. I. Kavanaugh, Kieran, 1928- II. Rodríguez, Otilio. III. Lisi, Carol, 1939- IV. Title.
    BX2179.T4M613 2010
    248.4'82--dc22   2010001632

10 9 8 7 6 5 4 3 2 1

ICS Publications dedicates this second edition of *The Interior Castle: Study Edition* to the memory of our beloved former publisher, translator, and author, Father Kieran Kavanaugh, O.C.D. May he rest in peace.

Father Kieran of the Cross, O.C.D.
February 19, 1928 — February 2, 2019

Contents

The Fifth Dwelling Places / 131

The Sixth Dwelling Places / 191

to fear, even though the experience is sublime and the favors are great. 207

Chapter 3 Deals with the same subject and tells of the manner in which God, when pleased, speaks to the soul. Gives counsel about how one should behave in such a matter and not follow one's own opinion. Sets down some signs for discerning when there is deception and when not. This chapter is very beneficial. 219

Chapter 4 Treats of when God suspends the soul in prayer with rapture or ecstasy or transport, which are all the same in my opinion, and how great courage is necessary to receive sublime favors from His Majesty. 237

Chapter 5 Continues on the same subject and deals with a kind of rapture in which God raises up the soul through a flight of the spirit, an experience different from that just explained. Tells why courage is necessary. Explains something about this delightful favor the Lord grants. The chapter is a very beneficial one. 256

Chapter 6 Tells about an effect of the prayer discussed in the previous chapter. How to understand whether this effect is true rather than deceptive. Discusses another favor the Lord grants so that the soul might be occupied in praising him. 268

Chapter 7 Discusses the kind of suffering those souls to whom God grants the favors mentioned feel concerning their sins. Tells what a great mistake it is, however spiritual one may be, not to practice keeping the humanity of our Lord and Savior

Abbreviations

St. Teresa of Ávila

All quotations of St. Teresa of Ávila are taken from the Kieran Kavanaugh, O.C.D., and Otilio Rodriguez, O.C.D., translation of *The Collected Works of St. Teresa of Avila*, 3 vols. (Washington, D.C.: ICS Publications, 1976–1985, 1987, 2012, 2019).

The abbreviations for St. Teresa's works are as follows:

C   *The Constitutions*
F   *The Book of the Foundations*
IC   *The Interior Castle*
L   *The Book of Her Life*
Ltr   *Letters* (same abbreviation for volumes 1 and 2, designating letter number and paragraph)
Sol   *The Soliloquies*
SS   *Meditations on the Song of Songs*
ST   *The Spiritual Testimonies*
W   *The Way of Perfection*

For the *Life*, *Interior Castle*, *Way of Perfection*, and *Foundations*, the first number refers to the chapter, and the second number refers to the paragraph.

Thus, L 3.5 refers to *The Book of Her Life*, chapter 3, paragraph 5.

Regarding *The Interior Castle*, the first number refers to the dwelling place; the second number refers to the chapter, and the third number refers to the paragraph.

Thus, IC 3.4.2 refers to the third dwelling place, chapter 4, paragraph 2.

For *Letters*, Ltr followed by the letter number and paragraph number. There is no mention of volume number, since letters are divided by number/date in the respective two volumes; thus: Ltr 123.4, Ltr 300.5.

Vatican Documents

All quotations from the documents of the Second Vatican Council are taken from Austin Flannery, ed., *The Basic Sixteen Documents of Vatican II* (Northport, N.Y.: Costello Publishing, 1996).

DV *Dei Verbum* (Dogmatic Constitution on Divine Revelation)

GS *Gaudium et Spes* (Pastoral Constitution on the Church in the Modern World)

LG *Lumen Gentium* (Dogmatic Constitution on the Church)

SC *Sacrosanctum Concilium* (Constitution on the Sacred Liturgy)

UR *Unitatis Redintegratio* (Decree on Ecumenism)

All quotations from the *Catechism of the Catholic Church* are taken from *Catechism of the Catholic Church*, 2nd Ed., (Washington, D.C.: United States Conference of Catholic Bishops, 2000).

CCC *Catechism of the Catholic Church*

Preface to the Study Edition

The Interior Castle is more than a book. It is a wonderful image of the mystery of the human person. It is the soul of its author, St. Teresa of Ávila, who journeys through the castle from dwelling place to dwelling place providing us with a unique road map of the Christian spiritual life. It is the last book written by Teresa, who five years before her death left to the best of her knowledge what in her experience she had been praising God for.

It is to be expected that to read a book like this, or better to enter the secret dwelling places of the castle, one would need to have recourse to a guide or expert, to go before us reading slowly, one by one, each chapter of the work. This is what we propose to do in these pages of the present volume. Our only objective is to serve as a kind of springboard of entry into Teresa's pages. For this reason, what we are trying to do is facilitate the reading and comprehension of the *Interior Castle*. Whether or not we succeed, reading Teresa herself is something that cannot be superseded. Thus we give first each chapter, dwelling place by dwelling place. After each chapter comes a chapter review in which the reader can run through the text and note the progress of Teresa's thought and its principal ideas. Each chapter will be placed in the context of the entire work so that Teresa's tendency to digress will be less likely to cause one to lose the thread of her whole thought.

The interpretive notes are the kind one would make in preparing a talk on a particular chapter. What interests us first is any light that Teresa herself might shed on the text in her other writings, which also contain doctrine and experience. In certain matters Teresa has her own lexicon; her terms call for clarification. The historical and social situations in which she found herself are often essential factors in coming to any, or at least a better, understanding of her words. Sometimes the notes and deletions of her censors have influenced the text, and it can be helpful to know what was taking place behind the scenes. Since Teresa had strong desires that her writings be in harmony with Sacred Scripture, we have pointed out some scriptural texts that stand behind or support various ideas of hers. In addition, present-day teachings of the church can show the correctness of Teresa's basic notions, but also advise us how to apply such principles in our times.

Especially valuable in the preparation of this study edition was the book by Tomás Alvarez, *Guia al Interior del Castillo*, published by Monte Carmelo, Burgos, Spain, 2000.

General Introduction

I n *The Way of Perfection*, Teresa assures her readers that the prayer of the Our Father leads to the fount of living waters. She then refers them to her *Life*, the book she had written in which she describes what the soul feels when it drinks this living water, how God satisfies and takes away thirst for earthly things.

Some ten or so years later, after she had labored much and increased the number of her new discalced monasteries to twelve, she was speaking again, on May 28, 1577, for basically the same reasons, of what was contained in her *Life*. But this time the result was the command to write another book since the *Life* was then in the scrupulously cautious hands of the Inquisition. The scene of the fateful incident took place at Toledo at the Carmel founded by Teresa. Father Jerome Gracián, her confessor and also enthusiastic supporter as a Carmelite friar in her reform, has left us his account of the event: "What happened with regard to the book of the *Dwelling Places* is that while I was superior and speaking with her once in Toledo of many things concerning her spirit, she said to me: 'Oh, how well this point was described in the book about my life which is in the Inquisition!' I answered: 'Since we cannot have it, recall what you can and other things and write another book, but put down the doctrine in a general way without naming the one to whom the things you mentioned there happened.' And thus I ordered her to write this book of the *Dwelling Places.*"[1]

Now sixty-two years old, Teresa had for five years been aware of the depth of spiritual life she describes as the ultimate stage of the mystical journey. She had come, then, to an experiential grasp of so much more than what she had written previously in her *Life*. In evidence of this, toward the outset of her *Interior Castle* she admits: "And although in other things I've written the Lord has given me some understanding I know there were certain things I had not understood as I have come to understand them now, especially certain more difficult things."[2]

Business Matters and Poor Health

If from the viewpoint of her own more evolved experience and understanding the command to undertake such a task again seemed well advised, from the standpoint of her physical sufferings and the external problems and trials that were being heaped upon her at this time the mere thought of writing a new book was painful to her. The prologue begins in complaint. Not many things that obedience had asked of her—and obedience had asked many difficult things—were as difficult as the chore of writing at this time yet another book. "I have been experiencing now for three months," she wearily reports, "such great noise and weakness in my head that I've found it a hardship even to write concerning necessary business matters."[3]

1. Antonio De San Joaquin, "Anotaciones al P. Ribera," *Año Teresiano*, 12 vols. (Madrid, 1733–1769), 8:149–50.

2. IC 1.2.7; see also 4.1.1; 4.2.7.

3. IC Prol 1.

In addition to this miserable health, the year was a troublesome and discouraging one; what she had struggled for zealously over the previous fifteen years could now be suppressed by the new authorities. Her work had become the center of a conflict that raged between Madrid and Rome. The jurisdictional complexities became so tangled and the misunderstandings, rivalries, and calumnies so much a part of everyday life that historians today find it difficult to judge objectively.[4]

In 1576 Father Jerónimo Tostado arrived in Spain with the faculties of visitator, reformer, and commissary general of the Spanish provinces and with the responsibility of carrying out the decrees of the order's chapter at Piacenza which had directed that the houses opened in Andalusia against the will of the general be abandoned. The "contemplative," or "primitive," fathers were forbidden to form a province or a congregation separate from the province of Castile. Mother Teresa was not to leave her monastery. The unpleasant rumor was that Tostado had come to quash Teresa's work; and his presence was the cause of considerable disquiet. But the papal nuncio in Spain, Nicolás Ormaneto, who favored Teresa and her foundation, advised Tostado to postpone his visit of Andalusia (where Gracián, under an assignment of the nuncio, was on a mission of reform among the Carmelites there) and to pass instead on to Portugal. In a letter dated September 7, 1576, Teresa thus wrote to María de San José: "But, as God has delivered us from Tostado,

---

4. For a detailed treatment of this whole question, see Efrén de La Madre de Dios and Otger Steggink, *Tiempo y vida de Santa Teresa* (Madrid, Spain: BAC, 1977), 701–805; see also Ildefonso Moriones, *El Carmelo Teresiano* (Vitoria, Spain: Ediciones El Carmen, 1978), 97–180. For a treatment of these questions from a different perspective, see Joachim Smet, *The Carmelites: The Post Tridentine Period*, vol. 2 (Darien, Ill.: Carmelite Spiritual Center, 1976), 1–131.

I hope His Majesty will help us in everything. You are not maligning him in describing how he has worked against the discalced fathers and against me, for he has given clear indications of having done so."[5]

In June of 1577, Ormaneto died, and without the nuncio's favor Teresa's followers now felt lost. With the death of Ormaneto, the mother foundress thought it would be better to return to her monastery of St. Joseph in Ávila and to remain there, "as a kind of prisoner" in accordance with the order of the general definitory.[6] To make matters worse, Ormaneto's successor, Felipe Sega, whose reference to Teresa as a "restless gadabout"[7] at least demonstrated a lack of firsthand information, immediately set out with his new authority to discard the plans of reform sponsored by Ormaneto.

About this time, as well, there appeared a scurrilous pamphlet denouncing Teresa and calumniating Gracián with a number of crimes, some too foolish and lurid to be believed but yet sufficient to arouse at least faint suspicions. Again, in October of 1577, Teresa was once more elected prioress of the Incarnation; she felt nothing but aversion toward taking up again such a responsibility. When this election became known, Tostado unwittingly came to Teresa's rescue and gave orders to annul the valid election. The nuns persisting to vote for Teresa in a second election were duly excommunicated. Though happy to be left in peace, Teresa protested the injustice: "Learned men say that the nuns are not excommunicated and that the friars are acting contrary to the council in

---

5. Ltr 120.2.
6. F 27.20.
7. Ltr 269.3.

confirming a prioress who received an insufficient number of votes. . . . all are stunned to see something like this which offends everyone."[8]

It was while she was in the midst of all these unpleasant and disturbing events that Teresa was engaged in writing her sublime book on prayer. The work was begun, appropriately, on the feast of the Holy Trinity, June 2, 1577. Within little more than a month, she had proceeded as far as the fifth dwelling place. We may suppose this from the copy made in Toledo and ending with chapter two of the fifth dwelling place when Teresa departed for Ávila in mid-July. Already in chapter two of the fourth dwelling place she had alluded to the inconvenience of interruptions: "God help me with what I have undertaken! I've already forgot what I was dealing with, for business matters and poor health have forced me to set this work aside just when I was at my best; and since I have a poor memory everything will come out confused because I can't go back to read it over."[9]

Nothing more was done on the work until the beginning of November, as she asserts at the outset of chapter four of the fifth dwelling place: "About five months have passed since I began, and because my head is in no condition to read over what I've written, everything will have to continue without order, and perhaps some things will be said twice."[10] She completed the remaining large section, more than half the work, by November 29, within less than a month. Thus the actual time spent on this spiritual masterpiece was a mere two months.

---

8. Ltr 211.4–5, October 22, 1577.
9. IC 4.2.1.
10. IC 5.4.1.

Inspiration

Despite her trials and ill health, Teresa held firmly to her belief that "obedience usually lessens the difficulty of things that seem impossible."[11] She prayed when beginning: "May He, in whose mercy I trust and who has helped me in other more difficult things so as to favor me, do this work for me."[12] Her prayer was heard. By the time she had reached the epilogue, her mood was entirely changed: "Although when I began writing this book I am sending you I did so with the aversion I mentioned in the beginning, now that I am finished I admit the work has brought me much happiness, and I consider the labor, though I confess it was small, well spent."[13]

At times she seemed to feel special inspiration, and that a work of such brilliance was brought to a conclusion so quickly is itself extraordinary. In one instance she wrote: "If what I have said up to now about this prayer is worthwhile, I know clearly that I'm not the one who has said it."[14] When she turns to the topic of mystical prayer she prays: "In order to begin to speak of the fourth dwelling places I really need to entrust myself, as I've already done, to the Holy Spirit and beg Him to speak for me from here on that I may say something about the remaining rooms in a way that you will understand."[15] Among those who actually saw Teresa writing this book was María del Nacimiento, who gave the following testimony: "When the said Mother Teresa of Jesus wrote

11. IC Prol 1.
12. IC Prol 1.
13. IC Epil 1.
14. IC 6.4.9.
15. IC 4.1.1; see also 5.4.11.

the book called *The Dwelling Places*, she was in Toledo, and this witness saw that it was after Communion that she wrote this book, and when she wrote she did so very rapidly and with such great beauty in her countenance that this witness was in admiration, and she was so absorbed in what she was writing that even if some noise was made there, it did not hinder her; wherefore this witness understood that in all that which she wrote and during the time she was writing she was in prayer."[16]

The Image of a Castle

The Interior Castle has come to be regarded as Teresa's best synthesis. In it the spiritual doctrine is presented through the unifying outline of seven dwelling places among which there is a division into two sections. The first three groups of dwelling places speak of what is achievable through human efforts and the ordinary help of grace. The remaining four groups deal with the passive, or mystical, elements of the spiritual life. By the term "supernatural prayer" (contemplation), Teresa refers to the whole series of forms and degrees of infused or mystical prayer. By the term "perfect contemplation," she refers only to those pure forms of contemplation found in the fifth, sixth, and seventh dwelling places.

The question has been raised, as one would expect in academics, as to how Teresa conceived the notion of using the castle as a symbol for the interior life. What she reveals leaves room for interpretation: "Today while beseeching our Lord to speak for me because I wasn't able to think of anything to

---

16. Silverio de Santa Teresa, ed., *Biblioteca Mística Carmelitana*, vol. 18 (Burgos, Spain: El Monte Carmelo 1934), 315.

say nor did I know how to begin to carry out this obedience, there came to my mind what I shall now speak about, that which will provide us with a basis to begin with. It is that we consider our soul to be like a castle made entirely out of a diamond or of very clear crystal, in which there are many rooms, just as in heaven there are many dwelling places."[17] Previously, in *The Way of Perfection*, with similar thoughts, Teresa had advised: "Well, let us imagine that within us is an extremely rich palace, built entirely of gold and precious stones; in sum, built for a Lord such as this. . . . Imagine, also, that in this palace dwells this mighty King."[18]

In an interesting account, one of her early biographers, Fr. Diego de Yepes, testifies that Teresa told him that on the eve of Trinity Sunday in 1577, God showed her in a flash the whole book. There was "a most beautiful crystal globe like a castle in which she saw seven dwelling places, and in the seventh, which was in the center, the King of Glory dwelt in the greatest splendor. From there He beautified and illumined all those dwelling places to the outer wall. The inhabitants received more light the nearer they were to the center. Outside of the castle all was darkness, with toads, vipers, and other poisonous vermin. While she was admiring this beauty which the grace of God communicates to souls, the light suddenly disappeared and, although the King of Glory did not leave the castle, the crystal was covered with darkness and was left as ugly as coal and with an unbearable stench, and the poisonous creatures outside the wall were able to get into the castle. Such was the state of a soul in sin."[19] This was told

---

17. IC 1.1.1.

18. W 28.9.

19. *Biblioteca Mística*, 18:276–278.

to Yepes, a former confessor of Teresa's, when she met him by chance one snowy day in an inn in Arévalo either in 1579 or 1580. Yepes also adds with a certain self-satisfaction that "although in the *Book of Her Life* and the *Dwelling Places* she mentions this, she doesn't in either of them communicate this vision as specifically as she did to me."[20] But if this vision came to Teresa in 1577, we are left wondering both how she could have referred to it in her *Life*, written in the 1560s, and about the value of Diego de Yepes' testimony. Nonetheless, Teresa's vague expression "there came to my mind" (*se me ofreció*) does not rule out the possibility of a vision as a basis of her symbol.

As described in her *Life*, she once did receive a mystical vision of God's presence and what it is for a soul to be in mortal sin: "Once while I was reciting with all the sisters the hours of the Divine Office, my soul suddenly became recollected; and it seemed to me to be like a brightly polished mirror, without any part on the back or sides or top or bottom that wasn't totally clear. In its center Christ, our Lord, was shown to me. . . . I was given understanding of what it is for a soul to be in mortal sin. It amounts to clouding this mirror with mist and leaving it black; and thus this Lord cannot be revealed or seen even though He is always present giving us being."[21] Later in the same chapter it seems from her reference that this experience influenced her thinking when she compares the Divinity to a very clear diamond in which everything is visible including sin with all its ugliness.[22]

20. *Biblioteca Mística*, 2:493.
21. L 40.5.
22. See L 40.10.

Whatever the speculation on matters like the above, the point must be made that *The Interior Castle* is principally the fruit of her own experience, and though Teresa makes the effort to hide her identity by referring to this other person she knows, her talents for concealing her identity were abysmally poor.

The Synthesis

Although the outer wall of the castle (the body) is ordinary, it nonetheless may lure the soul's attention from the inner brilliant castle.[23] Inside the castle are many dwelling places, above, below, and to the sides. In other words, the spiritual life that goes on within the castle is a complex matter involving the individual's capacities, the diversity of ways, and differing spiritual depths. The seven stages represent only types and allow for a wide range of variations. In speaking of the seven dwelling places, we must keep in mind that "in each of these there are many others, below and above and to the sides, with lovely gardens and fountains and labyrinths, such delightful things that you would want to be dissolved in praises of the great God who created the soul in His own image and likeness."[24] At the center of the castle is God's dwelling place.

The gate of entry is prayer.[25] Prayer is a door that opens up into the mystery of God and at the same time a means of communing with Him. It actuates the personal relationship with the Lord present in the very depths of the spirit.

---

23. See IC 1.1.2–3.
24. IC Epil 3.
25. See IC 1.1.7.

The first dwelling places. Setting aside those souls outside the castle, paralyzed and crippled, in need of special healing from the Lord Himself if they are to enter,[26] Teresa turns her attention to those who have entered the first area. Little of the glowing light from the King's royal chamber filters into these first dwelling places. Too many things entice and distract souls here and thus prevent them from taking the time to search for the true light. "So, I think, must be the condition of the soul. Even though it may not be in a bad state, it is so involved in worldly things and so absorbed with its possessions, honor, or business affairs, as I have said, that even though as a matter of fact it would want to see and enjoy its beauty these things do not allow it to; nor does it seem that it can slip free from so many impediments."[27] Such people do have some good desires, however; and they even pray on occasion. Their need, as is true of everyone, is for self-knowledge and for knowledge of the beauty of a soul in grace and of the ugliness of one in sin; in a word, for some insight into the Christian mystery of sin and grace. Self-knowledge and humility grow as the soul moves onward through the castle toward the center.

The second dwelling places. Here we have rooms set apart for those who have taken some first steps in the practice of prayer, who are more receptive to the promptings and invitations of Christ's grace which comes especially through external means such as books, sermons, good friendships, and through trials. The struggle with the forces of evil is now more keenly felt, and the time is ripe for the characteristically Teresian determination to persevere convinced that the

---

26. See IC 1.1.6, 8.
27. IC 1.2.14.

spiritual life cannot be grounded on consolations. Conformity with God's will must be the goal of one's strivings.

The third dwelling places. To persevere in prayer and the
struggle involved is to go forward.[28] Those who have come
to this stage begin to long not to offend His Majesty; they
guard against venial sin, are fond of both ascetical practices
and periods of recollection, seek to use their time well, practice charity toward their neighbor, and maintain balance in
the use of speech and dress and in the management of their
household. They are good Christians, and the Lord will not
deny these souls entrance into the final dwelling place if they
so desire.[29] Like the young man in the Gospel, however, they
could turn away upon hearing the requirements for becoming
perfect. Any threat to wealth or honor will quickly uncover
their attachments to these; and they are excessively discreet
about their health—to the point of fearing everything.[30] In
addition to their reluctance to part with wealth and honor,
they have a tendency to be too easily shocked by the faults
of others and quickly distraught by a little dryness.[31] Though
these persons find more consolation in the spiritual life than
they do in material comforts and distractions, they seldom
receive the deeper, more delectable peace and quiet of contemplation except occasionally as an invitation to prepare
better for what lies ahead.[32] They need someone who is free
of the world's illusions with whom they might speak.

Dealing less extensively with these first three dwelling places, Teresa says little about prayer; nor does she give

---

28. See IC 7.4.9.
29. See IC 3.1.5.
30. See IC 3.2.4–5, 7, 8.
31. See IC 3.2.13; 3.1.7.
32. See IC 3.2.9.

advice about methods. The impression left on her reader is that she is anxious to advance quickly to the part that deals more immediately with what God does; and she complains that while we are admonished to pray, only what we can do ourselves is explained and little said of what the Lord does, "I mean about the supernatural."[33] It is in response to this need souls have of knowing about passive prayer that Teresa felt she could contribute.

The question might be raised here: is it not useless for people to read about mystical prayer and favors when they do not themselves, for whatever reason, experience the same things? In answer to this, Teresa replies that learning about God's work will lead a receptive person to the prayer of praise. Characteristically, she reasons that if she who was so wretched was led to this praise when she read of such things, how much more will good and humble souls praise Him upon learning of them. Also, she thinks that these favors superabound with love and fortitude, enabling a person to do more good and to journey with less toil. Knowledge of these favors will make the readers aware of how much they may lose through their own fault. Furthermore, the testimony she gives of her contemplative experience, in which so many aspects of the Christian faith are illumined, provides the theologian with a rich abundance of material for reflection.[34]

The fourth dwelling places. The beginning of the supernatural or mystical marks off this section and presents Teresa with the problem of how to explain infused prayer.[35] She first seeks a solution through an analysis of the difference between

---

33. IC 1.2.7.

34. See Tomás de la Cruz, "Santa Teresa de Jesús contemplativa," *Ephemerides Carmeliticae* 13 (1962): 9–62.

35. See IC 4.1.1.

consolations (*contentos*) and spiritual delight (*gustos*); she notes that the former have their beginning in our human nature and end in God while the latter have their beginning in God and overflow to human nature.[36] The consolations, then, result from our own efforts accompanied by God's grace; the spiritual delight is received not through human efforts but passively. In this dwelling place the first degrees of infused prayer are discussed. Though there are no rules about the length of time required to reach this point, "the important thing is not to think much but to love much; and so do that which best stirs you to love."[37] In Teresa's thinking, love "doesn't consist in great delight but in desiring with strong determination to please God in everything, in striving, insofar as possible, not to offend Him, and in asking Him for the advancement of the honor and glory of His Son."[38]

This contemplative prayer begins with a passive experience of recollection, a gentle drawing of the faculties inward; it is different from recollection achieved at the cost of human effort.[39] This prayer of infused recollection is a less intense form of initial contemplation or, as called by Teresa, the prayer of quiet. While the will finds rest in the prayer of quiet, in the peace of God's presence, the intellect (in Teresa's terminology) continues to move about. One should let the intellect go and surrender oneself into the arms of love, for distractions, the wandering mind, are a part of the human condition and can no more be avoided than can eating and sleeping.[40]

---

36. See IC 4.1.4.
37. IC 4.1.7.
38. IC 4.1.7.
39. See IC 4.3.1–3.
40. See IC 4.3.8.

In a further effort to explain the difference between acquired and infused prayer, she turns to another analogy: the different ways in which two water troughs are filled. One trough is filled with water channelled through aqueducts, by the exercise of a great deal of ingenuity, while the other is filled by a spring bubbling up from the very spot where the trough is. However, the worth of one's prayer is not judged by its passive character; rather, "it is in the effects and deeds following afterward that one discerns the true value of prayer."[41]

Finally, in this dwelling place, since the passive prayer is in its beginning stages, the natural (active) and the supernatural (passive) are joined. It is not unusual for souls to enter here.

The fifth dwelling places. The prayer of union characterizes these rooms, an experience in which the faculties become completely silent, or, in Teresa's words, are suspended, and which leaves a certitude that the soul "was in God and God was in it."[42] Such certitude is not present when the union is merely partial as in the previous dwelling place.[43]

Here Teresa, never wanting in her attempts to find the best explanation, turns to another analogy. Leaving aside the castle and the troughs of water, she finds an unusual comparison as an example for explaining what is in her mind: the silkworm. Through the image of the silkworm she speaks ingeniously of death and of new life in Christ. In this prayer of union, God Himself becomes the dwelling place or cocoon in which a person dies. Once a soul is indeed dead to itself

---

41. See IC 4.2.3, 8, 9.
42. See IC 5.1.3–5, 9–10.
43. See IC 5.1.5, 11.

and its attachments, it breaks forth from the cocoon transformed as does a small white butterfly.[44]

Having made the point of the soul's death in Christ, Teresa introduces her final analogy, which serves to lead her readers through the remaining dwelling places to the center of the castle: marriage and its preparatory stages. In her day, before two people became engaged, they progressed through certain stages by which they sought to know first if there was any likeness between them and then whether there was any chance for love. If these were affirmatively established, they shared in additional meetings so as to deepen their knowledge of each other. In these experiences of union, then, His Majesty is desirous that the soul may get to know Him better.[45]

Teresa makes a final plea that love be not idle. One so intimate with His Majesty must walk with special care and attentiveness in the exercise of virtue and with particular emphasis on love of neighbor, humility (the desire to be considered the least), and the faithful performance of ordinary tasks.[46]

The sixth dwelling places. The longest section of *The Interior Castle* is devoted to this stage of the inward journey. Teresa deals here with many extraordinary mystical phenomena. Though the spiritual betrothal takes place in these rooms, the desires of the soul at a cost to itself must first increase.[47] Through both vehement desires for God and the sufferings these desires cause, the Lord enables the soul to have the courage to be joined with Him and take Him as its Spouse.[48]

---

44. See IC 5.2.2–5.
45. See IC 5.4.4.
46. See IC 5.4.9.
47. See IC 6.1.1.
48. See IC 6.2.1; 6.4.1.

Aware that readers will wonder why all this courage is necessary for something that should be looked upon as an attractive opportunity, Teresa asserts strongly: "I tell you there is need for more courage than you think."[49] Without the courage, which must be given by God, such a union would be impossible. This fortitude comes through many trials both exterior and interior: opposition from others; praise (itself becoming a trial); severe illnesses; inner sufferings, fears, and misunderstanding on the part of the confessor and the consequent anxiety that God will allow one to be deceived; and a feeling of unbearable inner oppression and even of being rejected by God.[50]

Other preparations for the betrothal come in the form of certain spiritual awakenings and impulses deep within the soul. These are of many kinds and include the woundings of love that can cause at one and the same time both pain and delight.[51]

The betrothal itself takes place when His Majesty "gives the soul raptures that draw it out of its senses. For if it were to see itself so near this great Majesty while in its senses, it would perhaps die."[52] Though the soul in ecstasy is without consciousness in its outward life, it was never before so awake to the things of God nor did it ever before have so deep an enlightenment and knowledge of God.[53]

Besides locutions from God with their beneficial effects, the soul may now also begin to receive through intellectual and imaginative visions understanding about the divine

---

49. IC 6.4.2.
50. See IC 6.1.3–4, 6–9.
51. See IC 6.2.
52. IC 6.4.2.
53. See IC 6.4.3–4.

mysteries.[54] The Lord shows it heavenly secrets. Some are
so sublime that it is incapable of explaining anything about
them; others can be explained to some extent. The supernatural realities that became the objects of Teresa's mystical
experience were so varied and complex that the scholar is left
disconcerted in his efforts to categorize them. Accompanying the discussion of these diverse favors are also many sharp
analyses and keenly perceptive rules for discerning authentic
mystical experiences from pseudo-mystical phenomena. The
effects the authentic favors leave in the soul are like the jewels the Spouse gives to the betrothed; they are knowledge of
the grandeur of God, self-knowledge together with humility,
and rejection of earthly things except of those that can be
used in the Lord's service.[55] Finally, joy will reach such an
excess that the soul will want to be a herald to the entire
world that all might help it praise the Lord.[56]

  When speaking of the intellectual and imaginative visions
of Christ, Teresa pauses to make some firm assertions about
the human and divine Christ present throughout one's spiritual pilgrimage. He is the one through whom all blessings
come. No state is so sublime that a person must always be
occupied with divinity and thus obliged to empty the mind of
all reference to the human Christ. "Life is long, and there are
in it many trials, and we need to look at Christ our model,
how He suffered them, and also at His apostles and saints,
so as to bear these trials with perfection. Jesus is too good
a companion for us to turn away from Him."[57] And here

---

54. See IC 6.4.5, 8.
55. See IC 6.5.10–11.
56. See IC 6.6.10–13.
57. IC 6.7.13.

Teresa makes an important distinction between discursive meditation about Christ and contemplative presence to Him. The inability of contemplative souls to engage in discursive thought about the mysteries of the Passion and life of Christ in their prayer is very common, she holds. But contemplating these mysteries, "dwelling on them with a simple gaze," in Teresa's words, "will not impede the most sublime prayer."[58] On the contrary, an effort to forget Christ and live in continual absorption in the Divinity will result in a failure to enter the last two dwelling places. Teresa is most insistent on this. The purification of the person is realized not merely through the sufferings inherent to the human condition but especially through contact with the person of Christ in his humanity and divinity.

Through these many favors and purifications, the desires of love are always increasing and the flight of the butterfly ever more restless. These desires reach a point of extreme spiritual torment, causing the soul a final purification of the spirit before entering the seventh dwelling place, "just as those who will enter heaven must be cleansed in purgatory."[59] Not only can this intense spiritual torment cause ecstasy, as can intense spiritual joy, but also it can place one in danger of death.[60] Nonetheless, the soul is aware that this spiritual suffering is a precious favor.

The seventh dwelling places. On account of these moments of great illumination, Teresa is able to teach that there are no closed doors between the sixth and the seventh dwelling places. If she divides them, it is "because there are things

---

58. See IC 6.7.6–7, 11–12.
59. IC 6.11.1, 6.
60. See IC 6.11.2, 4, 11.

in the last that are not revealed to those who have not yet reached it."[61] In the prayer of union explained in the fifth dwelling place and the raptures of the sixth, the Lord makes the soul blind and deaf as was St. Paul in his conversion. When God joins the soul to Himself, it doesn't understand anything of the nature and kind of favor enjoyed.[62] But in the seventh dwelling place the union is wrought differently: "Our good God now desires to remove the scales from the soul's eyes and let it see and understand, although in a strange way, something of the favor He grants it."[63] Now fortified, a person lifted up to these exalted mysteries no longer loses equilibrium or falls into ecstasy, but rather experiences them as a proper object, as connatural.

Entry into these last and most luminous dwelling places takes place through an amazing intellectual vision of the Most Blessed Trinity. Teresa places much emphasis on the depth at which this experience occurs, a spiritual profundity previously unrevealed, in "the extreme interior, in some place very deep within itself."[64] Though the presence of the Trinity remains and is felt habitually, it is not revealed in the fullness of light as at first or sometimes afterward when the Lord "desires that the window of the intellect be opened."[65] What seems awesome is that the habitual intellectual vision of the Trinity does not interfere with multiple and diverse daily duties carried out as acts of service.

The grace of spiritual marriage, of perfect union, is bestowed also in this center dwelling place and occurs through

---

61. IC 6.4.4.
62. See IC 7.1.5.
63. IC 7.1.6.
64. IC 7.1.7.
65. IC 7.1.8–9.

an imaginative vision of the Lord's most sacred humanity "so that the soul will understand and not be ignorant of receiving this sovereign gift."[66] The vision was so much at variance with previous ones that it left Teresa "stupefied," for, as does the vision of the Trinity, this takes place in that most interior depth of the spirit. In successive experiences of this grace, which is repeatable, the vision is an intellectual one. Suggesting the trait of inseparability,[67] the term "marriage" designates the union and the degree of His Majesty's love. It is so great and reaches such a point that the spirit is made one with God "just as those who are married cannot be separated."[68] With no allowance for division, as there is in spiritual betrothal (likened to the joining and separation of the two candles), the union of spiritual marriage makes Teresa think of the rain that has fallen into a river, or of a stream that enters the sea, or of the beams of light entering a room through different windows and becoming one.[69]

At this point the butterfly dies with the greatest joy because its new life is Christ. In St. Paul's words: "He that is joined or united to the Lord becomes one spirit with Him,"[70] and "for me to live is Christ."[71] The ultimate goal, then, of Teresa's journey, the spiritual marriage, is a union with Christ, now no longer living as the divine Logos but as the Word incarnate, risen and marked by the attributes of His earthly adventure, especially those of His resurrection. With

---

66. IC 7.2.1.
67. IC 7.2.2–4
68. IC 7.2.3.
69. See IC 7.2.4.
70. 1 Cor 6:17.
71. Phil 1:21; see IC 7.2.5.

the passing of time, the soul understands more clearly that its life is Christ.

Having examined the effects of this union, Teresa in the final chapter explains that the purpose of all these splendid favors is that one might live like Christ and that the fruit of the spiritual marriage must be good works. The interior calm fortifies these persons so that they may endure much less calm in the exterior events of their lives, that they might have the strength to serve.[72] The works of service may be outstanding ones, as in Teresa's case, but they need not be. One must concentrate on serving those who are in one's company. "The Lord doesn't look so much at the greatness of our works as at the love with which they are done."[73] His Majesty will join our sacrifice with that which He offered for us. "Thus even though our works are small they will have the value our love for Him would have merited had they been great."[74]

In the prologue Teresa states her intention to write about prayer, and anyone reading *The Interior Castle* would probably agree that it is indeed a book about prayer and its stages. But in a letter dated December 7, 1577, a week after completion of her manuscript, Teresa refers to her book and speaks of its theme differently. She says the book is about God ("it treats only of what He is"). This remark illustrates well how for Teresa the journey in prayer through the interior castle to the center room is nothing else than the magnificent work of God's love.[75]

72. See IC 7.4.4, 6, 9, 12.

73. IC 7.4.15.

74. IC 7.4.14–15.

75. See José Vicente Rodríguez, "Castillo interior o las moradas," in *Introducción a la lectura de Santa Teresa* (Madrid, Spain: Espiritualidad, 1978): 368–71.

The Autograph

The Interior Castle was not revised, although the manuscript does contain the marks of censors. Between June 13 and July 6, 1580 at the monastery of Carmelite nuns in Segovia, Father Gracián and the Dominican Father Diego de Yanguas went over the work with Teresa, pointing out their difficulties, cancelling passages, and making corrections. Many of Gracián's corrections annoyed Teresa's Jesuit biographer Francisco de Ribera, leading him to write on the opening page of the autograph a strong rebuke against censors of the work.[76] José Vicente Rodríguez surmises that Gracián was just killing time since he was in that part of Spain waiting for a brief to come from Rome.[77]

Teresa gave the new book to Gracián to guard, for her *Life* was still with the Inquisition. Gracián brought the work to Seville in 1580 and entrusted it for safekeeping to María de San José. Sometime between 1582 and 1585, while he was still provincial, Gracián gave the work as a gift to Don Pedro Cerezo Pardo, who was a generous benefactor of the Discalced Carmelites. Between 1586 and 1588 the autograph was in the hands of Fray Luis de León, who was at the time preparing the first edition of Teresa's works; and it was then returned to Don Pedro Cerezo. In 1618 Don Pedro's daughter, Doña Constancia de Ayala, made her profession of vows in the monastery of the Discalced Carmelite nuns in Seville. She had brought with her to the Carmel the autograph of *The Interior Castle*, and it has remained with the nuns in Seville ever since, with one exception. In 1961 it was

---

76. See IC 3.1.1n2.
77. See Rodríguez, "Castillo interior o las moradas," 318.

brought to Rome for repair, and in the following year, beautifully restored, the spiritual masterpiece was returned to the Carmelites in Seville. The red-bound book, referred to by its author as a jewel, is now set as a jewel in a reliquary that has walls like those of Ávila and in the shape of a castle surrounding and protecting it.

K. K.

THE INTERIOR CASTLE

Teresa of Jesus, a nun of Our Lady of Mount Carmel, wrote this treatise called *The Interior Castle* for her sisters and daughters, the Discalced Carmelite nuns.

IHS

Prologue

Not many things that I have been ordered to do under obedience have been as difficult for me as is this present task of writing about prayer. First, it doesn't seem the Lord is giving me either the spirit or the desire to undertake the work. Second, I have been experiencing now for three months such great noise and weakness in my head that I've found it a hardship even to write concerning necessary business matters. But knowing that the strength given by obedience usually lessens the difficulty of things that seem impossible, I resolved to carry out the task very willingly, even though my human nature seems greatly distressed. For the Lord hasn't given me so much virtue that my nature in the midst of its struggle with continual sickness and duties of so many kinds doesn't feel strong aversion toward such a task. May He, in whose mercy I trust and who has helped me in other more difficult things so as to favor me, do this work for me.

2. Indeed, I don't think I have much more to say than what I've said in other things they have ordered me to write;[1] rather, I fear that the things I write about will be nearly all alike. I'm, literally, just like the parrots that are taught to speak; they know no more than what they hear or are shown, and they often repeat it. If the Lord wants me to say something new, His Majesty will provide. Or, He will be pleased to make me remember what I have said at other times, for I would be happy even with this. My memory is so poor that I would be glad if I could repeat, in case they've been lost, some of the things which I was told were well said.[2] If the Lord doesn't make me remember, I will gain just by tiring myself and getting a worse headache for the sake of obedience—even if no one draws any benefit from what I say.

3. And so I'm beginning to comply today, the feast of the Most Blessed Trinity, in the year 1577, in this Carmelite monastery of St. Joseph in Toledo where I am at present.[3] In all that I say I submit to the opinion of the ones who ordered me to write, for they are persons of great learning.[4] If I should say something that isn't in conformity with what the holy Roman Catholic Church holds, it will be through ignorance and not through malice. This can be held as certain, and also that through the goodness of God I always am, and will be, and have been subject to her. May He be always blessed and glorified, amen.

1. An allusion to her *Life* and *The Way of Perfection*.

2. This is a veiled reference to her *Life*. The autograph of this work was requested by the Inquisition in 1576 and kept in its archives until 1588.

3. It was June 2, 1577. She completed the work in Ávila on November 29 of the same year.

4. These were Father Jerónimo Gracián and her confessor Dr. Alonso Velázquez, future bishop of Osma and later archbishop of Santiago de Compostela.

4. The one who ordered me to write told me that the nuns in these monasteries of our Lady of Mt. Carmel need someone to answer their questions about prayer and that he thought they would better understand the language used between women, and that because of the love they bore me they would pay more attention to what I would tell them. I thus understood that it was important for me to manage to say something. So, I shall be speaking to them while I write; it's nonsense to think that what I say could matter to other persons. Our Lord will be granting me favor enough if some of these nuns benefit by praising Him a little more. His Majesty well knows that I don't aim after anything else. And it should be very clear that if I manage to say something well the sisters will understand that this does not come from me since there would be no foundation for it, unless the Lord gave it to me; otherwise they would have as little intelligence as I little ability for such things.

OBEDIENCE USUALLY LESSENS THE DIFFICULTY OF THINGS

In the first paragraph of the prologue to *The Interior Castle*, Teresa reveals much about herself in a few words. We see her suffering poor health, especially in regard to the "great noise and weakness" in her head that interferes with her ability to carry out her ordinary business matters. The task of writing about prayer seems nearly impossible to her except for her trust that strength is given for things undertaken through obedience. She offers a prayer for the Lord's help.

Besides her general lack of enthusiasm for writing at this time, Teresa doubts that she has anything to add to what she has already written elsewhere. She fears that perhaps she won't even remember what she said at other times. She consoles herself with the thought that she will gain from her obedience.

Here Teresa expresses her deference to those persons of learning who ordered her to write and also expresses obedience to the authority of the Church regarding all that she writes.

We see that by the end of the prologue Teresa has already begun to change her tone in regard to her task. Thinking of the nuns' need to learn more about prayer, Teresa here doesn't mention her reluctance and writes that she understands that it is important for her to "manage to say something." She attributes to His Majesty any merit her words may have and says the Lord will be granting her a favor if some of the nuns benefit by praising him a little more. Perhaps we have to smile when she says she is speaking only to the nuns and writes, "it's nonsense to think that what I say could matter to other persons."

4

Interpretive Notes

In the opening page of her manuscript, Teresa explains that she wrote "this treatise called *The Interior Castle* for her sisters and daughters, the Discalced Carmelite nuns." In giving her book this title, she moves away from the simple autobiographical tone of *The Book of Her Life*, now kept in the hands of the Inquisition, toward a more doctrinal approach. She plans to expound the full, mysterious development of the spiritual life. Yet this in no way means that in her presentation she will not be drawing mainly from her own experience. So as to combine these two approaches, doctrinal and autobiographical, she makes use of a basic symbol: the castle. It will serve as a kind of literary filter through which she presents her material.

Teresa then speaks of her castle on three levels: experiential, symbolic, and theological. With regard to the first, this castle belongs to the author herself. Although she wants to hide her identity and refers only to "a person," "a certain person," or to "that person" who experienced the graces she is speaking of in her book, she obviously is referring to herself. The reader can be sure that it is Teresa passing through the rooms of her interior castle into its deepest and most intimate depths. Secondly, it was natural for Teresa to choose a symbol, or symbols, to express what was in reality inexpressible and awaken in the reader a certain sense of her own experience. Finally, Teresa wishes to explain to herself and to the reader the profound meaning of her experiences, to investigate the development of her spiritual life and the life of grace in general.

The symbol of the castle enabled her to begin her doctrinal part with the human person rather than the traditional outlines of beginner, proficient, and perfect. The human being, as made in the image of God, as a temple of the Holy Spirit, has a radical call to communion with God. But this call necessarily passes through Christ. The Christian grows into a full union with Jesus Christ.

The end phase of the journey through the castle, however, is Trinitarian and ecclesial. When persons reach the Trinitarian phase through their union with Christ, they focus especially on serving the Church.

In the prologue itself she speaks of her bad health and many other duties which seem to take away all inspiration and desire to write. She will be happy if she can remember some of the things she said well in her *Life*, which was now unavailable for public reading. But since she is writing for her sisters, she will write as though speaking to them and trust that some, at least, will benefit.

Questions for Discussion

1. For whom did Teresa write this work and why did she give it the title that she did?
2. What were some of the reasons she felt disinclined to begin this task?
3. What was the reason that others thought it important that she write this work?
4. It is often helpful to use symbols to express complex realities. What are some symbols people use to help others understand complex realities?

THE FIRST DWELLING PLACES

Contains Two Chapters

CHAPTER 1

Discusses the beauty and dignity of our souls. Draws a comparison in order to explain, and speaks of the benefit that comes from understanding this truth and knowing about the favors we receive from God and how the door to this castle is prayer.

Today while beseeching our Lord to speak for me because I wasn't able to think of anything to say nor did I know how to begin to carry out this obedience, there came to my mind what I shall now speak about, that which will provide us with a basis to begin with. It is that we consider our soul to be like a castle made entirely out of a diamond or of very clear crystal, in which there are many rooms, just as in heaven there are many dwelling places.[1] For in reflecting upon it carefully, sisters, we realize that the soul of the just person is

_____

1. Allusion to Jn 14:2. Teresa uses the Spanish words *moradas, aposentos,* and *piezas* in approximately the same sense; they refer to rooms or dwelling places within the castle. The fundamental text of Jn 14:2 has led previous translators to speak of these rooms as mansions. Most people today think of a mansion as a large stately house, not what Teresa had in mind with the term *moradas.* New versions of Scripture render Jn 14:2 as "in my Father's house there are many dwelling places." "Dwelling places" turns out to be a more precise translation of Teresa's *moradas* than is the classic "mansions," and more biblical and theological in tone.

nothing else but a paradise where the Lord says He finds His delight.[2] So then, what do you think that abode will be like where a King so powerful, so wise, so pure, so full of all good things takes His delight? I don't find anything comparable to the magnificent beauty of a soul and its marvelous capacity. Indeed, our intellects, however keen, can hardly comprehend it, just as they cannot comprehend God; but He Himself says that He created us in His own image and likeness.[3]

Well if this is true, as it is, there is no reason to tire ourselves in trying to comprehend the beauty of this castle. Since this castle is a creature and the difference, therefore, between it and God is the same as that between the Creator and His creature, His Majesty in saying that the soul is made in His own image makes it almost impossible for us to understand the sublime dignity and beauty of the soul.

2. It is a shame and unfortunate that through our own fault we don't understand ourselves or know who we are. Wouldn't it show great ignorance, my daughters, if someone when asked who he was didn't know, and didn't know his father or mother or from what country he came? Well now, if this would be so extremely stupid, we are incomparably more so when we do not strive to know who we are, but limit ourselves to considering only roughly these bodies. Because we have heard and because faith tells us so, we know we have souls. But we seldom consider the precious things that can be found in this soul, or who dwells within it, or its high value. Consequently, little effort is made to preserve its beauty. All our attention is taken up with the plainness of the diamond's setting or the outer wall of the castle; that is, with these bodies of ours.

---

2. Allusion to Prov 8:31.

3. Gen 1:26–27.

3. Well, let us consider that this castle has, as I said,[4] many dwelling places: some up above, others down below, others to the sides; and in the center and middle is the main dwelling place where the very secret exchanges between God and the soul take place.

It's necessary that you keep this comparison in mind. Perhaps God will be pleased to let me use it to explain something to you about the favors He is happy to grant souls and the differences between these favors. I shall explain them according to what I have understood as possible. For it is impossible that anyone understand them all since there are many; how much more so for someone as wretched as I. It will be a great consolation when the Lord grants them to you if you know that they are possible; and for anyone to whom He doesn't, it will be a great consolation to praise His wonderful goodness. Just as it doesn't do us any harm to reflect upon the things there are in heaven and what the blessed enjoy—but rather we rejoice and strive to attain what they enjoy—it doesn't do us any harm to see that it is possible in this exile for so great a God to commune with such foul-smelling worms; and, upon seeing this, come to love a goodness so perfect and a mercy so immeasurable. I hold as certain that anyone who might be harmed by knowing that God can grant this favor in this exile would be very much lacking in humility and love of neighbor. Otherwise, how could we fail to be happy that God grants these favors to our brother? His doing so is no impediment toward His granting them to us, and His Majesty can reveal His grandeurs to whomever He wants. Sometimes He does so merely to show forth His glory, as He said of the blind man whose sight He restored when His apostles asked

---

4. In IC 1.1.1.

Him if the blindness resulted from the man's sins or those of his parents.[5] Hence, He doesn't grant them because the sanctity of the recipients is greater than that of those who don't receive them but so that His glory may be known, as we see in St. Paul and the Magdalene, and that we might praise Him for His work in creatures.

4. One could say that these favors seem to be impossible and that it is good not to scandalize the weak. Less is lost when the weak do not believe in them than when the favors fail to benefit those to whom God grants them; and these latter will be delighted and awakened through these favors to a greater love of Him who grants so many gifts and whose power and majesty is so great. Moreover, I know I am speaking to those for whom this danger does not exist, for they know and believe that God grants even greater signs of His love. I know that whoever does not believe in these favors will have no experience of them, for God doesn't like us to put a limit on His works. And so, sisters, those of you whom the Lord doesn't lead by this path should never doubt His generosity.

5. Well, getting back to our beautiful and delightful castle, we must see how we can enter it. It seems I'm saying something foolish. For if this castle is the soul, clearly one doesn't have to enter it since it is within oneself. How foolish it would seem were we to tell someone to enter a room he is already in. But you must understand that there is a great difference in the ways one may be inside the castle. For there are many souls who are in the outer courtyard—which is where the guards stay—and don't care at all about entering the castle, nor do they know what lies within that

_____

5. Jn 9:2–3.

most precious place, nor who is within, nor even how many rooms it has. You have already heard in some books on prayer that the soul is advised to enter within itself;[6] well that's the very thing I'm advising.

6. Not long ago a very learned man told me that souls who do not practice prayer are like people with paralyzed or crippled bodies; even though they have hands and feet they cannot give orders to these hands and feet.[7] Thus there are souls so ill and so accustomed to being involved in external matters that there is no remedy, nor does it seem they can enter within themselves. They are now so used to dealing always with the insects and vermin that are in the wall surrounding the castle that they have become almost like them. And though they have so rich a nature and the power to converse with none other than God, there is no remedy. If these souls do not strive to understand and cure their great misery, they will be changed into statues of salt, unable to turn their heads to look at themselves, just as Lot's wife was changed for having turned her head.[8]

7. Insofar as I can understand, the door of entry to this castle is prayer and reflection. I don't mean to refer to mental more than vocal prayer, for since vocal prayer is prayer, it must be accompanied by reflection. A prayer in which a person is not aware of whom he is speaking to, what he is asking, who it is who is asking and of whom, I do not call prayer however much the lips move. Sometimes it will be so without this reflection, provided that the soul has these

---

6. She is probably alluding to Osuna's *Third Spiritual Alphabet* and Laredo's *Ascent of Mount Sion*, favorite books of hers. See L 4.7; 23.12.

7. She also received in an intellectual vision mystical understanding of this truth. See ST 20.

8. Gen 19:26.

reflections at other times. Nonetheless, anyone who has the habit of speaking before God's majesty as though he were speaking to a slave, without being careful to see how he is speaking, but saying whatever comes to his head and whatever he has learned from saying at other times, in my opinion is not praying. Please God, may no Christian pray in this way. Among yourselves, sisters, I hope in His Majesty that you will not do so, for the custom you have of being occupied with interior things is quite a good safeguard against falling and carrying on in this way like brute beasts.

8. Well now, we are not speaking to these crippled souls, for if the Lord Himself doesn't come to order them to get up—as He did the man who waited at the side of the pool for thirty years[9]—they are quite unfortunate and in serious danger. But we are speaking to other souls that, in the end, enter the castle. For even though they are very involved in the world, they have good desires and sometimes, though only once in a while, they entrust themselves to our Lord and reflect on who they are, although in a rather hurried fashion. During the period of a month they will sometimes pray, but their minds are then filled with business matters which ordinarily occupy them. They are so attached to these things that where their treasure lies their heart goes also.[10] Sometimes they do put all these things aside, and the self-knowledge and awareness that they are not proceeding correctly in order to get to the door is important. Finally, they enter the first, lower rooms. But so many reptiles get in with them that they are prevented from seeing the beauty of

---

9. Father Gracián added "and eight" after "thirty years," in accordance with Jn 5:5.

10. Allusion to Mt 6:21.

the castle and from calming down; they have done quite a bit just by having entered.

9. You may have been thinking, daughters, that this is irrelevant to you since by the Lord's goodness you are not among these people. You'll have to have patience, for I wouldn't know how to explain my understanding of some interior things about prayer if not in this way. And may it even please the Lord that I succeed in saying something, for what I want to explain to you is very difficult to understand without experience. If you have experience you will see that one cannot avoid touching upon things that—please God, through His mercy—do not pertain to us.

THE BEAUTY AND DIGNITY
OF OUR SOULS

1.1.1–2 Teresa explains that the idea for the castle came into her mind as she prayed for the Lord to speak for her in the challenging task of writing about prayer. She asks us to consider our soul to be like a castle made entirely out of diamond or very clear crystal, in which there are many rooms. She marvels at the beauty and value of our souls, created in the image and likeness of God. She laments that we attend more to our bodies than to our souls.

1.1.3 In this castle that is our soul, there are many dwelling places and in the center is the place where secret exchanges between God and the soul take place. Teresa states her purpose in writing—to explain the various favors God grants to souls. She thinks we should know about these favors, even if we don't receive them ourselves. If we don't receive such favors, we should be happy for those who do. We should praise God's wonderful goodness in giving these gifts. Those who do not believe in these favors will have no experience of them, for God doesn't like us to put a limit on his works.

1.1.5 Teresa realizes that her castle metaphor is imperfect, but explains why she thinks it is nevertheless useful. She refers to books on prayer that advise the soul to enter within itself; that is what she says she is advising also.

1.1.6 Teresa elaborates on the castle, describing the insects and vermin surrounding it. Souls who attend to external matters and who do not practice prayer are like sick people who are unable to enter the castle. Such souls must strive to understand and cure their great misery.

1.1.7 The door of entry to this castle is prayer and reflection. The essential aspect of prayer is attention to God, whether the prayer is vocal or mental.

1.1.8–9 Here Teresa clarifies and makes a distinction between two types of souls who have not yet entered the castle. The most impaired, those who have focused on external matters to such an extent that they have completely neglected prayer and the interior life, can no longer do anything to help themselves change; they need help from the Lord himself. She says she is not writing for such persons. Instead she addresses her work to persons who, though involved in the world, have good desires and make occasional efforts at prayer. They eventually enter the first lower rooms of the castle, but so many reptiles (worldly concerns) enter with them that they cannot appreciate the castle. Teresa assures the sisters that they are not among those in this least prayerful group, but asks their patience as she tries to write about this difficult topic. She thinks her task will be easier if she, so to speak, begins at the beginning.

Interpretive Notes

For those of us who are not accustomed to seeing castles, it might be of value to begin our notes with the idea a person in Teresa's time would have of a castle. It was a stronghold—a large, fortified residence for a king or lord of the territory in which he lived. It often included a high mound encircled by a ditch. The thickness of the castle walls varied. The defense of the outer wall of the castle was generally by one or more lines of moats, which could be traversed in front of the gateways by drawbridges. Teresa does not dwell on these outside fortifications of her castle but on the beauty of what lies within the castle with its many dwelling places.

This castle that Teresa places before our eyes is above all her own castle, her soul, her life. This castle that is Teresa's is also the Lord's. But Teresa's castle serves her as well to put before readers their own castles, and offers a kind of drawbridge by which they can enter into the world of her castle and her religious experiences.

Teresa begins on a positive note, speaking of the beauty and dignity of our souls. Actually, "soul" and "castle" are the same in the symbolic language of the work. And in our language today, the soul refers to the human person. So Teresa begins by speaking of the beauty and dignity of the human person. The *Catechism of the Catholic Church* speaks in this same vein: "Being in the image of God the human individual possesses the dignity of a person, who is not just something, but someone. He is capable of self-knowledge, of self-possession and of freely giving himself and entering into communion with other persons. And he is called by grace to a covenant with his Creator, to offer him a response of faith and love that no other creature can give in his stead" (CCC 357).

In explaining that we are made in the image and likeness of God, Teresa points out how we have a capacity for God that transcends the human person. Not only are we called to communion with God, but we are structured in such a way that God lives in his own dwelling place within us, more so than he does in the whole cosmos. Teresa, in choosing the symbol of a castle to express this deep truth, reveals its roots in her own mystical experience.

As Teresa develops her thoughts, her image of the castle as a beautiful jewel alternates with that of the castle as a location of struggle against enemies. This struggle against enemies prevails over the image of the castle as a beautiful jewel. Teresa is a struggling soul, one who has a combative idea of life. She wants to communicate this concept to readers so that they aren't left with a false peace about what awaits them in their journey through the rooms of the castle.

Alongside her symbol of the castle, Teresa sought support in the Word of God. She drew from it three affirmations: "In my Father's house there are many dwelling places" (Jn 14:2); "I found my delight in the human race" (Prov 8:31); "Let us make humankind in our image, after our likeness" (Gen 1:26). She finds her authority for her symbol of the castle in these biblical texts and evaluates the human person in a Christian key. Gradually, through her interior experience, these three biblical texts became a part of her and her convictions.

But to return to this beautiful castle, we need to know how to enter, and that is through prayer. Teresa knows that people can pour themselves out into the exterior world, even to the point of knowing nothing about the treasures they hold within. They become so used to dealing with the insects and vermin in the outer wall that they become like them. Teresa insists in the strongest manner possible that this turning away from one's own interior life is one of earth's greatest tragedies.

It may seem strange that the castle can only be entered through prayer. Couldn't a psychologist, for example, enter it by studying the psyche? But for Teresa, human interiority contains something sacred. The castle is inhabited by God. To enter it is to enter into relationship with God, who dwells in its inmost dwelling place. Not a profane, but a religious gesture is necessary. To pray is to enter into personal relationship with God.

Teresa mentions three biblical types who remain outside the castle and are invited to enter: the wife of Lot, who in turning to look at the burning city is turned into a pillar of salt (Gen 19:26); the paralytic at the pool in Bethesda (Jn 5:2–8); and the man born blind, who begins to see through his meeting with Jesus (Jn 9:1–7). Each of them was handicapped in some way and prevented from entering the castle and beholding the treasures that are there. They needed in some way to meet Jesus in order to enter the castle. If you want to enter the first dwelling places, you must look with trust to Jesus, who will enable you to see and enjoy the beauty of what lies within this mysterious castle.

Questions for Discussion

1. Why does Teresa use the symbol of a castle?
2. Before entering the castle, where do we tend to place all our attention?
3. What good does it do to talk about God's favors during times in our life when we don't seem to receive them ourselves?
4. Was there a time in your life when Jesus invited you to enter into a relationship with him? How does this experience parallel Teresa's description of entering the castle?

CHAPTER 2

Treats of how ugly a soul is when in mortal sin and how God wanted to let a certain person know something about this. Discusses, also, some matters on the theme of self-knowledge. This chapter is beneficial for there are noteworthy points. Explains what is meant by these dwelling places.

Before going on, I want to say that you should consider what it would mean to this so brilliantly shining and beautiful castle, this pearl from the Orient, this tree of life planted in the very living waters of life[1]—that is, in God—to fall into mortal sin; there's no darker darkness nor anything more obscure and black. You shouldn't want to know anything else than the fact that, although the very sun that gave the soul so much brilliance and beauty is still in the center, the soul is as though it were not there to share in these things. Yet, it is as capable of enjoying His Majesty as is crystal capable of reflecting the sun's brilliance. Nothing helps such a soul; and as a result all the good works it might do while in mortal sin are fruitless for the attainment of glory. Since these works do not proceed from that principle, which is God, who is the cause of our virtue being really virtue, and are separated from Him, they cannot be pleasing in His sight. Since, after all, the intention of anyone who commits a mortal sin is to please the devil, who is darkness itself, not God, the poor soul becomes darkness itself.

---

1. Allusion to Ps 1:3.

2. I know a person to whom our Lord wanted to show what a soul in mortal sin was like.[2] That person says that in her opinion if this were understood it would be impossible to sin, even though a soul would have to undergo the greatest trials imaginable in order to flee the occasions. So the Lord gave her a strong desire that all might understand this. May He give you, daughters, the desire to beseech Him earnestly for those who are in this state, who have become total darkness, and whose works have become darkness also. For just as all the streams that flow from a crystal-clear fount are also clear, the works a soul in grace, because they proceed from this fount of life, in which the soul is planted like a tree, are most pleasing in the eyes of both God and man. There would be no freshness, no fruit, if it were not for this fount sustaining the tree, preventing it from drying up, and causing it to produce good fruit. Thus in the case of a soul that through its own fault withdraws from this fount and plants itself in a place where the water is black and foul-smelling, everything that flows from it is equally wretched and filthy.

3. It should be kept in mind here that the fount, the shining sun that is in the center of the soul, does not lose its beauty and splendor; it is always present in the soul, and nothing can take away its loveliness. But if a black cloth is placed over a crystal that is in the sun, obviously the sun's brilliance will have no effect on the crystal even though the sun is shining on it.[3]

4. O souls redeemed by the blood of Jesus Christ! Understand and take pity on yourselves. How is it possible that in realizing these things you don't strive to remove the pitch

---

2. The person is Teresa herself. See ST 20.

3. For similar comparisons see L 40.5; ST 52.

from this crystal? See that if your life comes to an end you will never again enjoy this light. O Jesus, how sad a thing it is to see a soul separated from this light! How miserable is the state of those poor rooms within the castle! How disturbed the senses are, that is, the people who live in these rooms! And in the faculties, that is, among the custodians, the stewards, and the chief waiters, what blindness, what bad management! In sum, since the tree is planted where the devil is, what fruit can it bear?

5. I once heard of a spiritual man who was not surprised at things done by a person in mortal sin, but at what was not done. May God in His mercy deliver us from so great an evil. There is nothing, while we are living, that deserves this name "evil," except mortal sin, for such sin carries in its wake everlasting evils. This, daughters, is what we must go about in fear of and what we must ask God in our prayers to protect us against. For if He doesn't guard the city, our labor will be in vain since we are vanity itself.[4]

That person I mentioned[5] said she received two blessings from the favor God granted her: the first, an intense fear of offending Him, and so in seeing such terrible dangers she always went about begging Him not to let her fall; the second, a mirror for humility, in which she saw how none of our good deeds has its principle from ourselves but from this fount in which the tree, symbolizing our souls, is planted and from this sun that gives warmth to our works. She says that this truth was represented to her so clearly that in doing something good, or seeing it done, she gave heed to the source and understood how without this help we could do

---

4. Allusion to Ps 127:1.
5. In IC 1.2.2.

nothing. As a result she would begin immediately to praise God and usually not think of herself in any good thing that she did.

6. The time you spend in reading this, or I in writing it, sisters, would not be lost if we were left with these two blessings. Learned and wise men know about these things very well, but everything is necessary for our womanly dullness of mind; and so perhaps the Lord wills that we get to know comparisons like these. May it please His Goodness to give us grace to profit by them.

7. These interior matters are so obscure for our minds that anyone who knows as little as I will be forced to say many superfluous and even foolish things in order to say something that's right. Whoever reads this must have patience, for I have to have it in order to write about what I don't know. Indeed, sometimes I take up the paper like a simpleton, for I don't know what to say or how to begin. I understand well that it's important for you that I explain some things about the interior life as best I can. We always hear about what a good thing prayer is, and our constitutions oblige us to spend so many hours in prayer.[6] Yet only what we ourselves can do in prayer is explained to us; little is explained about what the Lord does in a soul, I mean about the supernatural.[7] By speaking about this heavenly interior building and explaining and considering it in many ways we shall find great comfort. It is so little understood by mortals, even though many walk through it. And although in other things I've written the Lord has given me some

---

6. See C 2, 7.

7. Teresa laments the fact there are few books that explain mystical (supernatural) prayer in depth. In IC 2.1.1, she asserts that there are many books dealing with ascetical matters. Thus, her orientation in this book is toward the mystical.

understanding[8] I know there were certain things I had not understood as I have come to understand them now, especially certain more difficult things. The trouble is that before discussing them, as I have said,[9] I will have to repeat matters that are well known; on account of my stupidity things can't be otherwise.

8. Well now, let's get back to our castle with its many dwelling places. You mustn't think of these dwelling places in such a way that each one would follow in file after the other; but turn your eyes toward the center, which is the room or royal chamber where the King stays, and think of how a palmetto[10] has many leaves surrounding and covering the tasty part that can be eaten. So here, surrounding this center room are many other rooms; and the same holds true for those above. The things of the soul must always be considered as plentiful, spacious, and large; to do so is not an exaggeration. The soul is capable of much more than we can imagine, and the sun that is in this royal chamber shines in all parts. It is very important for any soul that practices prayer, whether little or much, not to hold itself back and stay in one corner. Let it walk through these dwelling places which are up above, down below, and to the sides, since God has given it such great dignity. Don't force it to stay a long time in one room alone. Oh, but if it is in the room of self-knowledge! How necessary this room is—see that you understand me—even for those whom the Lord has

---

8. She is referring to the *Life* and *The Way of Perfection* and alludes to a divine influence in the composition of her mystical writings. See L 39.8: "many of the things I write about here do not come from my own head, but my heavenly Master told them to me."

9. In IC 1.2.7.

10. A plant about a foot in height, which grows in Andalusia and Valencia, resembling the palm tree. Only the center or heart, the tender part, is eaten.

brought into the very dwelling place where He abides. For never, however exalted the soul may be, is anything else fitting for it; nor could it be even were the soul to so desire. For humility, like the bee making honey in the beehive, is always at work. Without it, everything goes wrong. But let's remember that the bee doesn't fail to leave the beehive and fly about gathering nectar from the flowers. So it is with the soul in the room of self-knowledge; let it believe me and fly sometimes to ponder the grandeur and majesty of its God. Here it will discover its lowliness better than by thinking of itself, and be freer from the vermin that enter the first rooms, those of self-knowledge. For even though, as I say, it is by the mercy of God that a person practices self-knowledge, that which applies in lesser matters applies so much more in greater ones, as they say. And believe me, we shall practice much better virtue through God's help than by being tied down to our own misery.

9. I don't know if this has been explained well. Knowing ourselves is something so important that I wouldn't want any relaxation ever in this regard, however high you may have climbed into the heavens. While we are on this earth nothing is more important to us than humility. So I repeat that it is good, indeed very good, to try to enter first into the room where self-knowledge is dealt with rather than fly off to other rooms. This is the right road, and if we can journey along a safe and level path, why should we want wings to fly? Rather, let's strive to make more progress in self-knowledge. In my opinion we shall never completely know ourselves if we don't strive to know God. By gazing at His grandeur, we get in touch with our own lowliness; by looking at His purity, we shall see our own filth; by pondering His humility, we shall see how far we are from being humble.

10. Two advantages come from such activity. First, it's clear that something white seems much whiter when next to something black, and vice versa with the black next to the white. The second is that our intellects and wills, dealing in turn now with self, now with God, become nobler and better prepared for every good. And it would be disadvantageous for us never to get out of the mire of our miseries. As we said of those who are in mortal sin, that their streams are black and foul-smelling, so it is here; although not entirely—God deliver us—for we are just making a comparison. If we are always fixed on our earthly misery, the stream will never flow free from the mud of fears, faintheartedness, and cowardice. I would be looking to see if I'm being watched or not; if by taking this path things will turn out badly for me; whether it might be pride to dare begin a certain work; whether it would be good for a person so miserable to engage in something as lofty as prayer; whether I might be judged better than others if I don't follow the path they all do. I'd be thinking that extremes are not good, even in the practice of virtue; that, since I am such a sinner, I might have a greater fall; that perhaps I would not advance and would do harm to good people; that someone like myself has no need of anything special.

11. Oh, God help me, daughters, how many souls must have been made to suffer great loss in this way by the devil! These souls think that all such fears stem from humility. And there are many others I could mention. The fears come from our not understanding ourselves completely. They distort self-knowledge; and I'm not surprised if we never get free from ourselves, for this lack of freedom from ourselves, and even more, is what can be feared. So I say, daughters, that we should set our eyes on Christ, our Good, and on His

saints. There we shall learn true humility, the intellect will be enhanced,[11] as I have said, and self-knowledge will not make one base and cowardly. Even though this is the first dwelling place, it is very rich and so precious that if the soul slips away from the vermin within it, nothing will be left to do but advance. Terrible are the wiles and deceits used by the devil so that souls may not know themselves or understand their own paths.

12. I could give some very good proofs from experience of the wiles the devil uses in these first dwelling places. Thus I say that you should think not in terms of just a few rooms but in terms of a million;[12] for souls, all with good intentions, enter here in many ways. But since the devil always has such a bad intention, he must have in each room many legions of devils to fight off souls when they try to go from one room to the other. Since the poor soul doesn't know this, the devil plays tricks on it in a thousand ways. He's not so successful with those who have advanced closer to where the King dwells. But since in the first rooms souls are still absorbed in the world and engulfed in their pleasures and vanities, with their honors and pretenses, their vassals (which are these senses and faculties) don't have the strength God gave human nature in the beginning. And these souls are easily conquered, even though they may go about with desires not to offend God and though they do perform good works. Those who see themselves in this state must approach His Majesty as often as possible. They must take His Blessed Mother and His saints as intercessors so that these intercessors may fight

---

11. In IC 1.2.10.

12. See IC 1.2.8. Teresa avoids any arrangement of these dwelling places into neatly structured rows with set numbers. She thereby in her allegory makes it easy for us to imagine a marvelous depth and abundance of inner riches.

for them, for the soul's vassals have little strength to defend themselves. Truly, in all states it's necessary that strength come to us from God. May His Majesty through His mercy give it to us, amen.

13. How miserable the life in which we live! Because elsewhere I have said a great deal about the harm done to us by our failure to understand well this humility and self-knowledge,[13] I'll tell you no more about it here, even though this self-knowledge is the most important thing for us. Please God, I may have now said something beneficial for you.

14. You must note that hardly any of the light coming from the King's royal chamber reaches these first dwelling places. Even though they are not dark and black, as when the soul is in sin, they nevertheless are in some way darkened so that the soul cannot see the light. The darkness is not caused by a flaw in the room—for I don't know how to explain myself—but by so many bad things like snakes and vipers and poisonous creatures that enter with the soul and don't allow it to be aware of the light. It's as if a person were to enter a place where the sun is shining but be hardly able to open his eyes because of the mud in them. The room is bright but he doesn't enjoy it because of the impediment of things like these wild animals or beasts that make him close his eyes to everything but them. So, I think, must be the condition of the soul. Even though it may not be in a bad state, it is so involved in worldly things and so absorbed with its possessions, honor, or business affairs, as I have said,[14] that even though as a matter of fact it would want to see and enjoy its beauty these things do not allow it to; nor does it seem

---

13. In W 39.5. See also L 13.15.
14. In IC 1.1.8.

that it can slip free from so many impediments. If a person is to enter the second dwelling places, it is important that he strive to give up unnecessary things and business affairs. Each one should do this in conformity with his state in life. It is something so important in order for him to reach the main dwelling place that if he doesn't begin doing this I hold that it will be impossible for him to get there. And it will be even impossible for him to stay where he is without danger even though he has entered the castle, for in the midst of such poisonous creatures one cannot help but be bitten at one time or another.

15. Now then, what would happen, daughters, if we who are already free from these snares, as we are, and have entered much further into the castle to other secret dwelling places should turn back through our own fault and go out to this tumult? There are, because of our sins, many persons to whom God has granted favors who through their own fault have fallen back into this misery. In the monastery we are free with respect to exterior matters; in interior matters may it please the Lord that we also be free, and may He free us. Guard yourselves, my daughters, from extraneous cares. Remember that there are few dwelling places in this castle in which the devils do not wage battle. True, in some rooms the guards (which I believe I have said are the faculties)[15] have the strength to fight; but it is very necessary that we don't grow careless in recognizing the wiles of the devil, and that he not deceive us by changing himself into an angel of light.[16] There's a host of things he can do to cause us harm; he enters little by little, and until he's done the harm we don't recognize him.

---

15. In IC 1.2.4, 12.

16. Allusion to 2 Cor 11:14.

16. I've already told you elsewhere[17] that he's like a noiseless file, that we need to recognize him at the outset. Let me say something that will explain this better for you.

He gives a sister various impulses toward penance, for it seems to her she has no rest except when she is tormenting herself. This may be a good beginning; but if the prioress has ordered that no penance be done without permission, and the devil makes the sister think that in a practice that's so good one can be rightly daring, and she secretly gives herself up to such a penitential life that she loses her health and doesn't even observe what the rule commands, you can see clearly where all this good will end up.

He imbues another with a very great zeal for perfection. Such zeal is in itself good. But it could follow that every little fault the sisters commit will seem to her a serious breach; and she is careful to observe whether they commit them, and then informs the prioress. It could even happen at times that she doesn't see her own faults because of her intense zeal for the religious observance. Since the other sisters don't understand what's going on within her and see all this concern, they might not accept her zeal so well.

17. What the devil is hereby aiming after is no small thing: the cooling of the charity and love the sisters have for one another. This would cause serious harm. Let us understand my daughters, that true perfection consists in love of God and neighbor; the more perfectly we keep these two commandments the more perfect we will be. All that is in our rule and constitutions serves for nothing else than to be a means toward keeping these commandments with greater perfection. Let's forget about indiscreet zeal; it can do us a

---

17. In the W 38.2; 39 passim.

lot of harm. Let each one look to herself. Because I have said enough about this elsewhere,[18] I'll not enlarge on the matter.

18. This mutual love is so important that I would never want it to be forgotten. The soul could lose its peace and even disturb the peace of others by going about looking at trifling things in people that at times are not even imperfections, but since we know little we see these things in the worst light; look how costly this kind of perfection would be. Likewise, the devil could tempt the prioress in this way; and such a thing would be more dangerous. As a result much discretion is necessary. If things are done against the rule and constitutions, the matter need not always be seen in a good light. The prioress should be cautioned, and if she doesn't amend, the superior informed. This is charity. And the same with the sisters if there is something serious. And to fail to do these things for fear of a temptation would itself be a temptation. But it should be carefully noted—so that the devil doesn't deceive us—that we must not talk about these things to one another. The devil could thereby gain greatly and manage to get the custom of gossiping started. The matter should be discussed with the one who will benefit, as I have said. In this house, glory to God, there's not much occasion for gossip since such continual silence is kept; but it is good that we be on guard.

---

18. See L 13.8, 10; W 4; *Method for the Visitation of Monasteries* 17, 20, 21.

SIN AND DARKNESS

1.2.1–4 Teresa uses examples in her effort to convince us of the seriousness and consequences of mortal sin.

1.2.5–6 Having warned in the strongest terms of how abhorrent mortal sin should be to us, Teresa tells of two favors she received. The first was an intense fear of offending God, along with prayer begging God's help to keep her from falling. The second favor, which she calls a mirror for humility, was an understanding that God is the origin and source of any good that we do.

1.2.7 Teresa shares with her sisters her concerns about her ability to fulfill her writing task, worrying that she will have difficulty being concise. She also shares why she thinks her task of writing is important. Teresa points out that while the Carmelite constitutions oblige the nuns to spend many hours in prayer and all agree on the importance of prayer, help for those who wish to pray better was lacking. Instruction was provided on what we can do in prayer, but little was taught about what the Lord does in a soul. She says the interior life is little understood. Teresa proposes to help us understand the difficult things about the interior life that God has helped her understand.

1.2.8–13 Teresa explains more about the layout of the castle. The rooms don't follow one after the other in a fixed sequence. She compares the layout to a palmetto, which has many leaves surrounding the tender edible center. In this interior castle there are many spacious rooms surrounding the center where God dwells, and from where he illuminates the entire soul.

Although Teresa urges us to explore the many dwelling places which are up above, down below, and to the sides, she stresses the importance of the room of self-knowledge. This room is essential, even for those whom the Lord has brought to the very dwelling place where he abides. Teresa uses many examples and arguments to convince us of the tremendous importance of humility. Teresa says we will never completely know ourselves if we do not strive to know God. By gazing at his grandeur, we get in touch with our own lowliness.

1.2.10–11 Teresa warns about a false humility that arises from thinking too much of our own misery and not enough about God. This shift from focus on God to focus on self can keep persons from prayer and the practice of virtue. Their self-knowledge is distorted. We should set our eyes on Christ and his saints if we want to learn true humility.

In another view of the castle, Teresa says there are not just a few rooms, but rather millions, and souls enter the castle in many ways. She warns that the devil and his legions are at work in the outermost rooms (those farther from the center where the Lord dwells), trying to keep souls from advancing. Prayer is the best defense, asking God and the saints for help. She concludes by saying that humility and self-knowledge are the most important things for us.

1.2.14 Teresa tries in various ways to explain that souls in the first dwelling places have almost no perception of the light at the center of the castle where God dwells. Excessive preoccupation with worldly affairs absorbs their attention. Teresa understands that people living in the world cannot be completely free of worldly concerns, but to enter the second dwelling places, people must give up unnecessary things and unnecessary business affairs.

1.2.15–18 Teresa warns against the danger of turning back once we have entered the castle. She writes that many people have done so through their own fault. She explains that it is not only external matters that can preoccupy souls. She says that in the monasteries disobedience, even in matters that might seem good, such as doing penance, can cause harm. Another example is excessive zeal for perfection that leads to being critical of others while perhaps not seeing one's own faults. She adds that such zeal can lead to gossiping, to a decrease in charity, and can perhaps disturb the peace of others.

Interpretive Notes

How can human beings attain to the love of God, whom they do not see, unless God loves them first? No natural knowledge of God ascending from creatures discloses his hidden essence. All such natural knowledge—despite the analogy by which creature and Creator are linked—can comprehend him only as the totally Other. But in order to give ourselves to him in love we must first learn to know him as the divine lover. And only he himself can reveal himself to us in this capacity. This is accomplished by the word of revelation. The acceptance of divine revelation by faith already presupposes that God has turned to the soul in love. This gift of love is perfect when God gives himself to the soul in the life of grace and glory, when he draws the soul into his divine life. God lives in the innermost center of each soul, offering his gift of himself like the sun pouring forth its light.

Teresa begins this chapter with the darkness caused by mortal sin. From an ethical point of view, she knows well the disorder that it introduces into the castle. But much more her interest is seized by its theological dimension: mortal sin thwarts a person's relationship with God. It totally ruins the divine, primordial plan for every human being, which consists in a radical call to live in communion with God. The soul, which is so capable of shining like the sun and showing forth its beauty, is left totally dark. In fact, it really abandons its castle, living outside it in the dark ditch surrounded by poisonous snakes. *Gaudium et Spes* (Pastoral Constitution on the Church in the Modern World) puts it this way:

> For when humans look into their own heart they find that they are drawn towards what is wrong and sunk in many evils which cannot come from their good Creator. Often refusing to acknowledge God as their source, they have also upset the relationship which should tie them to their last end; and at the same time they have broken the right order that should reign within themselves, as well as between themselves and other human beings and all creatures. Humans therefore are divided in themselves. As a result, their whole life, both individual and social, shows itself to be a struggle, and a dramatic one, between good and evil, between light and darkness. Humans find that they are unable of themselves to overcome the assaults of evil successfully so that everyone feels as though bound by chains. (GS 13)

Who is this anonymous person that Teresa knows? It is Teresa herself. We remember that she was to hide her identity in this work, because *The Book of Her Life* was in the hands of the Inquisition and not allowed to be read because of its personal character. Since she is speaking of herself, we can identify her experience with the account she gives in her

Spiritual Testimonies of how the Lord showed what a soul is like both in grace and in mortal sin:

> Once while I was in prayer, the Lord showed me by a strange kind of intellectual vision what a soul is like in the state of grace. I saw this (through an intellectual vision) in the company of the most Blessed Trinity. From this company the soul received a power by which it had dominion over the whole earth. I was given an understanding of those words of the *Song of Songs* that say: "*Veniat dilectus meus in hortum suum et comedat* [Let my lover come to his garden and eat its choice fruits]" (Song 4:16). I was also shown how a soul in sin is without any power, but is like a person completely bound, tied, and blindfolded; for although wanting to see, such a person cannot, and cannot walk or hear, and remains in great darkness. Souls in this condition make me feel such compassion that any burden seems light to me if I can free one of them. I thought that by understanding this condition as I did— for it can be poorly explained—it wasn't possible for me to desire that anyone lose so much good or remain in so much evil. (ST 20)

Whenever Teresa touches on the theme of mortal sin, she begins to tremble: "Oh, oh, oh what a serious thing sin is" (Sol 10.1).

Teresa proposes the symbol of the "interior castle" to impress upon our minds the beauty and dignity of a human person. But we will not really know this beauty and dignity without knowing that we are capable of containing God, who dwells in us. We are not merely sparks of God, but God actually lives in us and makes us beautiful by his light. We are, however, at the same time capable of bringing evil into this beautiful castle and covering it with pitch. People must be aware of both dimensions. They must be aware of the darkness, but also of the light. They must turn their eyes toward the center, toward the light, toward the royal chamber where the King stays. This is the way to self-knowledge, which is "so important that I wouldn't want any relaxation ever in this regard, however high you may have climbed into the heavens. . . . In my opinion we shall never completely know ourselves if we don't strive to know God" (IC 1.2.9). Black and white seem blacker and whiter when next to each other. "Our intellects and wills, dealing in turn now with self, now with God, become nobler and better prepared for every good" (IC 1.2.10).

If we want to take full advantage of Teresa's symbol, we must not allow it to restrict our notion of the human person by thinking in terms of only seven rooms. There are numberless dwelling places in each category. We should think in terms of a million, she says (IC 1.2.12). The things of the soul must always be considered as "plentiful, spacious, and large" (IC 1.2.8). They do not follow in single file, but there are rooms everywhere, above, below, and to the sides. We are all capable of much more than we can imagine and the sun shines in all parts of the castle. Nor must we stay in one room a long time.

Life in the first dwelling places is not idyllic. Many enter the castle, but since they are absorbed with the things of the world, swallowed up with their own importance, pastimes, and pleasures of every kind, even becoming addicted to alcohol, drugs, sex, and gambling, they hardly live in the castle at all. Because of their many preoccupations, the light can barely touch them. But there is always the possibility for some prayer. Such people are easily vanquished, although they do experience from time to time some good desires. According to St. Augustine in his book *The City of God*, two loves have made two cities. Love of self to the despising of God has made the City of the world; love of God to the despising of self has made the City of God. Let us consult ourselves to see what we love, and we will find out to which city we belong.

Questions for Discussion

1. What effect should the thought of mortal sin have on us?
2. Teresa often found it difficult to write, but understood the necessity of teaching her sisters how to pray. Are there things that you find difficult or tiresome that have the potential to help others grow in their relationship with God? How can we overcome the barriers that keep us from fully accepting the actions God calls us to?
3. How must we think about the things of the soul?
4. How can we come to know ourselves completely?
5. What does Teresa want to do in this book?

THE SECOND DWELLING PLACES

This Section Has Only One Chapter

CHAPTER 1

Discusses the importance of perseverance if one is to reach the final dwelling places; the great war the devil wages; and the importance of taking the right road from the beginning. Offers a remedy that has proved very efficacious.

Now let us speak about the type of soul that enters the second dwelling places and what such a soul does in them. I'd like to say only a little, for I have spoken at length on this subject elsewhere.[1] And it would be impossible to avoid repeating much of it, for I don't remember a thing of what I said. If I could present the matter for you in a variety of ways, I know well that you wouldn't be annoyed since we never tire of books—as many as there are—that deal with it.

2. This stage pertains to those who have already begun to practice prayer and have understood how important it is not to stay in the first dwelling places. But they still don't have the determination to remain in this second stage without turning back, for they don't avoid the occasion of sin.

---

1. See L 11–13; W passim.

This failure to avoid these occasions is quite dangerous. But these persons have received a good deal of mercy in that they sometimes do strive to escape from snakes and poisonous creatures, and they understand that it is good to avoid them.

These rooms, in part, involve much more effort than do the first, even though there is not as much danger, for it now seems that souls in them recognize the dangers, and there is great hope they will enter further into the castle. I say that these rooms involve more effort because those who are in the first dwelling places are like deaf-mutes and thus the difficulty of not speaking is more easily endured by them than it is by those who hear but cannot speak. Yet, not for this reason does one have greater desire to be deaf, for after all it is a wonderful thing to hear what is being said to us. So these persons are able to hear the Lord when He calls. Since they are getting closer to where His Majesty dwells, He is a very good neighbor. His mercy and goodness are so bountiful; whereas we are occupied in our pastimes, business affairs, pleasures, and worldly buying and selling, and still falling into sin and rising again. These beasts are so poisonous and their presence so dangerous and noisy that it would be a wonder if we kept from stumbling and falling over them. Yet this Lord desires intensely that we love Him and seek His company, so much so that from time to time He calls us to draw near Him. And His voice is so sweet the poor soul dissolves at not doing immediately what He commands. Thus, as I say, hearing His voice is a greater trial than not hearing it.

3. I don't mean that these appeals and calls are like the ones I shall speak of later on.[2] But they come through words spoken by other good people, or through sermons, or

---

2. In IC 6.3.

through what is read in good books, or through the many things that are heard and by which God calls, or through illnesses and trials, or also through a truth that He teaches during the brief moments we spend in prayer; however lukewarm these moments may be, God esteems them highly. And you, sisters, don't underestimate this first favor, nor should you become disconsolate if you don't respond at once to the Lord. His Majesty knows well how to wait many days and years, especially when He sees perseverance and good desires. This perseverance is most necessary here. One always gains much through perseverance. But the attacks made by devils in a thousand ways afflict the soul more in these rooms than in the previous ones. In the previous ones the soul was deaf and dumb—at least it heard very little and resisted less, as one who has partly lost hope of conquering. Here the intellect is more alive and the faculties more skilled. The blows from the artillery strike in such a way that the soul cannot fail to hear. It is in this stage that the devils represent these snakes (worldly things) and the temporal pleasures of the present as though almost eternal. They bring to mind the esteem one has in the world, one's friends and relatives, one's health (when there's thought of penitential practices, for the soul that enters this dwelling place always begins wanting to practice some penance) and a thousand other obstacles.

4. O Jesus, what an uproar the devils instigate here! And the afflictions of the poor soul: it doesn't know whether to continue or to return to the first room. Reason, for its part, shows the soul that it is mistaken in thinking that these things of the world are not worth anything when compared to what it is aiming after. Faith, however, teaches it about where it will find fulfillment. The memory shows it where all these things end, holding before it the death of those who found great joy

in them. Through the memory it sees how some have suffered sudden death, how quickly they are forgotten by all. Some whom it had known in great prosperity are under the ground, and their graves are walked upon. This soul itself has often passed by these graves. It reflects that many worms are swarming over the corpses, and thinks about numerous other things. The will is inclined to love after seeing such countless signs of love; it would want to repay something; it especially keeps in mind how this true Lover never leaves it, accompanying it and giving it life and being. Then the intellect helps it realize that it couldn't find a better friend, even were it to live for many years, that the whole world is filled with falsehood, and that so too these joys the devil gives it are filled with trials, cares, and contradictions. The intellect tells the soul of its certainty that outside this castle neither security nor peace will be found, that it should avoid going about to strange houses since its own is so filled with blessings to be enjoyed if it wants. The intellect will ask who it is that finds everything he needs in his own house and, especially, has a guest who will make him lord over all goods provided that he wills to avoid going astray like the prodigal son and eating the husks of swine.[3]

5. These are reasons for conquering the devils. But, oh, my Lord and my God, how the whole world's habit of getting involved in vanities vitiates everything! Our faith is so dead that we desire what we see more than what faith tells us. And, indeed, we see only a lot of misfortune in those who go after these visible vanities. But these poisonous things we are dealing with are the cause of this misfortune, for just as all is poisoned if a viper bites someone and the wound swells,

---

3. Lk 15:16.

so we will be poisoned if we do not watch ourselves. Clearly many remedies are necessary to cure us, and God is favoring us a good deal if we do not die from the wound. Certainly the soul undergoes great trials here. If the devil, especially, realizes that it has all it needs in its temperament and habits to advance far, he will gather all hell together to make the soul go back outside.

6. Ah, my Lord! Your help is necessary here; without it one can do nothing.[4] In Your mercy do not consent to allow this soul to suffer deception and give up what was begun. Enlighten it that it may see how all its good is within this castle and that it may turn away from bad companions. It's a wonderful thing for a person to talk to those who speak about this interior castle, to draw near not only to those seen to be in these rooms where he is but to those known to have entered the ones closer to the center. Conversation with these latter will be a great help to him, and he can converse so much with them that they will bring him to where they are. Let the soul always heed the warning not to be conquered. If the devil sees that it has the strong determination to lose its life and repose and all that he offers it rather than return to the first room, he will abandon it much more quickly. Let the soul be manly and not like those soldiers who knelt down to drink before going into battle (I don't remember with whom),[5] but be determined to fight with all the devils and realize that there are no better weapons than those of the cross.

7. Even though I've said this at other times,[6] it's so important that I repeat it here: it is that souls shouldn't be thinking

---

4. Allusion to Jn 15:5.
5. Allusion to Judg 7:5.
6. See L 4.2; 11.10–15; W 20.2; 21.2; 23; 36; 41.

about consolations at this beginning stage. It would be a very poor way to start building so precious and great an edifice. If the foundation is on sand, the whole building will fall to the ground. They'll never finish being dissatisfied and tempted. These are not the dwelling places where it rains manna; those lie further ahead, where a soul finds in the manna every taste it desires;[7] for it wants only what God wants. It's an amusing thing that even though we still have a thousand impediments and imperfections and our virtues have hardly begun to grow—and please God they may have begun—we are yet not ashamed to seek spiritual delights in prayer or to complain about dryness. May this never happen to you, sisters. Embrace the cross your Spouse has carried and understand that this must be your task. Let the one who can do so, suffer more for Him; and she will be rewarded that much more. As for other favors, if the Lord should grant you one, thank Him for it as you would for something freely added on.

8. It will seem to you that you are truly determined to undergo exterior trials, provided that God favors you interiorly. His Majesty knows best what is suitable for us. There's no need for us to be advising Him about what He should give us, for He can rightly tell us that we don't know what we're asking for.[8] The whole aim of any person who is beginning prayer—and don't forget this, because it's very important—should be that he work and prepare himself with determination and every possible effort to bring his will into conformity with God's will. Be certain that, as I shall say later,[9] the greatest perfection attainable along the

---

7. Allusion to Wis 16:20.
8. Allusion to Mt 20:22.
9. In IC 5.3.3–12.

spiritual path lies in this conformity. It is the person who lives in more perfect conformity who will receive more from the Lord and be more advanced on this road. Don't think that in what concerns perfection there is some mystery or things unknown or still to be understood, for in perfect conformity to God's will lies all our good. Now then, if we err in the beginning, desiring that the Lord do our will at once and lead us according to what we imagine, what kind of stability will this edifice have? Let us strive to do what lies in our power and guard ourselves against these poisonous little reptiles, for the Lord often desires that dryness and bad thoughts afflict and pursue us without our being able to get rid of them. Sometimes He even permits these reptiles to bite us so that afterward we may know how to guard ourselves better and that He may prove whether we are greatly grieved by having offended Him.

9. Thus, if you should at times fall don't become discouraged and stop striving to advance. For even from this fall God will draw out good, as does the seller of an antidote who drinks some poison in order to test whether his antidote is effective. Even if we didn't see our misery—or the great harm that a dissipated life does to us—through any other means than through this assault that we endure for the sake of being brought back to recollection, that would be enough. Can there be an evil greater than that of being ill at ease in our own house? What hope can we have of finding rest outside of ourselves if we cannot be at rest within? We have so many great and true friends and relatives (which are our faculties) with whom we must always live, even though we may not want to. But from what we feel, these seem to be warring against us because of what our vices have done to them. Peace, peace, the Lord said, my sisters; and He urged

His apostle so many times.[10] [Well, believe me, if we don't obtain and have peace in our own house we'll not find it outside.] Let this war be ended. Through the blood He shed for us I ask those who have not begun to enter within themselves to do so; and those who have begun, not to let the war make them turn back. Let these latter reflect that a relapse is worse than a fall; they already see their loss. Let them trust in the mercy of God and not at all in themselves, and they will see how His Majesty brings them from the dwelling places of one stage to those of another and settles them in a land where these wild animals cannot touch or tire them, but where they themselves will bring all these animals into subjection and scoff at them. And they shall enjoy many more blessings than one can desire—blessings even in this life, I mean.

10. Since, as I've said in the beginning,[11] I've written to you about how you should conduct yourselves in these disturbances set up here by the devil and how you cannot begin to recollect yourselves by force but only by gentleness, if your recollection is going to be continual, I will not say anything else here than that in my opinion it is very important to consult persons with experience; for you will be thinking that you are seriously failing to do some necessary thing. Provided that we don't give up, the Lord will guide everything for our benefit, even though we may not find someone to teach us. There is no other remedy for this evil of giving up prayer than to begin again; otherwise the soul will gradually lose more each day—and please God that it will understand this fact.

11. Someone could think that if turning back is so bad it would be better never to begin but to remain outside the

---

10. Jn 20:19–21.
11. In IC 2.1.1.

castle. I have already told you at the beginning—and the Lord Himself tells you—that anyone who walks in danger perishes in it[12] and that the door of entry to this castle is prayer. Well now, it is foolish to think that we will enter heaven without entering into ourselves, coming to know ourselves, reflecting on our misery and what we owe God, and begging Him often for mercy. The Lord Himself says: *No one will ascend to My Father but through Me*[13] (I don't know if He says it this way—I think He does) and *whoever sees Me sees My Father.*[14] Well, if we never look at Him or reflect on what we owe Him and the death He suffered for us, I don't know how we'll be able to know Him or do works in His service. And what value can faith have without works and without joining them to the merits of Jesus Christ, our Good? Or who will awaken us to love this Lord?

May it please His Majesty to give us understanding of how much we cost Him, of how the servant is no greater than his master,[15] and that we must work in order to enjoy His glory. And we need to pray for this understanding so that we aren't always entering into temptation.[16]

---

12. Allusion to Sir 3:26.
13. Jn 14:6.
14. Jn 14:9.
15. Allusion to Mt 10:24.
16. Allusion to Mt 26:41.

PERSEVERANCE ON
THE RIGHT ROAD

2.1.1 Because she has already written on the topic, Teresa says she wishes to write only a little here about the type of souls that enter the second dwelling places and what souls do there.

2.1.2–3 Here Teresa introduces most of the ideas on which the discussion of the second dwelling places is based. Persons in these rooms have begun to practice prayer and understand the importance of moving forward in the spiritual life. They lack, however, the determination required to keep from turning back, for they don't avoid the occasions of sin. Teresa explains that there is a tension here that requires much more effort on the soul's part than was required in the first rooms. On the one hand, these souls are able to hear the Lord when he calls (although they don't hear his voice in the same way as do persons who have advanced further), whereas those in the first rooms could not. In the second dwelling places, the word of the Lord comes in various ways—through words spoken by good people, sermons, through what is read in books, trials, or truths understood in prayer. They want to do what he commands. On the other hand, however, there are more attacks by devils here, and perseverance is most necessary.

2.1.4 Teresa continues her discussion of the tensions in the second dwelling places. She portrays reason as an enemy that devalues the goals of the spiritual life in favor of those of the material world. Faith supports the soul by presenting its true goal and good, and memory reminds persons of their mortality. The will, she says, is inclined to love through gratitude for the loving presence which, it understands, sustains it and never leaves it. The intellect points out all the ways in which life within the castle is superior to life outside.

2.1.5–6 Teresa continues her discussion of the tensions and struggles in the second dwelling places. Faith is still weak, and trials and temptations are many. Teresa offers a prayer on behalf of these souls: ". . . do not consent to allow this soul to suffer deception and give up what was begun." Teresa emphasizes that strong determination on the soul's part is extremely important.

2.1.7–8 Teresa warns against thinking about consolations at this beginning stage. To do so, she says, would be like building a foundation in sand. Her advice is to embrace the cross, following the Lord's example. We must avoid prayer that tries to tell God what we think is best for us. Instead we must try in every way to bring our wills into conformity with God's will. In perfect conformity to God's will lies all our good. She says that here the Lord often desires that we experience dryness and that bad thoughts affect us without our being able to get rid of them; and sometimes he even permits these reptiles to bite us. The reason that God acts in this way is that we may thereby learn how to guard ourselves better in the future, and he may prove whether we are genuinely sorry for our offenses.

2.1.9 Teresa now offers some reassurance. Our failures should not discourage us or keep us from advancing. Trials and even our failures can teach us, through the misery that ensues, that we will never have peace outside of the castle; that is, in a dissipated life. She urges all to enter within themselves, trusting in God and not in themselves. There the Lord will bring them from the dwelling places of one stage to those of another. There, she says, they will enjoy more blessings than one can desire, even in this life.

2.1.10–11 Because persons in the second dwelling places can experience so many disturbances, Teresa thinks it is very important to consult persons with experience who can reassure and guide them. She adds that if we persevere, the Lord will guide everything for our benefit, even if we do not find an experienced person to teach us. She observes that there is no other remedy for the evil of giving up prayer except to begin again. Teresa anticipates an objection someone might raise: If going back is so bad, would it be better never to begin? She answers the objection, warning that anyone who walks in danger (that is, in the danger outside the castle) perishes in it, and the door of entry to the castle is prayer. Self-knowledge and reflection on what we owe God are essential if we wish to enter heaven. She presents strong arguments on the great value of prayer as essential to our growth in the spiritual life.

Interpretive Notes

This dwelling place represents a time of struggle because of the disorder introduced into the castle through a life that was lived outside of it. A radical decision must be made at the beginning. There must be an initial and progressive sensitivity to the word of God. By meditating on the biblical word, Christians in these dwelling places become aware of their situation as prodigal children of God, who once longed to feed on the husks of swine (Lk 15:16).

Teresa's castle is a real symbol. It represents human interiority, human struggle, and the call to transcendence. These three themes—interiority, struggle, and communion with God—are interwoven. In these first dwelling places, Teresa introduces the readers to interiority. She entreats them to enter within, insisting that they bring into their awareness this interior world, a spiritual point of view, their "soul," she says. You must enter the castle and remain within, going ever deeper toward the center.

To remain in the castle, especially in these beginnings, Teresa is convinced, requires struggle. The attractions and pull of the world surrounding one are extremely powerful. She refers to the struggle as a "great war." But it would be a mistake to think that this struggle is experienced only in the beginning dwelling places. The battle goes on as one moves deeper into the castle. Some today may not like this language of warfare when speaking of the spiritual life. But if we consider that it is a woman, not a man, who uses it, and a mystic, perhaps we can see that each of us carries within ourselves the root of this disharmony and conflict.

In speaking of conflict, Teresa uses such terms as reason, faith, memory, will, and intellect. She uses these terms to express how we must deal with the conflict because they were commonly used in her day by philosophers and theologians. She heard them in sermons and read about them in books. She employed them as best she could to express what she was trying to say without any precise training in philosophy or theology. Reason, for her, was the power by which we give to ourselves and others reasons for our thinking. Faith is a gift God pours into the soul by which we know and give assent to all that God reveals to us about himself and about the means by which we can reach him. It follows the stages of human growth and, through trials that test and perfect it, brings us toward an ever-deeper likeness to Christ. Memory is the power to recall past events and keep before our minds the things we have come to know in the past. The intellect is a power by which we come to know truths by drawing them out from other truths we already know. The will is the power to make choices and rest in the choices made. The supreme principle on which all human beings should make their choices is the will of God. The divine will is a personal project of love for all men and women which aims to bring them to their full and final happiness. The will of God can at times call us to painful sacrifice.

Teresa, then, introduces us in these second dwelling places to her special version of Christian asceticism before speaking of mysticism. Just as she does in the first and third dwelling places, she suggests a biblical text with which readers might identify: the soldiers of Gideon who lapped up the water. They were the valiant three hundred soldiers who Gideon took into battle and represent those in the second dwelling places determined not to be conquered. Actually, this view of the Christian life as a struggle against evil comes from St. Paul, who interprets his entire existence as a permanent combat. "I have fought the good fight" (2 Tim 4:7). He urges Christians to put on the armor of God, do all your duty requires, and hold your ground. "Our battle is against the rulers of this world of darkness" (Eph 6:11–17). Teresa belongs to this cohort of combative Christians. She situates her castle within these regions of Pauline, spiritual militancy. The spirituality she presents is not for cowards, the comfort-loving, or the lazy.

Sin is not a matter of a battle overcome definitively through pardon and a return to the castle. It has the sinister capacity of unleashing inordinate forces difficult to drive out of the dwelling places in the castle. Teresa begins by admiring the beauty of the castle, but she doesn't continue in this vein ingenuously. Human beings are at once both light and darkness: beauty and dignity in their being (the beauty of the castle), and darkness and misery in their life story (life within the castle).

Although souls are not in complete darkness as when outside the castle, so many vermin, poisonous reptiles, and beasts enter these first dwelling places from outside, and even bite people, that little light reaches them from the center. Perhaps we can simply explain Teresa's symbols with words of Jesus and St. Paul: "Evil thoughts, unchastity, theft, murder, adultery, greed, malice, deceit, licentiousness, envy, blasphemy, arrogance, folly" (Mk 7:21–22). "Evil, greed, and malice; full of envy, murder, rivalry, treachery, and spite. They are gossips and scandalmongers, and they hate God. They are insolent, haughty, boastful, ingenious in their wickedness, and rebellious toward their parents. They are senseless, faithless, heartless, ruthless" (Rom 1:29–31). At least we may be tempted much regarding many of these disorders, or vermin, as Teresa refers to them. She speaks at times as though God is tempting us to evil. But she insists that God only permits all that happens to us. If we fall, he allows it that we might learn a lesson and above all learn how to be sorry for our failures and grow in humility. We must come to know ourselves and reflect on our misery and get in the habit of looking at Jesus.

Gaudium et Spes (Pastoral Constitution on the Church in the Modern World) puts it this way:

> The whole of man's history has been the story of combat with the powers of evil, stretching, so our Lord tells us, from the very dawn of history until the last day. Finding himself in the midst of the battlefield, a person has to struggle to do what is right, and it is at great cost to himself, and aided by God's grace, that he succeeds in achieving his

own inner integrity. Hence the church of Christ, trusting in the design of the creator and admitting that progress can contribute to man's true happiness, still feels called upon to echo the words of the apostle: 'Do not be conformed to this world' (Rom 12:2). 'World' here means a spirit of vanity and malice whereby human activity from being ordered to the service of God and other humans is distorted into being an instrument of sin. (GS 37)

Questions for Discussion

1. How does Teresa compare those in this dwelling place with the people in the first?
2. What must the soul be determined to do in this dwelling place?
3. What good can come from the afflictions we undergo at this time?
4. What is the only remedy when one has given up prayer?
5. Can you recall an experience with sin and darkness where a more combative strategy was necessary? Did this strategy help you to grow stronger in your ability to fight against temptation in later occasions of sin?

THE THIRD
DWELLING PLACES

Contains Two Chapters

CHAPTER 1

Treats of what little security we can have while living in this exile, even though we may have reached a high state, and of how we should walk with fear. This chapter has some good points.

What shall we say to those who through perseverance and the mercy of God have won these battles and have entered the rooms of the third stage, if not: *Blessed is the man who fears the Lord?*[1] His Majesty has done no small thing in giving me understanding right now of what this verse means in the vernacular, for I am ignorant in matters like this. Certainly we are right in calling such a man blessed, since if he doesn't turn back he is, from what we can understand, on the secure path to his salvation.[2] Here you will see, sisters,

---

1. Ps 112:1.

2. Teresa commissioned Father Jerónimo Gracián to review her work. Gracián did so scrupulously and made corrections here and there throughout the manuscript. For example, in this passage he crossed out the word "secure" and substituted "right." In fact this whole chapter has a number of corrections by Gracián, who was fearful lest the saint affirm any certitude about the state of grace, or security about one's own salvation, that would have gone contrary to the teaching of the Council of Trent or have been similar to certain theories of the *Alumbrados*. Fortunately, Gracián made the deletion marks so as to leave the original completely legible. The

how important it was to win the previous battles. I am certain the Lord never fails to give a person like this security of conscience, which is no small blessing. I said "security" and I was wrong, for there is no security in this life; so always understand that I mean "if he doesn't abandon the path he began on."

2. It is a great misery to have to live a life in which we must always walk like those whose enemies are at their doorstep; they can neither sleep nor eat without weapons and without being always frightened lest somewhere these enemies might be able to break through this fortress. O my Lord and my Good, how is it that You want us to desire so miserable a life? For it isn't possible to stop wanting and asking You to take us out of it unless there is hope of losing it for You or of spending it very earnestly in Your service or, above

---

Jesuit Ribera, in turn, corrected Gracián's corrections with marginal comments such as the following: "One doesn't have to cross out any of the holy Mother's words." A further example of the skirmish that went on in the margins of Teresa's manuscript can be found in no. 8 of this chapter. In that delicate passage Teresa wrote: "Shouldn't we consider ourselves lucky to be able to repay something of what we owe Him for His service toward us? I say these words 'His service toward us' unwillingly; but the fact is that He did nothing else but serve us all the time He lived in this world." Gracián changed "His service toward us" to "having died for us" and crossed out what followed. Ribera again noted: "Nothing should be deleted; what the saint said has been very well said." All of this led to Ribera's written admonition on the first page of the autograph of *The Interior Castle*: "What the holy Mother wrote in this book is frequently crossed out, and other words are added or a gloss is made in the margin. Usually the cancellation is poorly conceived and the text is better the way it was first written . . . And since I have read and looked over this work with a certain amount of care, I think I should advise anyone reading it to read it as the holy Mother wrote it, for she understood and said things better, and to pay no attention to what was added or changed unless the correction was made by the saint herself in her own hand, which is seldom. And I ask out of charity anyone who reads this book to reverence the words and letters formed by so holy a hand and try to understand her correctly; and you will see that there is nothing to correct. Even if you do not understand, believe that she who wrote it knew better and that the words cannot be corrected well unless their meaning is fully understood. If their meaning is not grasped, what is very appropriately said will seem inappropriate. Such is the way books are ruined and lost."

all, of understanding what Your will is. If it is Your will, my God, may we die with You, as St. Thomas said;[3] for living without You and with these fears of the possibility of losing You forever is nothing else than dying often. That's why, daughters, I say that the blessedness we must ask for is that of being already secure with the blessed. For with these fears, what happiness can anyone have whose whole happiness is to please God? Consider that this happiness was had—and in much greater degree—by some saints who fell into serious sins and that we are not sure that God will help us to get free from these sins and to do penance for them.

3. Certainly, my daughters, I am so fearful as I write this that I don't know how I'm writing it or how I live when I think about it, which is very often. Pray, my daughters, that His Majesty may live in me always. If He doesn't, what security can a life as badly spent as mine have? And do not become sad in knowing that this life has been badly spent, as I have sometimes observed you become when I tell this to you; you continue to desire that I might have lived a very holy life— and you are right. I too would want to have so lived, but what can I do if I have lost holiness through my own fault! I will not complain about God who gave me enough help to carry out your desires. I cannot say this without tears and being very ashamed that I am writing something for those who can teach me. Doing so has been a hard command to obey! May it please the Lord that since it is being done for Him it may be of some benefit to you so that You may ask Him to pardon this miserable and bold creature. But His Majesty well knows that I can boast only of His mercy, and since I cannot cease being what I have been, I have no other

---

3. Jn 11:16.

remedy than to approach His mercy and to trust in the merits of His Son and of the Virgin, His mother, whose habit I wear so unworthily, and you wear. Praise Him, my daughters, for you truly belong to our Lady. Thus you have no reason to be ashamed of my misery since you have such a good mother. Imitate her and reflect that the grandeur of our Lady and the good of having her for your patroness must be indeed great since my sins and being what I am have not been enough to tarnish in any way this sacred order.

4. But one thing I advise you: not because you have such a mother or patroness should you feel secure, for David was very holy, and you already know who Solomon was. Don't pay any attention to the enclosure and the penance in which you live or feel safe in the fact that you are always conversing with God and practicing such continual prayer and being so withdrawn from the world of things and, in your opinion, holding them in abhorrence. These practices are all good, but not a sufficient reason, as I have said,[4] for us to stop fearing. So, continue to say this verse and often bear it in mind: *"Beatus vir qui timet Dominum* (Happy are those who fear the Lord)."[5]

5. I don't remember what I was speaking about, for I have digressed a great deal and in thinking of myself I feel helpless, as a bird with broken wings, when it comes to saying anything good. So I want to leave this matter aside for now. Let me get back to what I began telling you[6] concerning souls that have entered the third dwelling places, for the Lord has done them no small favor, but a very great one, in letting them

---

4. In IC 3.1.2.
5. Ps 112:1.
6. In IC 3.1.1.

get through the first difficulties. I believe that through the goodness of God there are many of these souls in the world. They long not to offend His Majesty, even guarding themselves against venial sins; they are fond of doing penance and setting aside periods for recollection; they spend their time well, practicing works of charity toward their neighbors; and are very balanced in their use of speech and dress and in the governing of their households—those who have them. Certainly, this is a state to be desired. And, in my opinion, there is no reason why entrance even into the final dwelling place should be denied these souls, nor will the Lord deny them this entrance if they desire it; for such a desire is an excellent way to prepare oneself; so that every favor may be granted.

6. O Jesus, and who will say that he doesn't want a good so wonderful, especially after having passed through the most difficult trial? No, nobody will. We all say that we want this good. But since there is need of still more in order that the soul possess the Lord completely, it is not enough to say we want it; just as this was not enough for the young man whom the Lord told what one must do in order to be perfect.[7] From the time I began to speak of these dwelling places I have had this young man in mind. For we are literally like him; and ordinarily the great dryness in prayer comes from this, although it also has other causes. And I'm leaving aside mention of some interior trials that many good souls undergo (unbearable trials and not at all due to their own fault), from which the Lord always frees them to their own great benefit, and mention of those who suffer from melancholy and other illnesses. Briefly, in all things we have to let God be the judge. What I've said, I believe, is what usually happens; for

---

7. Mt 19:16–22.

since these souls realize that they wouldn't commit a sin for anything—many wouldn't even advertently commit a venial sin—and that they conduct their lives and households well, they cannot accept patiently that the door of entry to the place where our King dwells be closed to them who consider themselves His vassals. But even though a king here on earth has many vassals, not all enter his chamber. Enter, enter, my daughters, into the interior rooms; pass on from your little works. By the mere fact that you are Christians you must do all these things and much more. It is enough for you to be God's vassals; don't let your desire be for so much that as a result you will be left with nothing. Behold the saints who entered this King's chamber, and you will see the difference between them and us. Don't ask for what you have not deserved, nor should it enter our minds that we have merited this favor however much we may have served—we who have offended God.

7. Oh, humility, humility! I don't know what kind of temptation I'm undergoing in this matter that I cannot help but think that anyone who makes such an issue of this dryness is a little lacking in humility. I said that I've omitted mention of those great interior trials I've referred to,[8] for those involve much more than just a lack of devotion. Let us prove ourselves, my sisters, or let the Lord prove us, for He knows well how to do this even though we often don't want to understand it. Let us speak now of those souls whose lives are so well ordered; let us recognize what they do for God, and we shall at once see how we have no reason for complaining of His Majesty. If, like the young man in the gospel, we turn our backs and go away sad[9] when the Lord tells us

8. In IC 3.1.6.
9. Mt 19:22.

what we must do to be perfect, what do you want His Majesty to do? [For He must give the reward in conformity with the love we have for Him. And this love, daughters, must not be fabricated in our imaginations but proved by deeds. And don't think He needs our works; He needs the determination of our wills.]

8. We seem to think that everything is done when we willingly take and wear the religious habit and abandon all worldly things and possession for Him—even though these possessions may amount to no more than the nets St. Peter possessed,[10] for he who gives what he has thinks he gives enough. This renunciation is a good enough preparation if one perseveres in it and doesn't turn back and become involved with the vermin in the first rooms, even if it be only in desire. There is no doubt that if a person perseveres in this nakedness and detachment from all worldly things he will reach his goal. But this perseverance includes the condition—and note that I am advising you of this—that you consider yourselves useless servants, as St. Paul, or Christ, says;[11] and believe that you have not put our Lord under any obligation to grant you these kinds of favors. Rather, as one who has received more, you are more indebted.[12] What can we do for a God so generous that He died for us, created us, and gives us being? Shouldn't we consider ourselves lucky to be able to repay something of what we owe Him for His service toward us? I say these words "His service toward us" unwillingly; but the fact is that He did nothing else but serve us all the time He lived in this world. And yet we ask Him again for favors and gifts.

---

10. Mt 19:27.

11. Teresa first wrote "as St. Paul says" then added between the lines "or Christ." Gracián crossed out both and wrote: "St. Luke says it in chapter 17." See Lk 17:10.

12. Allusion to Lk 12:48.

9. Reflect a great deal, daughters, on some of the things that are here pointed out, even though in a jumbled way, for I don't know how to explain them further. The Lord will give you understanding of them so that out of dryness you may draw humility—and not disquiet, which is what the devil aims after. Be convinced that where humility is truly present God will give a peace and conformity—even though He may never give consolations—by which one will walk with greater contentment than will others with their consolations. For often, as you have read,[13] the divine Majesty gives these consolations to the weaker souls; although I think we would not exchange these consolations for the fortitude of those who walk in dryness. We are fonder of consolations than we are of the cross. Test us, Lord—for You know the truth—so that we may know ourselves.

---

13. This is a vague reference, perhaps to W 17.2, 7.

PERSEVERANCE
AS USELESS SERVANTS

3.1.1 Teresa says that both perseverance and the mercy of God bring souls to the third stage. She applies to them the scriptural verse: "Blessed is the person who fears the Lord" (Ps 112:1). If they do not abandon the path they began on, the Lord will give these persons security of conscience. But then Teresa immediately checks herself and says that we can never be secure on this earth. Even though the soul has won the major battles of the first two dwelling places, it must still be on guard against offending the Lord.

3.1.2 Teresa interrupts the description of the third dwelling places to write about the human condition, which she believes requires constant vigilance against many enemies; these enemies, we infer, are sins and temptations. She says the blessedness we must ask for is that of being already secure with the blessed—that is, in death, if we wish to find happiness. If our whole happiness lies in pleasing God, we can never be truly happy if we are fearful of losing God through our sins.

She continues this theme, writing that she is so fearful as she writes that she doesn't know how she is writing or how she lives when she thinks about "it"; we infer that she is referring to the situation of uncertainty and insecurity she described in the preceding number. She laments that her life has been badly spent and says she is ashamed to write for those who can teach her. She asks the nuns to pray that His Majesty may live in her always.

3.1.3 She moves from her theme of fear to that of trust. She professes that she can boast only of God's mercy, and since she cannot cease being what she has been, her only remedy is to approach his mercy and trust in the merits of his Son and the Virgin his Mother.

3.1.4 Teresa returns to her theme of fear of the Lord and cautions that living in enclosure and penance, and prayer, and being withdrawn from the world and holding worldly things in abhorrence are not sufficient reasons to stop fearing. So no matter how holy we might be, we must still know that we can fall and keep often in mind the words: Blessed is the person who fears the Lord.

3.1.5–9 Teresa describes persons who have reached the third dwelling places as living commendable lives. She thinks these souls will reach the final dwelling place if they desire it. Then she goes on to explain what this desire must consist of. This desire cannot be a matter of words only. Souls must undergo many trials, including dryness in prayer. Teresa cautions against impatience in these good desires. The fact of their exemplary lives can, in some cases, be an impediment in that they may begin to think they deserve God's favors. Teresa thinks undue concern about dryness is a sign of lack of humility. We must prove our love by deeds, deeds that consist not of works, but of the determination of our wills. Renouncing possessions is less important than humility expressed in the gospel judgment that we are useless servants. We should not ask for favors. She trusts that God will help us understand that out of dryness may come humility and not disquiet. Where humility is present, God will give peace and conformity to his will. Teresa observes that we are fonder of consolations than we are of the cross.

Interpretive Notes

The first dwelling places consist in entering the castle, which means beginning the process of knowing oneself and entering a relationship with God. In the second, one must engage in battle, struggling against the forces of evil. And in entering the third, one might expect that the experience would be one of triumph, of victory and peace. But the asceticism continues, and vigilance and effort are necessary. Teresa speaks of proving one's love, of the risks of wishful or conceited thinking. Here one passes through a kind of spiritual adolescence.

In speaking of this period, Teresa recalls her own bittersweet experience of this stage, lasting in her case about ten years, from the time of her father's death (December 1543) when she was thirty years old until her conversion in 1554. It was a time filled with uncertainty and back and forth movement. Yet, with the death of her father she returned to a truth she saw in childhood, that everything is passing. She recovered her ideals, but not without a great struggle between her prayer life and all that warred against it, between, in her words, friendship with God and friendship with the world.

Teresa is certain, though, that we all will, in one way or another, have experiences similar to these. At times we will feel strong and self-sufficient, at other times weak and humiliated. We will know what it means to be determined, but then have evolving doubts. What has to be discovered through experience is our deep need for God's loving mercy.

The biblical text that first comes to Teresa's mind here comes from the Psalmist: "Blessed is the person who fears the Lord" (Ps 112:1). This biblical fear of God refers to a respect and loving awareness of God; persons have this fear when they have a deep and sincere love of his commandments. The second biblical text presents the image of the rich young man. He comes to Jesus enthusiastically searching, but goes away sad. This is a good picture of Teresa when in her thirties. She often approached her Lord enthusiastically, giving him her heart, only to withdraw it a while later. Those who live in this third dwelling place have to recognize that they need not only to offer themselves generously to the Lord but to recover from their failings. They have to become engaged in a more difficult task: accepting that God has plans that go far beyond one's present project, generous though it may be, and letting him take the initiative, especially when it is a surprise and upsets one's own strategies.

"Praise Him, my daughters, for you truly belong to our Lady. Thus you have no reason to be ashamed of my misery since you have such a good Mother. Imitate her" (IC 3.1.3). *Lumen Gentium* (Dogmatic Constitution on the Church) also directs us to Mary as our Mother and model:

Being of the race of Adam, she [the Mother of God] is at the same time also united to all those who are to be saved; indeed, she is clearly the mother of the members of Christ . . . since she has by her charity joined in bringing about the birth of believers in the Church, who are members of its head. Wherefore she is hailed as pre-eminent and as a wholly unique member of the Church, and as its type and outstanding model in faith and charity. The Catholic Church taught by the Holy Spirit honors her with filial affection and devotion as a most beloved mother. (LG 53)

Questions for Discussion

1. What are some of the characteristics of people in this third dwelling place?

2. What is the difference between me and the saints?

3. Are all things done when we abandon worldly possessions?

4. Why do we suffer dryness?

5. Teresa reminds her daughters that they belong to Mary. In which aspects of daily life can we specifically take Mary as our guide and example? For example, think of the various ways Mary accompanied Jesus throughout his life.

CHAPTER 2

Continues on the same topic; deals with dryness in prayer; with what, in her opinion, might take place at this stage; how it is necessary to test ourselves; and with the fact that the Lord does try those who are in these dwelling places.

I have known some souls and even many—I believe I can say—who have reached this state and have lived many years in this upright and well-ordered way both in body and soul, insofar as can be known. After these years, when it seems they have become lords of the world, at least clearly disillusioned in its regard, His Majesty will try them in some minor matters, and they will go about so disturbed and afflicted that it puzzles me and even makes me fearful. It's useless to give them advice, for since they have engaged so long in the practice of virtue they think they can teach others and that they are more than justified in feeling disturbed.

2. In sum, I have found neither a way of consoling nor a cure for such persons other than to show them compassion in their affliction—and, indeed, compassion is felt on seeing them subject to so much misery—and not contradict their reasoning. For everything in their minds leads them to think they are suffering these things for God, and so, they don't come to realize that their disturbance is an imperfection. This is another mistake of persons so advanced. There is no reason for us to be surprised at what they experience; although I do think the feeling stirred by such things should pass quickly. For God often desires that His chosen ones feel

their wretchedness, and He withdraws His favor a little. No more is necessary, for I would wager that we'd then soon get to know ourselves. The nature of this trial is immediately understood, for they recognize their fault very clearly. Sometimes seeing their fault distresses them more than the thing that disturbs them, for unable to help themselves they are affected by earthly happenings even though these may not be very burdensome. This distress, I think, is a great mercy from God; and although it is a defect, it is very beneficial for humility.

3. As for the persons I am speaking about, this is not so. But, as I have said, they canonize these feelings in their minds and would like others to do so. I want to mention some of these feelings so that we may understand and test ourselves before the Lord tests us. It is very important to be prepared and to have understood ourselves beforehand.

4. A rich person without children or anyone to whom he might want to leave his possessions happens to lose his wealth, but not to such an extent that he lacks necessities for himself and for the management of his household; he even has a surplus. If he should go about as worried and disturbed as he would be if not even a piece of bread were left, how can our Lord ask him to leave all for Him?[1] Here the person makes the excuse that he feels the way he does because he wants these things for the poor. But I believe that God has a greater desire that such a person conform to the divine will and that, though this person may try to procure such wealth, he keep his soul at rest rather than worry about charity of such a kind. And if the person doesn't do this, because the Lord has not brought him so far, well and good; but he

---

1. Allusion to the young man in the Gospel. See IC 3.1.6.

should understand that he lacks this freedom of spirit. And because the Lord will ask him for it, he should prepare himself so that the Lord may give it to him; he will be asking His Majesty for it.

A person has plenty to eat and even a surplus; the opportunity presents itself for him to acquire more wealth; all right, let him do so if it is offered to him. But if he strives for wealth and after possessing it strives for more and more, however good the intention may be (for he should have a good intention because, as I have said,[2] these are virtuous persons of prayer), he need have no fear of ascending to the dwelling places closest to the King.

5. There is a similar occurrence when an opportunity presents itself for these persons to be despised or to lose a little honor. God often grants them the favor of enduring such a thing; for He is very fond of favoring virtue publicly so that virtue itself will not undergo a loss of esteem. Or He will also do so because they have served Him, for this Beloved of ours is very good. But now they are left in such disquiet they cannot help themselves, nor can they quickly get rid of this disturbance. God help me! Aren't these the ones who for a long while now have considered how the Lord suffered and how good suffering is, and who have desired it? They would like everyone to live a life as well ordered as they do; and please God they will not think their grief is for the faults of others and in their minds turn it into something meritorious.

6. It must seem to you, sisters, that I'm not staying on the subject or not speaking to you, for these things don't take place here. Neither do we have wealth nor do we desire or strive for it, nor does anyone do injury to us. As a result the

---

2. In IC 3.2.1. See IC 3.1.5.

examples are not relevant to us. But from these examples many lessons can be learned about things which it would not be good to single out, nor would there be reason to do so. Through the above examples you will understand whether or not you are truly stripped of what you have left behind. For little things happen even though not of this kind, in which you can very well test and know whether or not you are the rulers of your passions. And believe me, the whole affair doesn't lie in whether or not we wear the religious habit but in striving to practice the virtues, in surrendering our will to God in everything, in bringing our life into accordance with what His Majesty ordains for it, and in desiring that His will, not ours, be done.[3] Since we may not have reached this stage—humility, as I have said![4] Humility is the ointment for our wounds because if we indeed have humility, even though there may be a time of delay, the surgeon, who is our Lord, will come to heal us.

7. The penance these souls do is well balanced, like their lives. They desire penance a great deal so as to serve our Lord by it. Nothing of this is wrong, and thus they are very discreet in doing it in a way so as not to harm their health. Have no fear that they will kill themselves, for their reason is still very much in control. Love has not yet reached the point of overwhelming reason. But I should like us to use our reason to make ourselves dissatisfied with this way of serving God, always going step by step, for we'll never finish this journey. And since, in our opinion, we are continually walking and are tired (for, believe me, it is a wearisome journey), we will be doing quite well if we don't go astray. But does it seem to

---

3. Allusion to Lk 22:42.
4. In IC 3.2.4. See IC 3.1.7.

you, daughters, that if we could go from one land to another
in eight days, it would be good to take a year through wind,
snow, rain, and bad roads? Wouldn't it be better to make the
journey all at once? For all these obstacles are present, as well
as danger from snakes. Oh what good proofs I could give of
these things. And please God I may have passed beyond this
stage, for often enough it seems to me I haven't.

8. Since we are so circumspect, everything offends us
because we fear everything; so we don't dare go further—as
if we could reach these dwelling places while leaving to other
persons the trouble of treading the path for us. Since this is
not possible, let us exert ourselves, my sisters, for the love
of the Lord; let's abandon our reason and our fears into His
hands; let's forget this natural weakness that can take up our
attention so much. Let the prelates take care of our bodily
needs; that's their business. As for ourselves, we should
care only about moving quickly so as to see this Lord. Even
though the comfort you have is little or none at all, we could
be deceived by worry about our health. This I know. And I
also know that the whole affair doesn't lie in what pertains
to the body, for this is what is the least important. The journey I am speaking of must be taken with great humility. For
if you have understood, it is in regard to humility, I believe,
that there is an obstacle for those who do not go forward. It
should seem to us that we have gone but a few steps, and we
should believe this to be so, and that those our sisters have
taken are rapid ones; and not only should we desire but we
should strive that they consider us the most miserable of all.

9. With humility present, this stage is a most excellent
one. If humility is lacking, we will remain here our whole
life—and with a thousand afflictions and miseries. For since
we will not have abandoned ourselves, this state will be

very laborious and burdensome. We shall be walking while weighed down with this mud of our human misery, which is not so with those who ascend to the remaining rooms. But in these rooms of which we're speaking, the Lord, as one who is just or even merciful, does not fail to pay; for He always gives much more than we deserve by giving us consolations far greater than those we find in the comforts and distractions of life. But I don't think He gives much spiritual delight unless sometimes in order to invite souls by the sight of what takes place in the remaining dwelling places and so that they will prepare themselves to enter them.

10. It will seem to you that consolations and spiritual delights are the same, so why should I make this distinction? To me it seems there is a very great difference between the two. Now I can be wrong. I'll say what I understand about this when I speak of the fourth dwelling places which come after these. For since something will have to be explained about the spiritual delights the Lord gives there, the discussion will be more appropriate at that time. And although the explanation may seem to be useless, it might help somewhat so that in understanding the nature of each thing you will be able to strive for what is best. Great solace comes to souls God brings there, and confusion to those who think they have everything. If souls are humble they will be moved to give thanks. If there is some lack in humility, they will feel an inner distaste for which they will find no reason. For perfection as well as its reward does not consist in spiritual delights but in greater love and in deeds done with greater justice and truth.

11. You will wonder, if this is true—as it is—what use it serves to explain and treat of these interior favors. I don't know. Ask him who ordered me to write, for I am not obliged

to dispute with superiors but to obey—nor would disputing
with them be right. What I can truthfully say to you is that
at one time I didn't have or even know about these favors
through experience or think that I would ever in my life
know about them in this way—and rightly so, for it was happiness enough for me to know, or by conjecture understand,
that I was pleasing God in something. But when I read in
books about these delights and favors the Lord grants souls
that serve Him, I was very much consoled and moved to give
great praise to God. Well, if my soul which was so wretched
did this, those souls that are good and humble will praise
Him much more. And if one alone is led to praise Him even
once, it is in my opinion very good that the subject be mentioned so that we know about the happiness and delight we
lose through our own fault. Moreover, if these favors are
from God, they come brimming over with love and fortitude
by which you can journey with less labor and grow in the
practice of works and virtues. Don't think that it matters little to lose such favors through our own fault; when it isn't
our fault, the Lord is just.[5] His Majesty will give you through
other paths what He keeps from you on this one because
of what He knows, for His secrets are very hidden; at least
what He does will without any doubt be what is most suitable for us.

12. What it seems to me would be highly beneficial for
those who through the goodness of the Lord are in this state
(for, as I have said,[6] He grants them no small mercy because
they are very close to ascending higher) is that they study

---

5. Allusion to Ps 119:137 . For a similar use of this text see L 19.9. On the following theme about God's different ways with souls, see W 16–18, especially 17.7.

6. In IC 3.1.1, 5, 8.

diligently how to be prompt in obedience. And even if they are not members of a religious order, it would be a great thing for them to have—as do many persons—someone whom they could consult so as not to do their own will in anything. Doing our own will is usually what harms us. And they shouldn't seek another of their own making, as they say—one who is so circumspect about everything; but seek out someone who is very free from illusion about the things of the world. For in order to know ourselves, it helps a great deal to speak with someone who already knows the world for what it is. And it helps also because when we see some things done by others that seem so impossible for us and the ease with which they are done, we become very encouraged. And it seems that through the flight of these others we also will make bold to fly, as do the bird's fledglings when they are taught; for even though they do not begin to soar immediately, little by little they imitate the parent. Receiving this help is most beneficial; I know. However determined they are to keep from offending the Lord, these persons will be right not to place themselves in the occasion of offending Him. Since they are close to the first dwelling places, they could easily return to them. Their fortitude is not founded on solid ground, as is the case with those who are tried in suffering, for these latter know about the storms of the world and what little reason there is to fear them or desire the world's consolations. But it would be possible for the former in a great persecution to return to these consolations. The devil knows well how to stir up tempests so as to do us harm, and these persons would be unable to bear the trials that would come from their zeal to prevent others from committing sin.

13. Let us look at our own faults and leave aside those of others, for it is very characteristic of persons with such

well-ordered lives to be shocked by everything. Perhaps we could truly learn from the one who shocks us what is most important, even though we may surpass him in external composure and our way of dealing with others. Although good, these latter things are not what is most important; nor is there any reason to desire that everyone follow at once our own path, or to set about teaching the way of the spirit to someone who perhaps doesn't know what such a thing is. For with these desires that God gives us, sisters, about the good of souls, we can make many mistakes. So it is better to carry out what our rule says, to strive to live always in silence and hope,[7] for the Lord will take care of these souls. If we ourselves are not negligent in beseeching His Majesty to do so, we shall, with His favor, do much good. May He be blessed forever.

---

7. Words from the Carmelite Rule (*The Rule of St. Albert*) and taken from Isa 30:15.

A WELL-ORDERED LIFE
UNTIL THE SOUL IS TRIED

3.2.1–9 Teresa continues her assessment of persons in the third dwelling places. She says these persons, because they have conducted well-ordered lives and practiced virtues, can be distressed by even minor trials. Loss of wealth, seeking to acquire greater wealth, and suffering damage to their reputations can all cause them disturbance. Teresa points out that these souls are well-balanced, not only in their lives, but in their penance. They let reason control their practice; love has not yet reached the point of overwhelming reason. She concludes that this stage is a most excellent one if humility is present. Without humility we will never progress. Though the Lord doesn't give much spiritual delight here, he does give consolations.

3.2.10–12 Teresa explains that she makes a distinction between consolations and spiritual delights, saying that she will discuss the matter further in her description of the fourth dwelling places. She takes care to be sure that we have a right attitude about favors. Humility is very important for souls in regard to favors. They should give thanks if they receive them, but also if they don't, for they can praise God for his generosity in giving favors to others.

Teresa thinks diligence in obedience is important for the nuns who are at this stage. Persons who are not members of a religious order should try to find someone to consult so as not to do their own will in anything. She says that doing our will is what usually harms us. She says we should try to find someone who is free from illusions about things of the world. She warns that persons in these dwelling places must take care to avoid occasions of offending God because their fortitude is not founded on solid ground. They are still close to the first dwelling places.

3.2.13 She concludes by saying we should look at our own faults and leave aside those of others. She recommends living in silence and hope, with confidence that God will take care of these souls who may seem less perfect to us.

Interpretive Notes

In this second chapter of the third dwelling places, Teresa brings to a conclusion the ascetical section of her book. One should not conclude that in the spiritual life of the Christian there comes a moment when the task of personal effort comes to an end. Struggle and effort continue to be demanded to the final day of one's life, even in the final dwelling places of this castle. But now Teresa wants to pass as quickly as possible to the other perspective: God's action in us. First, though, she gives some last touches to her description of people in this dwelling place. She has a great deal of experience with these persons who begin enthusiastically but get so caught up in themselves that they become unable to hand over the reins of their life to God.

They live well-ordered lives. But Teresa has some advice for them: that trials are from God, that in the spiritual life trials are necessary, and that ultimately, the trial is a test of love. Beyond our own array of daily projects, God has his own plans for us and may upset our plans. Trials may destroy what we have been working to build. What we need are the faith and love to submit to his will for us.

But Teresa does not get lost in theories. She proposes for her readers some concrete examples of these trials. They come to people who have entered the castle and struggled to get established within it by achieving a balanced arrangement in their lives and fidelity to their various obligations. A financial loss can cause them much more distress than might have been expected, and no one can find words to comfort these persons in their affliction. Or the opposite can happen: they can experience financial gain, but it is never enough and they seek more and more wealth without satisfaction. Or God may want to use them, because they are good people, to give examples of virtue to others and so allows them to undergo some persecution in which their reputation is damaged. They become terribly unhappy and disquieted over the loss of their prestige. Worry about health can be another problem to the extent that this worry harms their health. We have to see that the secret of our spiritual life lies in opening ourselves to the action of God. And God often desires that his chosen ones clearly see and feel their wretchedness and look toward him for any good they may come to possess. Otherwise they will remain in these rooms their whole lives, weighed down with the mud of human misery.

What Teresa advises as beneficial for people at this point in their spiritual journey is obedience. This advice may come as a surprise to modern readers, but if we look more closely, she is concerned with the avoidance of an isolated and self-sufficient style of existence. We need to consult with those who will help us to do not our own will, but God's, and who will encourage us even to fly toward him.

People who live with such composure can be easily shocked by the behavior of others and, under the appearance of zeal, complain and even gossip about the actions of others. Teresa advises that we look at our own faults and perhaps learn some worthwhile things from the very ones whose actions bother us.

Questions for Discussion

1. What does God want of someone who suffers financial loss?
2. How should we behave when we are disliked or our when our reputation is damaged by another person?
3. What is one of the ways in which we should use our reason?
4. Why is it good to have someone to consult?
5. In what concrete ways can we exercise obedience in daily life?

THE FOURTH
DWELLING PLACES

Contains Three Chapters

CHAPTER 1

Discusses the difference between consolations (or feelings of tenderness) in prayer and spiritual delights.[1] Tells of her happiness on learning the difference between the mind and the intellect. This knowledge is very beneficial for anyone who is greatly distracted in prayer.

In order to begin to speak of the fourth dwelling places I really need to entrust myself, as I've already done, to the Holy Spirit and beg Him to speak for me from here on that I may say something about the remaining rooms in a way that you will understand. For supernatural experiences begin here. These are something most difficult to explain, if His Majesty doesn't do so, as was said in another book I wrote fourteen years ago, more or less, in which I dealt with these

---

1. Teresa uses the Spanish word *contentos* (here rendered in English as consolations) to denote experiences (such as joy, peace, satisfaction) that are not infused; that is, experiences perceived as a result of prayer and virtue but similar to those derived from everyday events. On the other hand, she uses the Spanish word *gustos* (here rendered in English as spiritual delights) to denote infused experiences. Infused, "supernatural," or mystical prayer begins in these fourth dwelling places with the prayer of infused recollection (IC 4.3) and quiet, or spiritual delight (IC 4.2). Actually Teresa presents the fourth dwelling places as a stage of transition in which the natural and the supernatural (or the acquired and the infused) are intermingled.

experiences to the extent of my knowledge of them at that time. Although I think I now have a little more light about these favors the Lord grants to some souls, knowing how to explain them is a different matter.[2] May His Majesty help me to do so if it will be of some benefit; and if not, then no.

2. Since these dwelling places now are closer to where the King is, their beauty is great. There are things to see and understand so delicate that the intellect is incapable of finding words to explain them, although something might turn out to be well put and not at all obscure to the unexperienced; and anyone who has experience, especially when there is a lot of it, will understand very well.

It will seem that to reach these dwelling places one will have had to live in the others a long while. Although it is usual that a person will have to have stayed in those already spoken about, there is no certain rule, as you will have often heard. For the Lord gives when He desires, as He desires, and to whom He desires. Since these blessings belong to Him, He does no injustice to anyone.[3]

3. Poisonous creatures rarely enter these dwelling places. If they enter, they do no harm; rather, they are the occasion of gain. I hold that the situation is much better in this stage of prayer when these creatures do enter and wage war, for the devil could deceive one with respect to the spiritual delights given by God if there were no temptations, and do much

---

2. In her *Life*. She is alluding to the many chapters there that deal with mystical experiences. See L 14–32; 37–40. When Teresa wrote the *Life*, she had not yet come to the stage she describes in the seventh dwelling places. What she explains in her *Life* under the symbol of the fourth water corresponds to the sixth dwelling places. As a result, she points out that she has a better understanding of some matters concerning the spiritual life than she did in that book. See IC 1.2.7; 4.2.5.

3. Allusion to Mt 20:13. The absolute divine freedom in the granting or denying of mystical favors is frequently insisted upon in Teresa's writings. In this work see IC 4.2.9; 5.1.12; 6.4.12; 6.7.9; 6.8.5.

more harm than when temptations are felt. The soul would not gain so much; at least all the things contributing to its merit would be removed, and it would be left in a habitual absorption. [For when a soul is in one continual state, I don't consider it safe, nor do I think it is possible for the spirit of the Lord to be in one fixed state during this exile.]

4. Well now, in speaking about what I said I'd mention here[4] concerning the difference in prayer between consolations and spiritual delights, the term "consolations," I think, can be given to those experiences we ourselves acquire through our own meditation and petitions to the Lord, those that proceed from our own nature—although God in the end does have a hand in them; for it must be understood, in whatever I say, that without Him we can do nothing.[5] But the consolations arise from the virtuous work itself that we perform, and it seems that we have earned them through our own effort and are rightly consoled for having engaged in such deeds. But if we reflect upon this, we see that we experience the same joyful consolations in many of the things that can happen to us on earth; for example: when someone suddenly inherits a great fortune; when we suddenly see a person we love very much; when we succeed in a large and important business matter and of which everyone speaks well; when you see your husband or brother or son alive after someone has told you he is dead. I have seen the flow of tears from great consolations, and this has even happened to me at times. I think that just as these joyful consolations are natural so are those afforded us by the things of God, but these latter are of a nobler kind, although the others are not bad. In sum,

---

4. In IC 3.2.10.
5. Allusion to Jn 15:5.

joyful consolations in prayer have their beginning in our own
human nature and end in God.

The spiritual delights begin in God, but human nature
feels and enjoys them as much as it does those I mentioned—
and much more. O Jesus, how I long to know how to explain
this! For I discern, I think, a very recognizable difference, but
I don't have the knowledge to be able to explain myself. May
the Lord do so.

5. Now I remember a line that we say at Prime, in the latter part of the verse at the end of the last psalm: Cum dilatasti
cor meum.[6] For anyone who has had much experience these
words are sufficient to see the difference between consolations and spiritual delights; for anyone who has not, more
words are needed. The consolations that were mentioned do
not expand the heart; rather, they usually seem to constrain
it a little—although there is the greatest consolation at seeing
what is done for God. But some anxious tears come that in a
way, it seems, are brought on by the passions. I don't know
much about these passions of the soul—knowledge of them
might perhaps have enabled me to explain—and what proceeds from sensuality and from our human nature, for I am
very dull. If only I knew how to explain myself, for since I
have undergone this I understand it. Knowledge and learning
are a great help in everything.

6. My experience of this state (I mean of this joy and consolation that comes during meditation) is that if I began to
weep over the passion I didn't know how to stop until I got
a severe headache; if I did so over my sins, the same thing
happened. Our Lord granted me quite a favor. Yet I don't
want to examine now whether the one or the other is better,

Enlarging The heart

6. Ps 119:32.

but I would like to know how to explain the difference there is between the one and the other. It is for these reasons sometimes that these tears flow and desires come, and they are furthered by human nature and one's temperament; but finally, as I have said,[7] they end in God regardless of their nature. They are to be esteemed if there is the humility to understand that one is no better because of experiencing them, for it cannot be known whether they are all effects of love. When they are, the gift is God's.

For the most part, the souls in the previous dwelling places are the ones who have these devout feelings, for these souls work almost continually with the intellect, engaging in discursive thought and meditation. And they do well because nothing further has been given them; although they would be right if they engaged for a while in making acts of love, praising God, rejoicing in His goodness, that He is who He is, and in desiring His honor and glory. These acts should be made insofar as possible, for they are great awakeners of the will. Such souls would be well advised when the Lord gives them these acts not to abandon them for the sake of finishing the usual meditation.

7. Because I have spoken at length on this subject elsewhere,[8] I will say nothing about it here. I only wish to inform you that in order to profit by this path and ascend to the dwelling places we desire, the important thing is not to think much but to love much;[9] and so do that which best stirs you to love. Perhaps we don't know what love is. I wouldn't be very surprised, because it doesn't consist in great delight but

---

7. In IC 4.1.4.

8. In L 12; W 16–20.

9. One of Teresa's cherished maxims. See F 5.2.

in desiring with strong determination to please God in everything, in striving, insofar as possible, not to offend Him, and
in asking Him for the advancement of the honor and glory
of His Son and the increase of the Catholic Church. These
are the signs of love. Don't think the matter lies in thinking
of nothing else, and that if you become a little distracted all
is lost.

8. I have been very afflicted at times in the midst of this
turmoil of mind. A little more than four years ago I came
to understand through experience that the mind (or imagination, to put it more clearly) is not the intellect. I asked a
learned man and he told me that this was so; which brought
me no small consolation.[10] For since the intellect is one of
the soul's faculties, it was an arduous thing for me that it
should be so restless at times. Ordinarily the mind flies about
quickly, for only God can hold it fast in such a way as to
make it seem that we are somehow loosed from this body. I
have seen, I think, that the faculties of my soul were occupied
and recollected in God while my mind on the other hand was
distracted. This distraction puzzled me.[11]

9. O Lord, take into account the many things we suffer on this path for lack of knowledge! The trouble is that
since we do not think there is anything to know other than
that we must think of You, we do not even know how to ask
those who know nor do we understand what there is to ask.

---

10. We do not know who the learned man was. Some suggest that it may have
been St. John of the Cross, who was Teresa's director and confessor from 1572–1575.
But Teresa's ignorance of the difference between the imagination (*pensamiento*, or
mind, as she often refers to it) and the intellect was not total ignorance. See L 17.5.

11. For many years this wandering of the mind deeply troubled the Saint. See L
17.7; W 31.8. In this work she has come to a definite doctrinal position on the matter. The instability and rebellion of the imagination is a consequence of the disorder
produced in us through original sin. See IC 4.1.11.

Terrible trials are suffered because we don't understand ourselves, and that which isn't bad at all but good we think is a serious fault. This lack of knowledge causes the afflictions of many people who engage in prayer; complaints about interior trials, at least to a great extent, by people who have no learning; melancholy and loss of health; and even the complete abandonment of prayer. [For such persons don't reflect that there is an interior world here within us.] Just as [we cannot stop the movement of the heavens, but they proceed in rapid motion, so neither can we stop our mind; and then the faculties of the soul go with it,] and we think we are lost and have wasted the time spent before God. [But the soul is perhaps completely joined with Him in the dwelling places very close to the center while the mind is on the outskirts of the castle suffering from a thousand wild and poisonous beasts, and meriting by this suffering.] As a result we should not be disturbed; nor should we abandon prayer, which is what the devil wants us to do. For the most part all the trials and disturbance come from our not understanding ourselves.

10. While writing this, I'm thinking about what's going on in my head with the great noise there that I mentioned in the beginning.[12] It makes it almost impossible for me to write what I was ordered to. It seems as if there are in my head many rushing rivers and that these waters are hurtling downward, and many little birds and whistling sounds, not in the ears but in the upper part of the head where, they say, the higher part of the soul is. And I was in that superior part for a long time, for it seems this powerful movement of the spirit is a swift upward one. Please God I'll remember to mention the cause of this in discussing the dwelling places that

---

12. In IC Prol 1.

come further on, for this is not a fitting place to do so, and I wouldn't be surprised if the Lord gave me this headache so that I could understand these things better. For all this turmoil in my head doesn't hinder prayer or what I am saying, but the soul is completely taken up in its quiet, love, desires, and clear knowledge.

11. Now then, if the superior part of the soul is in the superior part of the head, why isn't the soul disturbed? This I don't know. But I do know that what I say is true. The pain is felt when suspension does not accompany the prayer. When suspension does accompany prayer, no pain is felt until the suspension passes. But it would be very bad if I were to abandon everything on account of this obstacle. And so it isn't good for us to be disturbed by our thoughts, nor should we be concerned. If the devil causes them, they will cease with this suspension. If they come, as they do, from one of the many miseries inherited through the sin of Adam, let us be patient and endure them for the love of God since we are likewise subject to eating and sleeping without being able to avoid it, which is quite a trial.

12. Let us recognize our misery and desire to go where no one will taunt us, for sometimes I recall having heard these words the bride says in the *Song of Songs*.[13] And indeed I don't find in all of life anything about which they can be more rightly said. It seems to me that all the contempt and trials one can endure in life cannot be compared to these interior battles. And disquiet and war can be suffered if we find peace where we live, as I have already said.[14] But that we desire to rest from the thousand trials there are in the

---

13. Song 8:1.
14. In IC 2.1.9.

world and that the Lord wants to prepare us for tranquility
and that within ourselves lies the obstacle to such rest and
tranquility cannot fail to be very painful and almost unbearable. So, Lord, bring us to the place where these miseries will
not taunt us, for they seem sometimes to be making fun of
the soul. Even in this life, the Lord frees the soul from these
miseries when it reaches the last dwelling place, as we shall
say if God wills.[15]

13. These miseries will not afflict or assail everyone as
much as they did me for many years because of my wretchedness. It seems that I myself wanted to take vengeance on
myself. And since the experience was something so painful for
me, I think perhaps that it will be so for you too. And I so
often speak of it here and there that I might sometime succeed
in explaining to you that it is an unavoidable thing and should
not be a disturbance or affliction for you but that we must let
the millclapper go clacking on, and must continue grinding
our flour and not fail to work with the will and the intellect.

14. There is a more and a less to this obstacle in accordance with one's health and age. Let the poor soul suffer even
though it has no fault in this; we have other faults, which
makes it right for us to practice patience. And since our reading and the counsels we receive (that is, to pay no attention to
these thoughts) don't suffice, I don't think that the time spent
in explaining these things for those of you with little knowledge and consoling you in this matter is time lost. But until the
Lord wants to enlighten us, these counsels will be of little help.
Yet, it is necessary and His Majesty wishes us to take the means
and understand ourselves; and let's not blame the soul for
what a weak imagination, human nature, and the devil cause.

---

15. See IC 7.2.11.

PERIOD OF TRANSITION

4.1.1–3 Teresa entrusts herself to the Holy Spirit, begging him to speak for her as she writes about the remaining rooms, for supernatural experiences begin here in the fourth dwelling places. She says that those who have experienced some of these things may find her words easier to understand than those who have no experience of them. Although usually a person will have remained in earlier dwelling places for a long while, there is no certain rule, and the Lord gives when he desires. If poisonous creatures enter here they can help, rather than do harm, for they can provide opportunities for the soul to gain merit by resisting them.

4.1.4–5 Teresa says she will talk about the difference in prayer between consolations (*contentos*) and spiritual delights (*gustos*). The term "consolations" can be given to those experiences we acquire through our own meditations and petitions to the Lord. Although God does have a hand in them, they proceed from our own nature. The consolations arise from the virtuous work that we perform. These consolations, even though related to things pertaining to God, are the same as those we experience in relation to earthly things. Joyful consolations in prayer have their beginning in our own human nature and end in God.

Spiritual delights begin in God, and human nature feels and enjoys them more than the consolations. A characteristic of spiritual delights is that they expand the heart.

4.1.6 Teresa gives examples of consolations that end in God. One must have humility to understand that one is no better for having experienced them because it cannot be known whether they are all effects of love. When they are, the gift is God's. Teresa says that sometimes during meditation God inspires persons to acts of love and praise. She says it is preferable to perform these acts that awaken the will, rather than to finish the usual meditation.

4.1.7 Teresa teaches that in order to profit by this path and advance to the dwelling places we desire, the important thing is not to think much, but to love much, and so to do that which best inspires you to love. Love, she says, doesn't consist in great delight, but in desiring with strong determination to please God in everything. She thinks becoming a little distracted shouldn't disturb us.

4.1.8–9 Teresa makes a distinction between the mind (which she says is the same as the imagination) and the intellect. Teresa laments how much souls suffer through lack of knowledge, even to the point of abandoning prayer. She urges perseverance.

4.1.10 Teresa suffers from noise in her head and from a headache. She uses these trials to explain that they don't hinder prayer or what she is saying (although a few sentences earlier she says that they make it almost impossible for her to write), and that the soul during this prayer of quiet is completely taken up in its quiet, love, desires, and clear knowledge.

4.1.11 The pain of Teresa's headaches is not experienced during the prayer that she will discuss in the fifth dwelling places. But we should not let pain or distractions cause us concern. They come from the miseries we have inherited from the sin of Adam, so we must be patient and endure our difficulties and sufferings for the love of God.

4.1.12–14 Teresa says that great pain comes from the fact that the obstacle to the rest and tranquility that we desire, and that God is preparing us for, lies within ourselves. Some persons experience this pain more than others. To clarify her advice that we should persevere in prayer despite distractions, she uses the metaphor of a noisy mill, saying that we must continue grinding our flour and not fail to work with the will and intellect, in spite of distractions. Teresa adds that health and age can affect the level of distractions persons experience. She concludes that it's a waste of time to give advice about ignoring distractions, because it isn't effective. But it is important to understand ourselves so that we don't blame the soul for what a weak imagination, human nature, and the devil cause.

Interpretive Notes

Readers of Teresa's *Life* may well remember what happened in her prayer at one point: "I sometimes experienced, as I said, although very briefly, the beginning of what I will now speak about. It used to happen, when I represented Christ within me in order to place myself in His presence, or even while reading, that a feeling of the presence of God would come upon me unexpectedly so that I could in no way doubt He was within me or I totally immersed in Him" (L 10.1). This experience marked something new in Teresa's prayer and represents what she will now begin to speak of in this fourth dwelling place.

Before dealing with this new prayer, however, a few words may still be necessary to clarify what Teresa has experienced in prayer up to this point, and the advice she gives to others. Spiritual writers of her day recommended discursive meditation for the beginner, which was a veritable torment for Teresa. This method, according to Teresa, consisted of reasoning "a great deal with the intellect, deducing many ideas from one idea, and working with concepts" (L 13.11; IC 6.7.10). It was an intellectual activity in which "the whole business lies in thinking" (F 5.2). This exercise required a form of thinking based on logic, a "hardworking intellect," one that could "concentrate" (L 13.12; W 19.1), as well as a capacity to picture things to oneself that could nourish the discourse with evocative images. "God did not give me talent for discursive thought or for a profitable use of the imagination . . . In fact, my imagination is so dull that I never succeeded even to think about and represent in my mind—as hard as I tried—the humanity of the Lord" (L 4.7). She doesn't deny the value of discursive meditation for others, although "they should not pass the whole time thinking. For although discursive meditation is very meritorious, they don't seem to realize that since their prayer is delightful there should be a Sunday or a time in which one is not working" (L 13.11, 22). For eighteen years Teresa suffered from this belief that she must practice discursive reflection in her prayer. What saved her were the books she used for her prayer. "With this recourse, which was like a partner or a shield by which to sustain the blows of my many thoughts, I went about consoled" (L 4.9).

When Teresa uses the scriptural text "you have expanded my heart" to explain the difference between consolations and spiritual delights, she appeals to experience and says that if you have the experience you will understand, and if you do not have it, you will have much more difficulty and need many words of explanation. Spiritual delights are given to the spirit, and that is why in these experiences there is the feeling of expansion, since the spirit is not in the body but the body is in the spirit. Our spirit is much more than the body and doesn't feel restricted by it when we begin to experience spirit more in infused prayer, which Teresa also calls "supernatural prayer" or "contemplation." "Infused" means that the prayer is given by God directly to the spirit. And in this initial stage it is experienced passively in the spirit—that is, in the depths of our being as quiet, peace, and love.

At the center of Teresa's life story lies her conversion experience of 1554, which occurred when she was thirty-nine years old, after she had lived about nineteen years as a nun at the Carmelite Monastery of the Incarnation. Her spiritual life before her conversion was marked by intense ascetical struggle; the life that followed was clearly mystical. The first stage lacked unity and continuity. It followed an undulating, winding path, with highs and lows and notable breakdowns. One way of presenting her life is to separate it into three periods. The first would cover her childhood and youth up to her entry into religious life (1515–1535). The second would include her initial years as a Carmelite nun. This would comprise her serious, painful illness, her return to prayer after her father's death in 1543, and the faint beginnings of her mystical life leading to her conversion in 1554. The third stage then follows in a continuous line the steps recounted in the fifth, sixth, and seventh dwelling places of this book.

What interests us here is the period that took place between 1535–1544. During this time we find intermittent waves of recollection and quiet and even some moments of union. These served to increase her desire for prayer in solitude. Noticeably in this stage, after Teresa had decided to return to prayer following the death of her father, she suffered through a veritable struggle between her prayer life and all that warred against it. As she worded it, the conflict was between friendship with God and friendship with the world.

In the midst of this struggle she began to perceive the first signs of passive prayer in the form of a contemplation which, though not "perfect" or "pure," was nonetheless "supernatural" or "infused " or "mystical." Although this grace was sporadic, it tended to recur, summoning Teresa to a more intense spiritual life until she reached the point of definitive change. When Teresa translated this period of her experience into theory, she placed it in this fourth dwelling place.

In the midst of her difficulty with discursive meditation, Teresa found no confessor who could help her. It was the Lord who came to her aid and taught her a manner of proceeding in prayer that gave her satisfaction (W 29.7). This manner of prayer she called "the prayer of recollection." "This prayer is called 'recollection' because the soul through its own efforts collects its faculties together and enters within itself to be with its God. And its divine Master comes more quickly to teach it and give it the prayer of quiet than He would through any other method it might use" (W 28.4).

> This method of keeping Christ present with us is beneficial in all stages and is a very safe means of advancing in the first degree of prayer, of reaching in a short time the second degree, and of walking secure against the dangers the devil can set up in the last degrees. Keeping Christ present [the Prayer of Recollection] is what we of ourselves can do. Whoever would desire to pass beyond this point and raise the spirit to an experience of spiritual delights that are not given would lose both the one and the other, in my opinion. (L 12.3–4)

Thus everyone, no matter what stage they are in or how far advanced, can best begin their prayer with this prayer of recollection, keeping Christ present.

There are two ways of maintaining this recollection that Teresa suggests. First, the repetition of a vocal prayer, such as the Our Father, the Hail Mary, or some other prayer like the Jesus Prayer while recollected in his presence. Second, the practice of being present to him, looking at and relating to him through scenes from the Gospel (W 28.4; 34.7; L 9.2). But, she says:

> The important thing is not to think much but to love much; and so do that which best stirs you to love. Perhaps we don't know what love is. I wouldn't be very surprised, because it doesn't consist in great delight, but in desiring with strong determination to please God in everything, in striving, insofar as possible, not to offend Him, and in asking Him for the advancement of the honor and glory of His Son and the increase of the Catholic Church. These are the signs of love. Don't think the matter lies in thinking of nothing else, and that if you become a little distracted all is lost. (IC 4.1.7)

The Constitution on the Sacred Liturgy of the Second Vatican Council (*Sacrosanctum Concilium*) states: "The spiritual life, however, is not limited solely to participation in the liturgy. The Christian is indeed called to pray with others, but he must also enter into his bedroom to pray with his father in secret (Mt 6:6); furthermore, according to the teaching of the apostle, he must pray without ceasing" (SC 12).

Questions for Discussion

1. Is it possible to predict how many years we will spend in each dwelling place?
2. What are consolations and how do they differ from spiritual delights?

3. Does love consist in consolations or in spiritual delights?

4. Is the intellect the same as the mind in Teresa's vocabulary?

5. Is it helpful to consider that prayer consists not in thinking much but in loving much? How can we distinguish between thinking and loving in prayer?

CHAPTER 2

Continues on the same subject and explains through a comparison the nature of spiritual delight and how this is attained by not seeking it.

God help me with what I have undertaken! I've already forgot what I was dealing with, for business matters and poor health have forced me to set this work aside just when I was at my best; and since I have a poor memory everything will come out confused because I can't go back to read it over. And perhaps even everything else I say is confused; at least that's what I feel it is.

It seems to me I have explained the nature of consolations in the spiritual life.[1] Since they are sometimes mixed with our own passions, they are the occasion of loud sobbing; and I have heard some persons say they experience a tightening in the chest and even external bodily movements that they cannot restrain. The force of these passions can cause nosebleeds and other things just as painful. I don't know how to explain anything about these experiences because I haven't had any. But they must nonetheless be consoling, for, as I'm saying,[2] the whole experience ends in the desire to please God and enjoy His Majesty's company.

2. The experiences that I call spiritual delight in God, that I termed elsewhere the prayer of quiet,[3] are of a very different kind, as those of you who by the mercy of God

---

1. In IC 4.1.4–6.
2. See IC 4.1.5.
3. See L 14–15.

have experienced them will know. Let's consider, for a better understanding, that we see two founts with two water troughs. (For I don't find anything more appropriate to explain some spiritual experiences than water; and this is because I know little and have no helpful cleverness of mind and am so fond of this element that I have observed it more attentively than other things. In all the things that so great and wise a God has created there must be many beneficial secrets, and those who understand them do benefit, although ⌈I believe that in each little thing created by God there is more than what is understood, even if it is a little ant.⌉

3. These two troughs are filled with water in different ways; with one the water comes from far away through many aqueducts and the use of much ingenuity; with the other the source of the water is right there, and the trough fills without any noise. If the spring is abundant, as is this one we are speaking about, the water overflows once the trough is filled, forming a large stream. There is no need of any skill, nor does the building of aqueducts have to continue; but water is always flowing from the spring.

The water coming from the aqueducts is comparable, in my opinion, to the consolations I mentioned[4] that are drawn from meditation. For we obtain them through thoughts, assisting ourselves, using creatures to help our meditation, and tiring the intellect. Since, in the end, the consolation comes through our own efforts, noise is made when there has to be some replenishing of the benefits the consolation causes in the soul, as has been said.[5]

---

4. In IC 3.2.9–10; 4.1.4–6.
5. In IC 4.1.5–6, 10.

4. With this other fount, the water comes from its own source which is God. And since His Majesty desires to do so—when He is pleased to grant some supernatural favor—He produces this delight with the greatest peace and quiet and sweetness in the very interior part of ourselves. I don't know from where or how, nor is that happiness and delight experienced, as are earthly consolations, in the heart. I mean there is no similarity at the beginning, for afterward the delight fills everything; this water overflows through all the dwelling places and faculties until reaching the body. This is why I said[6] that it begins in God and ends in ourselves. For, certainly, as anyone who may have experienced it will see, the whole exterior man enjoys this spiritual delight and sweetness.

5. I was now thinking, while writing this, that the verse mentioned above, *Dilatasti cor meum,*[7] says the heart was expanded. I don't think the experience is something, as I say, that rises from the heart, but from another part still more interior, as from something deep. I think this must be the center of the soul, as I later came to understand and will mention at the end.[8] For certainly I see secrets within ourselves that have often caused me to marvel. And how many more there must be! Oh, my Lord and my God, how great are Your grandeurs! We go about here below like foolish little shepherds, for while it seems that we are getting some knowledge of You it must amount to no more than nothing; for even in our own selves there are great secrets that we don't understand. I say "no more than nothing" because I'm comparing it to the many, many secrets that are in You, not because the grandeurs

---

6. In IC 4.1.4.

7. Ps 119:32. See IC 4.1.5.

8. In IC 7.1.3, 7, 10; 7.2.3, 9.

we see in You are not extraordinary; and that includes those we can attain knowledge of through Your works.

6. To return to the verse, what I think is helpful in it for explaining this matter is the idea of expansion. It seems that since that heavenly water begins to rise from this spring I'm mentioning that is deep within us, it swells and expands our whole interior being, producing ineffable blessings; nor does the soul even understand what is given to it there. It perceives a fragrance, let us say for now, as though there were in that interior depth a brazier giving off sweet-smelling perfumes. No light is seen, nor is the place seen where the brazier is; but the warmth and the fragrant fumes spread through the entire soul and even often enough, as I have said,[9] the body shares in them. See now that you understand me; no heat is felt, nor is there the scent of any perfume, for the experience is more delicate than an experience of these things; but I use the examples only so as to explain it to you. And let persons who have not experienced these things understand that truthfully they do happen and are felt in this way, and the soul understands them in a manner clearer than is my explanation right now. This spiritual delight is not something that can be imagined, because however diligent our efforts we cannot acquire it. The very experience of it makes us realize that it is not of the same metal as we ourselves but fashioned from the purest gold of the divine wisdom. Here, in my opinion, the faculties are not united but absorbed and looking as though in wonder at what they see.

7. It's possible that in dealing with these interior matters I might contradict something of what I said elsewhere. That's no surprise, because in the almost fifteen years[10]

---

9. In IC 4.2.4.

10. In IC 4.1.1, she says fourteen years. She finished the first redaction of her *Life* in 1562 and is writing these pages in the latter part of 1577.

since I wrote it the Lord may perhaps have given me clearer understanding in these matters than I had before. Now, as then, I could be completely mistaken—but I would not lie, because by God's mercy I'd rather suffer a thousand deaths. I speak of what I understand.

8. It seems clear to me the will must in some way be united with God's will. But it is in the effects and deeds following afterward that one discerns the true value of prayer; there is no better crucible for testing prayer. It is quite a great favor from our Lord if the person receiving the favor recognizes it, and a very great one if he doesn't turn back.

You will at once desire, my daughters, to obtain this prayer; and you are right, for, as I have said,[11] the soul will never understand the favors the Lord is granting there or the love with which He is drawing it nearer to Himself. It is good to try to understand how we can obtain such a favor; so I am going to tell you what I have understood about this.

9. Let's leave aside the times when our Lord is pleased to grant it because He wants to and for no other reason. He knows why; we don't have to meddle in this. After you have done what should be done by those in the previous dwelling places; humility! humility! By this means the Lord allows Himself to be conquered with regard to anything we want from Him. The first sign for seeing whether or not you have humility is that you do not think you deserve these favors and spiritual delights from the Lord or that you will receive them in your lifetime.

You will ask me how then one can obtain them without seeking them. I answer that for the following reasons there is no better way than the one I mentioned, of not striving for

---

11. In IC 4.2.5.

them. First, because the initial thing necessary for such favors is to love God without self-interest. Second, because there is a slight lack of humility in thinking that for our miserable services something so great can be obtained. Third, because the authentic preparation for these favors on the part of those of us who, after all, have offended Him is the desire to suffer and imitate the Lord rather than to have spiritual delights. Fourth, because His Majesty is not obliged to give them to us as He is to give us glory if we keep His commandments. (Without these favors we can be saved, and He knows better than we ourselves what is fitting for us and who of us truly loves Him. This is certain, I know. And I know persons who walk by the path of love as they ought to walk, that is, only so as to serve their Christ crucified; not only do these persons refuse to seek spiritual delights from Him or to desire them but they beseech Him not to give them these favors during their lifetime. This is true.) The fifth reason is that we would be laboring in vain; for since this water must not be drawn through aqueducts as was the previous water, we are little helped by tiring ourselves if the spring doesn't want to produce it. I mean that no matter how much we meditate or how much we try to squeeze something out and have tears, this water doesn't come in such a way. It is given only to whom God wills to give it and often when the soul is least thinking of it.

10. We belong to Him, daughters. Let Him do whatever He likes with us, bring us wherever He pleases. I really believe that whoever humbles himself and is detached (I mean in fact because the detachment and humility must not be just in our thoughts—for they often deceive us—but complete) will receive the favor of this water from the Lord and many other favors that we don't know how to desire. May He be forever praised and blessed, amen.

THE WATER OF SPIRITUAL DELIGHT
AND HOW IT IS ATTAINED

4.2.1 Here Teresa shares concerns about the writing task she has undertaken. She has been in poor health and preoccupied with business matters. She also says her memory is poor, and because she cannot go back and read what she has written, she fears that what she is writing will come out confused. She recalls that she was explaining the nature of consolations in the spiritual life. She says the consolations (*contentos*) are sometimes mixed with our own passions. They can be accompanied by physical phenomena such as sobbing, nosebleeds, and even uncontrollable bodily movements. Teresa says that she hasn't experienced these more extreme types of consolations and so can't say anything about them except that they must be consoling because the experiences end in the desire to please God. She contrasts these consolations with the experiences she calls spiritual delights (*gustos)*.

4.2.2–4 Teresa says that what she now calls spiritual delights (*gustos*) she has elsewhere referred to as the prayer of quiet. She begins by asking us to imagine two founts, each having a trough to catch the water. She digresses briefly to say how much she has enjoyed observing water, and adds that she believes that in each thing created by God there are many beneficial secrets and that those who understand them benefit, although there is always more to each thing than what is understood, even if it is a little ant. She continues the metaphor of the water troughs that are filled in different ways. One trough is filled with water that flows noisily through many aqueducts from far away. The other is filled from an abundant spring whose source is located at the trough itself. The water wells up silently in this second trough, fills it, and overflows into a large stream. There is no need of any skill or building of aqueducts in this second instance, and water is always flowing from the spring.

She says consolations are like the water coming from the aqueducts; they require human effort in the form of meditation. Spiritual delights are like the abundant spring. They flow from God and are accompanied by peace, quiet, and sweetness in the very interior part of ourselves. This spiritual delight is different from earthly consolations. The delight fills everything, overflowing through all the dwelling places and faculties, until reaching the body. She explains that because the whole exterior person enjoys this delight, we can say this spiritual delight begins in God and ends in ourselves.

4.2.5–7 Teresa begins with a reference to the verse mentioned earlier about expansion of the heart, and she shares her attempts not only to describe, but to analyze the experience of spiritual delight. It seems to her that the experience arises from something deep and even more interior than the heart, from what she thinks is the center of the soul. She marvels and praises God for what she calls the secrets within ourselves, and for the greatness and grandeurs of God. Returning to the verse, she says the idea of expansion of the heart helps explain spiritual delight. The experience that is deep within, like a deep spring of water, swells and expands our whole interior being, producing ineffable blessings, and the soul does not understand what is given to it there. The soul and even the body experience delightful effects without being able to perceive the origin of them. The spiritual delight is not something that can be imagined; it cannot be acquired through any of our efforts. She concludes by saying she is not sure if what she is writing now is the same as how she described the matter in a text written fifteen years earlier (her *Life)*. She believes she now has a clearer understanding than before, but even so says she could be mistaken.

4.2.8–10 Still referring to spiritual delight, Teresa says it seems that the will must be united in some way with God's will. She adds that the true value of prayer is in the effects and deeds that follow. Even to be able to recognize the favor of spiritual delight is a favor itself from the Lord, and it is a great favor also if the person does not turn back from this prayer.

Teresa advises how we should act in order to obtain the favor of this prayer of spiritual delight. She first repeats that the Lord can grant this prayer at any time for his own reasons, and says her advice does not cover such instances. She says that after having done what should be done in the earlier dwelling places, we must know that humility is of the greatest importance. Through our humility the Lord allows himself to be conquered with regard to anything we want from him. She says a first sign of humility is that we do not think we deserve these favors or that we will receive them in our lifetime. Anticipating objections, she says people will ask, then, how one can obtain these favors without seeking them. She repeats her conviction that one must not strive for them, and gives a number of reasons why. We must love God without self-interest. She sees a little lack of humility in thinking that anything we do could merit these favors. Further, she says that authentic preparation for these favors is the desire to suffer and imitate the Lord, rather than to have spiritual delights. A fourth reason, she says, is that His Majesty is not obliged to give these favors and we should be resigned to his will in the matter; she also says that some persons who seek only to serve the Lord without reward even pray not to receive these favors in their lifetime. She finishes her reasons by saying that our efforts or striving after these delights would be useless, anyway, since the favors are a pure gift. She concludes by repeating that we should accept God's will, but adds that she believes the Lord will give spiritual delight and many other favors to those who humble themselves and are detached.

Interpretive Notes

Teresa begins this chapter lamenting the fact that she had been forced to set this work aside and that she doesn't have time to read it over, and says she fears that everything will come out befuddled. What has happened is that the nuncio Nicolás Ormaneto died in Madrid fifteen days after Teresa began her writing of this work. He had played a key role, giving her strong support, in that other urgent project of hers, the founding of her new Carmelite communities. Now, Teresa had orders to move from Toledo to Ávila and await there the new nuncio, who, according to rumor, was bent on nullifying her efforts.

In her distinction between consolations (*contentos*) and spiritual delights (*gustos*), Teresa sees consolations as the result of our own efforts at prayer. Beginners in prayer do their part, which may involve a lot of work, to find consolation in prayer. Virtue and merit are found in all the things that cause the devotion acquired partly by the intellect (our thinking power), even though this devotion could not be merited or obtained if God did not give it. It is very good for a soul that hasn't gone beyond this point to refrain from striving to ascend further (L 12.1). "But when His Majesty doesn't give it [consolation], it isn't necessary . . . They should believe that their desire for consolation is a fault" (L 11.14). Teresa writes in *The Book of Her Life*:

> It is very important that no one be distressed or afflicted over dryness or noisy and distracting thoughts. . . . if the well is dry, we cannot put water into it. True, we must not become neglectful; when there is water, we should draw it out because then the Lord desires to multiply the virtues by this means. (L 11.17)

> [Otherwise, the soul should pay] little attention to whether this consolation and tenderness is lacking or whether the Lord gives it (or to whether the soul has much consolation or no consolation). (L 11.13)

For Teresa, the love of God does not consist in consolation but "in serving with justice and fortitude of soul and in humility" (L 11.13).

What type of prayer characterizes this dwelling place? Prayer, let us remember, is relationship with God. In her first book, her *Life*, Teresa spoke of the "prayer of quiet." Now she refers to this same experience as "spiritual delight," the enjoyment of God. The "prayer of quiet" in her *Life* corresponds to the second way of watering the garden of which Teresa speaks in chapters 14 and 15. The prayer of quiet represented the first form of mystical prayer, a kind of passive-contemplative prayer in which God takes the initiative. Its agent of expression is the will, the heart of the whole of a person's life. Teresa got the term "prayer of quiet" from books of her times. The term is in contrast with the noisy activity and complexity of discursive thought. It represents the silence and rest experienced by the will in the exercise of love rising above the agitation of the other powers of the soul, the mind and fantasy, which are still active. At this beginning stage of mystical experience, only the will, according to Teresa, is touched by grace so as to place it in the prayer of love and unite it for some moments to the mysterious object of love who is God, radiating in Christ the mystery of his goodness and tender love toward humans.

Now, in these fourth dwelling places, Teresa adds a nuance that is reflected in the new term, "spiritual delight." It is the entire person who is made joyfully aware of the presence of God. So Teresa speaks less of the will and more of the depth of the person, of the center of the soul, of a deepening of the entire life in the castle. It will be here in this mysterious depth where the relationship with God will cause the fount to flow and inundate the will and reach even the body with all its senses and activities.

Teresa writes: "These impulses [of love] are like some little springs I've seen flowing; they never cease to move the sand upward. This is a good example of, or comparison to, souls that reach this state: love is always stirring and thinking about what it will do" (L 30.19). This image forms the symbolic basis for Teresa's development of this fourth dwelling place. There are two sources of water. One is far away and requires human effort to obtain it. It corresponds to the ascetical life and the first three dwelling places. The other source is right there in the interior depths of the person. It corresponds to the experiences of the mystical life, the infused, passively bestowed (not acquired) prayer of the fourth and following dwelling places. This prayer or love comes from the interior depth, precisely because the deepest part of a person in the last dwelling place of the castle is a kind of radical opening to God and to the divine. This action of God gives the soul the sense of expansion in proportion to the amount of water that flows forth from the depths. This entrance into mystical experience is made by way of the will—that is, by way of the love of God that penetrates the human heart.

A certain illusion can take form in the person who prays when at the threshold of the mystical experience. The belief can easily arise that the prayer of quiet or any other form of mystical experience can be obtained through human effort. In the time of Teresa there were in vogue certain practices of mental emptying. But Teresa did not see this mental emptying or any other similar technique as a way to getting water from this inner fount. You cannot get this prayer, Teresa holds from the very chapter heading, by seeking it. It is an absolutely gratuitous gift from God. People can dispose themselves for this gift, but not through any psychosomatic techniques. The practices necessary for disposing oneself are humility and detachment.

Questions for Discussion

1. How does Teresa explain the difference between consolations and spiritual delights?
2. Can you think of some other analogy to use for explaining this difference?
3. How does one know the true value of one's prayer?
4. Is there any technique through which we can bring about these spiritual delights? What virtues are necessary to dispose ourselves to receiving and accepting these absolutely gratuitous gifts from God?
5. Teresa finds water to be a helpful symbol in the spiritual life. Can you think of examples from Sacred Scripture where water is an important theme? What can these examples teach us about prayer?

CHAPTER 3

Deals with the prayer of recollection which for the most part the Lord gives before the prayer just mentioned. Tells about its effects and about those that come from that spiritual delight, given by the Lord, that was discussed in the previous chapter.

The effects of this prayer are many. I shall mention some. But first, I want to mention another kind of prayer that almost always begins before this one. Since I have spoken of such a prayer elsewhere,[1] I shall say little. It is a recollection that also seems to me to be supernatural because it doesn't involve being in the dark or closing the eyes, nor does it consist in any exterior thing, since without first wanting to do so, one does close one's eyes and desire solitude. It seems that without any contrivance the edifice is being built, by means of this recollection, for the prayer that was mentioned. ⌈The senses and exterior things seem to be losing their hold because the soul is recovering what it had lost.⌉

2. They say that the soul enters within itself and, at other times, that it rises above itself.[2] With such terminology I wouldn't know how to clarify anything. This is what's

---

1. She spoke of the prayer of recollection in various places: L 14–15; W 28–29; ST 59.3. But Teresa is not consistent in her terminology. Sometimes she speaks of a recollection that is not infused (in *The Way of Perfection*); at other times of a recollection that is infused: in the *Life*, using the term indiscriminately with "quiet" to designate the first degree of infused prayer, and in the *Spiritual Testimonies* to designate the first faint experience of mystical prayer that prepares the way for the prayer of quiet. See IC 4.3.8.

2. She is alluding to works such as Osuna's *Third Spiritual Alphabet* 9.7; and Laredo's *Ascent of Mount Sion* 3.41. See L 12.1, 4–5, 7; 22.13, 18.

wrong with me: that I think you will understand by my way of explaining, while perhaps I'm the only one who will understand myself. Let us suppose that these senses and faculties (for I have already mentioned that these powers are the people of this castle,[3] which is the image I have taken for my explanation) have gone outside and have walked for days and years with strangers—enemies of the well-being of the castle. Having seen their perdition they've already begun to approach the castle even though they may not manage to remain inside because the habit of doing so is difficult to acquire. But still they are not traitors, and they walk in the environs of the castle. Once the great King, who is in the center dwelling place of this castle, sees their good will, He desires in His wonderful mercy to bring them back to Him. Like a good shepherd, with a whistle so gentle that even they themselves almost fail to hear it, He makes them recognize His voice and stops them from going so far astray so that they will return to their dwelling place. And this shepherd's whistle has such power that they abandon the exterior things in which they were estranged from Him and enter the castle.

3. I don't think I've ever explained it as clearly as I have now. When God grants the favor it is a great help to seek Him within where He is found more easily and in a way more beneficial to us than when sought in creatures, as St. Augustine says after having looked for Him in many places.[4] Don't think this recollection is acquired by the intellect striving to think about God within itself, or by the imagination imagining Him within itself. Such efforts are good and an excellent kind of meditation because they are founded on a

3. In IC 1.2.4, 12, 15.

4. In *Confessions* 10.27; or in the pseudo-Augustine's *Soliloquies* 31. See L 40.6; W 28.2.

truth, which is that God is within us. But this isn't the prayer of recollection because it is something each one can do—with the help of God, as should be understood of everything. But what I'm speaking of comes in a different way. Sometimes before one begins to think of God, these people are already inside the castle. I don't know in what way or how they heard their shepherd's whistle. It wasn't through the ears, because nothing is heard. But one noticeably senses a gentle drawing inward, as anyone who goes through this will observe, for I don't know how to make it clearer. It seems to me I have read where it was compared to a hedgehog curling up or a turtle drawing into a shell.[5] (The one who wrote this example must have understood the experience well.) But these creatures draw inward whenever they want. In the case of this recollection, it doesn't come when we want it but when God wants to grant us the favor. I for myself hold that when His Majesty grants it, He does so to persons who are already beginning to despise the things of the world. I don't say that those in the married state do so in deed, for they cannot, but in desire; for He calls such persons especially so that they might be attentive to interior matters. So I believe that if we desire to make room for His Majesty, He will give not only this but more, and give it to those whom He begins to call to advance further.

4. May whoever experiences this within himself praise God greatly because it is indeed right to recognize the favor and give thanks, for doing so will dispose one for other greater favors. And this recollection is a preparation for being able to listen, as is counselled in some books,[6] so that the soul,

---

5. In Osuna's *Third Spiritual Alphabet* 6.4.
6. See Laredo's *Ascent of Mount Sion* 3.27.

instead of striving to engage in discourse, strives to remain attentive and aware of what the Lord is working in it. If His Majesty has not begun to absorb us, I cannot understand how the mind can be stopped. There's no way of doing so without bringing about more harm than good, although there has been a lengthy controversy on this matter among some spiritual persons. For my part I must confess my lack of humility, but those in favor of stopping the mind have never given me a reason for submitting to what they say. One of them tried to convince me with a certain book by the saintly Friar Peter of Alcántara[7]—for I believe he is a saint—to whom I would submit because I know that he knew. And we read it together, and he says the same thing I do; although not in my words. But it is clear in what he says that love must be already awakened. It could be that I'm mistaken, but I have the following reasons.

5. First, in this work of the spirit the one who thinks less and has less desire to act does more. What we must do is beg like the needy poor before a rich and great emperor, and then lower our eyes and wait with humility. When through His secret paths it seems we understand that He hears us, then it is good to be silent since He has allowed us to remain near Him; and it will not be wrong to avoid working with the intellect—if we can work with it, I mean. But if we don't yet know whether this King has heard or seen us, we mustn't become fools. The soul does become quite a fool when it tries to induce this prayer, and it is left much drier; and the imagination perhaps becomes more restless through the effort made not to think of anything. But the Lord desires

---

7. Treatise on *Prayer and Meditation* by Granada and at that time attributed to St. Peter of Alcántara.

that we beseech Him and call to mind that we are in His presence; He knows what is suitable for us. I cannot persuade myself to use human diligence in a matter in which it seems His Majesty has placed a limit, and I want to leave the diligence to Him. What He did not reserve to Himself are many other efforts we can make with His help, such as penance, good deeds, and prayer—insofar as our wretchedness can do these things.

6. The second reason is that these interior works are all gentle and peaceful; doing something arduous would cause more harm than good. I call any force that we might want to use "something arduous"; for example, it would be arduous to hold one's breath. Leave the soul in God's hands; let Him do whatever He wants with it, with the greatest resignation to the will of God.

The third reason is that the very care used not to think of anything will perhaps rouse the mind to think very much.

The fourth reason is that what is most essential and pleasing to God is that we be mindful of His honor and glory and forget ourselves and our own profit and comfort and delight. How is a person forgetful of self if he is so careful not to stir or even to allow his intellect or desires to be stirred to a longing for the greater glory of God, or if he rests in what he already has? When His Majesty desires the intellect to stop, He occupies it in another way and gives it a light so far above what we can attain that it remains absorbed. Then, without knowing how, the intellect is much better instructed than it was through all the soul's efforts not to make use of it. Since God gave us our faculties that we might work with them and in this work they find their reward, there is no reason to charm them; we should let them perform their task until God appoints them to another greater one.

7. What I understand to be most fitting for the soul the Lord has desired to put in this dwelling place is that which has been said.[8] And without any effort or noise the soul should strive to cut down the rambling of the intellect—but not suspend either it or the mind; it is good to be aware that one is in God's presence and of who God is. If what it feels within itself absorbs it, well and good. But let it not strive to understand the nature of this recollection, for it is given to the will. Let the soul enjoy it without any endeavors other than some loving words, for even though we may not try in this prayer to go without thinking of anything, I know that often the intellect will be suspended, even though for only a very brief moment.

8. But as I said elsewhere,[9] the reason why in this kind of prayer—that is, the kind that is like the flowing spring in which the water does not come through aqueducts—the soul restrains itself or is restrained is its realization that it doesn't understand what it desires; and so the mind wanders from one extreme to the other, like a fool unable to rest in anything. (I am referring to the kind of prayer this dwelling place began with, for I have joined the prayer of recollection, which I should have mentioned first, with this one. The prayer of recollection is much less intense than the prayer of spiritual delight from God that I mentioned. But it is the beginning through which one goes to the other; for in the prayer of recollection, meditation, or the work of the intellect, must not be set aside.) The will has such deep rest in its God that the clamor of the intellect is a terrible bother to it. There is no need to pay any attention to this clamor, for doing so would

8. In IC 4.3.4–6; 4.2.9.

9. Perhaps she is referring to a parallel passage in W 31.3, 7.

make the will lose much of what it enjoys. But one should let
the intellect go and surrender oneself into the arms of love,
for His Majesty will teach the soul what it must do at that
point. Almost everything lies in finding oneself unworthy of
so great a good and in being occupied with giving thanks.

9. In order to deal with the prayer of recollection I post-
poned mention of the effects or signs in souls to whom God,
our Lord, gives this prayer of quiet. What an expansion or
dilation of the soul is may be clearly understood from the
example of a fount whose water doesn't overflow into a
stream because the fount itself is constructed of such material that the more water there is flowing into it the larger
the trough becomes. So it seems is the case with this prayer
and many other marvels that God grants to the soul, for He
enables and prepares it so that it can keep everything within
itself. Hence this interior sweetness and expansion can be
verified in the fact that the soul is not as tied down as it was
before in things pertaining to the service of God, but has
much more freedom. Thus, in not being constrained by the
fear of hell (because although there is even greater fear of
offending God it loses servile fear here), this soul is left with
great confidence that it will enjoy Him. The fear it used to
have of doing penance and losing its health has disappeared,
and it now thinks it will be able to do all things in God[10]
and has greater desire for penance than previously. The fear
it used to have of trials it now sees to be tempered. Its faith
is more alive; it knows that if it suffers trials for God, His
Majesty will give it the grace to suffer them with patience.
Sometimes it even desires them because there also remains a
strong will to do something for God. Since its knowledge of

---

10. Allusion to Phil 4:13.

God's grandeur grows, it considers itself to be more miserable. Because it has already experienced spiritual delight from God, it sees that worldly delights are like filth. It finds itself withdrawing from them little by little, and it is more master of itself for so doing. In sum, there is an improvement in all the virtues. It will continue to grow if it doesn't turn back now to offending God; because if it does, then everything will be lost, however high on the summit the soul may be. Nor should it be understood that if God grants this favor once or twice to a soul all these good effects will be caused. It must persevere in receiving them, for in this perseverance lies all our good.

10. One strong warning I give to whoever finds himself in this state is that he guard very carefully against placing himself in the occasion of offending God. In this prayer the soul is not yet grown but is like a suckling child. If it turns away from its mother's breasts, what can be expected for it but death? I am very afraid that this will happen to anyone to whom God has granted this favor and who withdraws from prayer—unless he does so for a particularly special reason—or if he doesn't return quickly to prayer, for he will go from bad to worse. I know there is a great deal to fear in this matter. And I know some persons for whom I have felt quite sorry—and I've seen what I'm speaking about—because they have turned away from One who with so much love wanted to be their friend and proved it by deeds. I advise them so strongly not to place themselves in the occasions of sin because the devil tries much harder for a soul of this kind than for very many to whom the Lord does not grant these favors. For such a soul can do a great deal of harm to the devil by getting others to follow it, and it could be of great benefit to God's Church. And even though the devil may

have no other reason than to see who it is to whom His Majesty shows particular love, that's sufficient for him to wear himself out trying to lead the soul to perdition. So these souls suffer much combat, and if they go astray, they stray much more than do others.

You, sisters, are free of dangers, from what we can know. From pride and vainglory may God deliver you. If the devil should counterfeit God's favors, this will be known by the fact that these good effects are not caused, but just the opposite.

11. There is one danger I want to warn you about (although I may have mentioned it elsewhere)[11] into which I have seen persons of prayer fall, especially women, for since we are weaker there is more occasion for what I'm about to say. It is that some have a weak constitution because of a great amount of penance, prayer, and keeping vigil, and even without these; in receiving some favor, their nature is overcome. Since they feel some consolation interiorly and a languishing and weakness exteriorly, they think they are experiencing a spiritual sleep (which is a prayer a little more intense than the prayer of quiet)[12] and they let themselves become absorbed. The more they allow this, the more absorbed they become because their nature is further weakened, and they fancy that they are being carried away in rapture. I call it being carried away in foolishness[13] because it amounts to nothing more than wasting time and wearing down one's health. These persons feel nothing through their senses, nor do they feel anything concerning God. One person happened to remain eight

---

11. In F 6. She will insist on this again in IC 6.7.13.

12. See L 16–17, where Teresa dwells at greater length on this *sleep of the faculties* as though dealing with a special stage in the degrees of mystical prayer.

13. Teresa makes a pun here with the Spanish words *arrobamiento* (rapture) and *abobamiento* (foolishness).

hours in this state. By sleeping and eating and avoiding so much penance, this person got rid of the stupor, for there was someone who understood her. She had misled both her confessor and other persons, as well as herself—for she hadn't intended to deceive. I truly believe that the devil was trying to gain ground, and in this instance indeed he was beginning to gain no small amount.

12. It must be understood that when something is truly from God there is no languishing in the soul, even though there may be an interior and exterior languishing, for the soul experiences deep feelings on seeing itself close to God. Nor does the experience last so long, but for a very short while—although one becomes absorbed again. In such prayer, if the cause of it is not weakness, as I said,[14] the body is not worn down nor is any external feeling produced.

13. For this reason let them take the advice that when they feel this languishing in themselves they tell the prioress and distract themselves from it insofar as they can. The prioress should make them give up so many hours for prayer so that they have only a very few and try to get them to sleep and eat well until their natural strength begins to return, if it has been lost through a lack of food and sleep. If a sister's nature is so weak that this is not enough, may she believe me that God does not want her to practice anything but the active life, which also must be practiced in monasteries. They should let her get busy with different duties; and always take care that she not have a great deal of solitude, for she would lose her health completely. It will be quite a mortification for her; in how she bears this absence is the way the Lord wants to test her love for Him. And He will be pleased to give her

---

14. In IC 4.3.11–12.

strength back after some time. If He doesn't, she will gain through vocal prayer and through obedience and will merit what she would have merited otherwise, and perhaps more.

14. There could also be some persons with such weak heads and imaginations—and I have known some—to whom it seems that everything they think about they see. This is very dangerous. Because I shall perhaps treat of it later on, I'll say no more here. I have greatly enlarged upon this dwelling place because it is the one which more souls enter. Since it is, and since the natural and the supernatural are joined in it, the devil can do more harm. In those dwelling places still to be spoken of, the Lord doesn't give him so much leeway. May His Majesty be forever praised, amen.

PASSIVE RECOLLECTION, THE PRAYER OF QUIET, AND A WARNING

4.3.1–4 Teresa thinks that before she talks about the effects of the prayer of spiritual delight (*gustos*), she should speak about another kind of prayer that almost always begins before the prayer of delight. It is a recollection that also seems to her to be supernatural because the initiative doesn't seem to come from oneself. There is a desire for solitude, and perhaps persons close their eyes; the senses and exterior things seem to lose their hold.

Teresa says that she thinks she can explain the matter better if she uses her own terminology and examples rather than terminology more common in her day. Returning to the castle metaphor, Teresa asks us to suppose that the people of the castle (the senses and faculties) have walked for years outside the castle. Sometimes they enter, but they cannot remain, even though they see the dangers outside. When the Lord sees their good will, he desires in his wonderful mercy to bring them to himself. Like a good shepherd, he makes them recognize his gentle whistle in a subtle way and keeps them from going so far astray that they can't return to their dwelling place. This shepherd's whistle has such power that they abandon the exterior things in which they were estranged from him and enter the castle.

Teresa continues her explanation of this type of recollection, emphasizing that it isn't the result of our efforts. Persons experience a gentle drawing inward that doesn't come from their own initiative. Teresa thinks God gives this gift to those who are already beginning to turn away from worldly things. She says that although married people cannot completely reject the world in deeds, they can do so in their desires.

This recollection is a preparation for the soul's being able to listen to how the Lord is working in it. Teresa here introduces an additional topic that she has given thought to—how the mind can be stopped. She believes that if His Majesty has not begun to absorb us, the mind cannot be stopped, and efforts to do so can be harmful. In this point of view she says she differs with some others of her day. She says that a book by Friar Peter of Alcántara supports her position that love must already be awakened for the mind to be stopped.

4.3.5 Teresa gives reasons why she believes love must be awakened (or, as she also puts it, His Majesty must begin to absorb us) before the mind is stopped in prayer. She says that in this work of the spirit, the one who thinks less and has less desire to act actually does more. To receive this supernatural recollection, we must beg in humility, like the needy poor before a rich and great emperor. When, through his secret paths, it seems we understand that God hears us, then it is good to be silent. In contrast, if we don't yet know whether this King has heard or seen us, we must continue to beseech him and call to mind that we are in his presence, even if we don't perceive that to be so. What we should not do is foolishly try to induce this prayer, which is of a type that is not in our power to effect. If we do try, the soul may be left much drier, and the imagination may become even more restless just because we are trying not to think of anything. Emphasizing that the initiative is God's, Teresa says she can't persuade herself to use human diligence in a matter in which it seems God has placed a limit; she wants to leave the diligence to him. However, she doesn't want to leave readers with the mistaken idea that because our efforts can't produce this prayer that we desire, we should therefore cease effort in everything. She says we should, with God's help, continue penance, good deeds, and prayer.

4.3.6 Teresa continues to elaborate on her view that we should not exercise effort in order to acquire supernatural recollection because it cannot be acquired, and that anything arduous we do would cause more harm than good. She terms any force we might want to use as something arduous and gives the example of holding one's breath. She says to leave the soul in God's hands, letting him do whatever he wants with it. Repeating an earlier argument, she says that the very care used not to think of anything will perhaps rouse the mind to think very much. Her fourth reason is that what pleases God most is our concern for his honor and glory alone, with forgetfulness of self. She thinks that we can't be forgetful of self if we are trying not to stir or even to allow our intellect or our desires to be stirred to a longing for the greater glory of God. When he desires the intellect to stop, the Lord can occupy it through an enlightenment so far above what we can attain ourselves that the intellect remains absorbed in God. Then, without knowing how, the intellect is much better instructed than it was through all the soul's efforts not to make use of it. Teresa argues that since God gave us our faculties to work with, we should let them perform their tasks until God gives them a greater one.

4.3.7 Here Teresa summarizes her reflections set forth in the preceding numbers on how the soul should act in regard to the prayer of supernatural recollection. We should not try to suspend either the intellect or the mind, but should try to focus the intellect, being aware that we are in God's presence and of who God is. If what the intellect feels within itself absorbs it, she says, that's well and good, but it should not strive to understand the nature of this recollection, for it is given to the will. She advises letting the soul enjoy this recollection without any effort other than some loving words. Suspension of the intellect will follow without effort, if only briefly.

4.3.8 Teresa points out now that the reason why the soul is restrained in this kind of supernatural prayer, is its realization that it doesn't understand what it desires, so that the mind wanders from one thing to another. The prayer of recollection is much less intense than the prayer of spiritual delight from God. She says the prayer of recollection is the beginning through which one goes to the prayer of delight.

4.3.9 After discussing at some length the prayer of recollection, Teresa returns to the topic of the effects or signs in souls to whom God gives the prayer of spiritual delight. She mentioned earlier that one effect is expansion or dilation of the soul. She returns to the fountain metaphor but with a difference. Now she asks us to imagine a fountain constructed of a material that can expand so that the more the water flows, the larger the water trough becomes. She says that in the prayer of delight, God prepares the soul so it can keep everything within itself. The soul has more freedom. The soul is no longer constrained by the fear of hell, although it has an even greater fear of offending God. The soul is left with great confidence that it will enjoy the Lord. Those who have experienced the prayer of spiritual delight have less fear of penance and trials. Sometimes they even desire suffering in order to do something for God. Worldly delights have no attraction, and there is improvement in all the virtues. If the soul does not turn back, it will continue to grow. She clarifies that these effects are not the result of only one or two instances of the prayer of delight. The soul must persevere in receiving and practicing these good effects, for in this perseverance lies all our good.

4.3.10 To those who have experienced the prayer of delight, Teresa warns in the strongest terms to guard against placing themselves in occasions of offending God because they are still weak and can go astray.

4.3.11–14 Teresa warns against the danger of a false experience of delight resulting from excessive hours of prayer, penance, and keeping vigils. Certain persons feel some consolation along with physical weakness and mistake the experience for deep prayer. If they continue, they are only wasting time and damaging their health. The cure is to get enough sleep, avoid so much penance, and resume eating well. Teresa contrasts this stupor induced by excessive deprivation with prayer truly from God. Genuine prayer is not accompanied by languishing in the soul, although there may be some interior and exterior languishing. Those who feel this languishing should tell the prioress and distract themselves from it as much as they can. The prioress should make them return to a more ordinary schedule of sleeping and eating well if deprivation has caused the languishing. If these things don't help, Teresa is convinced that such persons should practice an active life, which was possible in the monasteries. The nun might not be happy with this arrangement, but Teresa says she will gain through vocal prayer and obedience, and will merit what she would have merited otherwise and perhaps more.

Teresa mentions briefly another experience of some persons with weak heads and imaginations, who seem to see everything they think about. She concludes by saying she has spent so much effort in discussing this fourth dwelling place because it is one which more souls enter; also, because the natural and supernatural are joined in it, the devil can do more harm here than in the more advanced dwelling places.

Interpretive Notes

In the previous section, Teresa wrote: "God help me with what I have undertaken! I've already forgotten what I was dealing with, for business matters and poor health have forced me to set this work aside just when I was at my best; and since I have a poor memory everything will come out confused" (IC 4.2.1). This confusion in the unfolding of her teaching shows itself here in that Teresa begins to speak now of a prayer that should really precede the prayer of quiet (or *gustos*). In her description of the degrees of prayer given in her *Spiritual Testimony* (ST 59), she places this prayer in its proper order, as the first that, in her opinion, was supernatural, and calls it an "interior recollection." She hasn't changed her mind and now speaks of this passive recollection as a prayer coming before the previous one of spiritual delight. In her *Life* (L 15.1), she refers to quietude and recollection together as a prayer bestowed passively on the soul. In her *Way of Perfection* (W 28), however, she speaks of the "prayer of recollection" as an active exercise. We already pointed out how, in this prayer of active recollection, described in the *Way of Perfection*, the soul collects its faculties together and enters within itself to be with its God, and how this method of keeping Christ present is beneficial in all stages. Persons in any stage begin their prayer with this presence to Christ, which is equivalent to the prayer of active recollection. The transition from this active recollection to passive recollection can take place so subtly that one often hardly realizes it.

This chapter then has two different and important themes announced in the heading: the prayer of passive recollection (IC 4.3.1–7) and the effects of quiet (IC 4.3.8–14). "Recollection" was a common term in Teresa's day. Among some of the authors using it were St. Peter of Alcántara, Bernardino de Laredo, and Francisco de Osuna. These authors spoke of a path, along which one traveled, called the "prayer of recollection." Teresa recalls some of their terminology, such as "the soul enters within itself," or "ascends above itself," or strives to "think of nothing," but she doesn't limit herself to these terms to explain her experiences. She rejects completely the technique of not thinking of anything, of leaving the mind blank in hopes of some illumination. She does hold on to the expressive term "recollection," but uses the term freely to suit her various contexts. She shares Augustine's orientation to interiority:

> Late have I loved you, O beauty so ancient and so new; late have I loved you! For behold you were within me, and I outside; and I sought you outside and in my unloveliness fell upon those lovely things that you had made. You were with me and I was not with you. I was kept from you by those things, yet had they not been in you, they would not have been at all. (*Confessions*, 10.27)

She appropriates whatever fits the main symbol of her work: to enter into the castle of the soul—that is, to pray.

Teresa imagines the powers of the soul as people within the castle who have gone outside and walked for days and even years with strangers, enemies of their well-being. Recognizing their bad state, they come near the castle. In his wonderful mercy, the great King sees them and desires to bring them back to himself. She writes:

> Like a good shepherd, with a whistle so gentle that even they [the faculties] themselves almost fail to hear it, He makes them recognize His voice and stops them from going so far astray so that they will return to their dwelling place. And this shepherd's whistle has such power that they abandon the exterior things in which they were estranged from Him and enter the castle. (IC 4.3.2)

The only thing asked of these persons is that they disentangle themselves, at least for a while, from the strangers outside, who are enemies of their good, so as to give themselves over as much as possible to the action of God. They join this detachment from the world and surrender to God with expressions of humility, gratitude, love, and praise. The Spirit, who is present and active in all Christian prayer, has now taken the initiative, but very gently.

With regard to the technique taught by some in Teresa's time, not to think of anything (*no pensar nada*), Teresa insists that the mind cannot be stopped by our own efforts, but only by the infusion of a divine force. The mystical experience of God is absolutely gratuitous, and not something that we can obtain through our own techniques or efforts. We can, though, dispose ourselves for God's gifts by training ourselves to keep Christ present within us, which Teresa calls the prayer of active recollection and describes in chapters 26–29 of her *Way of Perfection*.

In the prayer of passive recollection and, although to a lesser extent, in the prayer of quiet, distractions are still a problem. Teresa's solution to this problem is to pay no attention to the wandering mind. "One should let the intellect go and surrender oneself into the arms of love" (IC 4.3.8). In other words, people should fix their gaze on the mystery of Christ in such a way that they do less thinking about, and more gazing with, love. At the same time, the will finds it possible to engage itself in loving, with a love that is infused. Although "to contemplate" means to gaze at with the eyes of the mind, here the contemplative is above all someone touched by love. But a vague perception prevails that both of these activities come from God's initiative. To use the term "passive" for this new manner of prayer is an inadequate expression employed merely to designate a kind of activity that does not emanate from the subject or flow from its ordinary sources of energy. There is Another who begins to shed his light on the horizon.

As Teresa goes on to ascend the mystical ladder with us, she points out how each stage of prayer brings about in the subject an ever-growing similarity to Christ. As a result of this prayer, the soul's faith becomes more alive, and it knows that if God sends trials, he will send the patience to suffer them. It finds itself withdrawing from worldly delights and improving in virtue. Especially, as its knowledge of God's grandeur grows, its humility increases.

Persons having a weak constitution, if they experience some mystical prayer, might be overcome and spend long hours in what they think is mystical prayer when it is no more than a loss of strength. Prayer that is truly from God gives the soul deep feelings on seeing itself close to God, and it doesn't last long. The body is not worn out through mystical prayer. These misguided persons need to regain their strength and not spend so many hours in prayer.

Questions for Discussion

1. What kind of prayer does Teresa speak of in this chapter?
2. What image does she use to convey her teaching about this prayer of recollection?
3. What is a good way to dispose oneself for this prayer?
4. What are some of the good effects of the prayer of "spiritual delight"?
5. What are some of the dangers Teresa warns about?
6. How do we know when our mortifications or ascetical practices begin to cause more harm than good?
7. Does Teresa advocate for an active process of trying to clear one's mind of all thoughts in prayer?

THE FIFTH
DWELLING PLACES

Contains Four Chapters

CHAPTER 1

Begins to deal with how the soul is united to God in prayer. Tells how one discerns whether there is any illusion.

O sisters, how can I explain the riches and treasures and delights found in the fifth dwelling places? I believe it would be better not to say anything about these remaining rooms, for there is no way of knowing how to speak of them; neither is the intellect capable of understanding them nor can comparisons help in explaining them; earthly things are too coarse for such a purpose.

Send light from heaven, my Lord, that I might be able to enlighten these Your servants—for You have been pleased that some of them ordinarily enjoy these delights—so that they may not be deceived by the devil transforming himself into an angel of light.[1] For all their desires are directed toward pleasing You.

2. And although I have said "some," there are indeed only a few who fail to enter this dwelling place of which I shall

---

1. Allusion to 2 Cor 11:14.

now speak. There are various degrees, and for that reason I say that most enter these places. But I believe that only a few will experience some of the things that I will say are in this room. Yet even if souls do no more than reach the door, God is being very merciful to them; although many are called, few are chosen.[2] So I say now that all of us who wear this holy habit of Carmel are called to prayer and contemplation. This call explains our origin; we are the descendants of men who felt this call, of those holy fathers on Mount Carmel who in such great solitude and contempt for the world sought this treasure, this precious pearl of contemplation that we are speaking about. Yet few of us dispose ourselves that the Lord may communicate it to us. In exterior matters we are proceeding well so that we will reach what is necessary; but in the practice of the virtues that are necessary for arriving at this point we need very, very much and cannot be careless in either small things or great. So, my sisters, since in some way we can enjoy heaven on earth, be brave in begging the Lord to give us His grace in such a way that nothing will be lacking through our own fault; that He show us the way and strengthen the soul that it may dig until it finds this hidden treasure.[3] The truth is that the treasure lies within our very selves. This is what I would like to know how to explain, if the Lord would enable me to do so.

3. I said "strengthen the soul" so that you will understand that bodily strength is not necessary for those to whom God does not give it. He doesn't make it impossible for anyone to buy His riches. He is content if each one gives what he has. Blessed be so great a God. But reflect, daughters, that

---

2. Allusion to Mt 22:14.
3. Allusion to Mt 13:44.

He doesn't want you to hold on to anything, so that you will be able to enjoy the favors we are speaking of. Whether you have little or much, He wants everything for Himself; and in conformity with what you know you have given you will receive greater or lesser favors. There is no better proof for recognizing whether our prayer has reached union or not.

4. Don't think this union is some kind of dreamy state like the one I mentioned before.[4] I say "dreamy state" because it only seems that the soul is asleep; for neither does it really think it is asleep nor does it feel awake. There is no need here to use any technique to suspend the mind since all the faculties are asleep in this state—and truly asleep—to the things of the world and to ourselves. As a matter of fact, during the time that the union lasts, the soul is left as though without its senses, for it has no power to think even if it wants to. In loving, if it does love, it doesn't understand how or what it is it loves or what it would want. In sum, it is like one who in every respect has died to the world so as to live more completely in God. Thus the death is a delightful one, an uprooting from the soul of all the operations it can have while being in the body. The death is a delightful one because in truth it seems that in order to dwell more perfectly in God the soul is so separated from the body that I don't even know if it has life enough to breathe. (I was just now thinking about this, and it seems to me that it doesn't—at least if it does breathe, it is unaware it is doing so.) Nonetheless, its whole intellect would want to be occupied in understanding something of what is felt. And since the soul does not have the energy to attain to this, it is so stunned that, even if consciousness is not completely lost, neither a hand nor a foot stirs, as we say

---

4. IC 4.3.11.

here below when a person is in such a swoon that we think he is dead. (shroom trip)

O secrets of God! I would never tire of trying to explain them if I thought I could in some way manage to do so; thus I will say a thousand foolish things in order that I might at times succeed and that we might give great praise to the Lord.

5. I said that this union was not some kind of dreamy state,[5] because even if the experience in the dwelling place that was just mentioned is abundant the soul remains doubtful that it was union. It doubts whether it imagined the experience; whether it was asleep; whether the experience was given by God; or whether the devil transformed himself into an angel of light.[6] It is left with a thousand suspicions. That it has them is good, for, as I have said,[7] even our own nature can sometimes deceive us in that dwelling place. Though there is not so much room for poisonous things to enter, some tiny lizards do enter; since these lizards have slender heads they can poke their heads in anywhere. And even though they do no harm, especially if one pays no attention to them, as I said,[8] they are often a bother since they are little thoughts proceeding from the imagination and from what I mentioned. But however slender they may be, these little lizards cannot enter this fifth dwelling place; for there is neither imagination, nor memory, nor intellect that can impede this good. And I would dare say that if the prayer is truly that of union with God the devil cannot even enter or do any damage. His Majesty is so joined and united with the essence of the soul

---

5. IC 5.1.3.

6. Another allusion to 2 Cor 11:14.

7. IC 4.3.11–14.

8. IC 4.1.8–12.

that the devil will not approach nor will he even know about this secret. And this is obvious. Since as they say, he doesn't know our mind, he will have less knowledge of something so secret; for God doesn't even entrust this to our own mind. Oh what a great good, a state in which this accursed one does us no harm! Thus the soul is left with such wonderful blessings because God works within it without anyone disturbing Him, not even ourselves. What will He not give, who is so fond of giving and who can give all that He wants?

6. It seems I have left you confused by saying "if it is union" and that there are other unions. And indeed how true it is that there are! Even though these unions regard vain things, the devil will use such things to transport us when they are greatly loved. But he doesn't do so in the way God does, or with the delight and satisfaction of soul, or with the peace and joy. This union is above all earthly joys, above all delights, above all consolations, and still more than that. It doesn't matter where those spiritual or earthly joys come from, for the feeling is very different, as you will have experienced. I once said[9] that the difference is like that between feeling something on the rough outer covering of the body or in the marrow of the bones. And that was right on the mark, for I don't know how to say it better.

7. It seems to me that you're still not satisfied, for you will think you can be mistaken and that these interior things are something difficult to examine. What was said will be sufficient for anyone who has experienced union. Yet, because the difference between union and the previous experience is great, I want to mention a clear sign by which you will be sure against error or doubts about whether the union is from God.

---

9. She made a similar observation in W 31.10.

His Majesty has brought it to my memory today, and in my opinion it is the sure sign. In difficult matters, even though it seems to me I understand and that I speak the truth, I always use this expression "it seems to me." For if I am mistaken, I am very much prepared to believe what those who have a great deal of learning say. Even though they have not experienced these things, very learned men have a certain "I don't know what"; for since God destines them to give light to His Church, He enlightens them that they might acknowledge a truth when presented with it. And if they do not live a dissipated life but are God's servants, they are never surprised by His grandeurs; they have come to understand well that He can do ever more and more. And, finally, even though some things are not so well explained, these learned men will find other things in their books that will show that these things could take place.

8. I have had a great deal of experience with learned men, and have also had experience with half-learned, fearful ones; these latter cost me dearly.[10] At least I think that anyone who refuses to believe that God can do much more or that He has considered and continues to consider it good sometimes to communicate favors to His creatures, has indeed closed the door to receiving them. Therefore, sisters, let this never happen to you, but believe that God can do far more and don't turn your attention to whether the ones to whom He grants His favors are good or bad; for His Majesty know this, as I have told you.[11] There is no reason for us to meddle in the matter, but with humility and simplicity of heart we should serve and praise Him for His works and marvels.

---

10. See L 5.3; 13.19; 25.22.
11. IC 4.1.2; 4.2.9

9. Well then, to return to the sign that I say is the true one,[12] you now see that God has made this soul a fool with regard to all so as better to impress upon it true wisdom. For during the time of this union it neither sees, nor hears, nor understands, because the union is always short and seems to the soul even much shorter than it probably is. God so places Himself in the interior of that soul that when it returns to itself it can in no way doubt that it was in God and God was in it. This truth remains with it so firmly that even though years go by without God's granting that favor again, the soul can neither forget nor doubt that it was in God and God was in it. This certitude is what matters now, for I shall speak of the effects of this prayer afterward.[13]

10. Now, you will ask me, how did the soul see this truth or understand if it didn't see or understand anything? I don't say that it then saw the truth but that afterward it sees the truth clearly, not because of a vision but because of a certitude remaining in the soul that only God can place there. I know a person who hadn't learned that God was in all things by presence, power, and essence, and through a favor of this kind that God granted her she came to believe it. After asking a half-learned man of the kind I mentioned[14]—he knew as little as she had known before God enlightened her—she was told that God was present only by grace. Such was her own conviction that even after this she didn't believe him and asked others who told her the truth, with which she was greatly consoled.[15]

---

12. See IC 5.1.7.
13. She speaks of them in the next chapter, IC 5.2.7–14.
14. In IC 5.1.8.
15. See L 18.15; ST 49.

11. Don't be mistaken by thinking that this certitude has to do with a corporal form, as in the case of the bodily presence of our Lord Jesus Christ in the Most Blessed Sacrament, even though we do not see Him. Here the matter isn't like that; it concerns only the divinity. How, then, is it that what we do not see leaves this certitude? I don't know; these are His works. But I do know I speak the truth. And I would say that whoever does not receive this certitude does not experience union of the whole soul with God, but union of some faculty, or that he experiences one of the many other kinds of favors God grants souls. In regard to all these favors we have to give up looking for reasons to see how they've come about. Since our intellect cannot understand this union, why do we have to make this effort? It's enough for us to see that He who is the cause of it is almighty. Since we have no part at all to play in bringing it about no matter how much effort we put forth, but it is God who does so, let us not desire the capacity to understand this union.

12. Now I recall, in saying that we have no part to play, what you have heard the bride say in the *Song of Songs*: *He brought me into the wine cellar* (or, placed me there, I believe it says).[16] And it doesn't say that she went. And it says also that she went looking about in every part of the city for her Beloved.[17] I understand this union to be the wine cellar where the Lord wishes to place us when He desires and as He desires. But however great the effort we make to do so, we cannot enter. His Majesty must place us there and enter Himself into the center of our soul. And that He may show His marvels more clearly, He doesn't want our will to have

---

16. Song 2:4.
17. Song 3:2.

any part to play, for it has been entirely surrendered to Him. Neither does He want the door of the faculties and of the senses to be opened, for they are all asleep. But He wants to enter the center of the soul without going through any door, as He entered the place where His disciples were when He said, *pax vobis;*[18] or as He left the tomb without lifting away the stone. Further on you will see in the last dwelling place[19] how His Majesty desires that the soul enjoy Him in its own center even much more than here.

13. O daughters, how much we shall see if we don't want to have anything more to do with our own lowliness and misery and if we understand that we are unworthy of being servants of a Lord who is so great we cannot comprehend His wonders! May He be forever praised, amen.

---

18. Jn 20:19.
19. See IC 7.2.3.

THE FACULTIES ARE ASLEEP
TO EVERYTHING BUT GOD

5.1.1–2 Teresa asks for help from heaven in order to speak about the delights of the fifth dwelling places. She says that most enter these dwelling places, but that there are various degrees, and there are some experiences that only a few souls will be given. She states that all who wear the holy habit of Carmel are called to prayer and contemplation. She refers to contemplation as enjoying heaven on earth, and says that it is a treasure that lies within ourselves. But before the Lord communicates with us, we must dispose ourselves for this gift through the practice of virtues, and we must not be careless in anything. We must beg the Lord to strengthen our souls.

5.1.3 Teresa says that God does not want us to hold on to anything; he wants everything for himself. She says that in conformity with what we know we have given, we will receive greater or lesser favors. She says, further, that there is no better proof than this disposition for recognizing whether our prayer has reached union or not.

5.1.4 Teresa compares the prayer of union in the fifth dwelling places to the prayer in the fourth dwelling places. In the fourth dwelling places, the soul experiences a state where it feels itself neither fully awake nor fully asleep. She calls this experience a "dreamy state."

In contrast, in the fifth dwelling places, all the faculties are asleep, both to things of the world and to self. The soul is so completely absorbed by its experience of God that it seems to have died to the world so as to live more completely in God.

5.1.5 Here Teresa returns to a comment on a type of experience from the fourth dwelling place, reviewing some characteristics of the earlier prayer. There the person might describe the experience as "dreamy," and the soul remains doubtful of the source and even the nature of it, wondering if it was asleep. Teresa thinks doubts in the fourth dwelling place are good and that they help protect the person from being deceived. She contrasts experiences in the fourth dwelling places with those of the fifth. In the fifth, neither imagination nor memory nor intellect nor even the devil can impede the prayer of union. The soul is left with wonderful blessings because God works in the soul without anyone disturbing him, not even ourselves.

5.1.6 Here Teresa explains that there are many kinds of union. The prayer of union is above all earthly joys, consolations, and delights, and it is experienced differently from these ordinary experiences. Teresa contrasts earthly delights with the joys of union by using a comparison of something experienced on the skin as opposed to something experienced in the marrow of the bones.

5.1.7-9 Teresa addresses concerns that might be raised by those who worry that the authenticity of these experiences in the fifth dwelling places can't be known for certain. She says anyone who has already had these experiences will be reassured by what she has already written. But she says His Majesty helped her remember what she thinks is a sure sign, although she defers to those with greater learning. After a digression praising learned men and warning against those whose learning is insufficient to advise others, Teresa returns to the topic of the true sign, which is that when it returns to itself, it can in no way doubt that it was in God and God was in it.

5.1.10–11 Teresa says that the soul doesn't understand anything during this union but that after it comes out of it, it has a certitude that the soul was in God and God was in it. This is a presence of God that we call "natural," not the presence through grace. When a priest told her that God was present in the soul only by grace, she couldn't believe it until by asking others she finally learned the truth—that God is in all things by his presence, power, and essence. And though she doesn't know how she had this certitude, she claims that anyone who doesn't think that God is present even in a sinner has not reached the prayer of union.

5.1.12–13 Teresa concludes chapter 1 with a reference to the *Song of Songs*. She says God must bring the soul to this union, as in the *Song of Songs* the bride is brought into the wine cellar, which is the center of the soul. This prayer cannot be attained through the soul's efforts, although through our love and complete surrender to God we can dispose ourselves to receive this favor. She concludes, "May he be forever praised, amen."

Interpretive Notes

Something of a religious trembling seizes Teresa as she approaches the fifth dwelling places, for there is no way by which we can understand or speak of them. They are the dwelling places of union, a term bland enough for us, but for a mystic like Teresa, one abounding with meaning and mystery, pointing like a sacrament to the culmination of the love God has for human beings. She hesitates, wondering if it would be better to say nothing more. But with the thought that most of her nuns enter these dwelling places, although there are various degrees, she turns to God for the light needed to go on describing this journey to the center of the castle. In fact, she reminds her readers at this point that all who wear the holy habit of Carmel are called to prayer and contemplation. The holy fathers on Mount Carmel, from whom they descend, sought this precious pearl of union in great solitude and contempt for the world. No other passage of her writing has affirmed so categorically the call to this contemplation, extended to those for whom she is writing. Since we can enjoy heaven on earth, be brave in begging the Lord that nothing will be lacking through our own fault, that with God's help we dig until we find this treasure. But this reminder to her Carmelite readers does not in any way subtract from her desire to attract all her readers to so sublime a blessing (L 18.8).

God is not only the most high, he is also the all-near as well. Teresa's discovery of the presence of God within every soul came in the light of a contemplative grace. She hadn't known that God was in all things. She thought this omnipresence of God was impossible. Those who had no learning confirmed her belief, telling her that he was present only by grace (L 18.15). It is true that God is also in us by grace—that is, that the Holy Trinity comes and dwells as a friend in anyone baptized who loves him and keeps his commandments. But if it is true that God is everywhere, both within us and outside of us, whether or not we are in grace, it is also true that we do not feel or perceive him as we do other objects. We do not experience his presence as we do that of a friend. We do not even experience him through our faith, because faith, like an opaque veil, separates our spirit from his. This barrier can be surmounted only through a gift from God, by a grace like the one given to Teresa at a precise moment in her spiritual journey.

I sometimes experienced, as I said, although very briefly, the beginning of what I will now speak about. It used to happen, when I represented Christ within me in order to place myself in His presence, or even while reading, that a feeling of the presence of God would come upon me unexpectedly so that I could in no way doubt He was within me or I totally immersed in Him. This did not occur after the manner of a vision. I believe they call the experience "mystical theology." (L 10.1).

A trickle of light shone through the opaque veil and Teresa experienced the presence of God in her soul.

Her statement that she hadn't learned that God was in all things through his presence, power, and essence probably reflects the explanations of her Dominican confessors, who took the terms from the *Summa Theologiae* of St. Thomas Aquinas: "God is in all things by his power inasmuch as all things are subject to his power; he is by his presence in all things, as all things are bare and open to his eyes; he is in all things by his essence, inasmuch as he is present to all as the cause of their being" (*Summa Theologiae* I, q. 8, a. 3).

What, then, is this prayer of union? Teresa compares it to sleep—a sleep in which all of our faculties are asleep to ourselves and to the things of the world. But they are not asleep to God, and this is how it differs from sleep. He makes them lose consciousness of everything but him. They don't understand, however, the way in which they are aware of God, nor can they describe it. This loss of consciousness of the world never lasts long—twenty minutes to a half hour or less—but it does seem that much less time passes to the one experiencing the union. It takes place in the center of our soul, a place where the Lord places us when and as he desires, but which we cannot enter on our own. How does one know for sure that one has reached the prayer of union if during the short time it lasts one neither sees, nor hears, nor understands? One knows for sure after one returns to consciousness, for then the soul can in no way doubt that it was in God and God was in it. This certitude remains, even though years may go by without God granting the favor again.

St. Teresa suffered a great deal from her confessors' doubts about her and from their lack of learning. Half-learned confessors, she says, did her soul a great deal of harm (L 5.3). As a result, she has a high esteem for learning and for learned confessors. But for beginners, a director who has good judgment and experience is sufficient. It was in her mystical life especially that Teresa needed the help of learned men, and even the learned men often doubted her or she found herself in disagreement with them. During the prayer itself, she experienced no doubts. It was afterward that her confessors succeeded in filling her with fears that the devil was causing all these experiences, and she forced herself to go along with their opinions (L 13.16; 25.14; 28.14).

Questions for Discussion

1. What did the holy fathers on Mount Carmel seek?
2. Where does the treasure lie?
3. What does God want from us?
4. What is the prayer of union?
5. What is the clear sign that someone has received the prayer of union?
6. What is the difference between the presence of God in someone in a state of mortal sin and in someone in the state of grace?

CHAPTER 2

Continues on the same topic. Explains the prayer of union through an exquisite comparison. Tells about the effects it leaves in the soul. The chapter is very important.

It will seem to you that everything has already been said about what there is to see in this dwelling place. Yet a lot is missing; for, as I said,[1] there are various degrees of intensity. With regard to the nature of union, I don't believe I'd know how to say anything more. But when souls to whom God grants these favors prepare themselves, there are many things to say about the Lord's work in them. I shall speak of some of these and tell about the state the soul is left in. To explain things better I want to use a helpful comparison; it is good for making us see how, even though we can do nothing in this work done by our Lord, we can do much by disposing ourselves so that His Majesty may grant us this favor.

2. You must have already heard about His marvels manifested in the way silk originates, for only He could have invented something like that. The silkworms come from seeds about the size of little grains of pepper. (I have never seen this but heard of it, and so if something in the explanation gets distorted it won't be my fault.) When warm weather comes and the leaves begin to appear on the mulberry tree, the seeds start to live, for they are dead until then. The worms nourish themselves on mulberry leaves until, having grown to full

---

1. In IC 5.1.2.

size, they settle on some twigs. There with their little mouths they themselves go about spinning the silk and making some very thick little cocoons in which they enclose themselves. The silkworm, which is fat and ugly, then dies, and a little white butterfly, which is very pretty, comes forth from the cocoon. Now if this were not seen but recounted to us as having happened in other times, who would believe it? Or what reasonings could make us conclude that a thing as non-rational as a worm or a bee could be so diligent in working for our benefit and with so much industriousness? And the poor little worm loses its life in the challenge. This is enough, sisters, for a period of meditation even though I may say no more to you; in it you can consider the wonders and the wisdom of our God. Well now, what would happen if we knew the property of every created thing. It is very beneficial for us to busy ourselves thinking of these grandeurs and delighting in being brides of a King so wise and powerful.

3. Let's return to what I was saying. This silkworm, then, starts to live when by the heat of the Holy Spirit it begins to benefit through the general help given to us all by God and through the remedies left by Him to His Church, by going to confession, reading good books, and hearing sermons, which are the remedies that a soul, dead in its carelessness and sins and placed in the midst of occasions, can make use of. It then begins to live and to sustain itself by these things, and by good meditations, until it is grown. Its being grown is what is relevant to what I'm saying, for these other things have little importance here.

4. Well, once this silkworm is grown—in the beginning I dealt with its growth[2]—it begins to spin the silk and build the

---

2. In IC 1–4.

house wherein it will die. I would like to point out here that this house is Christ. Somewhere, it seems to me, I have read or heard that our life is hidden in Christ or in God (both are the same), or that our life is Christ.[3] Whether the quotation is exact or not doesn't matter for what I intend.

5. Well see here, daughters, what we can do through the help of God: His Majesty Himself, as He does in this prayer of union, becomes the dwelling place we build for ourselves. It seems I'm saying that we can build up God and take Him away since I say that He is the dwelling place and we ourselves can build it so as to place ourselves in it. And, indeed, we can! Not that we can take God away or build Him up, but we can take away from ourselves and build up, as do these little silkworms. For we will not have finished doing all that we can in this work when, to the little we do, which is nothing, God will unite Himself, with His greatness, and give it such high value that the Lord Himself will become the reward of this work. Thus, since it was He who paid the highest price, His Majesty wants to join our little labors with the great ones He suffered so that all the work may become one.

6. Therefore, courage, my daughters! Let's be quick to do this work and weave this little cocoon by getting rid of our self-love and self-will, our attachments to any earthly things, and by performing deeds of penance, prayer, mortification, obedience, and of all the other things you know. Would to heaven that we would do what we know we must; and we are instructed about what we must do. Let it die; let this silkworm die, as it does in completing what it was created to do! And you will see how we see God, as well as ourselves placed inside His greatness, as is this little silkworm within

---

3. See Col 3:3–4.

its cocoon. Keep in mind that I say "see God" in the sense of what I mentioned[4] concerning that which is felt in this kind of union.

7. Now, then, let's see what this silkworm does, for that's the reason I've said everything else. When the soul is, in this prayer, truly dead to the world, a little white butterfly comes forth. Oh, greatness of God! How transformed the soul is when it comes out of this prayer after having been placed within the greatness of God and so closely joined with Him for a little while—in my opinion the union never lasts for as much as a half hour. Truly, I tell you that the soul doesn't recognize itself. Look at the difference there is between an ugly worm and a little white butterfly; that's what the difference is here. The soul doesn't know how it could have merited so much good—from where this good may have come I mean, for it well knows that it doesn't merit this blessing. It sees within itself a desire to praise the Lord; it would want to dissolve and die a thousand deaths for Him. It soon begins to experience a desire to suffer great trials without its being able to do otherwise. There are the strongest desires for penance, for solitude, and that all might know God; and great pain comes to it when it sees that He is offended. I shall treat of these things more particularly in the next dwelling place;[5] although what is in this dwelling place and the next are almost identical, the force of the effects is very different. As I have said,[6] if after God brings a soul here it makes the effort to advance, it will see great things.

---

4. In IC 5.1.10–11.

5. In IC 6.6.1; 6.11 passim.

6. In IC 5.1.2, 3, 13.

8. Oh, now, to see the restlessness of this little butterfly, even though it has never been quieter and calmer in its life, is something to praise God for! And the difficulty is that it doesn't know where to alight and rest. Since it has experienced such wonderful rest, all that it sees on earth displeases it, especially if God gives it this wine often. Almost each time it gains new treasures. It no longer has any esteem for the works it did while a worm, which was to weave the cocoon little by little; it now has wings. How can it be happy walking step by step when it can fly? On account of its desires, everything it can do for God becomes little in its own eyes. It doesn't wonder as much at what the saints suffered now that it understands through experience how the Lord helps and transforms a soul, for it doesn't recognize itself or its image. The weakness it previously seemed to have with regard to doing penance it now finds is its strength. Its attachment to relatives or friends or wealth (for neither its actions, nor its determination, nor its desire to withdraw were enough; rather, in its opinion, it was more attached to everything) is now so looked upon that it grieves when obliged to do what is necessary in this regard so as not to offend God. Everything wearies it, for it has learned through experience that creatures cannot give it true rest.

9. It seems I have been lengthy, but I could say much more; and whoever has received this favor from God will see that I've been brief. So, there is no reason to be surprised that this little butterfly seeks rest again since it feels estranged from earthly things. Well then, where will the poor little thing go? It can't return to where it came from; as was said,[7]

---

7. In IC 5.1.12; 4.2.9.

we are powerless, however much we do, to bring about this favor until God is again pleased to grant it. O Lord, what new trials begin for this soul! Who would say such a thing after a favor so sublime? Briefly, in one way or another⌠there must be a cross while we live⌡ And with respect to anyone who says that after he arrived here he always enjoyed rest and delight I would say that he never arrived but that perhaps he had experienced some spiritual delight—if he had entered into the previous dwelling place—and his experience had been helped along by natural weakness or perhaps even by the devil who gives him peace so as afterward to wage much greater war against him.

10. I don't mean to say that those who arrive here do not have peace; they do have it, and it is very deep. For the trials themselves are so valuable and have such good roots that although very severe they give rise to peace and happiness. ⌠From the very unhappiness caused by worldly things arises the ever-so-painful desire to leave this world⌡ Any relief the soul has comes from the thought that God wants it to be living in this exile; yet even this is not enough, because in spite of all these benefits it is not entirely surrendered to God's will, as will be seen further on[8]—although it doesn't fail to conform itself. But it conforms with a great feeling that it can do no more because no more has been given it, and with many tears. Every time it is in prayer this regret is its pain. In some ways perhaps the sorrow proceeds from the deep pain it feels at seeing that God is offended and little esteemed in this world and that many souls are lost, heretics as well as Moors; although those that grieve it most are Christians. Even though it sees that God's mercy is great—for, however

---

8. In IC 4.10.8; 7.3.4.

wicked their lives, these Christians can make amends and be saved—it fears that many are being condemned.

11. Oh, greatness of God! A few years ago—and even perhaps days—this soul wasn't mindful of anything but itself. Who has placed it in the midst of such painful concerns? Even were we to meditate for many years we wouldn't be able to feel them as painfully as does this soul now. Well, God help me, wouldn't it be enough if for many days and years I strove to think about the tremendous evil of an offense against God and that those souls who are condemned are His children and my brothers and about the dangers in which we live and how good it is for us to leave this miserable life? Not at all, daughters; the grief that is felt here is not like that of this world. We can, with God's favor, feel the grief that comes from thinking about these things a great deal, but such grief doesn't reach the intimate depths of our being as does the pain suffered in this state, for it seems that the pain breaks and grinds the soul into pieces, without the soul's striving for it or even at times wanting it. Well, what is this pain? Where does it come from? I shall tell you.

12. Haven't you heard it said of the bride—for I have already mentioned it elsewhere here but not in this sense[9]— that God brought her into the inner wine cellar and put charity in order within her?[10] Well, that is what I mean. Since that soul now surrenders itself into His hands and its great love makes it so surrendered that it neither knows nor wants anything more than what He wants with her (for God will never, in my judgment, grant this favor save to a soul that He takes for His own), He desires that, without its understanding how,

9. In IC 5.1.12.
10. Allusion to Song 2:4.

it may go forth from this union impressed with His seal. For
indeed the soul does no more in this union than does the
wax when another impresses a seal on it. The wax doesn't
impress the seal upon itself; it is only disposed—I mean by
being soft. And even in order to be disposed, it doesn't soften
itself but remains still and gives its consent. Oh, goodness of
God; everything must be at a cost to You! All You want is our
will and that there be no impediment in the wax.

*Free will;
the only thing
He doesn't
control?*

13. Well now, you see here, sisters, what our God does in
this union so that this soul may recognize itself as His own.
He gives from what He has, which is what His Son had in
this life. He cannot grant us a higher favor. Who could have
had a greater desire to leave this life? And so His Majesty said
at the Last Supper: *I have earnestly desired.*[11]

Well then, how is it, Lord, that you weren't thinking of
the laborious death You were about to suffer, so painful and
frightful? You answer: "No, my great love and the desire I
have that souls be saved are incomparably more important
than these sufferings; and the very greatest sorrows that I
have suffered and do suffer, after being in the world, are not
enough to be considered anything at all in comparison with
this love and desire to save souls."

14. This is true, for I have often reflected on the matter. I
know the torment a certain soul of my acquaintance[12] suffers
and has suffered at seeing our Lord offended. The pain is so
unbearable that she desires to die much more than to suffer
it. If a soul with so little charity when compared to Christ's—
for its charity could then be considered almost nonexistent—
felt this torment to be so unbearable, what must have been

---

11. Lk 22:15.
12. She is referring to herself. See L 38.18.

the feeling of our Lord Jesus Christ? And what kind of life must He have suffered since all things were present to Him and He was always witnessing the serious offenses committed against His Father? I believe without a doubt that these sufferings were much greater than were those of His most sacred passion. At the time of His passion He already saw an end to these trials and with this awareness as well as the happiness of seeing a remedy for us in His death and of showing us the love He had for His Father in suffering so much for Him, His sorrows were tempered. These sorrows are also tempered here below by those who with the strength that comes from love perform great penances, for they almost don't feel them; rather they would want to do more and more—and everything they do seems little to them. Well, what must it have been for His Majesty to find Himself with so excellent an occasion for showing His Father how completely obedient He was to Him, and with love for His neighbor? Oh, great delight, to suffer in doing the will of God! But I consider it so difficult to see the many offenses committed so continually against His Majesty and the many souls going to hell that I believe only one day of that pain would have been sufficient to end many lives; how much more one life, if He had been no more than man.

LET THIS SILKWORM DIE
IN ITS COCOON AND HOW
TRANSFORMED IT WILL BE

5.2.1–5 Teresa repeats, as she said in the first chapter of the fifth dwelling places, that the prayer of union may be experienced in various degrees of intensity. She makes a clarification, saying that she thinks she has said everything she can about the nature of union. What she does want to elaborate on is the Lord's work in those souls who prepare themselves for this favor. To help her readers understand better, Teresa describes what she understands to be the life cycle of a silkworm and makes a comparison to the transformation of souls in this prayer of union. By the help of the Holy Spirit, the soul benefits from general remedies in the spiritual life, such as going to confession, reading good books, and hearing sermons. The soul begins to be strengthened by these things and by good meditations until it is grown. In Teresa's story, the mature silkworm makes a house for itself, while the soul has a house in Christ. But actually what we can do is very little; it is really God who unites our little labors with the great ones he suffered.

5.2.6–8 Continuing with the silkworm metaphor, Teresa urges the nuns to be quick in weaving their cocoons by getting rid of self-love, self-will, and attachments, and by carrying out the deeds of a good life. Through those things the soul will die to the world and live in God through the prayer of union.

It is in the prayer of union that the metaphor is complete, and the soul, like the silkworm, is transformed. This union increases the soul's love. The soul longs for solitude and experiences increased desires to do penance and to suffer. The soul experiences a new type of restlessness. Its exterior calm isn't disturbed, but it has become tired of earthly things, since it has now experienced a wonderful rest in God. She says everything wearies it, for it has learned through experience that creatures can never give it true rest.

5.2.9–10 Teresa elaborates on the new suffering that arises from the experience of union. The soul feels estranged from earthly things. Again using the silkworm/butterfly metaphor, she asks, "Where will the poor little thing go?" It can't return at will to the prayer of union because we are powerless to bring about this favor; the initiative is God's. Teresa thinks this feeling of estrangement from earthly things, together with a longing to leave the world, is a sign of the authenticity of the experience of union. She goes on to try to explain the complexity of the spiritual feelings and desires that arise from the experience of this prayer of union. These souls suffer especially at the thought of the many ways people offend God and at the thought of the many souls who may be lost.

5.2.11–14 Teresa explains why she thinks the soul who has experienced the prayer of union suffers. She compares the soul to wax impressed with a seal. Like the wax, the soul is passive except for remaining still and giving consent to God. Teresa thinks that in the experience of union, God gives the soul a conformity with Christ in his love and obedience to the Father, his love of neighbor, and his willingness to suffer in doing the will of God. How much he must have suffered at seeing his Father offended, and Teresa shares this great pain now. It makes her want to leave this world, but yet at the same time she experiences a great love and desire to save souls.

Interpretive Notes

In the process of one's growth in the life of Christ, there comes a time when one reaches union with God. This word "union," as we saw in the previous chapter, points to a reality that has a deep meaning for the mystic. In its highest sense, it refers to the union in Jesus of his humanity with his divinity in the person of the Word. In the Christian, this union realized in Christ is repeated only in shadow. But this union of a human being with God requires one to pass through a kind of radical death to all previous forms of human life so limited by the dead weight of sin and evil. This passage through death is for the sake of being reborn in a wholly other manner of life, with a new horizon and new openness to God. It carries with it an insatiable appetite for a superior state of which one in this union gets a glimpse and foretaste. Teresa has spoken of union in the previous chapter. Now she will speak of the death and the new life that follows.

With regard to this death, the *Catechism of the Catholic Church* states:

> Because of Christ, Christian death has a positive meaning: "For to me to live is Christ, and to die is gain" (Phil 1:21). The saying is sure: "if we have died with him, we will also live with him" (2 Tim 2:11). What is essentially new about Christian death is this: through Baptism the Christian has already "died with Christ" sacramentally, in order to live a new life; and if we die in Christ's grace, physical death completes this "dying with Christ" and so completes our incorporation into him in his redeeming act: It is better for me to die in Christ than to reign over the ends of the earth. . . . Every action of yours, every thought, should be those of one who expects to die before the day is out. Death

would have no great terrors for you if you had a quiet conscience. . . . Then why not keep clear of sin instead of running away from death? If you aren't fit to face death today,
it's very unlikely you will be tomorrow. (CCC 1010, 1014)

Teresa had recently returned to Castile from Andalusia,
where she had learned of the marvelous way in which silk
was produced. In her monasteries they didn't have mulberry
trees or silkworms, but they probably saw baskets of cocoons,
or worked at spinning the silk, or above all heard accounts
of how the silkworm is transformed into a little white moth.
These accounts stirred Teresa's amazement at the wonders of
God's creation. The silkworm moth is the source of the silk.
The female lays between three hundred and five hundred eggs.
The natural food of the silkworm is mulberry leaves. Within a
forty-five-day growing period, it attains a maximum length of
about three inches. Pupation occurs within a cocoon of continuous white or yellow silken thread, averaging one thousand
yards. The thread is then preserved intact for commercial use.

Teresa found in the account of how silk came about a
wonderful example for explaining the mysterious work of
union with God. The Christian, like the silkworm, must first
grow through the ordinary remedies used in the struggle
against sin: the sacraments, reading good books, and prayer.
When it is grown, it begins to spin the silk by dying to self
and its attachments to earthly things and by performing good
works. The cocoon, fashioned in this way with the divine
help, is Christ, in whom one's life is hidden (Col 3:3). In
the prayer of union, the soul is placed gratuitously by God
in this cocoon. During the time of this prayer, the soul is so
united with Christ that it is dead to the world, and through
this dying is gradually transformed, as is the silkworm into a

little moth. In the end, then, it is not the human being who brings about this transformation, but God, who gives himself out of love.

In this mystical death, one triumphs over death itself. In her personal story, Teresa, a woman who suffered from broken-down health, experienced intensely the fear of death. For long years, her heart problems produced a gripping anxiety that would not even allow her to remain alone in her monastic cell. But with these experiences of union, all her fears of death vanished. "Likewise, little fear of death, which I always feared greatly remained. Now death seems to me to be the easiest thing for anyone who serves God, for in a moment the soul finds it is freed from this prison and brought to rest" (L 38.5).

After the death of the silkworm, Teresa gives a picture of herself, which carries traces of the life of every mystic. "Oh, now, to see the restlessness of this little butterfly, even though it has never been quieter and calmer in its life, is something to praise God for! And the difficulty is that it doesn't know where to alight and rest. Since it has experienced such wonderful rest, all that it sees on earth displeases it, especially if God gives it this wine often. . . . On account of its desires, everything it can do for God becomes little in its own eyes" (IC 5.2.8).

This dwelling place brings to mind another symbol: God brought her into the inner wine cellar and put charity in order in her. This is said of the bride in the *Song of Songs* (Song 2:4) and underlines the fact that through this union we have now come under the rule of love. This bridal imagery will be developed further as we proceed, but for the present it will be sufficient to say that one goes forth from this union impressed with his seal. In this image, the wax does not impress the seal on itself but only remains disposed by being soft—that is, it remains still and gives its consent. From this seal of love, impressed on the passive soul in this union, follows a deep pain felt by the soul at seeing that God is offended and little esteemed in this world.

Questions for Discussion

1. How does Teresa use the image of the silkworm?
2. What are some of the characteristics of the little white butterfly?
3. What kind of grief does the soul experience here?
4. What did God do for the soul in the "inner wine cellar"?
5. Teresa will begin to dive deeper into a bridal analogy of the love between God and the soul. What obstacles, present in our age, inhibit people from finding this analogy helpful? How might we go about dismantling these obstacles in our own lives?

CHAPTER 3

Continues on the same subject. Tells about another kind of union the soul can reach with God's help and of how important love of neighbor is for this union. The chapter is very useful.

Well now, let us get back to our little moth[1] and see something about what God gives it in this state. It must always be understood that one has to strive to go forward in the service of our Lord and in self-knowledge. For if a person does no more than receive this favor and if, as though already securely in possession of something, she grows careless in her life and turns aside from the heavenly path, which consists of keeping the commandments, that which happens to the silkworm will happen to her. For it gives forth the seed that produces other silkworms, and itself dies forever. I say that it "gives forth the seed" because I hold that it is God's desire that a favor so great not be given in vain; if a person doesn't herself benefit, the favor will benefit others. For since the soul is left with these desires and virtues that were mentioned, it always brings profit to other souls during the time that it continues to live virtuously; and they catch fire from its fire. And even when the soul has itself lost this fire, the inclination to benefit others will remain, and the soul delights in explaining the favors God grants to whoever loves and serves Him.

---

1. For Teresa, the little moth is equivalent to the little butterfly; she uses these images interchangeably. See IC 5.4.1; 6.2.1; 6.4.1; 6.6.1; 6.11.1; 7.3.1.

2. I know a person to whom this happened.[2] Although she had gone far astray, she enjoyed helping others through the favors God had granted her and showing the way of prayer to those who didn't understand it; and she did a great deal of good. Afterward the Lord again gave her light. It's true that she still hadn't experienced the effects that were mentioned; but how many there must be, like Judas, whom the Lord calls to the apostolate by communing with them, and like Saul, whom He calls to be king, who afterward through their own fault go astray! Thus we can conclude, sisters, that, in order to merit more and more and avoid getting lost like such persons, our security lies in obedience and refusal to deviate from God's law. I'm speaking to those to whom He has granted similar favors, and even to everyone.

3. It seems to me that despite all I've said about this dwelling place, the matter is still somewhat obscure. Since so much gain comes from entering this place, it will be good to avoid giving the impression that those to whom the Lord doesn't give things that are so supernatural are left without hope. True union can very well be reached, with God's help, if we make the effort to obtain it by keeping our wills fixed only on that which is God's will. Oh, how many of us there are who will say we do this, and it will seem to us that we don't want anything else and that we would die for this truth, as I believe I have said![3] Well, I tell you, and I will often repeat it, that if what you say is true you will have obtained this favor from the Lord, and you needn't care at all about the other delightful union that was mentioned. That which is most valuable in the delightful union

---

2. She is referring to herself. See L 7.10.
3. In IC 5.2.6–7.

is that it proceeds from this union of which I'm now speaking; and one cannot arrive at the delightful union if the union coming from being resigned to God's will is not very certain. Oh, how desirable is this union with God's will! Happy the soul that has reached it. Such a soul will live tranquilly in this life, and in the next as well. Nothing in earthly events afflicts it unless it finds itself in some danger of losing God or sees that He is offended: neither sickness, nor poverty, nor death—unless the death is of someone who will be missed by God's Church—for this soul sees well that the Lord knows what He is doing better than it knows what it is desiring.

4. You must note that there are different kinds of sufferings. Some sufferings are produced suddenly by our human nature, and the same goes for consolations, and even by the charity of compassion for one's neighbor, as our Lord experienced when He raised Lazarus.[4] Being united with God's will doesn't take these experiences away, nor do they disturb the soul with a restless, disquieting passion that lasts a long while. These sufferings pass quickly. As I have said concerning consolations in prayer,[5] it seems they do not reach the soul's depth but only the senses and faculties. They are found in the previous dwelling places; but they do not enter the last ones still to be explained, since the suspension of the faculties is necessary in order to reach these, as has been said.[6] The Lord has the power to enrich souls through many paths and bring them to these dwelling places, without using the shortcut that was mentioned.

---

4. See Jn 11:33–36.
5. In IC 5.1.6; 4.1.4–5; 4.2.3–5.
6. In IC 5.1.3–5.

5. Nonetheless, take careful note, daughters, that it is necessary for the silkworm to die, and, moreover, at a cost to yourselves. In the delightful union,[7] the experience of seeing oneself in so new a life greatly helps one to die; in the other union,[8] it's necessary that, while living in this life, we ourselves put the silkworm to death. I confess this latter death will require a great deal of effort, or more than that; but it has its value. Thus if you come out victorious the reward will be much greater. But there is no reason to doubt the possibility of this death any more than that of true union with the will of God. This union with God's will is the union I have desired all my life; it is the union I ask the Lord for always and the one that is clearest and safest.

6. But alas for us, how few there must be who reach it; although whoever guards himself against offending the Lord and has entered religious life thinks he has done everything! Oh, but there remain some worms, unrecognized until, like those in the story of Jonah that gnawed away the ivy,[9] they have gnawed away the virtues. This happens through self-love, self-esteem, judging one's neighbors (even though in little things), a lack of charity for them, and not loving them as ourselves. For even though, while crawling along, we fulfill our obligation and no sin is committed, we don't advance very far in what is required for complete union with the will of God.

7. What do you think His will is, daughters? That we be completely perfect. See what we lack to be one with Him and His Father as His Majesty asked.[10] I tell you I am writing

---

7. The delightful union is the infused prayer of union.
8. The union that arises from conformity of wills.
9. Jon 4:6–7.
10. Jn 17:22.

this with much pain upon seeing myself so far away—and all through my own fault. The Lord doesn't have to grant us great delights for this union; sufficient is what He has given us in His Son, who would teach us the way. Don't think the matter lies in my being so conformed to the will of God that if my father or brother dies I don't feel it, or that if there are trials or sicknesses I suffer them happily. Such an attitude is good, and sometimes it's a matter of discretion because we can't do otherwise, and we make a virtue of necessity. How many things like these the philosophers did, or even, though not like these, other things, such as acquiring much learning. Here in our religious life the Lord asks of us only two things: [love of His Majesty and love of our neighbor.] These are what we must work for. By observing them with perfection, we do His will and so will be united with Him. But how far, as I have said, we are from doing these two things for so great a God as we ought! May it please His Majesty to give us His grace so that we might merit, if we want, to reach this state that lies within our power.

8. The most certain sign, in my opinion, as to whether or not we are observing these two laws is whether we observe well the love of neighbor. We cannot know whether or not we love God, although there are strong indications for recognizing that we do love Him; but we can know whether we love our neighbor.[11] And be certain that the more advanced you see you are in love for your neighbor, the more advanced you will be in the love of God, for the love His Majesty has for us is so great that to repay us for our love of neighbor He will in a thousand ways increase the love we have for Him. I cannot doubt this.

---

11. Allusion to 1 Jn 4:20.

9. It's important for us to walk with careful attention to how we are proceeding in this matter, for if we practice love of neighbor with great perfection, we will have done everything. I believe that, since our nature is bad, we will not reach perfection in the love of neighbor if that love doesn't rise from love of God as its root. Since this is so important to us, sisters, let's try to understand ourselves even in little things, and pay no attention to any big plans that sometimes suddenly come to us during our prayer in which it seems we will do wonders for our neighbor and even for just one soul so that it may be saved. If afterward our deeds are not in conformity with those plans, there will be no reason to believe that we will accomplish the plans. I say the same about humility and all the virtues. Great are the wiles of the devil; to make us think we have one virtue—when we don't—he would circle hell a thousand times. And he is right because such a notion is very harmful, for these feigned virtues never come without some vainglory since they rise from that source; just as virtues from God are free of it as well as of pride.

10. I am amused sometimes to see certain souls who think when they are at prayer that they would like to be humiliated and publicly insulted for God, and afterward they would hide a tiny fault if they could; or, if they have not committed one and yet are charged with it—God deliver us! Well, let anyone who can't bear such a thing be careful not to pay attention to what he has by himself determined—in his opinion—to do. As matter of fact the determination was not in the will—for when there is a true determination of the will it's another matter—but a work of the imagination; it is in the imagination that the devil produces his wiles and deceits. And with women or unlearned people he can produce a great number, for we don't know how the faculties differ from one another

and from the imagination, nor do we know about a thousand other things there are in regard to interior matters. Oh, sisters, how clearly one sees the degree to which love of neighbor is present in some of you, and how clearly one sees the deficiency in those who lack such perfection![If you were to understand how important this virtue is for us, you wouldn't engage in any other study.]

11. When I see souls very earnest in trying to understand the prayer they have and very sullen when they are in it—for it seems they don't dare let their minds move or stir lest a bit of their spiritual delight and devotion be lost—it makes me realize how little they understand of the way by which union is attained; they think the whole matter lies in these things. No, sisters, absolutely not; [works are what the Lord wants!] He desires that if you see a sister who is sick to whom you can bring some relief, you have compassion on her and not worry about losing this devotion; and that if she is suffering pain, [you also feel it] and that, if necessary, you fast so that she might eat—not so much for her sake as because you know it is your Lord's desire. This is true union with His will, and if you see a person praised, the Lord wants you to be much happier than if you yourself were being praised. This, indeed, is easy, for if you have humility you will feel sorry to see yourself praised. But this happiness that comes when the virtues of the sisters are known is a very good thing; and [when we see some fault in them, it is also a very good thing to be sorry and hide the fault as though it were our own.]

12. I have said a lot on this subject elsewhere,[12] because I see, sisters, that if we fail in love of neighbors we are lost. May it please the Lord that this will never be so; for if you do

---

12. In W 7; F 5.

not fail, I tell you that you shall receive from His Majesty the union that was mentioned. When you see yourselves lacking in this love, even though you have devotion and gratifying experiences that make you think you have reached this stage, and you experience some little suspension in the prayer of quiet (for to some it then appears that everything has been accomplished), believe me you have not reached union. And beg our Lord to give you this perfect love of neighbor. Let His Majesty have a free hand, for He will give you more than you know how to desire because you are striving and making every effort to do what you can about this love. And force your will to do the will of your sisters in everything even though you may lose your rights; forget your own good for their sakes no matter how much resistance your nature puts up; and, when the occasion arises, strive to accept work yourself so as to relieve your neighbor of it. Don't think that it won't cost you anything or that you will find everything done for you. Look at what our Spouse's love for us cost Him; in order to free us from death, He died that most painful death of the cross.

TRUE UNION CAN BE REACHED
IF WE KEEP OUR WILLS
UNITED WITH GOD'S

5.3.1 Teresa stresses the importance of going forward in prayer and practices in the spiritual life. She says persons who grow careless will not benefit from the favors they experience, although they act in such a way that others benefit. Even if a soul has itself lost what she calls "the fire," it may delight in explaining the favor God grants to whoever loves and serves him.

5.3.2 Speaking in a veiled way about herself, Teresa describes a time when she enjoyed helping others learn to pray through the favors God had granted her, although she, as she puts it, had gone far astray. She advises obedience and refusal to deviate from God's law.

5.3.3 Those whom God has not favored with the prayer of union are not left without hope. True union can be reached, with God's help, if we make the effort to keep our wills fixed only on what is God's will. One cannot arrive at the prayer of union if there is no certainty of union with God's will. How happy the soul that has reached this union. Nothing in earthly events afflicts it unless it finds itself in some danger of losing God or sees that he is offended.

5.3.4 Teresa says that there are sufferings and consolations that proceed from our human nature, and being united with God's will doesn't take these experiences away. She says they pass quickly and do not reach the soul's depth, but only the senses and faculties. This kind of suffering and consolation will not be found in the dwelling places to come since the suspension of the faculties, necessary to enter these dwelling places, takes them away. But the Lord has many other paths by which he can enrich souls without using this shortcut, the suspension of the faculties in the prayer of union.

5.3.5 It is necessary for the soul to die at a cost to itself. The prayer of union greatly helps one to die. The other union requires much greater effort on our part. But if you come out victorious, the reward will be much greater. This union with God's will is the union Teresa has desired all her life.

5.3.6–7 Here Teresa laments that self-love, self-esteem, lack of charity, and other things keep us from advancing to what is required for complete union with the will of God. She says God's will is for us to be completely perfect. She explains that a person may still experience sorrow and may not be happy in suffering. She says that the Lord only asks of us love of His Majesty and love of our neighbor, and if we observe these with perfection we will do his will and be united with him. But she adds that we don't do these things as we should and asks for God's grace to reach this state.

5.3.8–9 Teresa says that while we cannot know for certain if we love God, we can know whether we love our neighbor. She believes that God will increase our love for him when he sees that we love our neighbor. Teresa believes that love of neighbor has its roots in love of God. She says we should not make grandiose plans and then not follow through with deeds in conformity with those plans. We should practice humility and not think we have virtues that we don't have.

5.3.10 Teresa points out how we can deceive ourselves about our own virtue. She gives the example of persons who think they would want to be humiliated publicly, but in fact try to hide their faults and would be upset if accused of faults they didn't commit. She warns against mistaking desires in the imagination for true determination in the will. She repeats how important love of neighbor is.

5.3.11 Teresa is critical of those who think the nature of the prayer of union is to sit silently without moving. She is very clear in stating that what the Lord wants is works. Caring for the sick and fasting so another might eat are things that demonstrate true union with the will of God. Further, she says we should be happier for others to be praised rather than ourselves, and also that we should be sorry for some fault in others and try to hide it as though it were our own.

5.3.12 Teresa concludes this chapter by saying that if we fail in love of neighbor we are lost. We must beg our Lord to give us this perfect love of neighbor. Without this love, a person can never receive the prayer of union with God. She gives advice which she admits is difficult to follow:

> And force your will to do the will of your sisters in every-
> thing even though you may lose your rights; forget your
> own good for their sakes no matter how much resistance
> your nature puts up; and, when the occasion arises, strive
> to accept work yourself so as to relieve your neighbor of it.
> Don't think that it won't cost you anything or that you will
> find everything done for you. Look at what our Spouse's
> love for us cost Him; in order to free us from death, He
> died that most painful death of the cross. (IC 5.3.12)

Interpretive Notes

The little moth or butterfly, as Teresa explains it, now flies about outside the cocoon in which the silkworm died. It flits from flower to flower, giving forth the seed from which other silkworms are produced. The soul, nonetheless, must be careful in striving to go forward in the practice of love. But even if persons fall away from the fruits of this prayer of union, they are left with great desires and they continue to help others; at least this was Teresa's experience. In her *Life* she tells how, after receiving the book *The Third Spiritual Alphabet* by Francisco de Osuna, which explained how to practice the prayer of recollection, she resolved to follow that path. The Lord so favored her efforts that she began to receive the prayer of quiet and sometimes the prayer of union (L 4.7). Then partly on account of her illness, Teresa lost her fervor, but she did not lose her enthusiasm for getting others to practice prayer and teaching them about it (L 7). Thus, Teresa holds that if through the prayer of union the person doesn't herself benefit anymore, the favor will continue to inspire her to be of benefit to others.

The prayer of union is not something that one should be preoccupied about receiving. What we must strive for with all our being is to keep our wills fixed only on what God wills. The soul that has reached this union will live happily and tranquilly in this life and the next. Nothing in earthly events will afflict it, for it sees that the Lord knows what he is doing better than it knows what it is desiring. Sufferings come about, but they pass quickly and do not reach the soul's depths or disturb it with a restless, disquieting passion that lasts a long while. This union with God's will is the union Teresa has always desired and urges us to desire.

Teresa's teaching, however, is different from that of some philosophers. She is probably thinking of the stoic philosophy that was popular in Spain partly because of Seneca. He was "the first of Spanish thinkers," born in Córdoba in the first century. According to the Stoics, God is everywhere and in every human being. Nothing happens but by the will of God. Thus everything is settled and arranged. If this is so, then there is left but one thing to do, and that is to give our assent. We can either accept the will of God willingly or we can struggle against it. The only thing that is in our power is the assent of the will. The will is everything, and so the supreme evil is emotion. The wise must be cleansed of all emotion, so that they can endure the greatest pain, and see even the death of their nearest and dearest, and say only that this is the will of God. In Teresa's mind some sufferings are produced suddenly by our human nature, and she gives the example of our Lord when he raised Lazarus. Being united with God's will does not eliminate all experiences of sadness. What Teresa looks for is the practice of the two loves: love of God and love of neighbor.

We can only know for certain, Teresa thinks, how much we love God by our practice of love of neighbor. Because our nature is so corrupt, we cannot love our neighbor with any kind of perfection unless this love of neighbor has God as its root. But the only way we can measure our love of God is by our love of neighbor. God so loves this virtue that he will repay our efforts to practice it by increasing in a thousand ways the love we have for him. It is foolish then, she thinks, to be so earnest in trying to decide what prayer you have. Works of love are what you should be solicitous about; and here we have Teresa's powerful words:

If you see a sister who is sick to whom you can bring some relief, you have compassion on her and not worry about losing this devotion; and that if she is suffering pain, you also feel it; and that, if necessary, you fast so that she might eat . . . and if you see a person praised, the Lord wants you to be much happier than if you yourself were being praised . . . and when we see some fault in them, it is also a very good thing to be sorry and hide the fault as though it were our own. (IC 5.3.11)

With regard to love of neighbor, some words of St. Edith Stein are appropriate here:

Our love for our fellow humans is the measure of our love for God. But it is different from a natural love of our neighbor. Natural love goes out to this one or that one, who may be close to us through the bond of blood or through a kinship of character or common interests. The rest then are strangers who do not concern us, who, it may be, eventually come to be repulsive, so that one keeps them as far away as possible from contact with us. For the Christian, there are no such strangers. Rather, he is the neighbor, this one who stands before us and who is in greatest need of our help; it doesn't matter whether he is related to us or not; whether we like him or not; whether he is morally worthy of help or not. The love of Christ knows no bounds, it never stops, it does not shrink back from ugliness and dirt. He came for the sake of sinners and not for the sake of the just. If the love of Christ lives in us then we will, like Him, go out after the lost sheep. (St. Edith Stein, *The Mystery of Christmas*)

Questions for Discussion

1. How do we grow careless in our lives?
2. What is most valuable about the delightful union?
3. What are some of the worms that gnaw away the ivy as in the story of Jonah?
4. Since by our nature we are not inclined to practice this love of neighbor, what is required to reach perfection in such love?
5. How does Teresa's understanding of the will differ from that of the Stoic philosophers?

CHAPTER 4

Continues with the same subject, explaining further this kind of prayer.[1] Tells how important it is to walk with care because the devil himself uses a great deal of care in trying to make one turn back from what was begun.

It seems to me you have a desire to see what this little moth is doing and where it rests since, as was explained, it rests neither in spiritual delights nor in earthly consolations. Its flight is higher, and I cannot satisfy your desire until the last dwelling place. May it please God that I then remember or have the time to write of this. About five months have passed since I began,[2] and because my head is in no condition to read over what I've written, everything will have to continue on without order, and perhaps some things will be said twice. Since this work is for my sisters, the disorder won't matter much.

2. Nonetheless, I want to explain more to you about what I think this prayer of union is. In accordance with my style, I shall draw a comparison. Later on we'll say more about this little butterfly. Although it is always bearing fruit by doing good for itself and for other souls, it never stops to rest, because it fails to find its true repose.

---

1. The prayer of union.

2. Having begun this work in Toledo, June 2, 1577, Teresa in less than a month and a half had got as far as chapter three of the fifth dwelling place. About the middle of July, she moved to Ávila where she probably wrote chapter three. She then abandoned all work on her book until the beginning of November. And by November 29, 1577, her task was completed.

3. You've already often heard that God espouses souls spiritually. Blessed be His mercy that wants so much to be humbled! And even though the comparison may be a coarse one, I cannot find another that would better explain what I mean than the sacrament of marriage. This spiritual espousal is different in kind from marriage, for in these matters that we are dealing with there is never anything that is not spiritual. Corporal things are far distant from them, and the spiritual joys the Lord gives when compared to the delights married people must experience are a thousand leagues distant. For it is all a matter of love united with love, and the actions of love are most pure and so extremely delicate and gentle that there is no way of explaining them, but the Lord knows how to make them very clearly felt.

4. It seems to me that the prayer of union does not yet reach the stage of spiritual betrothal. Here below when two people are to be engaged, there is a discussion about whether they are alike, whether they love each other, and whether they might meet together so as to become more satisfied with each other. So, too, in the case of this union with God, the agreement has been made, and this soul is well informed about the goodness of her Spouse and determined to do His will in everything and in as many ways as she sees might make Him happy. And His Majesty, as one who understands clearly whether these things about His betrothed are so, is happy with her. As a result He grants this mercy, for He desired her to know Him more and that they might meet together, as they say, and be united.[3] We can say that union is like this,

---

3. In her comparison, Teresa makes use of the stages that were followed in her day for the arrangement of a marriage: 1) meetings between the young man and woman; 2) exchanging of gifts; 3) falling in love; 4) the joining of hands; 5) betrothal; 6) marriage.

for it passes in a very short time. In it there no longer takes place the exchanging of gifts, but the soul sees secretly who this Spouse is that she is going to accept. Through the work of the senses and the faculties she couldn't in any way or in a thousand years understand what she understands here in the shortest time. But being who He is, the Spouse, from that meeting alone leaves her more worthy for the joining of hands, as they say. The soul is left so much in love that it does for its part all it can to avoid disturbing this divine betrothal. But if it is careless about placing its affection in something other than Him, it loses everything. And the loss is as great as the favors He was granting her, and cannot be exaggerated.

5. For this reason, I ask Christian souls whom the Lord has brought to these boundaries that for His sake they not grow careless but withdraw from occasions. Even in this state the soul is not so strong that it can place itself in the occasions as it will be after the betrothal is made. The betrothal belongs to the dwelling place we shall speak of after this one. This present communication amounts to no more than a meeting, as they say. And the devil will go about very carefully in order to fight against and prevent this betrothal. Afterward, since he sees the soul entirely surrendered to the Spouse he doesn't dare do so much, because he fears it. He has experienced that if sometimes he tries he is left with a great loss; and the soul, with further gain.

6. I tell you, daughters, that I have known persons who had ascended high and had reached this union, who were turned back and won over by the devil with his deep cunning and deceit. All hell must join for such a purpose because, as I have often said,[4] in losing one soul of this kind, not only

---

4. See, e.g., IC 4.3.9–10.

one is lost but a multitude. The devil already has experience in this matter. Look at the multitude of souls God draws to Himself by means of one. He is to be greatly praised for the thousands converted by the martyrs: for a young girl like St. Ursula; for those the devil must have lost through St. Dominic, St. Francis, and other founders of religious orders, and those he now loses through Father Ignatius, the one who founded the Society. Clearly, all of these received, as we read, similar favors from God. How would this have come about if they hadn't made the effort not to lose through their own fault so divine an espousal? Oh, my daughters, how prepared this Lord is to grant us favors now just as He has granted them to others in the past. And, in part, He is even more in need that we desire to receive them, for there are fewer now who care about His honor than there were then. We love ourselves very much; there's an extraordinary amount of prudence we use so as not to lose our rights. Oh, what great deception! May the Lord through His mercy enlighten us so that we do not fall into similar darknesses.

7. You will ask me or be in doubt concerning two things: First, if the soul is as ready to do the will of God as was mentioned,[5] how can it be deceived since it doesn't want to do anything but His will in all? Second, what are the ways in which the devil can enter so dangerously that your soul goes astray? For you are so withdrawn from the world, so close to the sacraments, and in the company, we could say, of angels, and through the Lord's goodness you have no other desire than to serve God and please Him in everything. With those who are already in the midst of worldly occasions such a turn backward would not be surprising. I say that you are right

---

5. In IC 5.4.4.

about this, for God has granted us a great deal of mercy. But when I see, as I have said,[6] that Judas was in the company of the Apostles and conversing always with God Himself and listening to His words, I understand that there is no security in these things.

8. In answer to the first, I say that if this soul were always attached to God's will it is clear that it would not go astray. But the devil comes along with some skilled deception and, under the color of good, confuses it with regard to little things and induces it to get taken up with some of them that he makes it think are good. Then little by little he darkens the intellect, cools the will's ardor, and makes self-love grow until in one way or another he withdraws the soul from the will of God and brings it to his own.

Thus, we have an answer to the second doubt. There is no enclosure so fenced in that he cannot enter, or desert so withdrawn that he fails to go there. And I still have something more to say: perhaps the Lord permits this so as to observe the behavior of that soul He wishes to set up as a light for others. If there is going to be a downfall, it's better that it happen in the beginning rather than later, when it would be harmful to many.

9. The diligence on our part that comes to my mind as being the most effective is the following. First, we must always ask God in prayer to sustain us, and very often think that if He abandons us we will soon end in the abyss, as is true; and we must never trust in ourselves since it would be foolish to do so. Then, we should walk with special care and attention, observing how we are proceeding in the practice of virtue: whether we are getting better or worse in some areas,

---

6. In IC 5.3.2.

especially in love for one another, in the desire to be considered the least among the sisters, and in the performance of ordinary tasks. For if we look out for these things and ask the Lord to enlighten us, we will soon see the gain or the loss. Don't think that a soul that comes so close to God is allowed to lose Him so quickly, that the devil has an easy task. His Majesty would regret the loss of this soul so much that He gives it in many ways a thousand interior warnings, so that the harm will not be hidden from it.

10. Let this, in sum, be the conclusion: that we strive always to advance. And if we don't advance, let us walk with great fear. Without doubt the devil wants to cause some lapse, for it is not possible that after having come so far, one will fail to grow. Love is never idle, and a failure to grow would be a very bad sign. A soul that has tried to be the betrothed of God Himself, that is now intimate with His Majesty, and has reached the boundaries that were mentioned, must not go to sleep.

That you, daughters, may see what He does with those He now considers to be His betrothed ones, we shall begin to speak of the sixth dwelling places. And you will see how little it all is that we can do to serve and suffer and accomplish so as to dispose ourselves for such great favors. It could be that our Lord ordained that they command me to write so that we might forget our little earthly joys because we will have our eyes set on the reward and see how immeasurable is His mercy—since He desires to commune with and reveal Himself to some worms—and because we will have these eyes set also on His greatness, and thus run along enkindled in His love.

11. May He be pleased that I manage to explain something about these very difficult things. I know well that this

will be impossible if His Majesty and the Holy Spirit do not move my pen. And if what I say will not be for your benefit, I beg Him that I may not succeed in saying anything. His Majesty knows that I have no other desire, insofar as I can understand myself, but that His name be praised and that we strive to serve a Lord who even here on earth pays like this. Through His favors we can understand something of what He will give us in heaven without the intervals, trials, and dangers that there are in this tempestuous sea. If there were no danger of losing or offending Him, it would be easy to endure life until the end of the world so as to labor for so great a God and Lord and Spouse.

May it please His Majesty that we may merit to render Him some service; without as many faults as we always have, even in good works, amen.

THEY MEET TOGETHER
SO AS TO BECOME MORE
SATISFIED WITH EACH OTHER

5.4.1–3 Teresa explains that her work may contain repetitions because her health doesn't permit re-reading the text and she has had to set it aside for about five months. She defers her use of the metaphor of the little butterfly so that she can develop another comparison to help her readers understand this prayer of union. She thinks the stages of courtship and marriage can help us better understand the stages of prayer.

5.4.4–6 Teresa says it seems that the prayer of union does not yet reach the stage of spiritual betrothal. She says it is here that God reveals more of himself and the soul is left in love. Even so, if the soul is careless about placing its affection on something other than him, it loses everything. Teresa warns that persons, even those who greatly desire to serve God, are not immune to temptations. She cautions the nuns to be diligent in asking God to sustain them, and says they must never trust in themselves. She advises monitoring the practice of virtue, and giving special attention to love for one another, to desiring to be considered the least of all, and to the performance of ordinary tasks. A soul, she says, must not go to sleep. She concludes the discussion of the fifth dwelling places with a reference to the sixth dwelling places with their great favors. She asks God's help in explaining these difficult topics.

5.4.7–8 How can the devil enter so dangerously that the soul goes astray? Even Judas was in the company of the apostles, conversing with Christ, and listening to his words. We can become deceived by the devil under the color of good. Then, little by little, he darkens the intellect and makes self-love grow. There is no enclosure or fence that he cannot enter, or desert so withdrawn that he fails to go there. God may permit this to observe the behavior of the soul he wishes to set up to be a light for others.

5.4.9 What must we do? First we must, Teresa insists, always ask God in prayer to sustain us and never trust in ourselves. Then we must observe how we are proceeding in the practice of virtue, and whether we are getting better or worse, especially in love for one another, in the desire to be considered the least, and in the performance of ordinary tasks. A soul who comes so close to God will not be allowed to lose him so quickly; the Lord gives the soul a thousand interior warnings.

5.4.10–11 Love is never idle, and a failure to grow in love is a very bad sign. How little is all we do to serve, suffer, and accomplish, so as to dispose ourselves for the great favors of the sixth dwelling places. "[May] His Majesty and the Holy Spirit . . . move my pen," Teresa entreats, "[so] that His name be praised and that we strive to serve a Lord who even here on earth pays [through favors like these] . . . [so that] we can understand something of what He will give us in heaven" (IC 5.4.11).

Interpretive Notes

Before thinking any further about this chapter, we must recall some facts. *The Interior Castle* is about mysticism; that is, Teresa is interested in explaining, above all, the final stages of the spiritual life. At the same time she is giving testimony of her own experiences of God so that his name might be praised. These final stages of the spiritual life correspond to the fifth, sixth, and seventh dwelling places. To enter this region of the experience of God, Teresa has recourse to two symbols. At the beginning of the fifth dwelling place, she makes use of the analogy of the silkworm that is transformed into a butterfly. To conclude her exposition, she turns to the *Song of Songs* and the symbol of married love. The first analogy is mainly Christological, and the second Trinitarian. The first serves her as an opportunity to explain how there is a time when our baptismal rebirth in Christ reaches its fullness. The second extols the primacy of love and grants Teresa an opportunity to point out a decisive difference between Christian mysticism and other forms of mysticism. It is a profoundly interpersonal relationship of love between the divine and human persons.

At the time Teresa began to write again, in Ávila, the new papal nuncio, Felipe Sega, who was opposed to Teresa, had arrived in Madrid from Seville. A number of calumnious reports written against Teresa, her nuns, and Father Gracián had arrived at the Spanish Court. Teresa was obliged to write to the king to defend herself and the others. At this time also the nuns at the Incarnation tried to elect Teresa again as prioress, but those who voted for her suffered excommunication for doing so. Teresa, only a short distance away, was informed of these events by St. John of the Cross, who was at the time confessor at the Incarnation. Teresa was also suffering so much from headaches during this period and was frequently unable to write her letters herself, but dictated to one of the nuns. On top of all this, she had to struggle to bring the monastery of St. Joseph in Ávila under the jurisdiction of the order, for it lay under that of the bishop, Don Alvaro de Mendoza, who was much loved by the nuns. It seemed impossible that she would find some calm moments to take up once more her work on her manuscript of *The Interior Castle*. She managed, though, to finish the work in a spurt of action during the month of November 1577. When she wrote the epilogue to her volume on November 29, the storm about her was raging. That very week St. John of the Cross was seized and taken prisoner to the monastery in Toledo. Teresa took up her pen again to write to the king and plead for freedom for that "little saint." But these outward events of her life at this time had no impact whatsoever on *The Interior Castle*; not the slightest mention of any outward troubles appears in her work.

Teresa sets aside her symbol of the little butterfly because it rests nowhere, neither in spiritual delights nor in earthly consolations. Its flight is higher and cannot be dealt with again until the last dwelling place. She looks for another comparison to explain for us what happens next, and she finds it in the notion that God espouses souls spiritually. At this time, St. John of the Cross was giving talks to the nuns at St. Joseph's. It was most likely from him that the nuns first heard talk about bridal love and the *Song of Songs*. It is reasonable, then, to suspect that in introducing her nuptial symbolism, Teresa had been listening to conferences given by John of the Cross, which followed in the tradition of Paul, Origen, Gregory of Nyssa, and up through St. Bernard of Clairvaux and Ruysbroeck. But Teresa, nonetheless, gives her own touch of originality to the ancient symbol. From the biblical poem, she moves quickly and spontaneously to the human reality of marriage. "And even though the comparison may be a coarse one, I cannot find another that would better explain what I mean than the sacrament of marriage" (IC 5.4.3).

Turning to marriage for her explanation, she turns as well to the marriage customs in the Spain of her day. In this ritual, there were three forward-moving periods representing the fifth, sixth, and seventh dwelling places. But before going any further she makes it clear that "in these matters that we are dealing with there is never anything that is not spiritual. Corporal things are far distant from them" (IC 5.4.3). In fact, she stresses further that the spiritual joys the Lord gives are a thousand leagues distant from what married delights must be. The "actions of love are most pure and so extremely delicate and gentle that there is no way of explaining them, but the Lord knows how to make them very clearly felt" (IC 5.4.3). This distance between the symbol and the symbolized cannot be exaggerated, according to Teresa.

The three successive periods that the symbol refers to are illustrated by Teresa in this way: meetings, betrothal, and marriage. The meetings are necessary on the social level so that the two can get to know each other and find out what they have in common. During betrothal the relationship passes from knowledge to love. In marriage each one surrenders completely to the other.

With regard to the meetings, the two get to know each other. But in this case, from the viewpoint of what is being symbolized, the enlightenment is not reciprocal. It lies in one direction, in that of Christ. It is Christ who makes himself known to the soul. He shows it in a secret way who this Bridegroom is that it is about to take. "Through the work of the senses and the faculties she couldn't in any way or in a thousand years understand what she understands here in the shortest time. But being who He is, the Spouse, from that meeting alone leaves her more worthy for the joining of hands, as they say" of the betrothal (IC 5.4.4).

Teresa's courtship imagery, with its increasingly intimate stages of meeting, betrothal, and marriage, is reminiscent of the *Song of Songs*. There have always been those who are uneasy or uncomfortable with this juxtaposition of the sensuous and the sublime. It seems, however, that the comparison, though inadequate, is the closest way for those who have experienced the indescribable to convey it to others. John of the Cross adopted this imagery as well. God is in love with his people. God *is* love—the phrase is so familiar that its meaning is sometimes lost. It is only natural to turn to the most intense forms of human love to express something of what is experienced of divine love.

Even after reaching experiences like this, one can grow careless, and Teresa warns us about this in the latter part of chapter 5. Teresa knows people who had reached this stage and then fallen back. She herself, in fact, was one of these. God has granted so much mercy to these souls—how can they fall back? Though it is true that, at this stage, one doesn't want to do anything but the will of God, one can be fooled under the color of good with regard to small matters. Little by little, then, the intellect is darkened and the will's ardor cooled. Our protection is in the realization that this can happen to us, and so we must always ask God in prayer to sustain us. Then we must walk with special attention as to how we are progressing, especially in love for one another, in the desire to be humble, and in the performance of ordinary tasks.

St. Bernard of Clairvaux is one of the best expositors of the nuptial analogy of the love between God and the soul. He writes in his *Commentary on the Song of Songs*:

> What a capacity this soul has, how privileged its merits, that it is found worthy not only to receive the divine

presence, but to be able to make sufficient room! What can I say of her who can provide avenues spacious enough for the God of majesty to walk in! She certainly cannot afford to be entangled in lawsuits nor by worldly cares; she cannot be enslaved by gluttony and sensual pleasures, by the lust of the eyes, the ambition to rule, or by pride in the possession of power. If she is to become heaven, the dwelling place of God, it is first of all essential that she be empty of all these defects. Otherwise how could she be still enough to know that he is God? . . . The soul must grow and expand, that it may be roomy enough for God. Its width is its love, if we accept what the Apostle says: "Widen your hearts in love." The soul being a spirit does not admit of material expansion, but grace confers gifts on it that nature is not equipped to bestow. Its growth and expansion must be understood in a spiritual sense; it is its virtue that increases, not its substance. . . . The capacity of any soul is judged by the amount of love one possesses. (St. Bernard of Clairvaux, *Commentary on the Song of Songs*, 27:10)

Questions for Discussion

1. Why did five months elapse since Teresa left off this work?

2. What were the stages leading up to marriage in the culture in which Teresa lived?

3. Why does the devil desire to turn back those souls who have reached this prayer of union?

4. What must you do to prevent your growing careless in the spiritual life?

5. Teresa holds that our love for God cannot be measured except proportionally to our love for one another. But how do we measure our love of neighbor?

6. How do we discern the best ways to better love our neighbor? How might this vary depending on our state in life?

THE SIXTH
DWELLING PLACES

Contains Eleven Chapters

CHAPTER 1

Discusses how greater trials come when the Lord begins to grant greater favors. Mentions some and how those who are now in this dwelling place conduct themselves. This chapter is good for souls undergoing interior trials.

Well then, let us, with the help of the Holy Spirit, speak of the sixth dwelling places, where the soul is now wounded with love for its Spouse and strives for more opportunities to be alone and, in conformity with its state, to rid itself of everything that can be an obstacle to this solitude.

That meeting[1] left such an impression that the soul's whole desire is to enjoy it again. I have already said that in this prayer nothing is seen in a way that can be called seeing, nor is anything seen with the imagination. I use the term "meeting" because of the comparison I made.[2] Now the soul is fully determined to take no other spouse. But the Spouse does not look at the soul's great desires that the betrothal

---

1. Allusion to the meeting referred to in IC 5.4.4.
2. See IC 5.1.9–11; 5.4.3–4.

take place, for He still wants it to desire this more, and He wants the betrothal to take place at a cost; it is the greatest of blessings. And although everything is small when it comes to paying for this exceptional benefit, I tell you, daughters, that for the soul to endure such delay it needs to have that token or pledge of betrothal that it now has. Oh, God help me, what interior and exterior trials the soul suffers before entering the seventh dwelling place!

2. Indeed, sometimes I reflect and fear that if a soul knew beforehand, its natural weakness would find it most difficult to have the determination to suffer and pass through these trials, no matter what blessings were represented to it—unless it had arrived at the seventh dwelling place. For once it has arrived there, the soul fears nothing and is absolutely determined to overcome every obstacle for God.[3] And the reason is that it is always so closely joined to His Majesty that from this union comes its fortitude. I believe it will be well to recount some of those trials that I know one will certainly undergo. Perhaps not all souls will be led along this path, although I doubt very much that those persons who sometimes enjoy so truly the things of heaven will live free of earthly trials that come in one way or another.

3. Although I hadn't intended to treat of these, I thought doing so would bring great consolation to some soul going through them, for it would learn that these trials take place in souls to whom God grants similar favors; for truly, when one is suffering the trials, it then seems that everything is lost. I will not deal with them according to the order in which they happen, but as they come to mind. And I want to begin with the smallest trials. There is an outcry by persons a sister

---

3. See IC 7.3.4–5.

is dealing with and even by those she does not deal with and who, it seems to her, would never even think of her; gossip like the following: "She's trying to make out she's a saint; she goes to extremes to deceive the world and bring others to ruin; there are other better Christians who don't put on all this outward show." (And it's worth noting that she is not putting on any outward show but just striving to fulfill well her state in life.) Those she considered her friends turn away from her, and they are the ones who take the largest and most painful bite at her: "That soul has gone astray and is clearly mistaken; these are things of the devil; she will turn out like this person or that other that went astray, and will bring about a decline in virtue; she has deceived her confessors" (and they go to these confessors, telling them so, giving them examples of what happened to some that were lost in this way); a thousand kinds of ridicule and statements like the above.

4. I know a person who had great fear that there would be no one who would hear her confession because of such gossip[4]—so much gossip that there's no reason to go into it all here. And what is worse, these things do not pass quickly, but go on throughout the person's whole life, including the advice to others to avoid any dealings with such persons.

You will tell me that there are also those who will speak well of that soul. Oh, daughters, how few there are who believe in such favors in comparison with the many who abhor them! Moreover, praise is just another trial greater than those mentioned! Since the soul sees clearly that if it has anything good this is given by God and is by no means its own—for just previously it saw itself to be very poor and

---

4. She is referring to herself. See L 28.14.

surrounded by great sins—praise is an intolerable burden to it, at least in the beginning. Later on, for certain reasons, praise is not so intolerable. First, because experience makes the soul see clearly that people are as quick to say good things as bad, and so it pays no more attention to the good things than to the bad. Second, because it has been more enlightened by the Lord that no good thing comes from itself but is given by His Majesty; and it turns to praise God, forgetful that it has had any part to play, just as if it had seen the gift in another person. Third, if it sees that some souls have benefited from seeing the favors God grants it, it thinks that His Majesty used this means, of its being falsely esteemed as for good, so that some blessings might come to those souls. Fourth, since it looks after the honor and glory of God more than its own, the temptation, which came in the beginning, that these praises will destroy it, is removed; little does dishonor matter to it if in exchange God might perhaps thereby just once be praised—afterward, let whatever comes come.

5. These reasons and others mitigate the great pain these praises cause; although some pain is almost always felt, except when one is paying hardly any attention. But it is an incomparably greater trial to see oneself publicly considered as good without reason than the trials mentioned. And when the soul reaches the stage at which it pays little attention to praise, it pays much less to disapproval; on the contrary, it rejoices in this and finds it a very sweet music. This is an amazing truth. Blame does not intimidate the soul but strengthens it. Experience has already taught it the wonderful gain that comes through this path. It feels that those who persecute it do not offend God; rather that His Majesty permits persecution for the benefit of the soul. And since it clearly

experiences the benefits of persecution, it acquires a special and very tender love for its persecutors. It seems to it that they are greater friends and more advantageous than those who speak well of it.

6. The Lord is wont also to send it the severest illnesses. This is a much greater trial, especially when the pains are acute. For in some way, if these pains are severe, the trial is, it seems to me, the greatest on earth—I mean the greatest exterior trial, however many the other pains. I say "if the pains are severe," because they then afflict the soul interiorly and exteriorly in such a way that it doesn't know what to do with itself. It would willingly accept at once any martyrdom rather than these sharp pains; although they do not last long in this extreme form. After all, God gives no more than what can be endured; and His Majesty gives patience first. But other great sufferings and illnesses of many kinds are the usual thing.

7. I know a person who cannot truthfully say that from the time the Lord began forty years ago to grant the favor that was mentioned she spent even one day without pains and other kinds of suffering (the lack of bodily health, I mean) and other great trials.[5] It's true that she had been very wretched and that everything seemed small to her in comparison with the hell she deserved. Others, who have not offended our Lord so much, will be led by another path. But I would always choose the path of suffering, if only to imitate our Lord Jesus Christ if there were no other gain, especially since there are always so many other benefits.

---

5. The "favor that was mentioned" is the prayer of union or the "meetings" between the two who will be betrothed, the prayer characteristic of the fifth dwelling place. The person Teresa refers to is herself. "Forty years ago" would have been 1537. For an account of these sufferings and trials see L 4–6; for her first experiences of union, see L 4.7.

Oh, were we to treat of interior sufferings these others would seem small if the interior ones could be clearly explained; but it is impossible to explain the way in which they come to pass.

8. Let us begin with the torment one meets with from a confessor who is so discreet and has so little experience that there is nothing he is sure of: he fears everything and finds in everything something to doubt because he sees these unusual experiences. He becomes especially doubtful if he notices some imperfection in a soul that has them, for it seems to such confessors that the ones to whom God grants these favors must be angels—but that is impossible as long as they are in this body. Everything is immediately condemned as from the devil or melancholy. And the world is so full of this melancholy that I am not surprised. There is so much of it now in the world, and the devil causes so many evils through this means, that confessors are very right in fearing it and considering it carefully. But the poor soul that walks with the same fear and goes to its confessor as to its judge, and is condemned by him, cannot help but be deeply tormented and disturbed. Only the one who has passed through this will understand what a great torment it is. For this is another one of the terrible trials these souls suffer, especially if they have lived wretched lives; thinking that because of their sins God will allow them to be deceived. Even though they feel secure and cannot believe that the favor, when granted by His Majesty, is from any other spirit than from God, the torment returns immediately since the favor is something that passes quickly, and the remembrance of sins is always present, and the soul sees faults in itself, which are never lacking. When the confessor assures it, the soul grows calm, although the disturbance will return. But when the confessor contributes

to the torment with more fear, the trial becomes something almost unbearable—especially when some dryness comes between the times of these favors. It then seems to the soul that it has never been mindful of God and never will be; and when it hears His Majesty spoken of, it seems to it as though it were hearing about a person far away.

9. All this would amount to nothing if it were not for the fact that in addition comes the feeling that it is incapable of explaining things to its confessors, that it has deceived them. And even though it thinks and sees that it tells its confessors about every stirring, even the first ones, this doesn't help. The soul's understanding is so darkened that it becomes incapable of seeing the truth and believes whatever the imagination represents to it (for the imagination is then its master) or whatever foolish things the devil wants to represent. The Lord, it seems, gives the devil license so that the soul might be tried and even be made to think it is rejected by God. Many are the things that war against it with an interior oppression so keen and unbearable that I don't know what to compare this experience to if not to the oppression of those that suffer in hell, for no consolation is allowed in the midst of this tempest. If they desire to be consoled by their confessor, it seems the devils assist him to torment it more. Thus, when a confessor was dealing with a person after she had suffered this torment (for it seems a dangerous affliction since there are so many things involved in it), he told her to let him know when she was in this state; but the torment was always so bad that he came to realize there was nothing he could do about it.[6] Well, then, if a person in this state who knows how

---

6. The person here is Teresa, and the confessor is Father Baltasar Alvarez, S.J. See L 30.13.

to read well takes up a book in the vernacular, he will find that he understands no more of it then if he didn't know how to read even one of the letters, for the intellect is incapable of understanding.[7]

10. In sum, there is no remedy in this tempest but to wait for the mercy of God. For at an unexpected time, with one word alone or a chance happening, He so quickly calms the storm that it seems there had not been even as much as a cloud in that soul, and it remains filled with sunlight and much more consolation. And like one who has escaped from a dangerous battle and been victorious, it comes out praising our Lord; for it was He who fought for the victory. It knows very clearly that it did not fight, for all the weapons with which it could have defended itself are seen to be, it seems, in the hands of its enemies. Thus, it knows clearly its wretchedness and the very little we of ourselves can do if the Lord abandons us.

11. It seems the soul has no longer any need of reflection to understand this, for the experience of having suffered through it, having seen itself totally incapacitated, made it understand our nothingness and what miserable things we are. For in this state grace is so hidden (even though the soul must not be without grace since with all this torment it doesn't offend God nor would it offend Him for anything on earth) that not even a very tiny spark is visible. The soul doesn't think that it has any love of God or that it ever had any, for if it has done some good, or His Majesty has granted it some favor, all of this seems to have been dreamed up or fancied. As for sins, it sees certainly that it has committed them.

---

7. See L 30.12.

12. O Jesus, and what a thing it is to see this kind of forsaken soul; and, as I have said,[8] what little help any earthly consolation is for it! Hence, do not think, sisters, if at some time you find yourselves in this state, that the rich and those who are free will have a better remedy for these times of suffering. Absolutely not, for being rich in this case seems to me like the situation of a person condemned to die who has all the world's delights placed before him. These delights would not be sufficient to alleviate his suffering; rather, they would increase the torment. So it is with this torment; it comes from above, and [earthly things are of no avail in the matter.] Our great God wants us to know our own misery and that He is king; and this is very important for what lies ahead.

13. Well then, what will this poor soul do when the torment goes on for many days? If it prays, it feels as though it hasn't prayed—as far as consolation goes, I mean. For consolation is not admitted into the soul's interior, nor is what one recites to oneself, even though vocal, understood. As for mental prayer, this definitely is not the time for that, because the faculties are incapable of the practice; rather, solitude causes greater harm—and also another torment for this soul is that it be with anyone or that others speak to it. And thus however much it forces itself not to do so, it goes about with a gloomy and ill-tempered mien that is externally very noticeable.

Is it true that it will know how to explain its experiences? They are indescribable, for they are spiritual afflictions and sufferings that one cannot name. The best remedy (I don't mean for getting rid of them, because I don't find any, but so that they may be endured) is to engage in external works

---

8. In IC 6.1.9–10.

of charity and to hope in the mercy of God who never fails those who hope in Him. May He be forever blessed, amen.

14. Other exterior trials the devils cause must be quite unusual; and so there's no reason to speak of them. Nor are they, for the most part, so painful; for, however much the devils do, they do not, in my opinion, manage to disable the faculties or disturb the soul in this way. In sum, there's reason for thinking that they can do no more than what the Lord allows them to do; and provided one doesn't lose one's mind, everything is small in comparison with what was mentioned.

15. We shall be speaking in these dwelling places of other interior sufferings, and dealing with different kinds of prayer and favors from the Lord. For even though some favors cause still more severe suffering than those mentioned, as will be seen from the condition in which the body is left, they do not deserve to be called trials. Nor is there any reason for us to write of them since they are such great favors from the Lord. In the midst of receiving them the soul understands that they are great favors and far beyond its merits. This severe suffering comes so that one may enter the seventh dwelling place. It comes along with many other sufferings, only some of which I shall speak of[9] because it would be impossible to speak of them all, or even to explain what they are; for they are of a different, much higher level than those mentioned in this chapter. And if I haven't been able to explain any more than I did about those of a lower kind, less will I be able to say of the others. May the Lord give His help for everything through the merits of His Son, amen.

---

9. She does so in IC 6.11.

GREATER TRIALS COME
WITH GREATER FAVORS

6.1.1 Teresa introduces important features of the experiences of the sixth dwelling places. She notes that greater trials accompany the greater favors. She says the soul is now wounded with love, and it strives for more opportunities to be alone. The soul's whole desire is to enjoy again the prayer of union.

6.1.2–7 Teresa repeats how difficult the trials of the sixth dwelling places are, saying that if the soul knew of them ahead of time, it might lack the determination to suffer and pass through them. She contrasts the fears of the sixth dwelling places with the situation in the seventh dwelling places, where the soul fears nothing and has great fortitude because it is always closely joined to God. She describes some of the trials of the sixth dwelling places. First she mentions misunderstanding, ridicule, and being the object of gossip. Even being praised is a trial, since the soul sees clearly that all it has comes from God and not from its own merits and efforts. Later, however, it comes to see these praises as having some benefit. Even though blame and persecution are trials, the soul is strengthened rather than harmed and learns to love its persecutors. She adds that the Lord also sends severe illness and pain. Even though she experienced severe pains over time, Teresa says that she prefers the path of suffering as a penitential way and also as a way to imitate our Lord Jesus Christ.

6.1.8–10 She describes the interior suffering caused by inexperienced and uneducated confessors. In particular, Teresa suffered at being told that her experiences were from the devil. Another torment comes from the frustration of not being able to explain the extraordinary experiences to one's confessor. She describes intense interior sufferings which she attributes to the devil, including the fear of being rejected by God. She concludes that a soul in this state can't be helped by confessors. There is no remedy. The only course is to wait for the mercy of God, who sometimes, at unexpected moments, gives the soul a respite.

6.1.11–13 Here Teresa gives more specifics concerning interior suffering in the sixth dwelling places. Through experience, without any need for reflection, the soul understands human nothingness. She says grace is not absent, but is so hidden that not even a spark is visible (even though the soul has great determination not to offend God). The soul doesn't think it has any love for God or that it ever had any, and any favors it has received seem imagined. It is aware only of the sins it has committed. Terrible as this self-knowledge and suffering are, they are important for what lies ahead. She continues that there is no consolation in prayer. Mental prayer is impossible, and vocal prayers recited seem to be empty words. A person in this suffering may be noticeably gloomy and ill-tempered. These afflictions, she says, are indescribable. The best remedy for enduring them is to engage in external works of charity and hope in the mercy of God.

6.1.14–15 Teresa says the exterior trials of this stage are less painful than the interior trials and usually do not disturb the soul. She concludes this chapter by saying she will speak further of other interior sufferings, prayers, and favors, all of which prepare the soul for the seventh dwelling places. She asks the Lord's help in her task.

Interpretive Notes

The sixth dwelling places break with the pattern Teresa was following in presenting the other dwelling places. Making up the largest section of the book and covering about a third of the material, eleven of the twenty-seven chapters of the book are in this section. The section deals with the ecstatic period in her own life, which lasted between the ages of forty-three and fifty-seven. Teresa intentionally wanted to abound with explanations about the experiences of this part of her life, since it was the part that caused her the most difficulty with her confessors. They failed to understand the graces God was giving her. Confessors, as well as some of her nuns and other readers, might benefit a great deal from learning of these favors from God. In her *Foundations*, she writes that if God brings most of the nuns in her houses to perfect contemplation (the prayer of union), some are so advanced as to reach rapture, revelations, and visions (F 4.8). But all of us readers can benefit from Teresa's explanations, in that knowledge of them will lead us to give praise to God for his mercies toward humans.

Teresa, however, had another purpose in expanding so much on these sixth dwelling places. It was because her writing on the topic had been poorly organized in her *Life*. She had written that book twelve years previous to this, when she was still in the midst of these graces without realizing fully where they were leading. In her own mystical process, graces were bestowed bountifully as a preparation for the final dwelling places, of which she knew nothing while writing her *Life*. Confronted now once again with this wealth of mystical graces, she proposes to treat them in a better order and describe them in a better style. Previously she had used the analogy of the four ways of watering a garden. In dealing with the third and fourth way of watering, she made a division that was not necessary. Now she joins these together into one dwelling place of her *Castle*, which we can refer to as the ecstatic period of the mystical process.

At the beginning of her work, Teresa referred to it as a treatise. *The Interior Castle*, then, takes on the air of a doctrinal exposition, of a treatise in spiritual theology, but it is a spiritual theology in a Teresian mold. Underlying the doctrinal exposition is her own autobiography. Together with the theological elucidation, the book contains the author's interior story, an account of her spiritual journey, discreetly camouflaged as belonging to an anonymous person. In these sixth dwelling places the autobiographical material is strengthened. In reality what happens in these sixth dwelling places is what happened interiorly to Teresa. The same holds true for the seventh dwelling places. We have, then, two splendid segments of her life systematically recounted by her within the theological outline of the book. These sixth dwelling places deal with material covered in her *Life* (L 16–21, 23–40), and the seventh dwelling places with material present in her *Spiritual Testimonies* (ST 31–65). But neither in her *Life* nor in the *Spiritual Testimonies* was the subject matter arranged as well as it is in these pages of *The Interior Castle*.

From the autobiographical viewpoint, the sixth dwelling places refer to a large section of Teresa's life, lasting about fifteen years. These are years in which Teresa struggled with the theologians of Ávila, who refused to endorse the authenticity of her mystical experiences. It was the period in which Christ promised to be for Teresa a living book, and when she experienced the transpiercing of her soul. They were the years in which she received her mission as a foundress and, after founding St. Joseph's in Ávila, traveled to Medina, Toledo, Malagón, and Valladolid for other foundations. Also during this time she recruited John of the Cross for the founding of the discalced Carmelites among the friars. In these years, she wrote her *Life* and *The Way of Perfection*. These years represent a period of irrepressible longings for God, frequent ecstasies, and raptures.

The first subject Teresa turns to in these dwelling places is what St. John of the Cross will later call in his writings the "dark night." Though Teresa does not use the technical term, the purifying reality of the mystical night (darkness, trials, the cross) is the first characteristic of which she treats in the sixth dwelling places. The soul in these dwelling places is now wounded with love for its Spouse. But in this first chapter she presents only one aspect of this fire of love—its painful aspect. Feeling incapable of describing it in depth, Teresa does propose a simple outline. We are dealing, according to her, with a painful and total trial coming from both without and within. In its relationship with others, the soul experiences total incomprehension and isolation. In its psychological dynamism, an interior darkness and powerlessness comes over the soul. In its relationship with God, it experiences feelings of his absence and being abandoned by him.

Beginning with exterior trials, she describes undergoing harassment and incomprehension from the assessors of her spirit. Teresa alludes to the terrible period in which they considered her to be possessed by the devil. They deprived her of Communion, obliged her not to think of Christ and to "make the fig" whenever he appeared to her (L 29.5). On top of this, she suffered from serious illnesses: "I know a person who cannot truthfully say that from the time the Lord began forty years ago to grant the favor that was mentioned she spent even one day without pains and other kinds of suffering (the lack of bodily health, I mean)" (IC 6.1.7). But the interior trials were the most intense: desolation in her relationship with God, a stifling remembrance of past sins, unbearable dryness, and darkness and confusion of mind. "Oh, God help me! Lord, how You afflict Your lovers! But everything is small in comparison with what You give them afterward" (IC 6.11.6). "In this pain the soul is purified . . . of what otherwise it would have to be purged of in purgatory" (L 20.16).

Questions For Discussion

1. What does the Spouse want of the soul?
2. What are the smallest trials Teresa begins to discuss?
3. Praise is an intolerable burden, but later on not so much. Why?
4. What is a much greater trial?
5. What troubles come from the confessor?
6. What can you say about the interior oppression the soul experiences at this time?

CHAPTER 2

Deals with some of the ways in which our Lord awakens the soul. It seems there is nothing in these awakenings to fear, even though the experience is sublime and the favors are great.

Seemingly we have left the little moth far behind; but we have not, [for these are the trials that make it fly still higher.] Well let us begin, then, to discuss the manner in which the Spouse deals with it and how, before He belongs to it completely, He makes it desire Him vehemently by certain delicate means the soul itself does not understand. (Nor do I believe I'll be successful in explaining them save to those who have experienced them). These are impulses so delicate and refined, for they proceed from very deep within the interior part of the soul, that I don't know any comparison that will fit.

2. They are far different from all that we can acquire of ourselves here below and even from the spiritual delights that were mentioned.[1] For often when a person is distracted and forgetful of God, His Majesty will awaken it. His action is as quick as a falling comet. And as clearly as it hears a thunder-clap, even though no sound is heard, the soul understands that it was called by God. So well does it understand that sometimes, especially in the beginning, it is made to tremble and even complain without there being anything that causes it pain. It feels that it is wounded in the most exquisite

---

1. In the fourth dwelling places.

way, but it doesn't learn how or by whom it was wounded. It knows clearly that the wound is something precious, and it would never want to be cured. It complains to its Spouse with words of love, even outwardly, without being able to do otherwise. It knows that He is present, but He doesn't want to reveal the manner in which He allows Himself to be enjoyed. And the pain is great, although delightful and sweet. And even if the soul does not want this wound, the wound cannot be avoided. But the soul, in fact, would never want to be deprived of this pain. The wound satisfies it much more than the delightful and painless absorption of the prayer of quiet.[2]

3. I am struggling, sisters, to explain for you this action of love, and I don't know how. For it seems a contradiction that the Beloved would give the soul clear understanding that He is with it and yet make it think that He is calling it by a sign so certain that no room is left for doubt and a whisper so penetrating that the soul cannot help but hear it. For it seems that when the Spouse, who is in the seventh dwelling place, communicates in this manner (for the words are not spoken), all the people in the other dwelling places keep still; neither the senses, nor the imagination, nor the faculties stir.

O my powerful God, how sublime are your secrets, and how different spiritual things are from all that is visible and understandable here below. There is nothing that serves to explain this favor, even though the favor is a very small one when compared to the very great ones You work in souls.

4. This action of love is so powerful that the soul dissolves with desire, and yet it doesn't know what to ask for since clearly it thinks that its God is with it.

---

2. See IC 4.3.11–14.

You will ask me: Well, if it knows this, what does it desire
or what pains it? What greater good does it want? I don't
know. I do know that it seems this pain reaches to the soul's
very depths and that when He who wounds it draws out the
arrow, it indeed seems, in accord with the deep love the soul
feels, that God is drawing these very depths after Him.[3] I was
thinking now that it's as though, from this fire enkindled in
the brazier that is my God, a spark leapt forth and so struck
the soul that the flaming fire was felt by it. And since the
spark was not enough to set the soul on fire, and the fire is so
delightful, the soul is left with that pain; but the spark merely
by touching the soul produces that effect. It seems to me this
is the best comparison I have come up with. This delightful
pain—and it is not pain—is not continuous, although sometimes it lasts a long while; at other times it goes away quickly.
This depends on the way the Lord wishes to communicate it,
for it is not something that can be produced in any human
way. But even though it sometimes lasts for a long while, it
comes and goes. To sum up, it is never permanent. For this
reason it doesn't set the soul on fire; but just as the fire is
about to start, the spark goes out and the soul is left with the
desire to suffer again that loving pain the spark causes.

5. Here there is no reason to wonder whether the experience is brought on naturally or caused by melancholy, or
whether it is some trick of the devil or some illusion. It is
something that leaves clear understanding of how this activity comes from the place where the Lord who is unchanging
dwells. The activity is not like that found in other feelings of
devotion, where the great absorption in delight can make us

_____

3. For a parallel passage from her personal experience see L 29.10; in L 29.13,
she describes her experience of the transverberation.

doubtful. Here all the senses and faculties remain free of any absorption, wondering what this could be, without hindering anything or being able, in my opinion, to increase or take away that delightful pain.

Anyone to whom our Lord may have granted this favor—for if He has, that fact will be recognized on reading this—should thank Him very much. Such a person doesn't have to fear deception. Let his great fear be that he might prove ungrateful for so generous a favor, and let him strive to better his entire life, and to serve, and he will see the results and how he receives more and more. In fact, I know a person[4] who received this favor for some years and was so pleased with it that had she served the Lord through severe trials for a great number of years she would have felt well repaid by it. May He be blessed forever, amen.

6. You may wonder why greater security is present in this favor than in other things. In my opinion, these are the reasons: First, the devil never gives delightful pain like this. He can give the savor and delight that seem to be spiritual, but he doesn't have the power to join pain—and so much of it—to the spiritual quiet and delight of the soul. For all of his powers are on the outside, and the pains he causes are never, in my opinion, delightful or peaceful, but disturbing and contentious. Second, this delightful tempest comes from a region other than those regions of which he can be lord. Third, the favor brings wonderful benefits to the soul, the more customary of which are the determination to suffer for God, the desire to have many trials, and the determination to withdraw from earthly satisfactions and conversations and other similar things.

---

4. She is alluding to herself. See ST 59.13.

7. That this favor is no fancy is very clear. Although at other times the soul may strive to experience this favor, it will not be able to counterfeit one. And the favor is something so manifest that it can in no way be fancied. I mean, one cannot think it is imagined, when it is not, or have doubts about it. If some doubt should remain, one must realize that the things experienced are not true impulses; I mean if there should be doubt about whether the favor was experienced or not. The favor is felt as clearly as a loud voice is heard. There's no basis for thinking it is caused by melancholy, because melancholy does not produce or fabricate its fancies save in the imagination. This favor proceeds from the interior part of the soul.

Now it could be that I'm mistaken, but until I hear other reasons from someone who understands the experience I will always have this opinion. And so I know a person who was quite fearful about being deceived but who never had any fear of this prayer.[5]

8. The Lord also has other ways of awakening the soul: unexpectedly, when it is praying vocally and not thinking of anything interior, it seems a delightful enkindling will come upon it as though a fragrance were suddenly to become so powerful as to spread through all the senses. (I don't say that it is a fragrance but am merely making this comparison.) Or the experience is something like this, and it is communicated only for the sake of making one feel the Spouse's presence there. The soul is moved with a delightful desire to enjoy Him, and thereby it is prepared to make intense acts of love

---

5. In ST 59.15 she speaks of how even the learned men she consulted were free of fears about this prayer. St. John of Ávila wrote to her assuring her that the prayer was good. For a description of her personal experience of this grace see also L 29–30.

and praise of our Lord. This favor rises out of that place I mentioned;[6] but there is nothing in it that causes pain, nor are the desires themselves to enjoy God painful. Such is the way the soul usually experiences it. Neither does it seem to me, for some of the reasons mentioned,[7] there is anything to fear; but one should try to receive this favor with gratitude.

---

6. See IC 6.2.1, 3, 5. These favors proceed "from very deep within the interior part of the soul," from "the Spouse, who is in the seventh dwelling place," there, "where the Lord who is unchanging dwells."

7. In IC 6.2.6.

HE MAKES IT DESIRE
HIM VEHEMENTLY

6.2.1–2 Teresa says that before the Spouse belongs completely to the soul, he makes the soul desire him greatly by delicate means that the soul itself doesn't understand. Here Teresa describes how God can awaken the soul to love and an awareness of himself. God does this in such a way that the soul feels that it is wounded in the most exquisite way, but it doesn't learn how or by whom it was wounded. Teresa explains that she knows that the experiences she is talking about will not be clearly understood except by those who have experienced them. This wound, she says, satisfies the soul more than the delightful and painless absorption of the prayer of quiet.

6.2.3 Here Teresa struggles to explain, for it may seem to be a contradiction that the soul would be called by the Lord and yet have clear understanding that he is with it. When the Spouse from the seventh dwelling places communicates in this manner, all the people in the other dwelling places keep still. How different spiritual things are from all that is visible and understandable here below.

6.2.4 Teresa continues trying to explain experiences that seem contradictory in terms of ordinary human experience. She raises a question that she can't answer to her satisfaction: If the soul clearly thinks God is with it, then how can it desire more, and what does its pain consist of? She uses the comparison of a wound caused by an arrow that reaches to the soul's depths. When he who wounds it draws out the arrow, it seems because of the soul's great love that God is drawing these very depths after him. She uses another example: The soul is struck by a spark from God that is not enough to set the soul aflame, but is enough to leave the soul with an intense longing. This experience may last for a long while, but is never permanent.

6.2.5 Teresa says this experience leaves a clear understanding that this activity comes from the place where the Lord dwells. Persons who experience this favor should thank the Lord very much and strive to better their entire lives and to serve God.

6.2.6–7 Teresa explains why there is greater security in this favor than in others (mentioned earlier). She says the devil doesn't have the power to join pain with spiritual quiet and spiritual delight. Second, she says this delight comes from a place the devil can't access. And third, she says the favor brings wonderful benefits to the soul, including the determination to suffer for God and the desire to have many trials.

Teresa gives examples to say that this favor can't be imagined and is accompanied by certitude. If there are doubts that the experience was imagined, these doubts would themselves be evidence that what was experienced was not this prayer experience that Teresa has been describing.

6.2.8 Teresa describes other ways that the Lord awakens the soul through making his presence felt. In these experiences there is nothing that causes pain. Instead the soul experiences delightful desire to enjoy God, and makes intense acts of love and praise. This type of experience is more common than the painful one described earlier, and here, as well, there is no reason to fear being deceived.

Interpretive Notes

These sixth dwelling places represent a region in which immense desires are experienced. Not arising from anything outside the soul, but coming from deep within it, the desires are as though produced by an arrow that wounds the soul. The wound, however, is both painful and delightful. The entire setting for these dwelling places, then, is marked off by these intense yearnings that God effects deep within the soul (IC 6.2). They culminate with such a great outburst of longings for God that the soul comes close to death (IC 6.6). Once again we are reminded that Teresa is giving us an account of her own experience when she tells us that she "knew a person who received this favor for some years" (IC 6.2.5).

In a prayer uttered in her *Life*, she gives an idea of the state she finds herself in as a result of these wounds of loving desire: "O true Lord and my Glory! How delicate and extremely heavy a cross You have prepared for those who reach this state! 'Delicate' because it is pleasing; 'heavy' because there come times when there is no capacity to bear it; and yet the soul would never want to be freed from it unless it were for the sake of being with You. . . . It doesn't know what it wants, but it well understands that it wants nothing other than You" (L 16.5). Her many-faceted desires are being strongly pulled now in one direction, toward Jesus Christ.

The desires to die to see Jesus Christ grow increasingly intense. "I die because I do not die" (P 1). When Teresa writes her *Life* the second time, she speaks of experiencing a desire which penetrates the whole soul at once. With this desire "the soul begins to grow so weary that it ascends far above itself and all creatures. God places it in a desert so distant from all things that however much it labors, it doesn't find a creature on earth that might accompany it—nor would it want to find one; it desires only to die in that solitude" (L 20.9). Later she says: "I sometimes really think that if this prayer continues as it does now, the Lord would be served if my life came to an end. In my opinion, a pain as great as this is sufficient to put an end to life, but I don't merit death. All my longing then is to die" (L 20.13).

In casting about for ways to explain this experience of love, Teresa, besides the wound, thinks of fire. It's as though a spark leapt forth from the fire enkindled in the brazier that is her God and so struck the soul that the flaming fire was felt by it. But the spark was not enough to set the soul ablaze; it only caused the fire to be felt in such a way as to touch off a delightful pain. Since the spark does not produce a permanent fire, the loving desires do not last in such intense form. The soul is left, though, with a desire to suffer again the loving pain caused by the spark. The awakening of desires is not always painful. So sometimes the enkindling will come upon it in a delightful way and is communicated for the sake of making the soul feel the Spouse's presence deep within. These loving desires for God are not painful but delightful only, and this is, in fact, the way the soul in this stage usually experiences its desires for God.

The description of the transpiercing of her soul recorded by Teresa in her *Life* (L 29.13) is well known, and it is given preeminence by Gian Lorenzo Bernini's renowned sculpture of the event found today in the church of Santa Maria della Vittoria in Rome. Noteworthy, however, is the fact that this accompanying vision was seen by Teresa more than once. Here, for example, is another description of the transpiercing of the soul in a more sober form in one of her *Spiritual Testimonies*:

> Another type of prayer quite frequent is a kind of *wound* in which it seems as though an arrow is thrust into the heart, or into the soul itself: Thus the wound causes a severe pain which makes the soul moan; yet the pain is so delightful the soul would never want it to go away. This pain is not in the senses, nor is the sore a physical one; but the pain lies in the interior depths of the soul without resemblance to bodily pain. Yet, since the experience cannot be explained save through comparisons, these rough comparisons are used (I mean rough when compared to what the experience is); but I don't know how to describe it any other way. For this reason these are not things to be written about or spoken of, because it's impossible to understand them unless one has experienced them. (ST 59.17)

In conclusion, we might add that for Teresa these are not events that can be explained through one's ordinary psychological experience—that is, reduced to the plane of one's natural conscious or unconscious makeup; they come from another, superior plane and are recognized by their effects: "The favor brings wonderful benefits to the soul, the more customary of which are the determination to suffer for God, the desire to have many trials, and the determination to withdraw from earthly satisfactions and conversations and other similar things" (IC 6.2.6).

Questions For Discussion

1. In what manner does the Lord allow himself to be enjoyed in this dwelling place?

2. How long does the delightful pain last?
3. Why can this experience not be explained by natural causes or melancholy?
4. What are some other ways in which the Lord awakens the soul?
5. What good does it do us to read about such favors?
6. Have you ever seen Bernini's sculpture of St. Teresa in Ecstasy? What is notable for you about the statue? What emotions does it express?

CHAPTER 3

Deals with the same subject and tells of the manner in which God, when pleased, speaks to the soul. Gives counsel about how one should behave in such a matter and not follow one's own opinion. Sets down some signs for discerning when there is deception and when not. This chapter is very beneficial.[1]

God has another way of awakening the soul. Although it somehow seems to be a greater favor than those mentioned,[2] it can be more dangerous, and therefore I shall pause a little to consider it. There are many kinds of locutions given to the soul. Some seem to come from outside oneself; others, from deep within the interior part of the soul; others, from the superior part; and some are so exterior that they come through the sense of hearing, for it seems there is a spoken word. Sometimes, and often, the locution can be an illusion, especially in persons with a weak imagination or in those who are melancholic, I mean who suffer noticeably from melancholy.

2. In my opinion no attention should be paid to these latter two kinds of persons even if they say they see and hear and understand. But neither should one disturb these persons by telling them their locutions come from the devil; one

---

1. This chapter restates what was said in L 25. In both places the prevailing effort is to distinguish between genuine locutions (coming from God or His saints) and false ones (from the imagination or the devil). In this chapter Teresa deals first with locutions in general (IC 6.3.1–11); then she goes on to treat of a more subtle kind of mystical locution accompanied by "a certain intellectual vision" (IC 6.3.12–18).

2. In IC 6.2.1–4, 8.

219

must listen to them as to sick persons. The prioress or confessor to whom they relate their locutions should tell them to pay no attention to such experiences, that these locutions are not essential to the service of God, and that the devil has deceived many by such means, even though this particular person, perhaps, may not be suffering such deception. This counsel should be given so as not to aggravate the melancholy, for if they tell her the locution is due to melancholy, there will be no end to the matter; she will swear that she sees and hears, for it seems to her that she does.

3. It is true that it's necessary to be firm in taking prayer away from her and to insist strongly that she pay no attention to locutions; for the devil is wont to profit from these souls that are sick in this way, even though what he does may not be to their harm but to the harm of others. But for both the sick and the healthy there is always reason to fear these things until the spirit of such persons is well understood. And I say that in the beginning it is always better to free these persons from such experiences, for if the locutions are from God, doing so is a greater help toward progress, and a person even grows when tested. This is true; nonetheless, one should not proceed in a way that is distressing or disturbing to a soul, because truly the soul can't help it if these locutions come.

4. Now then, to return to what I was saying about locutions, all the kinds I mentioned[3] can be from God or from the devil or from one's own imagination. If I can manage to do so, I shall give, with the help of the Lord, the signs as to when they come from these different sources and when they are dangerous; for there are many souls among prayerful people who hear them. My desire, sisters, is that you realize

------

3. In IC 6.3.1.

you are doing the right thing if you refuse to give credence to them, even when they are destined just for you (such as some consolation, or advice about your faults), no matter who tells you about them, or if they are an illusion, for it doesn't matter where they come from. One thing I advise you: do not think, even if the locutions are from God, that you are better because of them, for He spoke frequently with the Pharisees. [All the good comes from how one benefits by these words;] and pay no more attention to those that are not in close conformity with Scripture than you would to those heard from the devil himself. Even if they come from your weak imagination, it's necessary to treat them as if they were temptations in matters of faith, and thus resist them always. They will then go away because they will have little effect on you.

5. Returning, then, to the first of the different kinds of locutions; whether or not the words come from the interior part of the soul, from the superior part, or from the exterior part doesn't matter in discerning whether or not they are from God. The surest signs they are from God that can be had, in my opinion, are these: the first and truest is the power and authority they bear, for locutions from God effect what they say. Let me explain myself better. A soul finds itself in the midst of all the tribulation and disturbance that was mentioned,[4] in darkness of the intellect and in dryness; with one word alone of these locutions from the Lord ("don't be distressed"), it is left calm and free from all distress, with great light, and without all that suffering in which it seemed to it that all the learned men and all who might come together to give it reasons for not being distressed would be unable to remove its affliction no matter how hard they tried. Or, it is

---

4. In IC 6.1.7–15.

afflicted because its confessor and others have told it that its spirit is from the devil, and it is all full of fear; with one word alone ("it is I, fear not"), the fear is taken away completely, and the soul is most comforted, thinking that nothing would be sufficient to make it believe anything else. Or, it is greatly distressed over how certain serious business matters will turn out; it hears that it should be calm, that everything will turn out all right. It is left certain and free of anxiety. And this is the way in many other instances.[5]

6. The second sign is the great quiet left in the soul, the devout and peaceful recollection, the readiness to engage in the praises of God. O Lord, if a word sent to be spoken through one of Your attendants (for the Lord Himself does not speak the words—at least not in this dwelling place—but an angel) has such power, what will be the power You leave in the soul that is attached to You, and You to it, through love?

7. The third sign is that these words remain in the memory for a very long time, and some are never forgotten, as are those we listen to here on earth—I mean those we hear from men. For even if the words are spoken by men who are very important and learned, or concern the future, we do not have them engraved on our memory, or believe them, as we do these. The certitude is so strong that even in things that in one's own opinion sometimes seem impossible and in which there is doubt as to whether they will or will not happen, and the intellect wavers, there is an assurance in the soul itself that cannot be overcome. Even though it seems that everything is going contrary to what the soul understood, and years go by, the thought remains that God will find other

_____

5. In a veiled way she is alluding to her own experience described in her L 25.14–19.

means than those men know of and that in the end the words
will be accomplished; and so they are. Although, as I say, the
soul still suffers when it sees the many delays, for since time
has passed since it heard the words, and the effects and the
certitude that were present about their being from God have
passed, these doubts take place. The soul wonders whether
the locutions might have come from the devil or from the
imagination. Yet, none of these doubts remain in the soul,
but it would at present die a thousand deaths for that truth.
But, as I say, what won't the devil do with all these imaginings so as to afflict and intimidate the soul, especially if the
words regard a business matter which, when carried out,
will bring many blessings to souls, and works that will bring
great honor and service to God, and if there is great difficulty
involved? At least he weakens faith, for it does great harm
not to believe that God has the power to do things that our
intellects do not understand.

We Know Nothing

8. Despite all these struggles and even the persons who
tell one that the locutions are foolishness (I mean the confessors with whom one speaks about these things), and despite
the many unfortunate occurrences that make it seem the
words will not be fulfilled, there remains a spark of assurance
so alive—I don't know from where—that the words will be
fulfilled,[6] though all other hopes are dead, that even should
the soul desire otherwise, that spark will stay alive. And in
the end, as I have said, the words of the Lord are fulfilled.
And the soul is so consoled and happy it wouldn't want to do
anything but always praise His Majesty, and praise Him more
for the fact that what He had told it was fulfilled than for the
work itself, no matter how important the work is to the soul.

---

6. In IC 6.3.7.

9. I don't know why it is so important to the soul that these words turn out to be true, for if that soul were itself caught in some lies, I don't think it would regret the fact as much. And yet, there is nothing else it can do, for it merely says what it hears. Countless times, in this regard, a certain person thought of how the prophet Jonah feared that Nineveh would not be destroyed.[7] In sum, since the spirit is from God, it is right that the soul be faithful in its desire that the words be considered true, for God is the supreme truth. And so its happiness is great when through a thousand roundabout ways and in most difficult circumstances it sees them fulfilled. Even though great trials should come to the person herself from them, she would rather suffer such trials than the trial of seeing that what she knows for certain the Lord told her fails in fact to happen. Perhaps not all persons will have this weakness—if it is a weakness, for I cannot condemn it as bad.

10. If the locutions come from the imagination, there are none of these signs; neither certitude, nor peace, nor interior delight. But it could happen—and I even know some persons to whom it has happened—that while these imaginings come a person may be very absorbed in the prayer of quiet and spiritual sleep. Some have such a weak constitution and imagination, or I don't know the cause, that indeed in this deep recollection they are so outside themselves (for they don't feel anything exteriorly and all the senses are put to sleep) that they think as when they are asleep and dreaming (and perhaps it is true that they are asleep) that these locutions

---

7. See Jon 1 and 4. Though Teresa refers to Jonah about six times in her writings and could be referring to herself, she might, on the other hand, be thinking of Teresa de Layz, the benefactress of Alba, about whom she speaks in F 20, and especially in F 20.12.

are spoken to them and even that they see things. And they think these things are from God, but in the end the effects are like those of sleep. It can also happen that while with affection they are begging our Lord for something, they think the locution is telling them what they want to hear; this sometimes happens. But anyone who has had much experience of God's locutions will not be deceived by these that come, in my opinion, from the imagination.

11. With those locutions coming from the devil there is more to fear. But if the signs mentioned[8] are present, there can be a great deal of certainty that the locutions are from God. But the certainty shouldn't be so strong that if the locution concerns something serious about oneself and has to be carried out in deed, or business affairs involving third parties, anything should ever be done or pass through one's mind without the opinion of a learned and prudent confessor and servant of God. This is so even if the soul increasingly understands and thinks the locution is clearly from God. His Majesty wants the soul to consult in this way; and that it does so does not mean it is failing to carry out the Lord's commands, for He told us, where the words are undoubtedly His, to hold the confessor in His place.[9] And these words of His help to give courage if the task is a difficult one, and our Lord when He so desires will make the confessor believe that the locution comes from His spirit. If He doesn't, the confessor and the soul are no longer under obligation. To do otherwise and follow nothing but your own opinion in this, I hold to be very dangerous. And so, sisters, I warn you, on the part of our Lord, that you never let this happen to you.

---

8. In IC 6.3.5–7.
9. Allusion to Lk 10:16.

12. There is another way in which the Lord speaks to the soul—for I hold that it is very definitely from Him—with a certain intellectual vision, the nature of which I will explain further on.[10] The locution takes place in such intimate depths and a person with the ears of the soul seems to hear those words from the Lord Himself so clearly and so in secret that this very way in which they are heard, together with the acts that the vision itself produces, assures that person and gives him certitude that the devil can have no part to play in the locution. Wonderful effects are left so that the soul may believe; at least there is assurance that the locution doesn't come from the imagination. Furthermore, if the soul is attentive, it can always have assurance for the following reasons: First, there is a difference because of the clarity of the locution. It is so clear that the soul remembers every syllable and whether it is said in one style or another, even if it is a whole sentence. But in a locution fancied by the imagination the words will not be so clear or distinct but like something half-dreamed.

13. Second, in these locutions one often is not thinking about what is heard (I mean that the locution comes unexpectedly and even sometimes while one is in conversation), although many times it is a response to what passes quickly through the mind or to what did so previously. But it often refers to things about the future that never entered the mind, and so the imagination couldn't have fabricated it in such a way that the soul could be deceived in fancying what was not desired or wanted or thought of.

14. Third, the one locution comes as in the case of a person who hears, and that of the imagination comes as in the

---

10. She speaks of intellectual visions in IC 6.8 and 6.10; see also 6.5.8–9.

case of a person who gradually composes what he himself wants to be told.

15. Fourth, the words are very different, and with one of them much is comprehended. Our intellect could not compose them so quickly.

16. Fifth, together with the words, in a way I wouldn't know how to explain, [there is often given much more to understand than is ever dreamed possible without words.]

I shall speak more about this mode of understanding elsewhere,[11] for it is something very delicate and to the praise of our Lord. For in regard to these different kinds of locutions, there have been persons who were very doubtful and unable to understand themselves. A certain person, especially, experienced this doubt,[12] and so there will be others. And thus I know that she observed the differences with close attention because the Lord has often granted her this favor, and the greatest doubt she had in the beginning was whether she had imagined the locution. That the words come from the devil [can be more quickly understood] even though his wiles are so many, for he knows well how to counterfeit the Spirit of light. In my opinion the devil will say the words very clearly so that there will be certitude about their meaning, as is so with those coming from the Spirit of truth. But he will not be able to counterfeit the effects that were mentioned[13] or leave this peace or light in the soul; on the contrary he leaves restlessness and disturbance. But he can do little harm or none if the soul is humble and does what I have mentioned,[14] that is, doesn't make a move to do a thing of what he hears.

---

11. In IC 6.10; also in 6.4.
12. A reference to herself. See L 25.14–19.
13. In IC 6.3.12–16.
14. In IC 6.3.11.

17. If the locutions contain words of favor and consolation from the Lord, let the soul look attentively to see if
it thinks that because of them it is better than others. The
more it hears words of favor the more humble it should be
left; if it isn't, let it believe that the spirit is not from God.
One thing very certain is that when the spirit is from God
the soul esteems itself less, the greater the favor granted, and
it has more awareness of its sins and is more forgetful of its
own gain, and its will and memory are employed more in
seeking only the honor of God, nor does it think about its
own profit, and it walks with greater fear lest its will deviate
in anything, and with greater certitude that it never deserved
any of those favors but deserved hell. Since all the favors and
things it experienced in prayer produce these effects, the soul
does not walk fearfully but with confidence in the mercy of
the Lord, who is faithful[15] and will not let the devil deceive
it; although walking with fear is always good.

18. It could be that those whom the Lord does not lead
along this path think such souls could refuse to listen to these
words spoken to them—and, if the words are interior, distract
themselves in such a way that they not be admitted—and as a
result go about free of these dangers.

To this, I reply that it is impossible. I'm not speaking of
imaginary locutions, for by not being so desirous of a thing
or wanting to pay attention to their imaginings souls have a
remedy. In locutions from the Lord, they have none. For the
very spirit that speaks puts a stop to all other thoughts and
makes the soul attend to what is said. It does this in such a
way that I think, and I believe truly, that somehow it would
be more possible for a person with very good hearing not

---

15. Allusion to 1 Cor 10:13.

to hear someone else speaking in a loud voice. In this latter instance the person would be able to turn his attention away and center his mind and intellect on something else. But in the locution we are speaking about this cannot be done; there are no ears to stop, nor is there the power to think of anything but what is said to the soul. For He who was able to stop the sun (through Joshua's prayer, I believe)[16] can make the faculties and the whole interior stop in such a way that the soul sees clearly that another greater Lord than itself governs that castle. And this brings it deep devotion and humility. So there's no remedy for this kind of locution. May the divine Majesty provide a remedy that will enable us to place our eyes only on pleasing Him and to be forgetful of ourselves, as I said, amen.

Please God that I may have succeeded in explaining what I set out to; may it be helpful for whoever has had such experience.

---

16. Josh 10:12–13. See L 25.1.

THERE ARE MANY KINDS
OF LOCUTIONS

6.3.1–4 Teresa discusses locutions, which she says might seem a greater favor than some others she has mentioned, but which she says can be more dangerous. The danger is that the locution can be an illusion, especially in persons with a weak imagination, or in those who are melancholic. Teresa advises treating these types of persons kindly, but they should be told to pay no attention to the experiences.

Teresa says that locutions can be from God, from the devil, or from one's own imagination. Teresa warns that the safest path is to pay little attention to them.

6.3.6–7 Having said that paying little attention to locutions is the safest course, Teresa goes on to talk further about the locutions. She says the surest sign of authenticity is that the words effect what they say, and she gives several examples.

A second sign is the peace left in the soul along with a desire to praise God. A third sign is that the words remain in memory for a long time and the soul feels a certitude that in some way the words will be accomplished. But Teresa also seems to be working through her own experiences with locutions, where certitude alternated with doubts when events didn't follow as quickly as she had expected. She concludes that we must believe God has the power to do things that our intellects do not understand.

6.3.8–9 Teresa continues her thoughts about locutions. She repeats that they can be accompanied by certitude, even though the words of the locution seem to have described something that appears impossible. She says that the truth of the locutions is of great importance to the one who experiences them. Since the soul is very certain the words were from God, and since God is the supreme truth, the greatest trial would be that of seeing that the words she knows for certain the Lord told her were not ultimately fulfilled.

6.3.10 Teresa says that if locutions come from the imagination they won't be accompanied by certitude or peace or intense delight. Instead, some persons while deep in prayer may imagine locutions that tell them what they want to hear.

6.3.11 Teresa warns that there is more to fear if locutions are from the devil. The safest course is to consult one's confessor and never to act on locutions without such consultation. If the locution is from God, then God will make the confessor understand that it is true.

6.3.12–16 Teresa describes a locution in which the Lord speaks to the soul through an intellectual vision. The locution takes place in the intimate depths of the soul, and the person seems to hear the words with the ears of the soul, from the Lord himself. This type of locution is accompanied by certitude that it comes from God and also by wonderful effects left in the soul.

Teresa gives signs for discerning the authenticity of this type of locution. First, it is so clear that the soul remembers every syllable. Second, the locution comes unexpectedly and often refers to things about the future that the person never thought of. Third, the locution comes as something heard from another and is not simply composed in the mind to suit what a person wants to be told. Fourth, the words are very different, and with one of them much is comprehended. Finally, in a way Teresa says she can't fully explain, the person understands more than would be possible without words.

After giving these signs, Teresa adds that often these experiences are accompanied by doubts. She repeats what she said earlier (IC 6.3.11), that the safe path is not to act on any locution without consulting one's confessor.

6.3.17 Teresa states that humility is another sign of the authenticity of locutions and of other favors from God as well.

6.3.18 Teresa concludes her discussion of locutions by clarifying a point about them. Whereas in imagined locutions, as in ordinary conversation, a person can choose to be inattentive, locutions from the Lord cannot be ignored. God can command the soul's attention, and in seeing God's power, the soul is moved to deep devotion and humility.

Interpretive Notes

Words that are heard passively present a problem of discernment: What is their source? In fact, Teresa even says they can be dangerous. What are these words that I hear? Where do they come from? These are natural, healthy reactions of human beings. Through modern psychiatry and psychology, of which Teresa had no knowledge, much could be said about such experiences and their sources. But Teresa did have knowledge of the saints who heard words spoken by the Lord. Most famous among these was Paul of Tarsus, and among women there is the account of the well-known St. Joan of Arc, who heard voices and received messages for the salvation of France. But Teresa does also admit the fact that there are people who imagine these things—and she met some—for whom she uses the term "melancholic," a term often used for those with mental illness. Their locutions are an illusion, the result of what she calls a "weak imagination"—in fact, a very active imagination—that makes them think that everything they imagine really happens. Teresa is delicate in these matters. They should be told to pay no attention to such experiences, that these locutions are not essential to the service of God and that the devil has deceived many through them. But these persons should not be told that the source of what they hear is melancholy or there will be no end to the matter. They will insist over and over upon the truth of their hearing these words from God. One has to be firm with such persons even if it means taking prayer away from them.

This leads us to two different approaches, one of a religious person and the other of the psychiatrist. The religious person or theologian speaks freely of locutions or words from God, of a God who intervenes in history. God speaks to us not only through our ordinary meditations on the beauty of creation and the goodness of persons, but even by using our poor human words in a dialogue with human beings. In Scripture we hear Samuel petition the Lord: "Speak, Lord, for your servant is listening" (1 Sam 3:9); or in the prologue of Hebrews it is stated: "Long ago God spoke to our ancestors in many and various ways by the prophets" (Heb 1:1); or we read of episodes as real as that of St. Paul when he asks: "Who are you, Lord?" and he hears the words in reply: "I am Jesus, whom you are persecuting" (Acts 9:5). This is all normal and comprehensible for the Christian and the theologian from a basic presupposition: our religious life comes radically from revelation, through the words spoken to us by God.

For the psychiatrist or the scientist, it is different. We could even say it is diametrically opposed. Science, according to principle, restricts its investigation to the creature and its immanent laws. Anything that goes beyond the empirical either does not interest it, or is rejected by it, or is reduced to a paranormal phenomenon which is unexplainable today, but perhaps, through research, will be explained at a future date. Faced with the mystical phenomena reported by Teresa of Ávila, scientists would likely consider them to be part of a pathological alteration, more or less reducible to defects or known categories such as hysteria, epilepsy, or hallucinations. Thus the subject of locutions as described by Teresa in her *Interior Castle* presents us with a situation involving alternative choices: God, yes, or God, no. Or the one alternative: God for human beings, or God who exists for himself alone, who completely transcends the religious history of humankind. For Teresa, God has compassion on humans: God speaks, God loves, God saves.

In biblical history, God speaks at crucial moments. He speaks to chosen people, patriarchs, prophets, top leaders in salvation history. But this does not end with the *Book of Revelation*. God continues to speak, in the history of the Church as well, also to mystics and select prophets: Francis of Assisi, Catherine of Siena, Joan of Arc, and so on. For this reason, in her text, Teresa presents her discussion of locutions along two themes. In one theme she testifies that the Lord speaks to a person she knows. The second theme is theological: she defines how this comes about and assures us that these words from God differ clearly from hallucinations, manifesting all the suspicions that an expert psychiatrist or psychologist might show.

Once she has gotten beyond this, she needs to give testimony. She is convinced that at the heights of the spiritual life there are persons—mystics or prophets—to whom God speaks. He not only inspires them, but surprises them with his divine words.

It is important to note, however, that the words spoken by God to man can seem quite ordinary. The Dogmatic Constitution on Divine Revelation of the Second Vatican Council (*Dei Verbum*) states: "Indeed the words of God, expressed in the words of men, are in every way like human language, just as the Word of the eternal Father, when he took on himself the flesh of human weakness, became like men" (DV 13) (See also CCC 101).

Teresa in her work, then, brings to the reader two thematic lines of thought. In the first, she gives testimony that the Lord has spoken to her ("this person"), and her first mission is to testify to this. In the second, she must explain how this comes about. How can we be sure that the words come from God? Teresa has experienced this phenomenon herself and she is certain that at the heights of the spiritual life there are persons—mystics or prophets—to whom God directs his words. He does not just inspire them, but surprises them with his divine language. There are different ways in which God speaks to the soul: from the deep interior part, from the superior part, or from the exterior part. There are three signs that the words are from God. First is the power and authority the words carry with them; they effect what they say when they are from God. Second, they bring quiet and peace and recollection to the soul. Third, they remain fixed in the memory for a very long time. Some of his words are never forgotten. None of these signs are present when the locutions come from the imagination or, worse, from the devil. When the words are from God, there is given much more to understand than is ever dreamed possible without these words.

Questions for Discussion

1. How does God awaken the soul?
2. What are the different kinds of locutions?
3. What does Teresa mean by "those who are melancholic"?
4. Are locutions essential to the service of God?
5. How should one proceed in the matter of locutions?
6. What are the surest signs that locutions are from God?
7. What is a very certain sign that the favor is from God?
8. Can souls refuse to listen to words that come from the Lord?

CHAPTER 4

Treats of when God suspends the soul in prayer with rapture or ecstasy or transport, which are all the same in my opinion,[1] and how great courage is necessary to receive sublime favors from His Majesty.

With these trials and the other things that were mentioned, what kind of calm can the poor little butterfly have? All these sufferings are meant to increase one's desire to enjoy the Spouse. And His Majesty, as one who knows our weakness, is enabling the soul through these afflictions and many others to have the courage to be joined with so great a Lord and to take Him as its Spouse.[2]

2. You will laugh at my saying this and will think it's foolishness; it will seem to any one of you that such courage is unnecessary and that there's no woman so miserable who wouldn't have the courage to be married to the king. I believe this is true with respect to kings here on earth; but with respect to the King of Heaven, I tell you there is need for more courage than you think. Our nature is very timid and lowly when it comes to something so great, and I am certain that if God were not to give the courage, no matter how much you might see that the favor is good for us, it would be impossible for you to receive that favor. And thus you will see what His Majesty does to conclude this betrothal, which I

---

1. Regarding this terminology see L 20.1; ST 59.9.

2. The need for great courage in order to receive these mystical graces is often stated by Teresa. See L 13.2; 20.4; 39.21; ST 59.9; W 18; and in IC 6.5.1, 5, 12; 6.11.11.

understand comes about when He gives the soul raptures that draw it out of its senses. For if it were to see itself so near this great Majesty while in its senses, it would perhaps die. Let it be understood that I mean true raptures and not the weaknesses women experience here below, for everything seems to us to be a rapture or an ecstasy. And, as I believe I have said,[3] some have constitutions so weak that the prayer of quiet is enough to make them die.

I want to put down here some kinds of rapture that I've come to understand because I've discussed them with so many spiritual persons. But I don't know whether I shall succeed as I did when I wrote elsewhere about them[4] and other things that occur in this dwelling place. On account of certain reasons it seems worthwhile to speak of these kinds of rapture again, and, if for no other reason, so that everything related to these dwelling places will be put down here together.

3. One kind of rapture is that in which the soul, even though not in prayer, is touched by some word it remembers or hears about God. It seems that His Majesty from the interior of the soul makes the spark we mentioned[5] increase, for He is moved with compassion in seeing the soul suffer so long a time from its desire. All burnt up, the soul is renewed like the phoenix, and one can devoutly believe that its faults are pardoned. Now that it is so pure, the Lord joins it with Himself, without anyone understanding what is happening except these two; nor does the soul itself understand in a way that can afterward be explained. Yet, it does have interior understanding, for this experience is not like that of fainting

3. In IC 4.3.11–12; 6.3.10.
4. In L 20; ST 59.9.
5. In IC 6.2.4.

or convulsion; in these latter nothing is understood inwardly or outwardly.

4. What I know in this case is that the soul was never so awake to the things of God nor did it have such deep enlightenment and knowledge of His Majesty. This will seem impossible, for if the faculties are so absorbed that we can say they are dead, and likewise the senses, how can a soul know that it understands this secret? I don't know, nor perhaps does any creature but only the Creator. And this goes for many other things that take place in this state—I mean in these two dwelling places, [for there is no closed door between the one and the other.] Because there are things in the last that are not revealed to those who have not yet reached it, I thought I should divide them.

5. When the soul is in this suspension, the Lord likes to show it some secrets, things about heaven, and imaginative visions. It is able to tell of them afterward, for these remain so impressed on the memory that they are never forgotten. But when the visions are intellectual, the soul doesn't know how to speak of them. For there must be some visions during these moments that are so sublime that it's not fitting for those who live on this earth to have the further understanding necessary to explain them. However, when the soul is again in possession of its senses, it can say many things about these intellectual visions.

It could be that some of you do not know what a vision is, especially an intellectual one. I shall explain at the proper time,[6] for one who has the authority ordered me to do so.[7]

---

6. In IC 6.8, she will deal with intellectual visions and in 6.9, with imaginative ones.

7. Father Gracián; see IC Intro.

And although the explanation may not seem pertinent, it will perhaps benefit some souls.

6. Well, now you will ask me: if afterward there is to be no remembrance of these sublime favors granted by the Lord to the soul in this state, what benefit do they have? Oh, daughters, they are so great one cannot exaggerate! For even though they are unexplainable, they are well inscribed in the very interior part of the soul and are never forgotten.

But, you will insist, if there is no image and the faculties do not understand, how can the visions be remembered? I don't understand this either; but I do understand that some truths about the grandeur of God remain so fixed in this soul, that even if faith were not to tell it who God is and of its obligation to believe that He is God, from that very moment it would adore Him as God, as did Jacob when he saw the ladder. By means of the ladder Jacob must have understood other secrets that he didn't know how to explain, for by seeing just a ladder on which angels descended and ascended he would not have understood such great mysteries if there had not been deeper interior enlightenment.[8] I don't know if I'm guessing right in what I say, for although I have heard this story about Jacob, I don't know if I'm remembering it correctly.

7. Nor did Moses know how to describe all that he saw in the bush, but only what God wished him to describe.[9] But if God had not shown secrets to his soul along with a certitude that made him recognize and believe that they were from God, Moses could not have entered into so many severe trials. But he must have understood such deep things among the thorns of that bush that the vision gave him the courage to do

8. See Gen 28:12.
9. See Ex 3:1–16.

what he did for the people of Israel. So, sisters, we don't have to look for reasons to understand the hidden things of God. Since we believe He is powerful, clearly we must believe that a worm with as limited a power as ours will not understand His grandeurs. Let us praise Him, for He is pleased that we come to know some of them.

8. I have been wanting to find some comparison by which to explain what I'm speaking about, and I don't think there is any that fits. But let's use this one: you enter into the room of a king or great lord, or I believe they call it the treasure chamber, where there are countless kinds of glass and earthen vessels and other things so arranged that almost all these objects are seen upon entering. Once I was brought to a room like this in the house of the duchess of Alba where, while I was on a journey, obedience ordered me to stay because of this lady's insistence with my superiors.[10] I was amazed on entering and wondered what benefit could be gained from the conglomeration of things, and I saw that one could praise the Lord at seeing so many different kinds of objects, and now I laugh to myself upon realizing how the experience has helped me here in my explanation. Although I was in that room for a while, there was so much there to see that I soon forgot it all; none of those pieces has remained in my memory any more than if I had never seen them, nor would I know how to explain the workmanship of any of them. I can only say in general that I remember seeing everything. Likewise with this favor, the soul, while it is made one with God, is placed in this room of the empyreal heaven that we must have interiorly. For clearly, the soul has some of these dwelling places since God abides within it. And although the Lord must not want the soul to

---

10. This happened sometime during the first months of 1574. See F 20.1–2.

see these secrets every time it is in this ecstasy, for it can be so absorbed in enjoying Him that a sublime good like that is sufficient for it, sometimes He is pleased that the absorption decrease and the soul see at once what is in that room. After it returns to itself, the soul is left with that representation of the grandeurs it saw; but it cannot describe any of them, nor do its natural powers attain to any more than what God wished that it see supernaturally.

9. You, therefore, might object that I admit that the soul sees and that the vision is an imaginative one. But I'm not saying that, for I'm not dealing with an imaginative vision but with an intellectual one. Since I have no learning, I don't know how in my dullness to explain anything. If what I have said up to now about this prayer is worthwhile, I know clearly that I'm not the one who has said it.

I hold that if at times in its raptures the soul doesn't understand these secrets, its raptures are not given by God but caused by some natural weakness. It can happen to persons with a weak constitution, as is so with women, that any spiritual force will overcome the natural powers, and the soul will be absorbed, as I believe I mentioned in reference to the prayer of quiet.[11] These experiences have nothing to do with rapture. In a rapture, believe me, God carries off for Himself the entire soul, and, as to someone who is His own and His spouse, He begins showing it some little part of the kingdom that it has gained by being espoused to Him. However small that part of His kingdom may be, everything that there is in this great God is magnificent. And He doesn't want any hindrance from anyone, neither from the faculties nor from the senses, but he immediately commands the doors of all these

---

11. In IC 4.3.11–13.

dwelling places to be closed; and only that door to His dwelling place remains open so that we can enter. Blessed be so much mercy; they will be rightly cursed who have not wanted to benefit by it and who have lost this Lord.

10. Oh, my sisters, what nothingness it is, that which we leave! Nor is what we do anything, nor all that we could do for a God who thus wishes to communicate Himself to a worm! And if we hope to enjoy this blessing even in this present life, what are we doing? What is causing us to delay? What is enough to make us, even momentarily, stop looking for this Lord as the bride looked for Him in the streets and in the squares?[12] Oh, what a mockery everything in the world is if it doesn't lead us and help us toward this blessing even if its delights and riches and joys, as much of them as imaginable, were to last forever! It is all loathsome dung compared to these treasures that will be enjoyed without end. Nor are these anything in comparison with having as our own the Lord of all the treasures of heaven and earth.

11. Oh, human blindness! How long, how long before this dust will be removed from our eyes! Even though among ourselves the dust doesn't seem to be capable of blinding us completely, I see some specks, some tiny pebbles that, if we allow them to increase, will be enough to do us great harm. On the contrary, for the love of God, sisters, let us benefit by these faults so as to know our misery, and they will give us clearer vision as did the mud to the blind man cured by our Spouse.[13] Thus, seeing ourselves so imperfect, let us increase our supplications that His Majesty may draw good out of our miseries so that we might be pleasing to Him.

---

12. Allusion to Song 3:2.
13. Allusion to Jn 9:6–7.

12. I have digressed a great deal without realizing it. Pardon me, sisters, and believe me that having reached these grandeurs of God (I mean, reached the place where I must speak of them), I cannot help but feel very sorry to see what we lose through our own fault. Even though it is true that these are blessings the Lord gives to whomever He wills, His Majesty would give them all to us if we loved Him as He loves us. He doesn't desire anything else than to have those to whom to give. His riches do not lessen when He gives them away.

13. Well now, to get back to what I was saying,[14] the Spouse commands that the doors of the dwelling places be closed and even those of the castle and the outer wall. For in desiring to carry off this soul, He takes away the breath so that, even though the other senses sometimes last a little longer, a person cannot speak at all; although at other times everything is taken away at once, and the hands and the body grow cold so that the person doesn't seem to have any life; nor sometimes is it known whether he is breathing. This situation lasts but a short while, I mean in its intensity; for when this extreme suspension lets up a little, it seems that the body returns to itself somewhat and is nourished so as to die again and give more life to the soul. Nevertheless so extreme an ecstasy doesn't last long.

14. But it will happen that even though the extreme ecstasy ends, the will remains so absorbed and the intellect so withdrawn, for a day and even days, that the latter seems incapable of understanding anything that doesn't lead to awakening the will to love; and the will is wide awake to this love and asleep to becoming attached to any creature.]

14. In IC 6.4.9.

15. Oh, when the soul returns completely to itself, what bewilderment and how intense its desires to be occupied in God in every kind of way He might want! If the effects that were mentioned were produced by the former kinds of prayer, what will be the effects of a favor as sublime as this? The soul would desire to have a thousand lives so as to employ them all for God and that everything here on earth would be a tongue to help it praise Him. The desires to do penance are most strong, but not much help comes from performing it, because the strength of love makes the soul feel that all that is done amounts to little and see clearly that the martyrs did not accomplish much in suffering the torments they did because with this help from our Lord, such suffering is easy. Hence these souls complain to His Majesty when no opportunity for suffering presents itself.

16. When this favor is granted them in secret, their esteem for it is great; when it is given in the presence of other persons, their embarrassment and shame are so strong that the pain and worry over what those who saw it will think somehow take the soul away from what was being enjoyed.[15] For these persons know the malice of the world, and they understand that the world will not perhaps regard the experience for what it is, but that what the Lord should be praised for will perhaps be the occasion for rash judgments. In some ways it seems to me that this pain and embarrassment amount to a lack of humility, for if this person desires to be reviled, what difference does it make what others think? But the soul cannot control such feelings. One who was in this affliction heard from the Lord: "Don't be afflicted; either they will praise Me or criticize you, and in

---

15. See L 20.5.

either case you gain."[16] I learned afterward that this person was very much consoled and encouraged by these words, and I put them down here in case one of you might find herself in this affliction. It seems that our Lord wishes all to understand that that soul is now His, that no one should touch it. Well and good if its body, or honor, or possessions are touched, for this soul draws honor for His Majesty out of everything. But that one touch the soul—absolutely not; for if the soul does not withdraw from its Spouse through a very culpable boldness, He will protect it from the whole world and even from all hell.

17. I don't know if anything has been explained about the nature of rapture, for to explain it is completely impossible, as I have said.[17] But I don't believe anything has been lost by trying. For there are effects that are very different in feigned raptures. I do not say "feigned" because the one who has the experience wants to deceive but because that person is deceived. And since the signs and effects of the feigned raptures are not in conformity with such a great blessing, the true rapture is looked upon unfavorably; and afterward the one to whom the Lord grants it, justifiably is not believed. May He be blessed and praised forever, amen, amen.

---

16. She is alluding to herself. See L 31.13.
17. In IC 6.4.4–5.

GOD CONCLUDES
THE BETROTHAL WHEN HE
GIVES THE SOUL ECSTASY

6.4.1–2 Teresa returns to her metaphor of the butterfly. She explains that the favors which she has described earlier are experienced as afflictions in the sense that they cause great suffering by increasing the soul's desires for God. These afflictions strengthen the soul so that it will have the courage to be joined to the Lord and take him as its Spouse.

She further explains why courage is necessary. The timidity of our nature when confronted with the greatness of God is such that if God did not grant courage it would be impossible to receive the favor of the type of union she describes here, a type she calls rapture.

Teresa says that the spiritual betrothal comes about when God gives the soul raptures that draw it out of its senses. She thinks that this going out of the senses is necessary, for if the soul were to see itself so near to His Majesty while in its senses, it might die. As with other experiences, Teresa cautions against false raptures. She says that she thinks it worthwhile to describe certain types of raptures, even though she has spoken of them elsewhere.

6.4.3 Teresa describes a rapture in which a spark is increased within the soul, even though it is not in prayer. The soul, which was, to use Teresa's metaphor, all burnt up, is now renewed, and Teresa believes its sins are pardoned. In this rapture the Lord joins the soul with himself in a way that the soul understands to be true, but cannot afterward explain.

She contrasts this experience with fainting or convulsion, in which nothing is understood inwardly or outwardly.

6.4.4 Here Teresa begins to elaborate on her description of rapture. She says the soul was never before so awake to the things of God, nor did it ever before have such deep enlightenment and knowledge of His Majesty. The extent to which God reveals himself in secret to the soul is so all-absorbing that persons in this rapture, without losing consciousness as in a faint, are totally unaware of everything exterior. A person in this state doesn't engage in thought; this deep knowledge of God comes in a way that is distinct from ordinary ways of knowing.

6.4.5 Teresa says there are two types of visions that can be experienced in this rapture. Imaginative visions are one type. These can be told about in detail afterward because the visions are impressed on the memory in such a way that they are never forgotten. The second type of vision Teresa calls an intellectual vision. At first reading, her description of this type of vision seems to contain contradictions. She says the soul doesn't know how to speak of them, but then says that when the soul regains its senses it can say many things about the visions. Later she provides some clarification.

6.4.6–8 Readers of this section are confronted with two ways Teresa uses the concept of remembering. In the first sentence of the first paragraph of number six in this chapter, Teresa says that there is no remembrance afterward of the favors. But in the last sentence of this same paragraph she says that even though the favors are unexplainable, they are inscribed in the interior part of the soul and never forgotten.

In the remaining part of number six and in numbers seven and eight, Teresa uses examples from Scripture and from her own experience to help us understand a secret way that God can share knowledge of himself. Her example of seeing the duchess of Alba's treasure room helps us understand how a person can possess a general knowledge of a truth (in this example, the truth that the duchess possesses countless treasures and great wealth) without being able to provide supporting details that would let another person evaluate the knowledge or even allow the person to whom the intellectual vision came to reconstruct the experience in memory. What remains is the certain knowledge conveyed by the vision. This type of experience—where the soul knows it has received a wonderful favor from God but is unable to provide specific details about it—Teresa calls an intellectual vision. She contrasts this type of vision with imaginative visions, in which the soul sees clearly and is able to give details of the vision.

6.4.9–11 Teresa contrasts authentic raptures with other, merely natural experiences where nothing is learned. And she holds that if at times the soul in its rapture doesn't understand these secrets, its raptures are not given by God. She pauses in her description to remind us how great a favor raptures are. She says we should remember our faults. Seeing ourselves as imperfect, we should pray that God may draw good out of our miseries.

6.4.12 Teresa feels sorry at the blessings we lose through our own fault. She says the Lord loves to give his gifts, and his riches are not diminished when he gives them away.

6.4.13–14 Teresa describes some of the physical effects of ecstasy. A person may remain absorbed for some days after the extreme ecstasy ends, but the will is always engaged in love and unattached to any creature.

6.4.15 Teresa says that when the soul returns completely to itself, it has intense desires to be occupied in God in every

way that he might want. The soul has a desire to do penance
and to suffer.

6.4.16 Teresa says that although persons could suffer
embarrassment at being in the ecstatic state in public, they
should try to overcome these feelings. She reports what the
Lord told someone (referring in a veiled way to herself):
"Don't be afflicted; either they will praise Me or criticize you,
and in either case you gain." She adds that through the malice of the world, a person may suffer damage to body, honor,
or possessions, but God will protect the soul from all harm.

6.4.17 Teresa concludes her description of the nature of
raptures by wondering if she has explained it well enough,
for she says that even though she believes her description of
raptures is inadequate, she thinks the effort and what she has
been able to convey are worthwhile because they will help
in discerning between true and feigned raptures. She emphasizes that persons who experience feigned raptures are not
trying to deceive others; rather, they are the ones who are
deceived in believing that their experiences are true raptures.
Teresa says that the confusion between the two, and especially the effects of feigned raptures, are the cause for true
raptures being looked upon unfavorably by those who cannot
discern the difference.

Interpretive Notes

Around 1557, Teresa experienced her first ecstasy while living at the monastery of the Incarnation in Ávila. She was
forty-two years old at the time. About three or four years previous to this experience she underwent a conversion before a
"very devotional" statue of "the much wounded Christ." It
was a moment in which she, "being very distrustful of myself,

placed all my trust in God" (L 9.3). Although she went on improving, she still was not able to center her scattered heart entirely on the Lord. On the advice of her confessor, Juan de Prádanos, S.J., she began to commend the matter to God and recite a prayer to the Holy Spirit, the *Veni Creator Spiritus*. One day while reciting the hymn, after having spent a long time in prayer, "begging the Lord to help me please him in all things," a rapture "came upon me so suddenly that it almost carried me out of myself." It was the first time the Lord granted her that favor of rapture. And she heard these words deep within her spirit: "No longer do I want you to converse with men but with angels" (L 24.5–6). These words had a healing effect on her and cured her definitively of her affective weaknesses, and left her pure for what she later called in her *Interior Castle* "the betrothal of the soul with God" (IC 6.4.2). Now twenty years later, she takes up this topic of ecstasy once more, this time in a strictly doctrinal plan in these sixth dwelling places.

Today, the word "ecstasy" causes us to think of the world of drugs, something unforeseen in Teresa's time, and often creates serious suspicions in the minds of theologians and psychologists. Do such experiences, as Teresa describes them, really take place? But these pages of Teresa's perhaps bring the reader most directly to the zone of the supernatural: the Holy Spirit of God passing through human space. We can recall the attitude of the theologian Domingo Báñez when he was giving a talk on the Blessed Trinity to the community of nuns at St. Joseph's in Ávila. While he was doing so, Teresa fell into ecstasy; he interrupted his talk, uncovered his head, remained silent, and adored the Holy Spirit who was passing through her.

We ought, then, to define the meaning of the word "ecstasy" as used by St. Teresa: "I should like to know how to explain, with God's help, the difference there is between union and rapture, or as they call it, elevation of the spirit, or transport, which are all the same. I mean these latter terms, though different, refer to the same thing; it is also called ecstasy" (L 20.1). In her spiritual testimony she explains more:

> The difference between rapture and union is this: the rapture lasts longer and is felt more exteriorly, for your breathing diminishes in such a way that you are unable to speak or open your eyes. Although this diminishing of these bodily powers occurs in union, it takes place in this prayer with greater force, because the natural heat leaves the body, going I don't know where. When the rapture is intense (for in all these kinds of prayer there is a more and a less), when it is greater, as I say, the hands are frozen and sometimes stretched out like sticks, and the body remains as it is, either standing or kneeling. And the soul is so occupied with rejoicing in what the Lord represents to it that it seemingly forgets to animate the body and leaves the body abandoned. (ST 59.7)

The Spanish dictionary gives one of its definitions of ecstasy thus: "A state of soul, characterized by a certain mystical union with God by means of contemplation and love, and exteriorly through the suspension greater or less of the use of the senses." Webster's dictionary defines ecstasy in this manner: "an exalted state resembling a trance in which contemplation of what inspires the exaltation makes one oblivious of all else." Or rapture, it explains, "is a mystical phenomena in which the soul is borne out of itself and exalted to a knowledge of divine things." These are the religious meanings in which Teresa uses the word "ecstasy."

In chapter 6 of *The Book of Her Foundations*, Teresa explains a great deal about false ecstasies or seeming ecstasies. She writes:

> It must be noted that in rapture the power that takes away our power to be in control of ourselves lasts but a short while. But frequently it happens that there begins a kind of prayer of quiet, something that resembles spiritual sleep, that so absorbs the soul that if we do not understand how one is to proceed therein, much time could be lost and our strength diminished through our own fault and with little merit. (F 6.1)

She goes on to explain how some souls "of great virtue" she knew remained seven or eight hours in a kind of absorption:

> What I understand about this occurrence is that since the Lord begins to give delight, and our nature is very fond of delight, the soul becomes so occupied in the pleasure that it does not want to stir or lose that experience for anything. Indeed the pleasure is greater than any of the world's pleasures. And when the experience takes place in a weak nature, or comes from one's own natural inventiveness (or better, imagination), nature will make souls know a thousand delightful lies. (F 6.2)

Since the absorption and the rapture are the same in appearance, what is the difference? In rapture or union,

> of all the faculties, as I say, the duration is short, and great effects, interior light, and many other benefits are given, and the intellect doesn't work; it is the Lord who works in the will. In the absorption, things are very different, for although the body is captive, the will is not, nor is

the memory or the intellect. But these faculties carry on their delirious activity, and if they rest in something they will perhaps go back and forth over it with ifs and buts. I find no benefit in this bodily weakness. . . . It would be a greater help to use this time well than to remain in this absorption so long. (F 6.4–5)

Clearly, then, the ecstasy carries with it much interior light and never was it so awake to the divine things given to the soul by God as during this time.

But why is there a need in the spiritual life for the experience of ecstasy? The answer to this question, so normal for a utilitarian American, is given to us by Teresa. In addition to its work of increasing the desire of the soul to enjoy its Spouse, ecstasy is more than a corrective of our natural insufficiency; it is an overcoming of our limited natural being. "Our nature is very timid and lowly when it comes to something so great" (the experience of God), "and I am certain that if God were not to give the courage . . . it would be impossible for you to receive that favor" (IC 6.4.2). That is, you cannot receive the favor of God's nearness without passing through the fire of ecstasy. If the soul "were to see itself so near this great Majesty while in its senses, it would perhaps die" (IC 6.4.2). And the effects of this experience are also profound:

Oh, when the soul returns completely to itself, what bewilderment and how intense its desires to be occupied in God in every kind of way He might want! If the effects that were mentioned were produced by the former kinds of prayer what will be the effects of a favor as sublime as this? The soul would desire to have a thousand lives so as to employ them all for God and that everything here below would be a tongue to help it praise Him. . . . The strength of love makes the soul feel that all that is done amounts to little and see clearly that the martyrs did not accomplish much in suffering the torments they did because with this help from our Lord, such suffering is easy. Hence these souls complain to His Majesty when no opportunity for suffering presents itself. (IC 6.4.15)

As a result, the grace of ecstasy is merely a passing one. It prepares the human subject in its advance toward the final plenitude of the seventh dwelling places. In these sixth dwelling places the experience of ecstasy is frequent, and there is no means to avoid them. Not until it reaches the seventh dwelling places are all raptures taken away (IC 7.3.12). Teresa inserts this delicate matter of mystical ecstasy within the context of the complex and progressive development of the spiritual life of the believer. Outside this context, this jewel could not be evaluated nor would it even be comprehensible.

Questions for Discussion

1. Why is ecstasy necessary?
2. Are there false ecstasies?
3. What are the characteristics of a true ecstasy?
4. Does this topic have anything to say to me, or is it completely alien to my experience?
5. Does the soul eventually move on from experiencing ecstasies?

CHAPTER 5

Continues on the same subject and deals with a kind of rapture in which God raises up the soul through a flight of the spirit, an experience different from that just explained. Tells why courage is necessary. Explains something about this delightful favor the Lord grants. The chapter is a very beneficial one.

There is another kind of rapture—I call it flight of the spirit—which, though substantially the same as other raptures, is interiorly experienced very differently.[1] For sometimes suddenly a movement of the soul is felt so swift that it seems the spirit is carried off, and at a fearful speed especially in the beginning. This is why I have told you[2] that strong courage is necessary for the one to whom God grants these favors, and even faith and confidence and a full surrender to our Lord so that He may do what He wants with the soul. Do you think it is a small disturbance for a person to be very much in his senses and see his soul carried off (and in the case of some, we have read, even the body with the soul) without knowing where that soul is going, what or who does this, or how? At the beginning of this swift movement there is not so much certitude that the rapture is from God.[3]

2. Well, now, is there some means by which one can resist it? None at all; rather, to resist makes matters worse,

---

1. On the difference between rapture and flight of the spirit see L 18.7; 20.1; ST 59.9–10.

2. In IC 6.4.1.

3. See the account of her personal experience in L 20.3–7.

for I know this was so with a certain person.[4] It seems God wishes that the soul that has so often, so earnestly, and with such complete willingness offered everything to Him should understand that in itself it no longer has any part to play; and it is carried off with a noticeably more impetuous movement. It is determined now to do no more than what the straw does when drawn by the amber—if you have noticed—and abandon itself into the hands of the One who is all powerful, for it sees that the safest thing to do is to make a virtue of necessity. And that I mentioned a straw is certainly appropriate, for as easily as a huge giant snatches up a straw, this great and powerful Giant of ours carries away the spirit.[5]

3. It seems the trough of water we mentioned (I believe it was in the fourth dwelling place, for I don't recall exactly)[6] filled so easily and gently, I mean without any movement. Here this great God, who holds back the springs of water and doesn't allow the sea to go beyond its boundaries,[7] lets loose the springs from which the water in this trough flows. With a powerful impulse, a huge wave rises up so forcefully that it lifts high this little bark that is our soul. A bark cannot prevent the furious waves from leaving it where they will; nor does the pilot have the power, nor do those who take part in controlling the little ship. So much less can the interior part of the soul stay where it will, or make its senses or faculties do other than what they are commanded; here the soul doesn't care what happens in the exterior senses.

---

4. She is speaking of herself; see L 20.5–6.

5. For parallel passages see L 22.13; 20.4.

6. In IC 4.2.2–5.

7. Allusion to Prov 8:29.

4. It is certain, sisters, that just from writing about it I am amazed at how the immense power of this great King and Emperor is shown here. What will be the amazement of the one who experiences it! I hold that if His Majesty were to reveal this power to those who go astray in the world as He does to these souls, the former would not dare offend Him; this out of fear if not out of love. Oh, how obliged, then, will those persons be who have been informed through so sublime a path to strive with all their might not to displease this Lord! For love of Him, sisters, I beg you, those of you to whom His Majesty has granted these favors, or others like them, that you don't grow careless and do nothing but receive. ⌈Reflect that the one who owes a lot must pay a lot.[8]⌉

5. In this respect, too, great courage is necessary, for this favor is something frightening. If our Lord were not to give such courage, the soul would always go about deeply distressed. For it reflects on what His Majesty does for it and turns back to look at itself, at how little it serves in comparison with its obligation, and at how the tiny bit it does is full of faults, failures, and weaknesses. So as not to recall how imperfectly it performs some work—if it does—it prefers striving to forget its works, keeping in mind its sins, and placing itself before the mercy of God. Since it doesn't have anything with which to pay, it begs for the pity and mercy God has always had toward sinners.

6. Perhaps He will respond as He did to a person who before a crucifix was reflecting with deep affliction that she had never had anything to give to God, or anything to give up for Him. The Crucified, Himself, in consoling her told her He had given her all the sufferings and trials He had

---

8. Allusion to Lk 12:48.

undergone in His passion so that she could have them as her own to offer His Father.[9] The comfort and enrichment was such that, according to what I have heard from her, she cannot forget the experience. Rather, every time she sees how miserable she is, she gets encouragement and consolation from remembering those words.

I could mention here some other experiences like this, for since I have dealt with so many holy and prayerful persons, I know about many such experiences; but I want to limit myself lest you think I am speaking of myself. What I said seems to me very beneficial to help you understand how pleased our Lord is that we know ourselves and strive to reflect again and again on our poverty and misery and on how we possess nothing that we have not received. So, my sisters, courage is necessary for this knowledge and for the many other graces given to the soul the Lord has brought to this stage. And when there is humility, courage, in my opinion, is even more necessary for this knowledge of one's own misery. May the Lord give us this humility because of who He is.

7. Well, now, to return to this quick rapture of the spirit.[10] It is such that the spirit truly seems to go forth from the body. On the other hand, it is clear that this person is not dead; at least, he cannot say whether for some moments he was in the body or not. It seems to him that he was entirely in another region different from this in which we live, where there is shown another light so different from earth's light that if he were to spend his whole life trying to imagine that light, along with the other things, he would be unable to do

---

9. She is speaking of herself. See ST 46.

10. She returns to the theme taken up in IC 6.5.1.

so. It happens that within an instant so many things together
are taught him that if he were to work for many years with
his imagination and mind in order to systematize them he
wouldn't be able to do so, not with even one-thousandth part
of one of them. This is not an intellectual but an imaginative
vision, for the eyes of the soul see much better than do we
with bodily eyes here on earth, and without words understanding of some things is given; I mean that if a person sees
some saints, he knows them as well as if he had often spoken
with them.

8. At other times, along with the things seen through the
eyes of the soul by an intellectual vision, other things are represented, especially a multitude of angels with their Lord.
And without seeing anything with the eyes of the body or the
soul, through an admirable knowledge I will not be able to
explain, there is represented what I'm saying and many other
things not meant to be spoken of. Anyone who experiences
them, and has more ability than I, will perhaps know how
to explain them; although doing so seems to me very difficult indeed. Whether all this takes place in the body or not,
I wouldn't know; at least I wouldn't swear that the soul is in
the body or that the body is without the soul.[11]

9. I have often thought that just as the sun while in the
sky has such strong rays that, even though it doesn't move
from there, the rays promptly reach the earth, so the soul and
the spirit, which are one,[12] could be like the sun and its rays.
Thus, while the soul remains in its place, the superior part
rises above it. In a word, I don't know what I'm saying. What

11. Allusion to 2 Cor 12:2–4.
12. Concerning the distinction between the soul and the spirit, see IC 7.1.11; ST
59.11; 25.1; L 20.14.

is true is that with the speed of a ball shot from an arque-
bus, when fire is applied, an interior flight is experienced—I
don't know what else to call it—which, though noiseless,
is so clearly a movement that it cannot be the work of the
imagination. And while the spirit is far outside itself, from
all it can understand, great things are shown to it. When it
again senses that it is within itself, the benefits it feels are
remarkable, and it has so little esteem for all earthly things
in comparison to the things it has seen that the former seem
like dung. From then on its life on earth is very painful, and
it doesn't see anything good in those things that used to seem
good to it. The experience causes it to care little about them.
It seems the Lord, like those Israelites who brought back
signs from the promised land,[13] has desired to show it something about its future land so that it may suffer the trials of
this laborious path, knowing where it must go to get its final
rest. Even though something that passes so quickly will not
seem to you very beneficial, the blessings left in the soul are
so great that only the person who has this experience will be
able to understand its value.

10. Wherefore, the experience, obviously, is not from the
devil; it would be impossible for the imagination or the devil
to represent things that leave so much virtue, peace, calm,
and improvement in the soul. Three things, especially, are left
in it to a very sublime degree: knowledge of the grandeur of
God, because the more we see in this grandeur the greater is
our understanding; self-knowledge and humility upon seeing
that something so low in comparison with the Creator of so
many grandeurs dared to offend Him (and neither does the
soul dare look up at Him); the third, little esteem of earthly

13. Num 13:18–27.

things save for those that can be used for the service of so great a God.

11. These are the jewels the Spouse begins to give the betrothed, and their value is such that the soul will not want to lose them. For these meetings[14] remain so engraved in the memory that I believe it's impossible to forget them until one enjoys them forever, unless they are forgotten through one's own most serious fault. But the Spouse who gives them has the power to give the grace not to lose them.

12. Well, to get back to the courage that is necessary,[15] does it seem to you that this is so trivial a thing? For it truly seems that because the soul loses its senses, and doesn't understand why, that it is separated from the body. It's necessary that He who gives everything else give the courage also. You will say that this fear is well paid. So do I. May it please His Majesty to give us the courage so that we may merit to serve Him, amen.

---

14. She continues to use the symbolic language (jewels and meetings) introduced in IC 5.4.3.

15. See IC 6.5.1–5; 6.4.1–2.

FLIGHT OF THE SPIRIT

6.5.1–3 Teresa intends in this chapter to explain another kind of rapture that she calls a "flight of the spirit." She says that while persons are very much in their senses, they can experience a sudden, swift movement of the soul so that it seems that the spirit is carried off. The soul is completely passive in the experience, and Teresa compares the soul to a straw attracted to amber through static electricity. To describe the intensity and powerful nature of this experience, Teresa uses the example of great waves of water that cannot be resisted.

6.5.4–6 Teresa shares her awe at the power of God experienced in this flight of the spirit. She thinks anyone who experiences it would not dare to offend God. This experience can cause powerful feelings in the soul. The soul feels tremendous gratitude, a sense of obligation to serve, and awareness of its own weakness and imperfections. Teresa says there is particularly an awareness of one's poverty, of having nothing to give or to give up for God. An answer to this problem came to her as she reflected before a crucifix. The Lord told her that she could have all his sufferings and trials to offer to the Father. Teresa took great comfort from this experience.

6.5.7–8 Teresa returns to her description of rapture of the spirit (called "flight of the spirit" in the first paragraph of this chapter). She says that in this rapture, persons are not sure whether they are in or out of the body. They seem to be in another region of extraordinary light where many things are taught to them. These things are experienced as imaginative visions. Understanding is given without words. She says that at other times the soul experiences intellectual visions, and without seeing anything with the eyes of the body or the soul, knowledge is represented in a way Teresa can't explain.

6.5.9–12 Teresa attempts to clarify further what she understands of flights of the spirit, but finds comparisons inadequate. She rephrases some of the things she stated earlier about how the spirit is taken outside itself and shown great things. When the soul recovers, it feels great benefits and values earthly things very little in comparison to the things it has seen, and she says life on earth afterward is very painful. Even so, the soul is left with great blessings. It is these blessings that give assurance that the experience was from God because the devil could not give such gifts. Teresa concludes by calling these experiences jewels that the Spouse begins to give the betrothed. She says these meetings remain engraved in the memory unless they are forgotten through one's own serious fault, but the one who gives them has the power to give the grace not to lose them. Teresa gives one final reminder about the courage necessary to receive this favor.

Interpretive Notes

In a way, Teresa's experience of ecstasy as explained in the previous chapter was an experience of going deep within herself, where she went beyond herself and entered into the orbit of the divine. In fact, in *The Interior Castle*, which symbolizes the soul, she will explain in the last dwelling places, the deepest of the human spirit, that the soul borders on the divine. God has reserved these seventh dwelling places for himself. He dwells in them.

Now, in these sixth dwelling places, another kind of ecstasy takes place, not by going within oneself but by going outside. The soul is taken out of itself and elevated to the divine. The biblical passage that supports Teresa's explanation of this experience is that of St. Paul:

> I must go on boasting, however useless it may be, and speak of visions and revelations of the Lord. I know a man in Christ who, fourteen years ago, whether he was in or outside his body I cannot say, only God can say—a man who was snatched up to the third heaven. I know that this man— whether in or outside the body I do not know, God knows— was snatched up to Paradise to hear words which cannot be uttered, words which no man may speak. (2 Cor 12:1–4)

This "flight of the spirit," as Teresa names it, is substantially the same as ecstasy, but it is experienced differently. It seems that the spirit is carried off at a fearful speed, and there is no possibility of resisting. Sometimes even the body is carried aloft with the soul. The safest thing to do is to make a virtue of necessity and abandon oneself into the hands of God. "For as easily as a huge giant snatches up a straw, this great and powerful Giant of ours carries away the spirit" (IC 6.5.2).

Teresa writes in her *Life* of this experience of flight of the spirit:

> I say that one understands and sees oneself carried away and does not know where. Although this experience is delightful, our natural weakness causes fear in the beginning. It is necessary that the soul be resolute and courageous—much more so than for the prayer already described—in order to risk all, come what may, and abandon oneself into the hands of God and go willingly wherever it is brought since,

like it or not, one is taken away. So forceful is this enrapturing that very many times I wanted to resist and used all my energy, especially sometimes when it happened in public or other times when in secret and I was afraid of being deceived. At times I was able to accomplish something, but with a great loss of energy, as when someone fights with a giant and afterward is worn out. At other times it was impossible for me to resist, but it carried off my soul and usually, too, my head along with it, without my being able to hold back—and sometimes the whole body until the body was raised from the ground. (L 20.4)

At times, but rarely, her entire body levitated in such a way that this could be seen by others. Again she gives witness to this experience in her writings:

Once it happened when we were together in the choir ready to go up to receive Communion and while I was kneeling. I was very distressed because the experience seemed to me to be something most extraordinary and it would then become widely known. So I ordered the nuns—for this happened recently while I held the office of prioress—not to say anything about it. But at other times when I began to see the Lord was going to do the same (and once when there were some ladies of nobility present in order to hear a sermon, for it was our titular feast), I stretched out on the floor and the nuns came and held me down; nonetheless, this was seen. I begged the Lord very much not to give me any more favors that would involve any outward show. (L 20.5)

From this text and the one in the previous number, we see Teresa's experience of God's power but at the same time the delight she experienced in God by receiving these favors. That Teresa tried to resist, especially if any show were involved, is a good sign of God's good spirit. Also she mentions the great courage it took for her to receive these favors from God. She says the soul reflects on what His Majesty has done for it and turns back to look at itself, at how the tiny bit it does is full of faults, failures, and weaknesses. So, Teresa finds her best stance is to place herself before the mercy of God.

Questions for Discussion

1. Why does Teresa deal with so rare an experience?
2. What are some of the effects of this grace from God?
3. Why would courage be so necessary to receive it?
4. What might have been some of the effects on others who witnessed this grace given to Teresa?
5. Did she want to be seen by others?

CHAPTER 6

Tells about an effect of the prayer discussed in the previous chapter. How to understand whether this effect is true rather than deceptive. Discusses another favor the Lord grants so that the soul might be occupied in praising Him.

As a result of these wonderful favors the soul is left so full of longings to enjoy completely the One who grants them that it lives in a great though delightful torment. With the strongest yearnings to die, and thus usually with tears, it begs God to take it from this exile. Everything it sees wearies it. When it is alone it finds some relief, but soon this torment returns; yet when the soul does not experience this pain, something is felt to be missing. In sum, this little butterfly is unable to find a lasting place of rest; rather, since the soul goes about with such tender love, any occasion that enkindles this fire more makes the soul fly aloft. As a result, in this dwelling place the raptures are very common and there is no means to avoid them even though they may take place in public. Hence, persecutions and criticism. Even though the soul may want to be free from fears, others do not allow this freedom. For there are many persons who cause these fears, especially confessors.

2. And even though, on the one hand, the soul seems to feel very secure in its interior part, especially when it is alone with God, on the other hand, it goes about in deep distress because it fears the devil may in some way beguile it into offending the One whom it loves so much. Little does it

suffer over criticism, unless the confessor himself distresses it, as if it could do more. It does nothing but ask prayers from all and beg His Majesty to lead it by another path, for they all tell it to take another; they say that the path it is on is very dangerous. But since the soul has found this path to be so greatly beneficial, it sees that such a path is leading it along the way to heaven, according to what it reads, hears, and knows about God's commandments. Even if it wanted to, it could not really desire anything else but to abandon itself into God's hands. And even this powerlessness distresses it, for it thinks it is not obeying its confessor. Obeying and not offending our Lord, it thinks, is the complete remedy against deception. Thus, in its opinion, it would not commit knowingly a venial sin even were others to crush it to pieces. It is intensely afflicted upon seeing that it cannot free itself from unknowingly committing many venial sins.

3. God gives these souls the strongest desire not to displease Him in anything, however small, and the desire to avoid if possible every imperfection. For this reason alone, if for no other, the soul wants to flee people, and it has great envy of those who have lived in deserts. On the other hand, it would want to enter into the midst of the world to try to play a part in getting even one soul to praise God more. A woman in this stage of prayer is distressed by the natural hindrance there is to her entering the world, and she has great envy of those who have the freedom to cry out and spread the news abroad about who this great God of hosts is.

4. Oh, poor little butterfly, bound with so many chains which do not let you fly where you would like! Have pity on it, my God! Ordain that it might somehow fulfill its desires for your honor and glory. Do not be mindful of the little it deserves and of its lowly nature. You have the power, Lord, to make

the great sea and the large river Jordan roll back and allow the children of Israel to pass.[1] Yet, do not take pity on this little butterfly! Helped by your strength, it can suffer many trials; it is determined to do so and desires to suffer them. Extend Your powerful arm,[2] Lord, that this soul might not spend its life in things so base. Let Your grandeur appear in a creature so feminine and lowly, whatever the cost to her, so that the world may know that this grandeur is not hers at all and may praise You. This praise is what she desires, and she would give a thousand lives—if she had that many—if one soul were to praise You a little more through her; and she would consider such lives very well spent. She understands in all truth that she doesn't deserve to suffer for You a tiny trial, much less die.

5. I don't know what my goal was in saying this, sisters, nor why I said it, for these words were not planned. Let us realize that such effects are undoubtedly left by these suspensions and ecstasies. The desires are not passing but remain, and when an occasion arises to manifest their presence, one sees that they are not feigned. Why do I say they remain? Sometimes the soul feels, and in the smallest things, that it is a coward and so timid and frightened it doesn't think that it has the courage to do anything. I understand that the Lord leaves it then to its own human nature for its own greater good. It then sees that if it had been able to do something, the power was given by His Majesty. This truth is seen with a clarity that leaves the soul annihilated within itself and with deeper knowledge of God's mercy and grandeur—attributes the Lord desired to show to something so low. But usually its state is like that we've just mentioned.

---

1. Ex 14:21–22; Josh 3:13–17.
2. Allusion to Gen 8:8–9, used again in IC 7.3.13.

6. Note one thing, sisters, about these great desires to see our Lord: they sometimes afflict so much that you must necessarily avoid fostering them and must distract yourselves; if you can, I mean, for in other instances which I shall mention further on,[3] this cannot be done, as you will see. As for these initial desires, it's sometimes possible to distract oneself from them because there is every reason to be conformed to the will of God and say what St. Martin said.[4] A person can reflect upon St. Martin's words if the desires afflict a great deal. Since it seems these desires are characteristic of very advanced persons, the devil could instigate them so that we might think we are advanced. It is always good to walk with fear. But my opinion is that he would not be able to give the quiet and peace this suffering gives the soul; he would be stirring some passion, as happens when we suffer over worldly things. But a person who has no experience of the authentic and the inauthentic desires will think his desires are something great and will help them along as much as he can and will do serious harm to his health. For this suffering is continual, or at least very habitual.

7. Also note that a weak constitution is wont to cause these kinds of suffering, especially in the case of tender persons who will weep over every little thing. A thousand times they will be led to think they weep for God, but they will not be doing so. And it can even happen, when tears flow in abundance (I mean, that for a time every little word the soul hears or thinks concerning God becomes the cause of tears), that some humor has reached the heart thereby contributing

---

3. In IC 6.11.

4. "Lord, if I am still necessary to your people I don't refuse to live; may Your will be done." See the liturgical office for St. Martin in the Roman Breviary.

more to the tears than does love for God; for seemingly these persons will never finish weeping. Since they have already heard that tears are good, they will not restrain themselves nor would they desire to do anything else; and they help the tears along as much as they can. The devil's aim here is that these persons become so weak they will afterward be unable either to pray or to keep their rule.

8. It seems to me I can see you asking what you should do since I mark danger everywhere and in something as good as tears I think there can be deception; you are wondering if I may be the one who is deceived. And it could be that I am. But believe me, I do not speak without having seen that these false tears can be experienced by some persons; although not by me, for I am not at all tender. Rather, I have a heart so hard that sometimes I am distressed; although when the inner fire is intense, the heart, no matter how hard, distills like an alembic. You will indeed know when this fire is the source of the tears, for they are then more comforting and bring peace not turbulence, and seldom cause harm. The good that lies in the false tears—when there is any good—is that the damage is done to the body (I mean when there is humility) and not to the soul. But even if there is no harm done to the body, it won't be wrong to be suspicious about tears.

9. Let's not think that everything is accomplished through much weeping but set our hands to the task of hard work and virtue. These are what we must pay attention to; let the tears come when God sends them and without any effort on our part to induce them. These tears from God will irrigate this dry earth, and they are a great help in producing fruit. The less attention we pay to them the more there are, for they are the water that falls from heaven. The tears we draw out by tiring ourselves in digging cannot compare with the

tears that come from God, for often in digging we shall get worn out and not find even a puddle of water, much less a flowing well. Therefore, sisters, I consider it better for us to place ourselves in the presence of the Lord and look at His mercy and grandeur and at our own lowliness, and let Him give us what He wants, whether water or dryness. He knows best what is suitable for us. With such an attitude we shall go about refreshed, and the devil will not have so much chance to play tricks on us.

10. In the midst of the experiences that are both painful and delightful together, our Lord sometimes gives the soul feelings of jubilation and a strange prayer it doesn't understand. I am writing about this favor here so that if He grants it to you, you may give Him much praise and know what is taking place. It is, in my opinion, a deep union of the faculties; but our Lord nonetheless leaves them free that they might enjoy this joy—and the same goes for the senses—without understanding what it is they are enjoying or how they are enjoying. What I'm saying seems like gibberish, but certainly the experience takes place in this way, for the joy is so excessive the soul wouldn't want to enjoy it alone but wants to tell everyone about it so that they might help this soul praise our Lord. All its activity is directed to this praise. Oh, how many festivals and demonstrations the soul would organize, if it could, that all might know its joy! It seems it has found itself and that, like the father of the prodigal son, it would want to prepare a festival and invite all[5] because it sees itself in an undoubtedly safe place, at least for the time being. And I hold that there is reason for its desires. The devil cannot give this experience, because there is so much interior

---

5. Lk 15:22–32.

joy in the very intimate part of the soul and so much peace; and all the happiness stirs the soul to the praises of God.

11. To be silent and conceal this great impulse of happiness when experiencing it is no small pain. St. Francis must have felt this impulse when the robbers struck him, for he ran through the fields crying out and telling the robbers that he was the herald of the great King; and also other saints must feel it who go to deserts to be able to proclaim as St. Francis these praises of their God. I knew a saint named Friar Peter of Alcántara—for I believe from the way he lived that he was one—who did this very thing,[6] and those who at one time listened to him thought he was crazy. Oh, what blessed madness, sisters! If only God would give it to us all! And what a favor He has granted you by bringing you to this house where, when the Lord gives you this favor and you tell others about it, you will receive help rather than the criticism you would receive in the world. This proclamation is so unusual there that one is not at all surprised at the criticism.

12. Oh, how unfortunate the times and miserable the life in which we now live; happy are they whose good fortune it is to remain apart from the world. Sometimes it is a particular joy for me to see these sisters gathered together and feeling such great joy at being in the monastery that they praise our Lord as much as possible. It is seen very clearly that their praises rise from the interior of the soul. I would want you to praise Him often, sisters; for the one who begins, awakens the others. In what better way can you, when together, use your tongues than in the praises of God since we have so many reasons for praising Him?

---

6. She tells about St. Peter of Alcántara's manner of life in L 27.16–20; 30.2–7.

13. May it please His Majesty to give us this prayer often since it is so safe and beneficial; to acquire it is impossible because it is something very supernatural. And it may last a whole day. The soul goes about like a person who has drunk a great deal but not so much as to be drawn out of his senses; or like a person suffering melancholy who has not lost his reason completely but cannot free himself from what is in his imagination—nor can anyone else.

These are inelegant comparisons for something so precious, but I can't think up any others. The joy makes a person so forgetful of self and of all things that he doesn't advert to, nor can he speak of anything other than the praises of God which proceed from his joy.

Let us all help this soul, my daughters. Why do we want to have more discretion? What can give us greater happiness? And may all creatures help us forever and ever, amen, amen, amen!

A DELIGHTFUL TORMENT
AND FEELINGS OF JUBILATION

6.6.1–4 Teresa says that those who have experienced the flight of the spirit have a great longing for God and wish to leave the world so as to enjoy him completely. Everything earthly wearies such souls. Their love makes raptures common and they may suffer persecution and criticism as a result. Teresa, although seeming to write about no particular person, is actually telling of her own suffering, doubts, and trials with her confessors because of her extraordinary experiences in prayer. One cause of distress for her was the contemporary view of appropriate roles for women, which prevented her from being able to speak in public about the greatness of God. She offers a prayer that God will take pity on the weakness of the little butterfly and allow his power to be seen at work in her so that he might be praised.

6.6.5 Teresa writes that the prayer in the preceding paragraph was not planned, but was a manifestation of the effects of suspension and ecstasies. She contrasts the desires the soul experiences to do great things with other feelings that it can do nothing.

6.6.6–9 Teresa advises that when souls experience the great desires to see our Lord they should distract themselves as much as possible and be conformed to the will of God.

Teresa says that this suffering gives a peace to the soul that the devil could not counterfeit. She says persons who are naturally emotional tend to cry over everything. Such persons may think they are weeping for God, but they will not be doing so. They may deceive themselves, thinking their tears are a sign of their love of God and make an effort to sustain their weeping. Teresa says the devil is at work here because such persons may become so weak that they can neither pray nor keep their rule.

After discussing further the danger of false tears, Teresa urges: "Let's not think that everything is accomplished through much weeping but set our hands to the task of hard work and virtue" (IC 6.6.9). She says the best course is to place ourselves in the presence of the Lord and look to his mercy and our lowliness, and let God give what is suitable for us, whether or not it is tears.

6.6.10–13 Teresa concludes the sixth chapter with yet another type of prayer. It consists of feelings of jubilation and a strange prayer that the soul doesn't understand. The defining characteristics of this prayer are the great desires to praise God and to engage others in praising him as well. There is a tremendous intense joy, inspired by the grandeur of God, that the soul wants to share with the whole world. Teresa encourages the nuns to praise God often. She concludes with a prayer that God will give this type of prayer often and that it may last for a long time so that, forgetful of self, we may praise God.

Interpretive Notes

When Teresa comes out of her ecstasy, having been brought from everyday life into the sphere of the divine, even though only for some moments, she returns to the daily round, wounded. In this chapter she deals with the life of mystics when they return from the ecstasy to their ordinary life, of their internal tensions and their new manner of dealing with life.

When she looked over her work so as to divide it into chapters, she divided this chapter into two sections. In numbers 1–9, she speaks of the effects that the ecstasies spoken of in the previous chapter leave in the soul. Then, in numbers 10–13, she speaks of another favor the Lord sometimes gives the soul, which are feelings of jubilation.

In chapter 2 of this dwelling place, she spoke of the great desires for God experienced by the soul. Now she takes up the topic again, but the soul now lives in a great—though delightful—torment with powerful longings to die. "I die because I do not die" is the refrain from one of her poems (P 1). The little butterfly cannot find a place of rest on this earth where it can be freed from this painful torment. Teresa is speaking here out of her own experience. Adding to her torment is the fear that the devil may in some way trick her into offending the One whom she loves with all this excruciatingly painful desire. She begs God to lead her by another path, as advised by her confessors, but at the same time she sees clearly that his path is good for her and leading her along the way to heaven. All she can do, in the end, is abandon herself into the hands of God.

These desires for God are not passing but remain, and sometimes afflict so much that you must avoid fostering them and distract yourselves, if possible, by saying what St. Martin said: "Lord, if I am still necessary to your people I don't refuse to live; may Your will be done." This torment, though, in no way takes away the quiet and peace; in fact, it seems to increase them just as it increases one's desire for God's will to be done. And when the desires overflow into tears, the sign that the tears caused by these desires are authentic is that they bring peace, not disturbance. So, in regard to these desires and tears, let God give what he wants. He knows best what is suitable for us. We must set our hands to the tasks of hard work and virtue.

To this end, Teresa longs for death, or at least to go off to the desert in order to flee people, live apart from everything in this world, and avoid—if possible—every imperfection. In fact, she tells in her *Life* how she seriously considered transferring to another, faraway monastery of the order that was much more enclosed than the one she lived in. But at the same time, she experienced the contradictory longing to enter into the midst of the world to try to play a part in getting at least one soul to praise God more. And this is the way her life actually played out. She became enmeshed in all the very human complications involved in her mission of founding discalced Carmelite monasteries of friars and nuns, a mission which ultimately proved fruitful, despite the difficulties she encountered.

In the midst of these painful and delightful experiences, the Lord sometimes gives the soul feelings of jubilation. This is the next subject in our present chapter that Teresa addresses. What are these feelings of jubilation? They are like explosions of joy from deep within Teresa. This is the first time that Teresa, in all her writings, refers to this experience. Where did this term "jubilation" come from? Scholars think she got it from a Latinized biblical passage that alludes to Jerusalem in festivity read in the liturgy of Advent: "Rejoice heartily, O daughter Zion, shout for joy, O daughter Jerusalem" (Zech 9:9). This shows the profoundly religious character of the overflowing joy that connects with a genuine aspect of the Teresian psyche: her constant spirit of joy. Her native quality of joy opens her soul to a joy so excessive that the soul does not want to enjoy it alone but wants to tell everyone about it so that they might help her praise our Lord.

"Oh, how many festivals and demonstrations the soul would organize, if it could, that all might know its joy!" (IC 6.6.10). At the same time there is much interior joy in the intimate part of the soul—and much peace—and all this happiness stirs the soul to the praises of God. She finds examples of this in the experience of the saints, especially St. Francis of Assisi, who ran through the fields crying out and telling the robbers that he was the herald of the great King. Joy is a special part of the Teresian charism that she introduced into her newly founded communities. "Sometimes," she says, "it is a particular joy for me to see these sisters gathered together and feeling such great joy at being in the monastery that they praise our Lord as much as possible. It is seen very clearly that their praises rise from the interior of the soul" (IC 6.6.12). So, Teresa encourages her sisters in joyfully praising God. Finally, Teresa thinks this prayer is very safe. But to acquire such joy is impossible, for it is God's gift and something very supernatural, as Teresa notes.

Questions for Discussion

1. What is the torment the soul feels here? Why does she long to die?
2. What is the state of the little butterfly?
3. What are her fears in this state?
4. What can one do when one experiences these great desires?
5. What is the state of jubilation the Lord sometimes gives souls?
6. Does His Majesty want us all to experience these favors?
7. What are the effects of jubilation?

CHAPTER 7

Discusses the kind of suffering those souls to whom God grants the favors mentioned feel concerning their sins. Tells what a great mistake it is, however spiritual one may be, not to practice keeping the humanity of our Lord and Savior Jesus Christ present in one's mind; also His most sacred Passion and life, His glorious Mother, and the saints. The chapter is very helpful.

You will think, sisters, that these souls to whom the Lord communicates Himself in this unusual way will already be so sure of enjoying Him forever that they will have nothing to fear nor sins to weep over. Those especially who have not attained these favors from God will think this, for if they had enjoyed them, they would know what I'm going to say. But to think the above would be a great mistake because suffering over one's sins increases the more one receives from our God. And, for my part, I hold that until we are there where nothing can cause pain this suffering will not be taken away.

2. True, sometimes there is greater affliction than at other times; and the affliction is also of a different kind, for the soul doesn't think about the suffering it will undergo on account of its sins but of how ungrateful it has been to One to whom it owes so much and who deserves so much to be served. For in these grandeurs God communicates to it, it understands much more about Him. It is astonished at how bold it was; it weeps over its lack of respect; it thinks its foolishness was so excessive that it never finishes grieving over that foolishness

when it recalls that for such base things it abandoned so great a Majesty. Much more does it recall this foolishness than it does the favors it receives, though these favors are as remarkable as the ones mentioned or as those still to be spoken of. These favors are like the waves of a large river in that they come and go; but the memory these souls have of their sins clings like thick mire. It always seems that these sins are alive in the memory, and this is a heavy cross.

3. I know a person[1] who, apart from wanting to die in order to see God, wanted to die so as not to feel the continual pain of how ungrateful she had been to One to whom she ever owed so much and would owe. Thus it didn't seem to her that anyone's wickedness could equal her own, for she understood that there could be no one else from whom God would have had so much to put up with and to whom He had granted so many favors. As for the fear of hell, such persons don't have any. That they might lose God, at times—though seldom—distresses them very much. All their fear is that God might allow them out of His hand to offend Him, and they find themselves in as miserable a state as they were once before. In regard to their own suffering or glory, they don't care. If they don't want to stay long in purgatory, the reason comes from the fact of their not wanting to be away from God—as are those who are in purgatory—rather than from the sufferings undergone there.

4. I wouldn't consider it safe for a soul, however favored by God, to forget that at one time it saw itself in a miserable state. Although recalling this misery is a painful thing, doing so is helpful for many. Perhaps it is because I have been so wretched that I have this opinion and am always mindful of

---

1. She is referring to herself. See L 26.2; 34.10; ST 1.26; 48.1; 59.12.

my misery. Those who have been good will not have to feel this pain, although [there will always be failures as long as we live in this mortal body.] No relief is afforded this suffering by the thought that our Lord has already pardoned and forgotten the sins. Rather, it adds to the suffering to see so much goodness and realize that favors are granted to one who deserves nothing but hell. I think such a realization was a great martyrdom for St. Peter and the Magdalene. Since their love for God had grown so deep and they had received so many favors and come to know the grandeur and majesty of God, the remembrance of their misery would have been difficult to suffer, and they would have suffered it with tender sentiments.

5. It will also seem to you that anyone who enjoys such lofty things will no longer meditate on the mysteries of the most sacred humanity of our Lord Jesus Christ. Such a person would now be engaged entirely in loving. This is a matter I wrote about at length elsewhere.[2] They have contradicted me about it and said that I don't understand, because these are paths along which our Lord leads, and that when souls have already passed beyond the beginning stages it is better for them to deal with things concerning the divinity and flee from corporeal things. Nonetheless, they will not make me admit that such a road is a good one. Now it could be that I'm mistaken and that we are all saying the same thing. But I myself see that the devil tried to deceive me in this matter, and thus I have so learned my lesson from experience that I think, although I've spoken on this topic at other times,[3] I will speak of it again here that you will proceed very carefully in this matter. And take notice that I dare say you should not believe anyone who

---

2. In L 22.
3. In L 22.2–3.

tells you something else. I'll try to explain myself better than I did elsewhere. If anyone perhaps has written what a certain person told me, this would be good if the matter is explained at length, but to speak of it so summarily could do much harm to those of us who are not well informed.[4]

6. It will also seem to some souls that they cannot think about the passion, or still less about the Blessed Virgin and the lives of the saints; the remembrance of both of these latter is so very helpful and encouraging. I cannot imagine what such souls are thinking of. To be always withdrawn from corporeal things and enkindled in love is the trait of angelic spirits, not of those who live in mortal bodies. It's necessary that we speak to, think about, and become the companions of those who having had a mortal body accomplished such great feats for God. How much more is it necessary not to withdraw through one's own efforts from all our good and help which is the most sacred humanity of our Lord Jesus Christ. I cannot believe that these souls do so, but they just don't understand; and they will do harm to themselves and to others. At least I assure them that they will not enter these last two dwelling places. For if they lose the guide, who is the good Jesus, they will not hit upon the right road. It will be quite an accomplishment if they remain safely in the other dwelling places. The Lord Himself says that He is the way; the Lord says also that He is the light and that no one can go to the Father but through Him, and "anyone who sees me sees my Father."[5] They will say that another meaning is given to these words. I don't know about those other meanings; I have got along very well with this one that my soul always feels to be true.

---

4. The person to whom Teresa refers is unknown. The passage is intentionally somewhat enigmatic.

5. See Jn 8:12; 14:6, 9.

7. There are some souls—and there are many who have spoken about it to me—who, brought by our Lord to perfect contemplation, would like to be in that prayer always; but that is impossible. Yet this favor of the Lord remains with them in such a way that afterward they cannot engage as before in discursive thought about the mysteries of the passion and life of Christ. I don't know the reason, but this inability is very common, for the intellect becomes less capable of meditation. I believe the reason must be that since in meditation the whole effort consists in seeking God and that once God is found the soul becomes used to seeking Him again through the work of the will, the soul doesn't want to tire itself by working with the intellect. Likewise, it seems to me that since this generous faculty, which is the will, is already enkindled, it wants to avoid, if it can, using the other faculty; and it doesn't go wrong. But to avoid this will be impossible, especially before the soul reaches these last two dwelling places; and the soul will lose time, for the will often needs the help of the intellect so as to be enkindled.

8. And note this point, sisters; it is important, and so I want to explain it further: The soul desires to be completely occupied in love and does not want to be taken up with anything else, but to be so occupied is impossible for it even though it may want to; for although the will is not dead, the fire that usually makes it burn is dying out, and someone must necessarily blow on the fire so that heat will be given off. Would it be good for a soul with this dryness to wait for fire to come down from heaven to burn this sacrifice that it is making of itself to God, as did our Father Elijah?[6] No, certainly not, nor is it right to expect miracles. The Lord

---

6. 1 Kings 18:30–39.

works them for this soul when He pleases, as was said and will be said further on.[7] But His Majesty wants us to consider ourselves undeserving of them because of our wretchedness, and desires that we help ourselves in every way possible. I hold for myself that until we die such an attitude is necessary, however sublime the prayer may be.

9. It is true that anyone whom the Lord places in the seventh dwelling place rarely, or hardly ever, needs to make this effort. (I will give the reason for this fact when speaking of that dwelling place, if I remember.)[8] But such a person walks continually in an admirable way with Christ, our Lord, in whom the divine and the human are joined and who is always that person's companion. As for the above, when the fire in the will that was mentioned[9] is not enkindled and God's presence is not felt, it is necessary that we seek this presence. This is what His Majesty wants us to do, as the bride did in the *Song of Songs*,[10] and He wants us to ask creatures who it is who made them—as St. Augustine says, I believe, in his Meditations or *Confessions*[11]—and not be like dunces wasting time waiting for what was given us once before. At the beginning of the life of prayer it may be that the Lord will not give this fire in a year, or even in many years. His Majesty knows why; we must not desire to know nor is there any reason why we should. Since we know the path by which we must please God, which is that of the commandments and counsels, we should follow it very diligently, and think of His life and death and of the many things we owe Him; let the rest come when the Lord desires.

7. In IC 6.11.8.
8. In IC 7.2.3, 9–10; 7.3.8, 10–11; 7.4.1–2.
9. At the end of IC 6.7.7.
10. Song 3:1–3.
11. See St. Augustine, *Confessions* 10.6.9–10.

10. At this point, someone may respond that he cannot dwell on these things, and, because of what was said,[12] perhaps he will in a certain way be right. You already know that discursive thinking with the intellect is one thing and representing truths to the intellect by means of the memory is another. You may say, perhaps, that you do not understand me, and indeed it could be that I don't know how to explain the matter; but I shall do the best I can. By meditation I mean much discursive reflection with the intellect in the following way: we begin to think about the favor God granted us in giving us His only Son, and we do not stop there, but go on to the mysteries of His whole glorious life; or we begin to think about the prayer in the garden, but the intellect doesn't stop until He is on the cross; or we take a phase of the passion like, let us say, the arrest, and we proceed with this mystery, considering in detail the things there are to think of and feel about the betrayal of Judas, the flight of the apostles, and all the rest; this kind of reflection is an admirable and very meritorious prayer.

11. This prayer is the kind that those whom God has brought to supernatural things and to perfect contemplation are right in saying they cannot practice. As I have said,[13] I don't know the reason, but usually they cannot practice discursive reflection. But I say that a person will not be right if he says he does not dwell on these mysteries or often have them in mind, especially when the Catholic Church celebrates them. Nor is it possible for the soul to forget that it has received so much from God, so many precious signs of love, for these are living sparks that will enkindle it more in

---

12. In IC 6.7.7.
13. In IC 6.7.9–10.

its love for our Lord. But I say this person doesn't understand himself, because the soul understands these mysteries in a more perfect manner. The intellect represents them in such a way, and they are so stamped on the memory, that the mere sight of the Lord fallen to the ground in the garden with that frightful sweat is enough to last the intellect not only an hour but many days, while it looks with a simple gaze at who He is and how ungrateful we have been for so much suffering. Soon the will responds even though it may not do so with tender feelings, with the desire to serve somehow for such a great favor and to suffer something for One who suffered so much, and with other similar desires relating to what the memory and intellect are dwelling upon. I believe that for this reason a person cannot go on to further discursive reflection on the passion, and this inability makes him think that he cannot think about it.

12. If he doesn't dwell on these mysteries in the way that was mentioned, it is good that he strive to do so, for I know that doing so will not impede the most sublime prayer. I don't think it's good to fail to dwell often on these mysteries. If as a result the Lord suspends the intellect, well and good; for even though the soul may not so desire, He will make it abandon what it was dwelling on. And I am very certain that this procedure is not a hindrance but a very great help toward every good; the hindrance would come from a great deal of work with the discursive reflection I mentioned in the beginning. I hold that one who has advanced further along cannot practice this discursive reflection. It could be that one can, for God leads souls by many paths. But let not those who can travel by the road of discursive thought condemn those who cannot, or judge them incapable of enjoying the sublime blessings that lie enclosed in the mysteries of our good, Jesus

Christ. Nor will anyone make me think, however spiritual he may be, that he will advance by trying to turn away from these mysteries.

13. There are some principles and even means that certain souls use, by which it is thought that when a person begins to experience the prayer of quiet and to relish the enjoyment and spiritual delights given by the Lord, the important thing is to remain always in that state of delight. Well, now, let them believe me and not be so absorbed, as I have said elsewhere.[14] Life is long, and there are in it many trials, and we need to look at Christ our model, how He suffered them, and also at His apostles and saints, so as to bear these trials with perfection. Jesus is too good a companion for us to turn away from Him and His most Blessed Mother, and He is very pleased that we grieve over His sufferings even though we sometimes leave aside our own consolation and delight. Moreover, daughters, enjoyment in prayer is not so habitual that there is not time for everything. I would be suspicious of anyone who says this delight is continual; I mean, who can never do what was mentioned. And you should be suspicious too, and strive to free yourselves from this error and avoid such absorption with all your strength. If your efforts aren't enough, tell the prioress so that she might give you some task demanding such care that this danger is removed. For if this absorption continues, it is extremely dangerous at least for the brain and the head.

14. I believe I've explained that it is fitting for souls, however spiritual, to take care not to flee from corporal things to the extent of thinking that even the most sacred humanity causes harm. Some quote what the Lord said to His disciples

---

14. In IC 6.4.2, 9; L 22.10.

that it was fitting that He go.[15] I can't bear this. I would wager that He didn't say it to His most Blessed Mother, because she was firm in the faith; she knew He was God and man, and even though she loved Him more than they did, she did so with such perfection that His presence was a help rather than a hindrance. The apostles must not have been as firm then in the faith as they were afterward and as we have reason to be now. I tell you, daughters, that I consider this a dangerous path and think the devil could make one lose devotion for the most Blessed Sacrament.

15. The mistake it seemed to me I was making wasn't so extreme; rather, it consisted of not delighting so much in the thought of our Lord Jesus Christ but in going along in that absorption, waiting for that enjoyment. And I realized clearly that I was proceeding badly. Since it wasn't possible for me to experience the absorption always, the mind wandered here and there. My soul, it seems to me, was like a bird flying about that doesn't know where to light; and it was losing a lot of time and not making progress in virtue or improving in prayer. I didn't understand the reason, nor would I have understood it, in my opinion, because it seemed to me that what I was doing was very correct, until a person with whom I was discussing my prayer, who was a servant of God, warned me. Afterward, I saw clearly how wrong I had been, and I never stop regretting that there had been a time in which I failed to understand that I could not gain much through such a great loss. And even if I could gain, I wouldn't want any good save that acquired through Him from whom all blessings come to us. May He be always praised, amen.

---

15. Jn 16:7.

SUFFERING OVER ONE'S SINS
AND KEEPING CHRIST PRESENT

6.7.1–4 Teresa discusses at some length the suffering of souls whom God has favored with ecstasies and visions. The suffering, in addition to the great longing for God mentioned in the previous chapters, consists of a perpetual awareness of having offended God and sorrow for having done so. She says this affliction is greater at some times than at others, but never leaves entirely. Teresa, speaking of herself in a veiled way, says that she knows a person who wanted to die so as not to feel the continual pain of how ungrateful she had been to the Lord to whom she owed so much. The greatest fear of such persons is that God might allow them out of his hand to offend him. Teresa says that, no matter how many favors from God a soul receives, it should never forget that at one time it was in a miserable state. Even the thought that the Lord has already pardoned and forgotten our sins, instead of providing relief, adds to the suffering because of seeing so much goodness granted to ones who deserve nothing but hell.

6.7.5–6 The remaining divisions of chapter 7 deal with Teresa's belief in the great importance of meditating on the mysteries of the most sacred humanity of our Lord Jesus Christ. Some told her this view was wrong, telling her that when souls pass the beginning stages in the spiritual life they should then deal with things concerning the divinity rather than corporeal things. While allowing that there could be some mutual misunderstanding between her and them, Teresa is very firm in her position. Since we live in mortal bodies in this world, it is necessary for us to take strength and comfort and encouragement from thinking about the Blessed Virgin and the lives of the saints, and much more so from the life and passion of our Lord Jesus Christ. We need to be companions of those who, having had a mortal body, accomplished great feats for God. She takes her argument from Scripture, quoting Jesus' words that he is the way and the light, and no one can go to the Father except through him; and also that anyone who sees Jesus sees the Father. She says that they will say there is another meaning given to these words of Jesus. She adds that she doesn't know about those other meanings, but she gets along very well with this one that her soul always feels to be true.

6.7.7–8 Teresa begins to explain how keeping in mind the humanity of Christ is practiced at various stages in the spiritual life. She says that souls who have experienced perfect contemplation would like to be in that prayer always, but that is impossible. On the other hand, for some reason these souls are less able than before to engage in discursive thought about the mysteries of the Passion and the life of Christ. She gives some reasons for why this change is true. The problem is that although the soul wants to be completely occupied with love and not be taken up with anything else, such a state is impossible. The fire of love must be renewed and maintained either by God himself, when he chooses, or by our efforts. What these efforts consist of she explains in later paragraphs of this chapter.

6.7.9 Teresa explains that persons whom the Lord places in the seventh dwelling place don't often need to make an effort to keep the fire of love enkindled. They walk continually with Christ, in whom the divine and the human are joined, and he is always their companion. Until we reach that dwelling place, however, we should follow the path by which we please God, and that is by keeping the commandments and counsels and thinking of Christ's life and death and of the many things we owe him.

6.7.10–12 Teresa explains a distinction between meditation (discursive reflection) and another way of keeping in mind the humanity of Christ. She says that at a certain point many persons will no longer be able to engage in detailed thought about all the details of Christ's life, even though this type of reflection is an admirable and very meritorious prayer.

Even if souls can't practice discursive reflection, they can still dwell on these mysteries of Christ's life or often have them in mind, and also remember how much they have received from God. These thoughts are living sparks that will enkindle more love for our Lord. Teresa clarifies that there are many ways to pray and says those who can practice discursive thought should not condemn those who cannot; nor, on the other hand, should anyone think that it is possible to advance by trying to turn away from these mysteries.

6.7.13 Teresa writes about the error of thinking that it is important to remain in a state of delight in prayer for an extended period. She says life is long and there are many trials, and we should look to the example of Christ and the saints to see how to bear trials with perfection. She thinks extended absorption in prayer is dangerous for the brain and the head, and should be avoided. If one's own efforts aren't enough to resist this temptation to remain in absorption, then she recommends getting help from another, and perhaps taking on tasks that require full attention.

6.7.14–15 Teresa concludes by summing up her position that souls, no matter how spiritual, must never think that there is a time when it is harmful to think of the humanity of Christ. She says her own error was in going along, waiting for past enjoyment of the Lord to return. She says that she realized that she was proceeding badly. Her mind wandered and she made no progress in virtue or improving her prayer. Through the advice of a servant of God, she understood that she should follow the way she advocates in this chapter.

Interpretive Notes

You would think that on reaching these heights one would experience little bother over one's past and forgiven sins. Those sinners who read Teresa wonder what her sins were that she laments so much. Indeed, it is very difficult to decide precisely what her sins were from her writings. But this chapter begins with a question that anyone would have in reading this material: When persons reach this stage of the spiritual life, do they still have anything to fear or sins to weep over? It would seem not. But Teresa has just the opposite answer: "suffering over one's sins increases the more one receives from our God" (IC 6.7.1). The second question also has to do with these heights: Must you keep the humanity of Christ present in your mind after you have experiences like these? She deals with the first question in numbers 1–4. The second topic gets taken up later, in numbers 5–15.

The reason the soul suffers so much affliction is not due to the sufferings it will undergo because of sins but at the thought of "how ungrateful it has been to One to whom it owes so much and who deserves so much to be served" (IC 6.7.2). For in what God communicates to her, she understands so much more about him, and her desires to serve him keep increasing. Teresa, no matter how high she flies, always leaves us clearly aware that she never loses touch with the world in which she lives. Clearly, for her, friendship with God purified and intensified her capacity for friendship with other human beings. Her *Letters* give ample testimony to this. Actually, her friendship with God put the final touches on her view of the whole human venture, from the "farce of this so poorly harmonized life" (L 21.6), as she refers to it, to the hidden mystery of each person's interior castle.

Teresa is also someone who has experienced a conversion, and she shares with us the religious psychology of the person who is converted. In her story there are no crimes committed, nor even serious sins. Yet Teresa was capable of resisting God. For many years she dragged her feet when it came to serving God. She lost precious time. More than once she begged her Lord to give her back the time that was lost. In *The Interior Castle* she speaks of sin once at the beginning, again in the middle—in chapter 6 of the sixth dwelling places—and even in the epilogue: "As for me, ask Him to pardon my sins" (IC Epil 4). Before this, in her disguised anonymity she tells us: "I know a person who, apart from wanting to die in order to see God, wanted to die so as not to feel the continual pain of how ungrateful she had been to One to whom she ever owed so much and would owe" (IC 6.7.3).

Teresa writes that she "wouldn't consider it safe for a soul, however favored by God, to forget that at one time it saw itself in a miserable state. Although recalling this misery is a painful thing, doing so is helpful for many. Perhaps it is because I have been so wretched that I have this opinion and am always mindful of my misery" (IC 6.7.4). It doesn't help to think that God has forgiven and forgotten your sins, she says. Rather, it adds to the pain to see so much goodness.

When Teresa speaks so repeatedly of her wretchedness, the problem of Teresa's humility is situated at a deeper depth.

We are dealing with the abyss at which the mystic feels and measures human evil and the entire negative mass of all the crimes committed by humans throughout history. It can only be explained by the solidarity and a symbiosis of the mystic with all that makes up the universal, human condition. Just as the innocent Jesus is weighed down by the sins of this world, so in human history there have been those who have shared this experience with Jesus and exercise a mysterious, vicarious priesthood, which causes them to feel weighed down by the weight of the evil incurred or committed by other human beings throughout history. The tremendous evils of the twentieth century cannot lead us to a kind of pseudo-optimism. They are too enormous and overwhelming. It all seems to demonstrate that there are historical events in which evil surpasses human limits. Mystics, with their experience of "great evils," do not cancel history. But as Christians, they share and actualize the mysterious catharsis realized by Jesus. They purify and elevate humanity from evil to good. For this reason, Teresa places the remembrance of sin in the marvelous context of the sixth dwelling places. In a world that tends to extinguish the awareness of sin, the experience of the mystics keeps awakening to this reality.

In the *Book of Her Life*, chapter 22, Teresa approaches the same problem that she does in this seventh chapter of the sixth dwelling places. With regard to the twelve years existing between the two writings, we can ask ourselves if Teresa reveals any change of thought in her teaching about the place of the humanity of Christ in the spiritual life. After reading both texts, one can only conclude that Teresa, in both texts, has a decisive message about the radical centrality of the humanity of Christ for the entire Christian life.

When Teresa speaks of the humanity of Jesus, she is thinking of the Jesus of salvation history. First of all, she is thinking of the historical Jesus, marked by time, place, and persons, by his being, actions, and sufferings. This includes all the interior feelings and external happenings in his life, his words, and his love. It includes the paschal mystery that Jesus went through, his Passion, death, and glorious resurrection. And always in referring to the humanity of Christ she includes a special emphasis on the presence of Jesus in the Eucharist. At the same time, the humanity of Christ is integrated into the mystery of his person in whom both divine and human are joined, constituting the mysterious framework of his being and history.

As for the physical body, certainly Teresa does not reduce the humanity of the Lord to a bodily component. But neither does she sidestep it. As is the case with every lover, the body draws her attention—his hands, pierced and glorious, his presence, his manner of speaking. All of this speaks to us not only about the historical Jesus but just as much about the glorious and transfigured Jesus.

In chapter 22 of her *Life*, Teresa speaks as well of a mistake she made, which she always regretted: thinking when she began to receive the prayer of quiet that the humanity of Christ, as something bodily, would be an impediment to further progress in prayer. For centuries, Christian spirituality underwent a Neoplatonic temptation to spiritualize life by paying no attention to whatever is material, including the bodily humanity of Jesus. Books under such influence taught that when one is brought to contemplation, one should strive to cooperate with this new mystical experience by setting aside all recourse to the humanity of Christ in prayer and let oneself be drawn instead into a non-bodily contemplation of the mystery of his divinity.

I had no master and was reading these books in which I
thought I was gradually coming to understand something . . . (And afterward I understood that if the Lord
didn't show me, I was able to learn little from books,
because there was nothing I understood until His Majesty gave me understanding through experience, nor did
I know what I was doing.) As a result, when I began to
experience something of supernatural prayer, I mean of
the prayer of quiet, I strove to turn aside from everything
bodily. But it seemed to me that I felt the presence of God,
as was so, and I strove to recollect myself in his presence.
This is a pleasing prayer, if God helps in it, and the delight
is great. Since I felt that benefit and consolation, there was
no one who could have made me return to the humanity of
Christ; as a matter of fact, I thought the humanity was an
impediment. O Lord of my soul and my Good, Jesus Christ
crucified! At no time do I recall this opinion I had without
feeling pain; it seems to me I became a dreadful traitor—
although in ignorance. (L 22.3)

This happened just before the Lord began to favor Teresa
with raptures and visions. It is noteworthy that in every favor
the Lord granted her, whether visions or revelations, her soul
gained something; through some visions it gained a great
deal. An example of the grace that came to her from visions
of Christ can be seen in the following:

The vision of Christ left upon me an impression of his
most extraordinary beauty, and the impression remains
today; one time is sufficient to make this imprint. How
much deeper it becomes as the Lord grants this favor
more often! The benefit I received was most advantageous, and this is what it consisted of: I had a serious fault

that did me much harm; it was that when I began to know that certain persons like me, and I found them attractive, I became so attached that my memory was bound strongly by the thought of them. There was no intention to offend God, but I was happy to see these persons and think about them and about the good things I saw in them. This was something so harmful it was leading my soul seriously astray. After I beheld the extraordinary beauty of the Lord, I didn't see anyone who in comparison with him seemed to attract me or occupy my thoughts. By turning my gaze just a little inward to behold the image I have in my soul, I obtained such freedom in this respect that everything I see here below seems loathsome when compared to the excelling and beautiful qualities I beheld in this Lord. (L 37.4)

This Christ-centeredness we find in Teresa means that for her the faith and Christian life are not founded in abstractions or in philosophies, but on the special existence of a historical person who is called Jesus Christ. He is the center of our life, which is "a life in Christ." Without him, the Christian life loses its meaning. Grace, life, salvation— all these we receive from Jesus in a descending flow from him to us, but also in the entire process of the Christian life, in all its stages and manifestations, we ascend through him to the Father. In him is realized and accomplished our union with God. Through him are received the highest graces of sanctity. Anyone who would try to abstract from him in the journey to God: "I assure . . . that they will not enter these last two dwelling places [sixth and seventh]. For if they lose the guide, who is the good Jesus, they will not hit upon the right road" (IC 6.7.6).

Though Teresa presents discursive meditation as the work of beginners, she knew well from experience that there were many beginners who were unable to practice discursive meditation and she counted herself among them, asserting that she could not reflect discursively with the intellect (L 9.4; 13.11). Discursive meditation requires imagination as well. In this area, too, Teresa felt helpless. She acknowledged that she could never picture things in her imagination (L 9.6). But looking at Christ in the awareness that he is looking at us, speaking and listening to him—these were what Teresa found most attractive and helpful in meditative prayer. Wishing, perhaps subtly, to instruct some of her theologian friends, she says they should take some time out to delight in the presence of Christ and not wear themselves out composing syllogisms (L 13.11). When asked by her sisters to write something about prayer, she wrote *The Way of Perfection*, and openly confessed in it that she had nothing to say about discursive meditation since there were excellent books on the matter for those "who can form the habit of following this method of prayer" (W 19.1). She was going to present a method for those who could not recollect their minds through discursive thought (W 21.3; 24.1); that is, she intended to teach them how to pray through the use of words—vocal prayer, particularly the *Our Father* (W 24.5).

> Represent the Lord himself as close to you and behold how lovingly and humbly he is teaching you. Believe me, you should remain with so good a friend as long as you can. If you grow accustomed to having him present at your side, and he sees that you do so with love and that you go about striving to please him, you will not be able—as they say— to get away from him; he will never fail you. . . . Do you

think it is a small matter to have a friend like this at your side? O sisters, those of you who cannot engage in much discursive reflection with the intellect or keep your mind from distractions, get used to this practice. (W 26.1–2)

While explaining these matters, Teresa almost unnoticeably moves from our being present to the Master at our side, outside of us, to finding him within us. Turning within to be with the Master is what Teresa calls the "prayer of recollection." She promises us that if we practice this method of enclosing ourselves within ourselves "in this little heaven of our soul," where the Master is present, and grow accustomed to refusing to look in the direction of the exterior senses and their distractions, we will not fail to drink water from the fount (W 28.5). For Teresa, then, being present to Christ by means of the prayer of recollection, whether in meditation or in the repetition of words from Scripture, amounts to what we ourselves can do. Then all that is necessary is to persevere (L 8.5).

They must have a great and very determined determination to persevere until reaching the end, come what may, happen what may, whatever work is involved, whatever criticism arises, whether they arrive or whether they die on the road, or even if they don't have courage for the trials that are met, or if the whole world collapses. (W 21.2)

Teresa writes: "This method of keeping Christ present with us is beneficial in all stages and is a very safe means of advancing in the first degree of prayer, of reaching in a short time the second degree, and of walking secure against the dangers the devil can set up in the last degrees. Keeping Christ present is what we of ourselves can do" (L 12.3–4). What we do, then, is quite simple: keep Christ present. The representation of Christ is not a matter of how clearly you can image him to yourself, but of your faith. You represent him to yourself through faith.

Questions for Discussion

1. Is the soul now freed from pain over the thought of its own sins?
2. Do these souls fear hell? Do they fear purgatory?
3. Should we forget our past sins?
4. Must we always meditate on the mysteries of the life of Christ?
5. What is the path by which we must please God?
6. What kind of prayer do those whom God has brought to perfect contemplation find they cannot practice?
7. What mistake can such persons make?

CHAPTER 8

Discusses how God communicates Himself to the soul through an intellectual vision; gives some counsels. Tells about the effects such a vision causes if it is genuine. Recommends secrecy concerning these favors.

For you to see, sisters, that what I have told you is true and that the further a soul advances the more it is accompanied by the good Jesus, we will do well to discuss how, when His Majesty desires, we cannot do otherwise than walk always with Him. This is evident in the ways and modes by which His Majesty communicates Himself to us and shows us the love He bears us. He does this through some very wonderful apparitions and visions. That you might not be frightened if He grants you some of these, I want briefly to mention something about these visions—if the Lord be pleased that I succeed—so that we might praise Him very much even though He may not grant them to us. We would be praising Him because though He is filled with majesty and power He nonetheless desires to communicate thus with a creature.

2. It will happen while the soul is heedless of any thought about such a favor being granted to it, and though it never had a thought that it deserved this vision, that it will feel Jesus Christ, our Lord, beside it. Yet, it does not see Him, either with the eyes of the body or with those of the soul. This is called an intellectual vision; I don't know why. I saw the person[1] to whom God granted this favor, along with

---

1. This person is Teresa herself. See L 27.2–5.

303

other favors I shall mention further on, quite worried in the beginning because since she didn't see anything she couldn't understand the nature of this vision. However, she knew so certainly that it was Jesus Christ, our Lord, who showed Himself to her in that way that she couldn't doubt; I mean she couldn't doubt the vision was there. As to whether it was from God or not, even though she carried with her great effects to show that it was, she nonetheless was afraid. She had never heard of an intellectual vision, nor had she thought there was such a kind. But she understood very clearly that it was this same Lord who often spoke to her in the way mentioned.[2] For until He granted her this favor I am referring to, she never knew who was speaking to her, although she understood the words.

3. I know that since she was afraid about this vision (for it isn't like the imaginative one that passes quickly, but lasts many days and sometimes even more than a year), she went very worried to her confessor. He asked her how, since she didn't see anything, she knew that it was our Lord; what kind of face He had.[3] She told him she didn't know, that she didn't see any face, and that she couldn't say any more than what she had said, that what she did know was that He was the one who spoke to her and that the vision had not been fancied. And although some persons put many fears in her, she was still frequently unable to doubt, especially when the Lord said to her: "Do not be afraid, it is I."[4] These words had so much power that from then on she could not doubt the vision, and she was left very much strengthened and happy

<hr />

2. In IC 6.3.
3. See L 27.3.
4. See L 25.18; ST 22.1; 31; 48; 58.16; IC 6.3.5.

over such good company. She saw clearly that the vision was a great help toward walking with a habitual remembrance of God and a deep concern about avoiding anything displeasing to Him, for it seemed to her that He was always looking at her. And each time she wanted to speak with His Majesty in prayer, and even outside of it, she felt He was so near that He couldn't fail to hear her. But she didn't hear words spoken whenever she wanted; only unexpectedly when they were necessary. She felt He was walking at her right side, but she didn't experience this with those senses by which we can know that a person is beside us. This vision comes in another unexplainable, more delicate way. But it is so certain and leaves much certitude; even much more than the other visions do because in the visions that come through the senses one can be deceived, but not in the intellectual vision. For this latter brings great interior benefits and effects that couldn't be present if the experience were caused by melancholy; nor would the devil produce so much good; nor would the soul go about with such peace and continual desires to please God, and with so much contempt for everything that does not bring it to Him. Afterward she understood clearly that the vision was not caused by the devil, which became more and more clear as time went on.

4. Nonetheless, I know that at times she went about very much frightened; at other times, with the most intense confusion, for she didn't know why so much good had come to her. We were so united, she and I, that nothing took place in her soul of which I was ignorant; so I can be a good witness. And believe me, all I have said of this matter is the truth.

It is a favor from the Lord that she bears in herself the most intense confusion and humility. If the vision were from the devil, the effects would be contrary. And since the vision is something definitely understood to be a gift from God and human effort would not be sufficient to produce this experience, the one who receives it can in no way think it is his own good but a good given through the hand of God. And even though, in my opinion, some of those favors that were mentioned are greater, this favor bears with it a particular knowledge of God. This continual companionship gives rise to a most tender love for His Majesty, to some desires even greater than those mentioned[5] to surrender oneself totally to His service, and to a great purity of conscience because the presence at its side makes the soul pay attention to everything. For even though we already know that God is present in all we do, our nature is such that we neglect to think of this. Here the truth cannot be forgotten, for the Lord awakens the soul to His presence beside it. And even the favors that were mentioned[6] became much more common since the soul goes about almost continually with actual love for the One who it sees and understands is at its side.

5. In sum, with respect to the soul's gain, the vision is seen to be a most wonderful and highly valuable favor. The soul thanks the Lord that He gives the vision without any merits on its part and would not exchange that blessing for any earthly treasure or delight. Thus, when the Lord is pleased to take the vision away, the soul feels very much alone. But all the efforts it could possibly make are of little avail in bringing back that companionship. The Lord gives it when He desires, and it cannot be acquired. Sometimes also the vision is of some saint, and this too is most beneficial.

---

5. In IC 6.6.1–6.

6. The series of favors mentioned in the preceding chapters.

6. You will ask how if nothing is seen one knows that it is Christ, or a saint, or His most glorious mother. This, the soul will not know how to explain, nor can it understand how it knows, but it does know with the greatest certitude. It seems easier for the soul to know when the Lord speaks; but what is more amazing is that it knows the saint, who doesn't speak but seemingly is placed there by the Lord as a help to it and as its companion. Thus there are other spiritual things that one doesn't know how to explain, but through them one knows how lowly our nature is when there is question of understanding the sublime grandeurs of God, for we are incapable even of understanding these spiritual things. But let the one to whom His Majesty gives these favors receive them with admiration and praise for Him. Thus He grants the soul particular graces through these favors. For since the favors are not granted to all, they should be highly esteemed; and one should strive to perform greater services since God in so many ways helps the soul to perform these services. Hence the soul doesn't consider itself to be any greater because of this, and it thinks that it is the one who serves God the least among all who are in the world. This soul thinks that it is more obligated to Him than anyone, and any fault it commits pierces to the core of its being, and very rightly so.

7. These effects from the vision that were mentioned[7] and that are left in the soul can be recognized by anyone of you whom the Lord has brought by this road. Through them you can know that the vision is not an illusion or a fancy. As I have said,[8] I hold that it would be impossible for a vision caused by the devil to last so long and benefit the soul so remarkably,

---

7. In IC 6.8.3–5.
8. In IC 6.8.3.

clothing it with so much interior peace. It is not customary for something so evil to do something so good, nor can the devil even though he may want to. If he could, there would at once be some outward show of self-esteem and thought of being better than others. But that the soul goes about always so attached to God and with its thoughts so occupied in Him causes the devil such rage that even though he might try he would not often return. And God is so faithful[9] that He will not allow the devil much leeway with a soul that doesn't aim for anything else than to please His Majesty and spend its life for His honor and glory; He will at once ordain how it may be undeceived.

8. My theme is and will be that since, as a result of these favors from God, the soul walks in the way here mentioned, His Majesty will make it be the one to gain. And if He sometimes permits the devil to tempt the soul, He will so ordain that the evil one will be defeated. As a result, daughters, if someone should walk along this road, as I have said, do not be astonished. It is good that there be fear and that we walk with more care. Nor should you be self-confident, for since you are so favored you could grow more careless. If you do not see in yourselves the effects that were mentioned,[10] it will be a sign the favor is not from God. It is good that at the beginning you speak about this vision under the seal of confession with a very learned man, for learned men will give us light. Or, with some very spiritual person, if there be one available; if there isn't, it's better to speak with a very learned man. Or with both a spiritual person and a learned man if both are at hand. And should they tell you the vision is

---

9. Allusion to 1 Cor 10:13. See IC 6.3.17. She also refers to this statement of St. Paul in her L 23.15.

10. In IC 6.8.1.

fancied, do not be concerned, for the fancy can do little good or evil. Commend yourself to the divine Majesty that He not let you be deceived. If they should tell you your vision is from the devil, it will be a greater trial, although no one will say this if he is indeed learned and the effects mentioned are present. But if he says so, I know that the Lord Himself who walks with you will console you, assure you, and give the confessor light that he may give it to you.

9. If the confessor is a person whom, although he practices prayer, the Lord has not led by this path, he will at once be frightened and condemn it. For this reason I advise you to have a confessor who is very learned and, if possible, also spiritual. The prioress should give permission for such consultation. Even though, judging by the good life you live, you may be walking securely, the prioress will be obligated to have you speak with a confessor so that both you and she may walk securely. And once you have spoken with these persons, be quiet and don't try to confer about the matter with others; at times the devil causes some fears so excessive that they force the soul, without its having anything really to fear, not to be satisfied with one consultation. If, especially, the confessor has little experience, and the soul sees that he is fearful, and he himself makes it continue to speak of the matter, that which by rights should have remained very secret is made public, and this soul is persecuted and tormented. For while it thinks the matter is secret, it finds out that the visions are publicly known. As a result many troublesome things happen to it and could happen to its religious order, the way these times are going.[11] Hence a great deal of discretion is necessary in this matter, and I highly recommend it to the prioresses.

---

11. She is alluding probably to interventions of the Spanish Inquisition.

10. A prioress should not think that since a sister has experiences like these she is better than the others. The Lord leads each one as He sees is necessary. This path is a preparation for becoming a very good servant of God, provided that one cooperate. But sometimes God leads the weakest along this path. And so there is nothing in it to approve or condemn. One should consider the virtues and who it is who serves our Lord with greater mortification, humility, and purity of conscience; this is the one who will be the holiest. Yet, little can be known here below with certitude; we must wait until the true Judge gives to each one what is merited. In heaven we will be surprised to see how different His judgment is from what we can understand here below. May He be forever praised, amen.

HOW GOD COMMUNICATES
THROUGH AN
INTELLECTUAL VISION

6.8.1 Teresa states her purpose for the chapter. She says the more the soul advances, the more it is accompanied by Jesus, and it will be beneficial to discuss how, through various communications, the Lord commands our attention so that we cannot do otherwise than walk with him always. This experience she calls an intellectual vision, and she explains it further in subsequent chapters of the sixth dwelling places.

6.8.2–5 Teresa says that it can happen that the soul can become aware of Jesus Christ beside it, even though the soul had never thought of such a favor being granted to it. The soul doesn't see with the eyes of the body or the soul. This experience, she says, is called an intellectual vision. She goes on to give more details of her own experience, referring to herself as if speaking of another person. She shares her earlier worries about the experience caused by her ignorance of how such a vision could be possible.

The anxiety-producing aspect of intellectual visions is that the soul is aware of possessing knowledge, such as that Jesus is present, or some truth that has been communicated to it, but the means by which the knowledge came is completely hidden and mysterious. Without seeing or hearing or thinking or imagining, the soul somehow knows. Because persons cannot provide a description of how they came to some knowledge or awareness, their efforts to share the experience with their confessors may be met with skepticism or disapproval. Nevertheless, the power of the vision is such that the person cannot doubt it.

Teresa goes on to give more details about intellectual visions, especially about the awareness of Christ's presence. In 6.8.4, Teresa emphasizes the reliability of her description of the experience of intellectual visions, saying that she was very close to the hypothetical person (actually herself) who had these experiences.

Teresa says that these visions produce an intense confusion and humility, and the person cannot doubt that they came from God. The presence of the Lord produces in the soul great love, great care to try to avoid every fault, and greater desire to surrender totally to his service.

She concludes (in 6.8.5) that this vision is a wonderful favor that benefits the soul greatly. She says the soul thanks the Lord that he gives this vision without any merit on its part and says the soul would not exchange the vision for any earthly treasure or delight. When the Lord is pleased to take the vision away, she says the soul feels very much alone. Teresa says no amount of effort on the soul's part can bring back that companionship; the Lord gives it when he desires and it can't be acquired. She adds that sometimes the vision is of some saint and that, too, is beneficial.

6.8.6–7 Teresa takes up the question of how a person can be convinced of the identity of the Lord or a saint whom it knows is present, and she has no answer. She concludes that through this mystery we understand how lowly our nature is when there is a question of understanding the sublime grandeurs of God. Teresa says great benefit comes to the soul through this type of vision, and the soul goes about always attached to God and with its thoughts occupied in him.

6.8.8–9 Here Teresa mixes advice to those who experience intellectual visions with narrative about the trials these persons can experience. The ideal situation would be to have access to a very learned, very spiritual confessor who has experience with these visions. If such a confessor isn't available, Teresa advises seeking out more than one person, each of whom may have one of these qualities (spirituality or learning), and speaking with them. In 6.8.9, she advises a person to be satisfied after consulting with a person who is learned and, if possible, spiritual, and then be quiet. Otherwise the matter can become public and many troublesome things can happen.

In this section we see a tension in Teresa's thought. On the one hand, she has experienced the intellectual vision of the presence of the Lord as absolutely convincing. On the other hand, because the experience is so different from ordinary experience, she was fearful at first at not understanding how such visions are possible, and so she sought advice. But in a subtle way, Teresa is saying that intellectual visions authenticate themselves by virtue of the great certitude of the Lord's presence and the accompanying habitual remembrance of God, and the deep concern one has to avoid displeasing him in anything. While she clearly advises seeking out a spiritual and learned confessor, she doesn't advise doubting or being fearful of this type of vision, even if a confessor condemns it. In the previous dwelling places, Teresa believed there was much greater opportunity for being deceived by the devil or by one's imagination, but not here.

6.8.10 Teresa concludes with a point that is frequently disregarded. There is a tendency to believe that only the greatest saints experience intellectual visions. Teresa, on the other hand, was writing for the nuns with the expectation that some of them could have these experiences. She says that persons who have these experiences may or may not be greater in holiness than persons who don't have these experiences. She says God sometimes leads the weakest along this path. But looking at the weakness or apparent holiness of the person is not the way to judge the authenticity of the visions. The important things are that the love of God and desire to serve and to avoid displeasing him are present, along with the soul's great conviction that the vision is of divine origin.

Interpretive Notes

Here God communicates with Teresa a favor in a way that at first caused her great fear, as did most of her mystical experiences at first. He manifested himself to her in a manner which she had great trouble in explaining to others. Probably she learned the name for the favor from some of the confessors she consulted. She had been receiving the locutions and been advised by confessors that they were dangerous and to pray to God to lead her by another, safer path because this one, with the locutions and ecstasies, was suspect and dangerous. Even though she was obeying and begging God to do so, she wasn't doing it with complete conviction, for she knew the good that these favors were doing her. However, she didn't at this time know who it was in her locutions who was speaking to her. Teresa then begins to tell us about this next favor so that if the Lord gives it to us we won't be frightened by it and so that even if he doesn't, we can always praise him for giving such favors to others.

Teresa reacted against the teaching of the Neoplatonists on a personal biographical plane in her *Life* (L 22) and on a doctrinal, theological plane in the previous chapter of these dwelling places. She did so definitely and clearly, without reservation. She is certain that the person "walks continually in an admirable way with Christ, our Lord, in whom the divine and the human are joined and who is always that person's companion" (IC 6.7.9). The human and divine are joined and not separated. And the human does not cut itself off from the bodily, historical, and earthly life of Jesus Christ. We could present many of Teresa's arguments in favor of this thesis of hers. But now we are interested in a new argument, an argument lived by her. The decisive event in her mystical experience is the Lord Jesus Christ, both God and man.

In her *Life*, Teresa was content to tell about this event (L 27), after having argued against the spiritualists, who were opposed to the body. Now, on the doctrinal plane of *The Interior Castle*, chapters seven and eight of the sixth dwelling places form a kind of Christological diptych. First, she assents to the doctrine that Christ, both God and man, is the mediator of all the divine graces on the ascending as well as the descending scale (IC 6.7). Second, her argument is as follows: in following the process of the mystical experiences that lead to union with God, Teresa experiences what she calls the intellectual vision of Jesus Christ's humanity. She begins her explanation in this way: "For you to see, sisters, that what I have told you is true and that the further a soul advances the more it is accompanied by the good Jesus, we will do well to discuss how, when His Majesty desires, we cannot do otherwise than walk always with Him" (IC 6.8.1).

The reason Teresa didn't understand the nature of this vision is that she didn't see anything, either with the eyes of her body or with those of the soul (the interior sense faculties). Yet she knew certainly that it was Jesus Christ, the Lord, who showed himself to her. As we have mentioned, Teresa in

The Interior Castle speaks of her experience as happening to a third party, since she is disguising her identity. She speaks of this grace also in her *Life*, as being given to herself: "It seemed to me that Jesus Christ was always present at my side; but since this wasn't an imaginative vision, I didn't see any form. Yet I felt very clearly that He was always present at my right side and that He was witness of everything I did. At no time in which I was a little recollected, or not greatly distracted, was I able to ignore that He was present at my side" (L 27.2). Or again in that same chapter of her *Life* she writes: "the vision is represented through knowledge given to the soul that is clearer than sunlight. I don't mean that you see the sun or brightness, but that a light, without your seeing light, illumines the intellect so that the soul may enjoy such a great good. The vision bears with it wonderful blessings" (L 27.3).

In the Bible, the prophet generally arises as the result of a strong experience of God or of Christ. After the theophany at the burning bush, Moses, the shepherd in the region of Sinai, was converted into a prophet and leader of the people. After the experience of Christ that happened on the road to Damascus, Saul, a persecutor of Christians, was converted into an apostle of Jesus. Both of these two were suddenly reborn. In Teresa's case, this Christological experience changed her life.

This extraordinary favor, the intellectual vision of Christ, took place in 1560, a date that divides the story of Teresa's spiritual life into two parts. Before this year, Teresa struggled with herself up to the point of a total conversion in which she received a whole series of mystical graces. Yet she had not yet done anything with regard to what was to become her mission in the Church. There was still nothing of the prophet, or the doctor, or the foundress. All of her writings will have a date later than 1560, from her first *Spiritual Testimony* in 1560 up to the last account in her *Foundations*. Only after this extraordinary fact in 1560 did she decide to make her vow of always doing the more perfect thing. All her foundations of Carmelites came after this personal encounter with Christ, her Lord. Only after this date did she change her name from Teresa de Ahumada to Teresa of Jesus. "In sum, with respect to the soul's gain, the vision is seen to be a most wonderful and highly valuable favor. The soul thanks the Lord that He gives the vision without any merits on its part and would not exchange that blessing for any earthly treasure or delight" (IC 6.8.5).

Questions for Discussion

1. What did Teresa understand in this intellectual vision?
2. Why did Teresa fear this experience?
3. What were some of the good effects of this vision?
4. Have you experienced any particular moments that changed the course of your life? How does your experience relate to Teresa's?
5. The grace of an experience of Jesus changed the lives of many saints. How has your relationship with Jesus changed your own life?

CHAPTER 9

Treats of how the Lord communicates with the soul through an imaginative vision; gives careful warning against desiring to walk by this path and the reasons for such a warning. The chapter is very beneficial.

Now let us come to imaginative visions, for they say the devil meddles more in these than in the ones mentioned,[1] and it must be so. But when these imaginative visions are from our Lord, they in some way seem to me more beneficial because they are in greater conformity with our nature. I'm excluding from that comparison the visions the Lord shows in the last dwelling place; no other visions are comparable to those.

2. Well now, let us consider what I have told you in the preceding chapter[2] about how this Lord is present. It is as though we had in a gold vessel a precious stone having the highest value and curative powers. We know very certainly that it is there although we have never seen it. But the powers of the stone do not cease to benefit us provided that we carry it with us.[3] Although we have never seen this stone, we do not on that account cease to prize it, because through experience we have seen that it has cured us of some illnesses for which it is suited. But we do not dare look at it

---

1. In IC 6.8; the intellectual visions.

2. In IC 6.8.2–3.

3. A popular belief in Teresa's time was that certain stones had curative powers; for example, the bezoar.

or open the reliquary, nor can we, because the manner of opening this reliquary is known solely by the one to whom the jewel belongs. Even though he lent us the jewel for our own benefit, he has kept the key to the reliquary and will open it, as something belonging to him when he desires to show us the contents, and he will take the jewel back when he wants to, as he does.

3. Well, let us say now that sometimes he wants to open the reliquary suddenly in order to do good to the one to whom he has lent it. Clearly, a person will afterward be much happier when he remembers the admirable splendor of the stone, and hence it will remain more deeply engrained in his memory. So it happens here: when our Lord is pleased to give more delight to this soul, He shows it clearly His most sacred humanity in the way He desires; either as He was when He went about in the world or as He is after His resurrection. And even though the vision happens so quickly that we could compare it to a streak of lightning, this most glorious image remains so engraved on the imagination that I think it would be impossible to erase it until it is seen by the soul in that place where it will be enjoyed without end.

4. Although I say "image" let it be understood that, in the opinion of the one who sees it, it is not a painting but truly alive, and sometimes the Lord is speaking to the soul and even revealing great secrets. But you must understand that even though the soul is detained by this vision for some while, it can no more fix its gaze on the vision than it can on the sun. Hence this vision always passes very quickly, but not because its brilliance is painful, like the sun's to the inner eye. It is the inner eye that sees all of this. I wouldn't know how to say anything about a vision that comes through the exterior sense of sight, because this person mentioned, of whom

I can speak so particularly,[4] had not undergone such a vision, and one cannot be sure about what one has not experienced. The brilliance of this inner vision is like that of an infused light coming from a sun covered by something as transparent as a properly-cut diamond. The garments seems made of a fine Dutch linen. Almost every time God grants this favor the soul is in rapture, for in its lowliness it cannot suffer so frightening a sight.

5. I say "frightening" because although the Lord's presence is the most beautiful and delightful a person could imagine even were he to live and labor a thousand years thinking about it (for it far surpasses the limitations of our imagination or intellect), this presence bears such extraordinary majesty that it causes the soul extreme fright. Certainly it's not necessary here to ask how the soul knows, without having been told, who the Lord is, for it is clearly revealed that He is the Lord of heaven and earth. This is not true of earthly kings, for in themselves they would be held in little account were it not for their retinue, or unless they tell who they are.

6. O Lord, how we Christians fail to know You! What will that day be when You come to judge, for even when You come here with so much friendliness to speak with Your bride, she experiences such fear when she looks at You? Oh, daughters, what will it be like when He says in so severe a voice, *depart you who are cursed by My Father?*[5]

7. As a result of this favor granted by God, let us keep in mind the above thought, for it will be no small blessing. Even St. Jerome, though he was a saint, kept it in mind. And thus

---

4. Teresa is referring to herself. See L 28, especially 28.4; ST 58.15, in which she states that "she never saw anything with her bodily eyes."

5. Mt 25:41.

all that we suffer here in the strict observance of the religious life will seem to us nothing; for, however long it lasts, it lasts but a moment in comparison with eternity. I tell you truthfully that as wretched as I am I have never had fear of the torments of hell, for they would be nothing if compared to what I recall the condemned will experience upon seeing the anger in these eyes of the Lord, so beautiful, meek, and kind. It doesn't seem my heart could suffer such a sight. I've felt this way all my life. How much more will the person fear this sight to whom the Lord has thus represented Himself since the experience is so powerful that it carries that person out of his senses. The reason the soul is suspended must be that the Lord helps its weakness, which is joined to His greatness in this sublime communication.

8. When the soul can remain a long while gazing upon this Lord, I don't believe it will be experiencing a vision but some intense reflection in which some likeness is fashioned in the imagination; compared with a vision, this likeness is similar to something dead.

9. It happens to some persons (and I know this is true, for they have spoken with me—and not just three or four but many) that their imagination is so weak, or their intellect so effective, or I don't know what the cause is, that they become absorbed in their imagination to the extent that everything they think about seems to be clearly seen. Yet, if they were to see a real vision, they would know without any doubt whatsoever their mistake, for they themselves are composing what they see with their imagination. This imagining doesn't have any effect afterward, but they are left cold—much more than if they were to see a devotional image. It's very wise not to pay any attention to this kind of imagining and thus what was seen is forgotten much more than a dream.

10. In the vision we are dealing with the above is not so: rather, while the soul is very far from thinking that anything will be seen, or having the thought even pass through its mind, suddenly the vision is represented to it all at once and stirs all the faculties and senses with a great fear and tumult so as to place them afterward in that happy peace. Just as there was a tempest and tumult that came from heaven when St. Paul was hurled to the ground,[6] here in this interior world there is a great stirring; and in a moment, as I have said,[7] all remains calm, and this soul is left so well instructed about so many great truths that it has no need of any other master. For without any effort on the soul's part, true Wisdom has taken away the mind's dullness and leaves a certitude, which lasts for some time, that this favor is from God. However much the soul is told the contrary, others cannot then cause it fear that there could be any deception. Afterward, if the confessor puts fear in it, God allows it to waver and think that because of its sins it could possibly be deceived. But it does not believe this; rather, as I have said concerning those other things,[8] the devil can stir up doubts, as he does with temptations against matters of faith, that do not allow the soul to be firm in its certitude. But the more the devil fights against that certitude, the more certain the soul is that the devil could not have left it with so many blessings, as they really are, for he cannot do so much in the interior of the soul. The devil can present a vision, but not with this truth and majesty and these results.

11. Since the confessors cannot witness this vision—nor perhaps, can it be explained by the one to whom God grants

6. Acts 9:3–4.
7. In IC 6.8.3.
8. In IC 6.8.4, 8.

this favor—they fear and rightly so. Thus it's necessary to proceed with caution, wait for the time when these apparitions will bear fruit, and move along little by little looking for the humility they leave in the soul and the fortitude in virtue. If the vision is from the devil, he will soon show a sign, and will be caught in a thousand lies. If the confessor has experience and has undergone these experiences, he needs little time for discernment; immediately in the account given he will see whether the vision is from God or the imagination or the devil, especially if His Majesty has given him the gift of discernment of spirits. If he has this latter as well as learning, even though he may have no experience, he will recognize the true vision very well.

12. What is necessary, sisters, is that you proceed very openly and truthfully with your confessor. I don't mean in regard to telling your sins, for that is obvious, but in giving an account of your prayer. If you do not give such an account, I am not sure you are proceeding well, nor that it is God who is teaching you. He is very fond of our speaking as truthfully and clearly to the one who stands in His place as we would to Him and of our desiring that the confessor understand all our thoughts and even more our deeds, however small they be. If you do this you don't have to go about disturbed or worried. Even if the vision is not from God, it will do you no harm if you have humility and a good conscience. His Majesty knows how to draw good from evil, and the road along which the devil wanted to make you go astray will be to your great gain. Thinking that God grants you such wonderful favors, you will force yourselves to please Him more and be always remembering His image. As a very learned man said,[9]

---

9. She is referring to Father Domingo Báñez, O.P. See F 8.3.

the devil is a great painter and that if the devil were to show him a living image of the Lord, he wouldn't be grieved but allow the image to awaken his devotion, and that he would thereby wage war on the devil with that evil one's own wickedness. [Even though a painter may be a very poor one, a person shouldn't on that account fail to reverence the image he makes if it is a painting of our every Good.]

13. That learned man was strongly opposed to the advice some gave about making the fig[10] when seeing a vision, for he used to say that wherever we see a painting of our King we must reverence it. And I see that he is right, because even here below a similar action would be regretted: If a person knew that before a portrait of himself another whom he loved manifested such contempt, he would be unhappy about the act. Well how much greater reason there is always to have respect for any crucifix or portrait we see of our Emperor? Although I have written of this elsewhere,[11] I am glad to write of it here, for I saw that a person went about in distress when ordered to use this remedy.[12] I don't know who invented a thing that could so torment a person who wasn't able to do anything else than obey, if the confessor gave her this counsel, because she thought she would go astray if she didn't obey. My counsel is that even though a confessor gives you such advice, you should humbly tell him this reason and not accept his counsel. The good reasons given me by that learned man I found very acceptable.

14. A wonderful benefit the soul draws from this favor of the Lord is that when it thinks of Him or of His life and

---

10. See L 29.5–6.

11. In F 8.3.

12. This person is herself. See L 29.5–6.

passion it remembers His most meek and beautiful countenance. This remembrance is the greatest consolation, just as here below it would be far more consoling to see a person who has done a great deal of good for us than someone we had never met. I tell you that so delightful a remembrance brings much consolation and benefit.

Many are the other blessings these visions bring, but since so much has been said about such effects, and more will be said, I don't want to tire myself, or tire you, but advise you strongly that when you learn or hear that God grants these favors to souls you never beseech Him or desire Him to lead you by this path.

15. Although this path may seem to you very good, one to be highly esteemed and reverenced, desiring it is inappropriate for certain reasons: First, the desire to be given what you have never deserved shows a lack of humility, and so I believe that whoever desires this path will not have much humility. Just as the thoughts of a lowly workman are far from any desire to be king since such a thing seems impossible to him, and he thinks he doesn't deserve it, so too with the humble person in similar matters. I believe that these favors will never be given to those who desire them, because before granting them God gives a deep self-knowledge. For how will he who has such desires understand in truth that he is being granted a very great favor at not being in hell? Second, such a person will very certainly be deceived or in great danger because the devil needs nothing more than to see a little door open before playing a thousand tricks on us. Third, the imagination itself, when there is a great desire, makes a person think that he sees what he desires and hears it, as with those who desiring something during the day and thinking a great deal about it happen to dream of it at night. Fourth, it

would be extremely bold to want to choose a path while not knowing what suits me more. Such a matter should be left to the Lord who knows me—for He leads me along the path that is fitting—so that in all things I might do His will. Fifth, do you think the trials suffered by those to whom the Lord grants these favors are few? No, they are extraordinary and of many kinds. How do you know you would be able to bear them? Sixth, by the very way you think you will gain, you will lose, as Saul did by being king.[13]

16. In sum, sisters, besides these reasons there are others; believe me, the safest way is to want only what God wants. He knows more than we ourselves do, and He loves us. Let us place ourselves in His hands so that His will may be done in us, and we cannot err if with a determined will we always maintain this attitude. And you must note that greater glory is not merited by receiving a large number of these favors; rather, on the contrary the recipients of these favors are obliged to serve more since they have received more. The Lord doesn't take away from us that which, because it lies within our power, is more meritorious. So there are many holy persons who have never received one of these favors; and others who receive them but are not holy. And do not think the favors are given continually; rather, for each time the Lord grants them there are many trials. Thus, the soul doesn't think about receiving more but about how to serve for what it has received.

17. It is true that this vision must be a powerful help toward possessing the virtues with higher perfection, but the person who has gained them at the cost of his own labors will merit much more. I know a person or two persons—one was

---

13. See 1 Sam 15:10–11.

a man—to whom the Lord had granted some of these favors, who were so desirous of serving His Majesty at their own cost, without these great delights, and so anxious to suffer that they complained to our Lord because He bestowed the favors on them, and if they could decline receiving these gifts they would do so.[14] I am speaking not of the delights coming from these visions—for in the end these persons see that the visions are very beneficial and to be highly esteemed—but of those the Lord gives in contemplation.

18. It is true that these desires also, in my opinion, are supernatural and characteristic of souls very much inflamed in love. Such souls would want the Lord to see that they do not serve Him for pay. Thus, as I have said,[15] they never, as a motive for making the effort to serve more, think about receiving glory for anything they do. But their desire is to satisfy love, and it is love's nature to serve with deeds in a thousand ways. If it could, love would want to discover ways of consuming the soul within itself. And if it were necessary to be always annihilated for the greater honor of God, love would do so very eagerly. May He be praised forever, amen. For in lowering Himself to commune with such miserable creatures, He wants to show His greatness.

---

14. She is speaking of herself. The man could have been St. John of the Cross, who was confessor at the monastery of the Incarnation in Ávila when St. Teresa was prioress there from 1571–1574.

15. In IC 6.9.16; 4.2.9.

HOW GOD COMMUNICATES
THROUGH IMAGINATIVE VISIONS

6.9.1 Teresa writes here about imaginative visions, which she says can seem more beneficial than intellectual visions in that they are more in conformity with our nature. She warns, however, that the devil meddles more in these visions than in intellectual visions.

6.9.2–3 She introduces the metaphor of a precious, curative stone held inside a reliquary to illustrate how the Lord can give glimpses of himself to a soul. She says these visions happen very quickly, but appear in such a way that the image is never forgotten. Specifically, this type of vision is of the Lord's sacred humanity.

6.9.4–9 Here Teresa begins to explain imaginative visions in more detail. She says that such a vision passes quickly because of its intensity. The vision does not come through exterior senses, but through an inner vision. Teresa says that the soul understands clearly that the vision is of the Lord of heaven and earth, and she gives many details of the profound effects on the soul of one who experiences this type of vision. She also contrasts aspects and the effects of authentic visions with other types of experiences which are not supernatural.

6.9.10–12 Teresa compares the experience of an imaginative vision to St. Paul's conversion experience. She also advises how persons who believe they are experiencing imaginative visions should conduct themselves. The devil may stir up doubts, but he will fail because the soul understands how much it has benefited. Confessors who have not had these experiences may have fears about the authenticity of a vision, and rightly proceed with caution, looking for the effects left in the soul. Confessors who have undergone the experience will be able to discern more quickly.

6.9.13–14 Teresa shares her distress at being told by one confessor to make an irreverent gesture (the so-called "fig") when she saw a vision of the Lord. She repeats good advice given her by another confessor to reverence images of the Lord always, since whether the images are from God or from the devil they merit reverence because they represent the Lord. She writes of the great benefit and consolation she received from remembering the beautiful countenance of the Lord.

6.9.15–16 Teresa warns that however good this path of imaginative visions may seem, one should not desire it. To do so shows a lack of humility. Second, through desire, the person may easily be deceived by the devil. Third, the imagination may make persons see what they want to see. Fourth, one should leave the matter to the Lord, who will choose the best path. Fifth, the trials of the path are great and hard to bear. Sixth, a person might lose instead of gain. She says the safest way is to want only what God wants.

6.9.17–18 Teresa concludes her discussion of imaginative visions by saying that although they may be a great help toward possessing virtues, persons who gain virtues through their own labors will merit more. Teresa believes that desiring to serve without the consolation of visions is characteristic of souls very much inflamed by love. She sees such love—that loves without any self-serving motive—as the greatest love.

Interpretive Notes

The word "Christophany" is one to which we are unaccustomed, especially in our culture. Teresa herself never uses it.

The theologian or biblical scholar is the one most likely to use it to refer to a manifestation of Christ in his risen, glorious body to our sense experience. As a result, the word is sometimes used to refer, on the part of the believer or mystic, to the human perception of this reality of the glorious, risen Lord. We have an affirmation of the power of the Lord of glory to enter into our history and be present there. The Christophany that Paul experienced on the road to Damascus as presented in the *Acts of the Apostles* and elsewhere by Paul himself is a point of reference for us. But here we find the classic words used, such as "He appeared to me" (apparition) or "I saw Him" (vision). Teresa prefers, as do most mystics, the term "vision" to express this same experience of Paul that now happened to her. And that she is convinced happens with a certain normality in the enlightened experience of the mystics. Because of this she introduces the theme in her doctrinal synthesis of *The Interior Castle*.

> Now let us come to imaginative visions, for they say the devil meddles more in these than in the ones mentioned, and it must be so. But when these imaginative visions are from our Lord, they in some way seem to me more beneficial because they are in greater conformity with our nature. I'm excluding from that comparison the visions the Lord shows in the last dwelling place; no other visions are comparable to those. (IC 6.9.1)

This opening text from this chapter is remarkable. As in other passages, Teresa repeats her conviction that alongside the mystical visions are those that are not from God. For this reason, she takes up in this chapter the task of distinguishing or discerning the mystical vision from other visions or hallucinations. Another aspect of this short introduction is the evidence of her acquaintance with what theologians and others say about these imaginative visions: that one who receives them is more liable to abnormalities or being deceived by the devil. But, finally, when they are from the Lord, truly mystical experiences, they are more beneficial than the purely spiritual experiences "for they are more in conformity with our nature." It was theologians like St. Thomas Aquinas and St. Augustine who distinguished the intellectual visions from the imaginative ones. What is more important in our case is that this ladder of mystical experiences reflects Teresa's own history. Her favors began with the purely spiritual experiences (intellectual visions) of the Lord. Then came the experiences of his physical humanity (imaginative visions). Finally, this process will culminate in the Trinitarian experiences of the seventh dwelling places.

How does Teresa discern the true mystical experience from the false visions? We know, because she tells us, that she had a great deal of experience with people whose imaginations, or their intellects, were so effective, or she didn't know what the cause was, that they become absorbed in the imagination to the extent that everything they think about seems clearly to be seen. Teresa maintains that they are composing what they see with their imagination. Their imagining has no effect afterward, but they are left cold. The true vision comes all at once and stirs all the faculties and senses with a great fear and tumult so as to place them afterward in that happy peace. Just as there was a "tumult that came from heaven when St. Paul was hurled to the ground, here in this interior world there is a great stirring" (IC 6.9.10), and then in a moment all remains calm. The soul is left well instructed about so many great truths that it has no need of any other master. But this does not mean that it should not proceed very openly and truthfully with its confessor in giving an account of its prayer. And Teresa suffered extensive agony because of the ignorance of her confessors.

The Lord's beauty and majesty are in no way imaginable by any human effort. And there is no need, then, to ask how the soul knows that it is the Lord, for it is clearly revealed in this beauty and majesty that he is the Lord of heaven and earth. Seeing the beauty of the Lord was equivalent to loving him with all her being. But beyond the affective plane of love, the visions introduced her to light and truth. The experience of Paul, who was thrown to the ground on the road to Damascus, is in a certain way repeated.

Finally, Teresa warns, one should never desire or beseech the Lord to lead it by this path. Among those reasons mentioned by Teresa, two stand out: the true followers of Christ base their journey on humility and so are far from aiming after such privileges; and true lovers show their love in sacrifice and the cross much more than in enjoyments. Teresa never had the opportunity to read the writings of St. John of the Cross about how the inordinate appetites for visions and ecstasies can impede union with God. But she probably heard the doctrine directly from her conversations with him:

> I know a person or two persons—one was a man—to whom the Lord had granted some of these favors, who were so desirous of serving His Majesty at their own cost, without these great delights, and so anxious to suffer that they complained to our Lord because He bestowed the favors on them, and if they could decline receiving these gifts they would do so. (IC 6.9.17)

These two are evidently John of the Cross and Teresa herself.

Teresa's detachment from extraordinary visions by no means impedes or contradicts the Church's teaching on the veneration of Christ in art and images, which has been defended by the Church throughout its history:

> At the same time, the Church has always acknowledged that in the body of Jesus "we see our God made visible and so are caught up in love of the God we cannot see" (*Roman Missal*, Preface of Christmas). The individual character- istics of Christ's body express the divine person of God's Son. He has made the features of his human body his own, to the point that they can be venerated when portrayed in a holy image, for the believer "who venerates the icon is venerating in it the person of the one depicted" (Council of Nicaea II). (CCC 477)

Questions for Discussion

1. Why are imaginative visions in some way more beneficial than intellectual ones?
2. Can the soul gaze on these visions?
3. Should you avoid speaking of these favors to your confes- sor when he is inexperienced in these matters?
4. Why should we not desire to follow this path of visions from God?
5. Since God was made visible in the Incarnation, do you think it is helpful to meditate on the bodily appearance of Jesus through his depiction in art?

CHAPTER 10

Tells about other favors God grants the soul, in a way different from those just mentioned, and of the great profit that comes from them.

In many ways does the Lord communicate Himself to the soul through these apparitions. He grants some of them when it is afflicted; others, when a great trial is about to come; others, so that His Majesty might take His delight in the soul and give delight to it. There's no reason to go into further detail about each, since my intention is only to explain the different favors there are on this road, insofar as I understand them. Thus you will know, sisters, their nature and their effects, lest we fancy that everything imagined is a vision. When what you see is an authentic vision, you won't go about disturbed or afflicted if you understand that such a thing is possible. [The devil gains much and is extremely pleased to see a soul afflicted and disquieted, for he knows that disturbance impedes it from being totally occupied in loving and praising God.]

His Majesty communicates Himself in other ways that are more sublime, and less dangerous because the devil, I believe, will be unable to counterfeit them. Thus, since these latter are something very secret, it is difficult to explain them, whereas the imaginative visions are easier to explain.

2. It will happen, when the Lord is pleased, that while the soul is in prayer and very much in its senses a suspension will suddenly be experienced in which the Lord will reveal deep secrets. It seems the soul sees these secrets in

God Himself, for they are not visions of the most sacred humanity. Although I say the soul sees, it doesn't see anything, for the favor is not an imaginative vision but very much an intellectual one. In this vision it is revealed how all things are seen in God and how He has them all in Himself.[1] This favor is most beneficial. Even though it passes in a moment, it remains deeply engraved in the soul and causes the greatest confusion. The evil of offending God is seen more clearly, because while being in God Himself (I mean being within Him) we commit great evils. I want to draw a comparison—if I succeed—so as to explain this to you. For although what I said is true, and we hear it often, either we do not pay attention to this truth or we do not want to understand it. If the matter were understood, it doesn't seem it would be possible to be so bold.

3. Let's suppose that God is like an immense and beautiful dwelling or palace and that this palace, as I say, is God Himself.[2] Could the sinner, perhaps, so as to engage in his evil deeds leave this palace? No, certainly not; rather, within the palace itself, that is within God Himself, the abominations, indecent actions, and evil deeds committed by us sinners take place. Oh, frightful thought, worthy of deep reflection, and very beneficial for those of us who know little. We don't completely understand these truths, for otherwise it wouldn't be possible to be so foolishly audacious! Let us consider, sisters, the great mercy and compassion of God in not immediately destroying us there, and be extremely thankful to Him, and let us be ashamed to feel resentment about anything that is said or done against us. The greatest evil of the world is

---

1. See L 40.9.
2. For the origin of this comparison see L 40.10.

that God, our Creator, suffers so many evil things from His creatures within His very self and that we sometimes resent a word said in our absence and perhaps with no evil intention.

4. Oh, human misery! When, daughters, will we imitate this great God? Oh, let us not think we are doing anything by suffering injuries, but we should very eagerly endure everything, and let us love the one who offends us since this great God has not ceased to love us even though we have offended Him very much. Thus the Lord is right in wanting all to pardon the wrongs done to them.[3]

I tell you, daughters, that even though this vision passes quickly it is a great favor from our Lord if one desires to benefit from it by keeping it habitually present.

5. It also happens very quickly and ineffably that God will show within Himself a truth that seems to leave in obscurity all those there are in creatures, and one understands very clearly that God alone is Truth, unable to lie.[4] What David says in a psalm about every man being a liar is clearly understood.[5] However frequently the verse may be heard, it is never understood as it is in this vision. God is everlasting Truth. I am reminded of Pilate, how he was often questioning our Lord when during the passion he asked Him, "What is truth?"[6] and of the little we understand here below about this supreme Truth.

6. I would like to be able to explain more about this, but it is unexplainable. Let us conclude, sisters, that in order to live in conformity with our God and Spouse in something, it will be well if we always study diligently how to walk in this

---

3. Allusion to Mt 6:12, 15; Lk 6:37.
4. Teresa gives a personal account of this experience in L 40.1–4.
5. Ps 116:11.
6. Jn 18:36–38.

truth.] I'm not merely saying that we should not tell lies, for in that regard, glory to God, I already notice that you take great care in these houses not to tell a lie for anything. I'm saying that we should walk in truth before God and people in as many ways as possible. Especially, there should be no desire that others consider us better than we are. And in our works we should attribute to God what is His and to ourselves what is ours and strive to draw out the truth in everything. [Thus, we shall have little esteem for this world, which is a complete lie and falsehood, and as such will not endure.]

7. Once I was pondering why our Lord was so fond of this virtue of humility, and this thought came to me—in my opinion not as a result of reflection but suddenly: It is because God is supreme Truth; and to be humble is to walk in truth, for it is a very deep truth that of ourselves we have nothing good but only misery and nothingness. Whoever does not understand this walks in falsehood. The more anyone understands it the more he pleases the supreme Truth because he is walking in truth. Please God, sisters, we will be granted the favor never to leave this path of self-knowledge, amen.

8. Our Lord grants these favors to the soul because, as to one to whom He is truly betrothed, one who is already determined to do His will in everything, He desires to give it some knowledge of how to do His will and of His grandeurs. There's no reason to deal with more than these two things I mentioned[7] since they seem to me very beneficial. In similar things there is nothing to fear; rather, the Lord should be praised because He gives them. The devil, in my opinion, and even one's own imagination have little capacity at this level, and so the soul is left with profound satisfaction.

---

7. In IC 6.10.2, 5.

DEEP SECRETS ARE
REVEALED WHILE THE SOUL
IS IN SUSPENSION

6.10.1 In this chapter Teresa writes about yet a different type of favor. Some, she says, are given to comfort or strengthen, and others are given to provide delight to the soul. She says that she won't go into great detail, but she hopes to give information so that people who experience these visions will not be upset since they will understand that their experiences are from the Lord. On the other hand, she wants to provide enough description so that persons won't think that everything they imagine is a vision. Some of these experiences Teresa says are more difficult to explain than the imaginative visions discussed in chapter 9.

6.10.2 Although in the first part of this chapter Teresa referred to these favors as apparitions, in this second paragraph she calls them intellectual visions. When she wrote about intellectual visions in chapter 8, she described them as experiencing the Lord as present. Here she describes the visions as being a revelation of how things are seen in God and how he has them all in himself.

6.10.3-4 Here Teresa changes her metaphor and tells us to think of God as a great palace in which we live. In this metaphor, God is everywhere, and we always dwell in him, and even commit sins in him. God, our creator, suffers so many things from his creatures within his very self. When will we imitate this great God? Let us not think we do anything by suffering injuries, but very eagerly endure them and love the one who offends us.

6.10.5–7 Teresa describes another favor. She says God can show himself to be Truth itself, a standard by which human truth seems lesser and inadequate. Teresa says that she cannot explain anything further about this unexplainable truth, but urges us to walk in this truth in as many ways as we can. She gives examples of what she means. She says that humility and self-knowledge are ways to walk in truth.

6.10.8 Teresa writes that the Lord gives these favors to those to whom he is betrothed so they will better understand his grandeurs and how to do his will. In these favors, she says, neither the devil nor a person's imagination can interfere and the soul enjoys profound satisfaction.

Interpretive Notes

As Teresa approaches the last dwelling places, those in the deepest center of her being, those containing the greatest secrets, she dwells in these last two chapters, chapters ten and eleven, in a kind of waiting room. She must pass through two zones first, one of light and the other of fire. First is the light of truth—or better put, the light of the Truth. Of this she treats in chapter ten. Then follows the zone of uncontainable desires, so impetuous and great that they actually place her in danger of death. These will be dealt with in the last chapter of the sixth dwelling places, as a kind of prelude to the seventh. So, truth and desire are the two wings with which Teresa takes flight into the mysterious region of the last dwelling place.

The truth will make you free. Recalling the episode in the Gospels where Pilate questions Jesus, "What is truth?" but then turns away without waiting for an answer, Teresa is very interested in the question, but she underlines the fact that we understand very little here below about the supreme

Truth. In her own personal history, she comes to the stage addressed by the final chapter of her *Life*. She speaks of how her soul began to be enkindled and there came upon her a spiritual rapture in which she was carried into and filled with God's majesty. In that experience she was given knowledge of a truth that is the fulfillment of all truths. She clearly understood that it was Truth itself telling her: "all the harm that comes to the world comes from its not knowing the truths of Scripture in clarity and truth; not one iota of Scripture will fall short" (L 40.1). To enter into the last dwelling place one must be free of every lie. In the depths of all of us there lurks something of the lie. Teresa understood clearly "that which I observe as not being directed toward the service of God seems to me to be such vanity and deception that I wouldn't know how to describe the manner in which I understand this" (L 40.2). So Teresa clearly understands what David says about every man being a liar.

Once, while thinking about why God was so fond of the virtue of humility, the thought suddenly came to Teresa, not as a result of reflection, she insists:

> It is because God is supreme Truth; and to be humble is to walk in truth, for it is a very deep truth that of ourselves we have nothing good but only misery and nothingness. Whoever does not understand this walks in falsehood. The more anyone understands it the more he pleases the supreme Truth because he is walking in truth. (IC 6.10.7)

The *Catechism of the Catholic Church* states:

> In Jesus Christ, the whole of God's truth has been made manifest. "Full of grace and truth," he came as the "light of the world," he is *the Truth*. "Whoever believes in me may

not remain in darkness." The disciple of Jesus continues in his word so as to know "the truth [that] will make you free" and that sanctifies. To follow Jesus is to live in "the Spirit of truth," whom the Father sends in his name and who leads "into all the truth." To his disciples Jesus teaches the unconditional love of truth: "Let what you say be simply 'Yes or No.'" (CCC 2466)

This experience of God as Truth is the highest experience with which Teresa, some years previously, closed her *Life*. Now she not only recalls that experience, but she proposes it as a stage in approaching the final dwelling places. "Blessed is the soul the Lord brings to the understanding of truth!" (L 21.1). Now at this point in *The Interior Castle*, Teresa returns to speak of the liberating efficacy of this experience of truth: "This favor is most beneficial. Even though it passes in a moment, it remains deeply engraved in the soul and causes the greatest confusion. The evil of offending God is seen more clearly, because while being in God Himself (I mean being within Him) we commit great evils" (IC 6.10.2).

We might here give a little attention to how Teresa changes her metaphor and says that God is like a palace in which we all live. Everything we do and think takes place in him and we cannot ever escape from this palace. Most modern philosophical explanations infer that God is the highest member of the order of being. However, unlike orthodox Catholic doctrine, these models do not account for God's immanent presence in the world. An opposite model, also rejected by the Catholic Church, is called pantheism ("all is God"), which erases the difference between created and uncreated, thereby collapsing God and the world into each other. The model that allows for the most intelligible interpretation of this presence, as it was revealed to Teresa, is neither of these two modern explanations. Instead, Teresa envisions a relationship whereby everything abides in God, who in turn holds everything in existence. This is the God as understood by St. Paul in Ephesians, "above all and through all and in all" (Eph 4:6).

Questions for Discussion

1. When is God likely to communicate these apparitions?
2. What is an example of a deep secret that God reveals to the soul?
3. Where do the evil deeds of sinners take place?
4. What does this tell us about God?

CHAPTER 11

Treats of some desires God gives the soul that are so powerful and vehement they place it in danger of death. Treats also of the benefits caused by this favor the Lord grants.

Do you think that all these favors the Spouse has bestowed on the soul will be sufficient to satisfy the little dove or butterfly—don't think I have forgotten it—so that it may come to rest in the place where it will die? No, certainly not; rather, this little butterfly is much worse. Even though it may have been receiving these favors for many years, it always moans and goes about sorrowful because they leave it with greater pain. The reason is that since it is getting to know ever more the grandeurs of its God and sees itself so distant and far from enjoying Him, the desire for the Lord increases much more; also, love increases in the measure the soul discovers how much this great God and Lord deserves to be loved. And this desire continues gradually growing in these years so that it reaches a point of suffering as great as that I shall now speak of. I have said "years" so as to be in line with the experience of that person I've mentioned here,[1] for I well understand that one must not put limits on God; in a moment He can bring a soul to the lofty experience mentioned here. His Majesty has the power to do whatever He wants and is eager to do many things for us.

2. Well, here is what happens sometimes to a soul that experiences these anxious longings, tears, sighs, and great

_____
1. The person is herself. See IC 6.10.2–5.

impulses that were mentioned[2] (for all of these seem to proceed from our love with deep feelings, but they are all nothing in comparison with this other experience that I'm going to explain, for they resemble a smoking fire that though painful can be endured). While this soul is going about in this manner, burning up within itself, a blow is felt from elsewhere (the soul doesn't understand from where or how). The blow comes often through a sudden thought or word about death's delay. Or the soul will feel pierced by a fiery arrow.[3] I don't say that there is an arrow, but whatever the experience, the soul realizes clearly that the feeling couldn't come about naturally. Neither is the experience that of a blow, although I said "blow"; but it causes a sharp wound. And, in my opinion, it isn't felt where earthly sufferings are felt, but in the very deep and intimate part of the soul, where this sudden flash of lightning reduces to dust everything it finds in this earthly nature of ours; for while this experience lasts nothing can be remembered about our being. In an instant the experience so binds the faculties that they have no freedom for anything except those things that will make this pain increase.

3. I wouldn't want what I say to appear to be an exaggeration. Indeed, I see that my words fall short because the experience is unexplainable. It is an enrapturing of the faculties and senses away from everything that is not a help, as I said, to feeling this affliction. For the intellect is very alive to understanding the reason why the soul feels far from God; and His Majesty helps at that time with a vivid knowledge of Himself in such a way that the pain increases to a point

---

2. In IC 6.2.1; 6.6.6; 6.8.4.

3. Teresa describes an equivalent experience of hers that took place at Salamanca in 1571. See ST 12.1–5.

that makes the one who experiences it begin to cry aloud. Though she is a person who has suffered and is used to suffering severe pains, she cannot then do otherwise. This feeling is not in the body, as was said,[4] but in the interior part of the soul. [As a result, this person understood how much more severe the feelings of the soul are than those of the body,] and she reflected that such must be the nature of the sufferings of souls in purgatory, for the fact that these souls have no body doesn't keep them from suffering much more than they do through all the bodily sufferings they endure here on earth.

4. I saw a person in this condition; truly she thought she was dying, and this was not so surprising because certainly there is great danger of death.[5] And thus, even though the experience lasts a short while, it leaves the body very disjointed, and during that time the heartbeat is as slow as it would be if a person were about to render his soul to God. This is no exaggeration, for the natural heat fails, and the fire so burns the soul that with a little more intensity God would have fulfilled the soul's desires. This is true not because a person feels little or much pain in the body; although it is disjointed, as I said, in such a way that for three of four days afterward one feels great sufferings and doesn't even have the strength to write. And it even seems to me always that the body is left weaker. The reason one doesn't feel the pain must be that the interior feeling of the soul is so much greater that one doesn't pay any attention to the body. When one experiences a very sharp bodily pain, other bodily pains are hardly felt even though there may be many. I have indeed experienced this. With the presence of this spiritual pain, I

---

4. In IC 6.11.2.

5. She is speaking of herself. See ST 59.14; L 20.12–14.

don't believe that physical pain would be felt, little or much, even if the body were cut in pieces.

5. You will tell me that this feeling is an imperfection and ask why the soul doesn't conform to the will of God since it is so surrendered to Him. Until now it could do this, and has spent its life doing so. As for now, the reasoning faculty is in such a condition that the soul is not the master of it, nor can the soul think of anything else than of why it is grieving, of how it is absent from its Good, and of why it should want to live. It feels a strange solitude because no creature in all the earth provides it company, nor do I believe would any heavenly creature, not being the One whom it loves; rather, everything torments it. But the soul sees that it is like a person hanging, who cannot support himself on any earthly thing; nor can it ascend to heaven. On fire with this thirst, it cannot get to the water; and the thirst is not one that is endurable but already at such a point that nothing will take it away. Nor does the soul desire that the thirst be taken away save by that water of which our Lord spoke to the Samaritan woman.[6] Yet no one gives such water to the soul.

6. Oh, God help me! Lord, how You afflict Your lovers! But everything is small in comparison with what You give them afterward. [It's natural that what is worth much costs much.] Moreover, if the suffering is to purify this soul so that it might enter the seventh dwelling place—just as those who will enter heaven must be cleansed in purgatory—it is as small as a drop of water in the sea. Furthermore, in spite of all this torment and affliction, which cannot be surpassed, I believe, by any earthly afflictions (for this person had suffered many bodily as well as spiritual pains, but they all seemed nothing

6. Jn 4:7–14.

in comparison with this suffering), the soul feels that the pain is precious; so precious—it understands very well—that one could not deserve it. However, this awareness is not of a kind that alleviates the suffering in any way. But with this knowledge the soul suffers the pain very willingly and would suffer it all its life, if God were to be thereby served; although the soul would not then die once but be always dying, for truly the suffering is no less than death.

7. Well, let us consider, sisters, those who are in hell, who do not have this conformity or this consolation and spiritual delight which is placed by God in the soul; nor do they see that their suffering is beneficial, but they always suffer more and more. The torments of the soul are so much more severe than those of the body, and the torment souls in hell suffer is incomparably greater than the suffering we have here mentioned, and must, it is seen, last forever and ever. What, then, will the suffering of these unfortunate souls be? And what can we do or suffer in so short a life that would amount to anything if we were thereby to free ourselves of those terrible and eternal torments? I tell you it would be impossible to explain how keenly felt is the suffering of the soul, and how different it is from that of the body, if one had not experienced these things. And the Lord Himself desires that we understand this so that we may know the extraordinary debt we owe Him for bringing us to a state in which through His mercy we hope He will free us and pardon our sins.

8. Well, to return to what we were dealing with[7]—for we left this soul with much pain—this pain lasts only a short while in such intensity. At the most it will last three or four hours, in my opinion, because if it were to last a long while,

---

7. In IC 6.11.2, 4.

natural weakness would not be able to endure it unless by a miracle. It has happened that the experience lasted no more than a quarter of an hour but left the soul in pieces. Truly, that time the person lost her senses completely, and the pain came in its rigor merely from her hearing a word about life not ending. This happened while she was engaged in conversation during Easter week, the last day of the octave, after she had spent all of Easter in so much dryness she almost didn't know it was Easter. In no way can the soul resist. It can no more do so than it can, if thrown in a fire, stop flames from having heat and burning it. This feeling is not one that can be concealed from others, but those who are present are aware of the great danger in which the person lies, although they cannot be witnesses to what is taking place interiorly. True, they provide some company, as though they were shadows; and so, like shadows, do all earthly things appear to that person.

9. And that you realize, in case you might sometime have this experience, what is due to our weakness, it happens at times that while in that state, as you have seen, the soul dies with the desire to die. For the fire afflicts so much that seemingly hardly anything keeps the soul from leaving the body. The soul truly fears and lest it end up dying would want the pain to abate. The soul indeed understands that this fear is from natural weakness, because on the other hand its desire to die is not taken away. Nor can a remedy be found to remove this pain until the Lord Himself takes it away, usually by means of a great rapture, or with some vision, where the true Comforter consoles and strengthens the soul that it might desire to live as long as God wills.

10. This experience is a painful one, but the soul is left with the most beneficial effects, and fear of the trials that can

come its way is lost. When compared to the painful feeling experienced in the soul, the trials don't seem to amount to anything. The benefits are such that one would be pleased to suffer the pain often. But one can in no way do this, nor is there any means for suffering the experience again. The soul must wait until the Lord desires to give this favor, just as there is no way to resist it or remove it when it comes. The soul is left with greater contempt for the world than before because it sees that nothing in the world was any help to it in that torment, and it is much more detached from creatures because it now sees that only the Creator can console and satisfy it. And it has greater fear of offending Him, taking more care not to do so, because it sees that He can also torment as well as console.

11. Two experiences, it seems to me, which lie on this spiritual path, put a person in danger of death: the one is this pain, for it truly is a danger, and no small one; the other is overwhelming joy and delight, which reaches so extraordinary a peak that indeed the soul, I think, swoons to the point that it is hardly kept from leaving the body—indeed, its happiness could not be considered small.

Here you will see, sisters, whether I was right in saying that courage is necessary,[8] and whether when you ask the Lord for these favors He is right in answering as He did the sons of Zebedee, *are you able to drink the chalice?*[9]

12. I believe all of us, sisters, will answer yes; and very rightly so, for His Majesty gives strength to the one He sees has need of it. He defends these souls in all things; when they are persecuted and criticized, He answers for them as He did

---

8. See IC 6.4.
9. Mt 20:22.

for the Magdalene[10]—if not through words, through deeds. And in the very end, before they die, He will pay for everything at once, as you will now see. May He be blessed forever, and may all creatures praise Him, amen.

---

10. Lk 7:40–48.

THESE FAVORS LEAVE
THE LITTLE BUTTERFLY
WITH GREATER PAIN

6.11.1–3 Teresa proposes to explain some of the soul's deep desires for God. She returns to the butterfly or little moth; it never seems to be able to rest in anything. She says the more favors the soul receives, the more it suffers in seeing itself still so distant from God and far from enjoying him. She says even though these desires are painful, they are bearable. But in souls who suffer in this way another thing can happen. She says the soul experiences a sharp, sudden wound, as from an arrow, that reduces everything of our earthly nature to dust. The soul's whole attention is held by this experience, and the intense knowledge of God imparted in the experience causes deepest pain as the soul understands two things—an enrapturing knowledge of God and at the same time the feeling that God is far away. Teresa reflects that this must be the pain of souls in purgatory.

6.11.4 Teresa describes the physical sensations that accompany this experience of God, but she says that the spiritual pain is much greater than the physical pain.

6.11.5 She answers criticisms that might be raised in response to her description. She says that some might think the suffering experienced by persons favored with this knowledge is a sign of lack of conformity to the will of God. She says in this case the soul is not master of reason. The soul is suspended in torment between earthly things that hold no attraction for it and the God whom it loves and desires above all things and finds unattainable. Yet the pain is such that the soul does not want to be deprived of it. Teresa uses the example of the Samaritan woman to explain this desire.

6.11.6–7 Teresa continues her description of the soul's suffering, but adds that the pain is small in comparison to the reward that the soul receives later. She also says the suffering purifies the soul to prepare it to enter the seventh dwelling places. She compares this suffering with the suffering in hell, which she says is incomparably greater and lasts forever. She says the Lord wants souls to understand spiritual suffering so we can know the debt we owe him for bringing us to a state in which, through his mercy, we hope, he will free us and pardon our sins.

6.11.8 Teresa says that the greatest intensity of the pain lasts only a short while—perhaps, at most, for three or four hours. She describes one instance in which a quarter hour of this pain was enough to leave the soul in pieces. Such an experience is irresistible and can come in an instant. Persons who witness another so overcome can do very little for the suffering one beyond providing some company.

6.11.9–11 Teresa sums up by saying that the soul dies of the desire to die (and so be with God). Only the Lord can provide a remedy and strengthen the soul with determination to live for as long as God wills. Teresa describes many good effects that follow this favor of intense longing. Teresa says two experiences on this path put a person in danger of death. One is the pain of longing and the other is an intense joy. She says for these reasons great courage is necessary, and she quotes the Lord's words: "Are you able to drink this chalice?" (Mt 20:22). Her belief is that we will answer yes, for the Lord will give the strength necessary for this path.

Interpretive Notes

Teresa was always a woman of great desires. In her *Life* she writes: "Although in this matter of desires I have always had great ones" (L 13.6). Later she writes, "I am imperfection incarnate, except in desires" (L 30.17). But these desires she speaks of now come from a different region, arising from the deepest part of her soul, beyond the depths of our visceral instincts or of our rational cravings and longings. In Teresa's intimate history, she relates an experience that serves as a point of reference. The episode took place on Easter 1571, in Salamanca during community recreation. A young novice, Isabel de Jimena, sang with a beautiful voice a song about longing love: "*Veante mis ojos / dulce Jesús bueno. / veante mis ojos / muerame yo luego.*" (Let my eyes see you / O sweet, gentle Jesus. / Let my eyes see you / and I will die at once.) In her *Meditations on the Song of Songs* (SS 7.2), she tells again of how a person she knew (she is referring to herself) would have easily died if the beautiful singing that was the cause of her ecstasy had not stopped. In listening to those words and the accompanying music, Teresa fell into a profound ecstasy and they had to carry her to the most hidden spot in the monastery. She speaks in more detail of this experience in *Spiritual Testimonies* (ST 59.14–16).

Teresa had often experienced a relationship with our Lord similar to St. Mary Magdalene's. In this vein she wrote in one of her *Spiritual Testimonies*:

> The desires and impulses for death, which were so strong, have left me, especially since the feast day of St. Mary Magdalene; for I resolved to live very willingly in order to render much service to God. There is the exception

sometimes when no matter how much I try to reject the desire to see Him, I cannot. (ST 17)

Only some months after this episode of Isabel's singing, Teresa, returning to the monastery of the Incarnation as prioress, placed herself under the direction of St. John of the Cross. She was in her fifties at the time and he was only thirty. But both knew through their mystical experience of these great desires to die. Both, in fact, wrote a poem on this refrain: *Que muero porque no muero (I die because I do not die)*. This period of great desires ended for Teresa with her entry into the seventh dwelling places. She herself gives us the date: November 18, 1572, after receiving the Eucharist from John of the Cross (ST 31).

Why does Teresa experience this storm of desires—and desires for what? The answer to the question flows from the special human situation of the mystic. There comes a time in her life when she perceives in the most refined point of her spirit the absence of God in her own life—the absence and transcendence of someone absolutely necessary and indispensable if she is going to live, love, and possess. And at the same time this someone is unobtainable on account of the earthly condition of our life, wherein the soul is inserted and rooted in a sensible world that little by little is diminishing, growing weaker and becoming less sufficient for life. It's as if the whole world of creation had fallen into a zone of emptiness and insufficiency. This produces in the mystic the sensation of a total solitude:

It feels a strange solitude because no creature in all the earth provides it company, nor do I believe would any heavenly creature, not being the One whom it loves; rather, everything torments it . . . On fire with this thirst, it cannot get to the water; and the thirst is not one that is endurable . . . Yet no one gives such water to the soul. (IC 6.11.5)

This pain lasts only a short while in such intensity. At the most it will last only three or four hours, in my opinion, because if it were to last a long while, natural weakness would not be able to endure unless by a miracle. It has happened that the experience lasted no more than a quarter of an hour but left the soul in pieces. (IC 6.11.8)

In her *Spiritual Testimonies* we read another account of this pain of love:

The fact is that it seems everything the soul understands then adds to its pain, and that the Lord doesn't want it to profit in its entire being from anything else. Nor does its will appear to be alive, but it seems to be in so great a solitude and so forsaken by all that this abandonment cannot be described in writing. For the whole world and its affairs give it pain, and no created thing provides it with company, nor does it want any company but only the Creator; and it seems that having such company is impossible unless it dies. Since it must not kill itself, it so dies with the longing to die that there is true danger of death; and it finds itself as though hanging between heaven and earth. (ST 59.14)

As for the benefits of such an experience:

The soul must wait until the Lord desires to give this favor, just as there is no way to resist it or remove it when it comes. The soul is left with greater contempt for the world than before because it sees that nothing in the world was any help to it in that torment, and it is much more detached from creatures because it now sees that only the Creator can console and satisfy it. And it has greater fear of offending Him, taking more care not to do so, because it sees that He can also torment as well as console. (IC 6.11.10)

Questions for Discussion

1. Why do God's favors leave the soul with greater pain?
2. Where does the pain described here exist?
3. Why doesn't the soul, rather than wanting to die, just practice conformity to God's will?
4. Can the soul with such experiences ever feel dryness?
5. Why does it become more detached from creatures after experiencing this pain?
6. What are the benefits to such a pain?

THE SEVENTH DWELLING PLACES

Contains Four Chapters

CHAPTER 1

Treats of the great favors God grants souls that have entered the seventh dwelling places. Tells how in her opinion there is a certain difference between the soul and the spirit, although the soul is all one. The chapter contains noteworthy doctrine.

You will think, sisters, that since so much has been said about this spiritual path it will be impossible for anything more to be said. Such a thought would be very foolish. Since the greatness of God is without limits, His works are too. Who will finish telling of His mercies and grandeurs? To do so is impossible, and thus do not be surprised at what was said, and will be said, because it is but naught in comparison to what there is to tell of God. He grants us a great favor in having communicated these things to a person through whom we can know about them. Thus the more we know about His communication to creatures the more we will praise His grandeur and make the effort to have esteem for souls in which the Lord delights so much. Each one of us has a soul, but since we do not prize souls as is deserved by creatures made in the image of God, we do not understand the deep secrets that lie in them.

May it please His Majesty, if He may thereby be served to move my pen and give me understanding of how I might say something about the many things to be said and which God reveals to the one whom He places in this dwelling place. I have earnestly begged this of His Majesty since He knows that my intention is to make known His mercies that His name may be more praised and glorified.

2. I hope, not for myself but for you, sisters, that He may grant me this favor. Thus you will understand how important it is for you not to impede your Spouse's celebration of this spiritual marriage with your souls, since this marriage brings so many blessings, as you will see. O great God! It seems that a creature as miserable as I should tremble to deal with a thing so foreign to what I deserve to understand. And, indeed, I have been covered with confusion wondering if it might not be better to conclude my discussion of this dwelling place with just a few words. For it seems to me that others will think I know about it through experience. This makes me extremely ashamed; for, knowing what I am, such a thought is a terrible thing. On the other hand, the thought of neglecting to explain this dwelling place seemed to me to be a temptation and weakness on my part, no matter how many of the above judgments you make about me. May God be praised and understood a little more, and let all the world cry out against me; how much more so in that I will perhaps be dead when what I write is seen. May He be blessed who lives, and will live, forever, amen.

3. When our Lord is pleased to have pity on this soul that He has already taken spiritually as His spouse because of what it suffers and has suffered through its desires, He brings it, before the spiritual marriage is consummated, into His dwelling place, which is this seventh. For just as in heaven, so

in the soul His Majesty must have a room where He dwells alone. Let us call it another heaven. It's very important for us, sisters, not to think the soul is something dark. Since we do not see the soul, it usually seems that there is no such thing as interior light but only the exterior light which we all see, and that a certain darkness is in our soul. As for the soul that is not in grace, I confess this is so, but not through any fault of the Sun of Justice who dwells within it giving it being but because such a soul is incapable of receiving the light, as I believe I have said in the first dwelling place, according to what a certain person understood.[1] For these unfortunate souls are as though in a dark prison, bound hands and feet, in regard to doing anything good that would enable them to merit, and blind and deaf. We can rightly take pity on them and reflect that at one time we were ourselves in this condition and that the Lord can also have mercy on them.

4. Let us take special care, sisters, to beg this mercy of Him and not be careless, for it is a most generous alms to pray for those who are in mortal sin. Suppose we were to see a Christian with his hands fastened behind his back by a strong chain, bound to a post, and dying of hunger, not because of lack of food, for there are very choice dishes beside him, but because he cannot take hold of the food and eat, and even has great loathing for it; and suppose he sees that he is about to breathe his last and die, not just an earthly death but an eternal one. Wouldn't it be a terrible cruelty to stand looking at him and not feed him? Well, then, what if through your prayer the chains could be loosed? The answer is obvious. For the love of God I ask you always to remember in your prayers souls in mortal sin.

---

1. In IC 1.2.1–3.

5. We are not speaking about them now but about those who already by the mercy of God have done penance for their sins and are in the state of grace. Thus we are not reflecting on something restricted to a corner but on an interior world where there is room for so many and such attractive dwelling places, as you have seen; and indeed it is right that the soul be like this since within it there is a dwelling place for God.

Infinite

Now then, when His Majesty is pleased to grant the soul this divine marriage that was mentioned,[2] He first brings it into His own dwelling place. He desires that the favor be different from what it was at other times when He gave the soul raptures. I really believe that in rapture He unites it with Himself, as well as in the prayer of union that was mentioned.[3] But it doesn't seem to the soul that it is called to enter into its center, as it is here in this dwelling place, but called to the superior part. These things matter little; whether the experience comes in one way or another, the Lord joins the soul to Himself. But He does so by making it blind and deaf, as was St. Paul in his conversion,[4] and by taking away perception of the nature and kind of favor enjoyed, for the great delight the soul then feels is to see itself near God. Yet when He joins it to Himself, it doesn't understand anything; for all the faculties are lost.

6. In this seventh dwelling place the union comes about in a different way: our good God now desires to remove the scales from the soul's eyes and let it see and understand, although in a strange way, something of the favor He grants it. When the soul is brought into that dwelling place, the

---

2. In IC 7.1.3.

3. In the fifth dwelling place.

4. Acts 9:8.

Most Blessed Trinity, all three Persons, through an intellectual vision, is revealed to it through a certain representation of the truth. First there comes an enkindling in the spirit in the manner of a cloud of magnificent splendor; and these Persons are distinct, and through an admirable knowledge the soul understands as a most profound truth that all three Persons are one substance and one power and one knowledge and one God alone. It knows in such a way that what we hold by faith, it understands, we can say, through sight—although the sight is not with the bodily eyes nor with the eyes of the soul, because we are not dealing with an imaginative vision. Here all three Persons communicate themselves to it, speak to it, and explain those words of the Lord in the Gospel: that He and the Father and the Holy Spirit will come to dwell with the soul that loves Him and keeps His commandments.[5]

7. Oh, God help me! How different is hearing and believing these words from understanding their truth in this way! Each day this soul becomes more amazed, for these Persons never seem to leave it any more, but it clearly beholds, in the way that was mentioned,[6] that they are within it. In the extreme interior, in some place very deep within itself, the nature of which it doesn't know how to explain, because of a lack of learning, it perceives this divine company.

8. You may think that as a result the soul will be outside itself and so absorbed that it will be unable to be occupied with anything else. On the contrary, the soul is much more occupied than before with everything pertaining to the service of God; and once its duties are over it remains with that enjoyable company. If the soul does not fail God, He will

---

5. Jn 14:23. For another description of this grace see ST 13.
6. Through an intellectual vision; see IC 7.1.6.

never fail, in my opinion, to make His presence clearly known to it. It has strong confidence that since God has granted this favor He will not allow it to lose the favor. Though the soul thinks this, it goes about with greater care than ever not to displease Him in anything.

9. It should be understood that this presence is not felt so fully, I mean so clearly, as when revealed the first time or at other times when God grants the soul this gift. For if the presence were felt so clearly, the soul would find it impossible to be engaged in anything else or even to live among people. But even though the presence is not perceived with this very clear light, the soul finds itself in this company every time it takes notice. Let's say that the experience resembles that of a person who after being in a bright room with others finds himself, once the shutters are closed, in darkness. The light by which he could see them is taken away. Until it returns he doesn't see them, but not for that reason does he stop knowing they are present. It might be asked whether the soul can see them when it so desires and the light returns. To see them does not lie in its power, but depends on when our Lord desires that the window of the intellect be opened. Great is the mercy He shows in never departing from the soul and in desiring that it perceive Him so manifestly.

10. It seems that the divine Majesty desires, through this wonderful company, to prepare the soul for more. Clearly, the soul will be truly helped in every way to advance in perfection and to lose the fear it sometimes had of the other favors He granted it, as was said.[7] Such was the experience of this person,[8] for in everything she found herself improved,

---

7. In IC 6.3.3, 17; 6.6.6; 6.7.3; 6.8.3–4.

8. Teresa is referring to herself.

and it seemed to her, despite the trials she underwent and the business affairs she had to attend to, that the essential part of her soul never moved from that room. As a result, it seemed to her that there was, in a certain way, a division in her soul. And while suffering some great trials a little after God granted her this favor, she complained of that part of the soul, as Martha complained of Mary,[9] and sometimes pointed out that it was there always enjoying that quietude at its own pleasure while leaving her in the midst of so many trials and occupations that she could not keep it company.

11. This will seem to you, daughters, to be foolishness, but it truly happens in this way. Although we know that the soul is all one, what I say is no mere fancy; the experience is very common. Wherefore I said[10] that interior things are seen in such a way that one understands with certitude that there is some kind of difference, a difference clearly recognized, between the soul and the spirit, even though they are both one. So delicate a division is perceived that sometimes it seems the one functions differently from the other, and so does the savor the Lord desires to give them seem different. It also seems to me that the soul and the faculties are not one but different. There are so many and such delicate things in the interior that it would be boldness on my part to set out to explain them. In heaven we will see all this, if the Lord in His mercy grants us the favor of bringing us there where we shall understand these secrets.

---

9. Lk 10:40.
10. In IC 6.5.1, 9.

WE DO NOT UNDERSTAND
THE DEEP SECRETS
THAT LIE IN OUR SOULS

7.1.1 Teresa writes that no one can finish telling of the mercies and grandeurs of God. The more we know about God's communications to creatures, the more we will praise him and make the effort to value souls in which the Lord delights so much. Each of us has a soul, but we do not understand their deep secrets because we do not prize souls as is deserved by creatures made in the image of God. She prays for the Lord's inspiration to her in writing about things revealed in the seventh dwelling places.

7.1.2 Teresa tells the sisters that it is important not to impede their Spouse's celebration of the spiritual marriage in their souls because it brings so many blessings. She has misgivings about dealing with things so foreign to what she says she deserves to understand.

7.1.3–5 Before the spiritual marriage is consummated, the Lord brings the soul that he has already taken spiritually as his betrothed into his dwelling place, which is the seventh. In this place God dwells alone; Teresa calls it another heaven. After saying that it is important not to think of the soul in grace as something dark, Teresa is reminded of the contrary—the condition of souls not in grace. She says we should pity them and pray for them. But she returns then to her main topic of souls in grace who are favored with the spiritual marriage. She believes this union is different from previous unions in which the soul felt great delight but did not understand anything.

7.1.6–10 In the seventh dwelling places the union comes about in a different way. God desires to let the soul see and understand, although in a strange way, something of the favor he grants it. The Blessed Trinity, all three Persons, is revealed through a certain representation of the truth in an intellectual vision. Here all three Persons communicate themselves to the soul and explain the Lord's words in the Gospel: that he and the Father and the Holy Spirit will come to dwell with the soul that loves him and keeps his commandments. The soul clearly sees that the Persons of the Trinity are with it. Contrary to what you might think, rather than being totally absorbed and unable to do anything, the soul is more occupied than before in serving God. The soul takes greater care than ever not to displease him in anything. Teresa explains that the soul is able to continue its active service to God because the presence is only rarely perceived with a clear light. It is God and not the soul who determines the clarity and the intensity of the experience of presence. But it always enjoys this presence and when its duties are over it remains with that enjoyable presence.

7.1.11–12 This experience of the presence of the Trinity seems to prepare the soul for more. The soul advances in perfection. Teresa says the experience made her aware of a division in her soul, the division characterized by Mary and Martha in the Gospel account. Teresa complained at times, she says, as did Martha, that a part of her soul enjoyed quietude while leaving her in the midst of so many trials that she could not keep it company. Teresa says that the soul is one, but she thinks that there are differences between soul and spirit even though they are both one. She says it seems to her that the soul and faculties are different also.

Interpretive Notes

Teresa says she should tremble to speak of something so foreign to what she deserves to understand, but the thought of neglecting to explain this dwelling place so that God may be praised and understood a little more seemed to her to be a temptation. Now, because of what the soul has been suffering because of its desires, God brings it into his dwelling place, which is the seventh, the dwelling place of sanctity. Four chapters make up Teresa's discussion of this place. First of all, sanctity is a Trinitarian fact which takes place within the soul of the Christian and transforms it (7.1). Now, holiness for the Christian derives from the holiness of Jesus Christ and is realized through the relationship of a human being with Christ (7.2). So sanctity, or holiness, in its anthropological dimension is a fact of human plenitude: of the maturity of the new self in the development of its new life (7.3). Finally, sanctity is something that overflows the strict limits of the subject; it is grace for others, for the human community, for the sake of assuming the condition of a servant of God. This means that Christian holiness has an ecclesiastical dimension, and by that fact entails the charism of service of one's brothers and sisters (7.4).

Teresa begins her testimony about this dwelling place in this manner:

> When our Lord is pleased to have pity on this soul that He has already taken spiritually as His spouse, because of what it suffers and has suffered through its desires, He brings it, before the spiritual marriage is consummated, into His dwelling place, which is this seventh. For just as in heaven, so in the soul His Majesty must have a room where He dwells alone. Let us call it another heaven. (IC 7.1.3)

This grace is different from that of the fifth and sixth dwelling places in which God unites the soul with himself. Now he unites the soul with himself, not by making it blind and deaf as he does in these other two dwelling places of union; in this dwelling place, God desires to remove the scales from its eyes and let it see and understand, although in a strange way, something of the favor he grants it. Then Teresa goes on to explain more: "When the soul is brought into that dwelling place, the Most Blessed Trinity, all three Persons, through an intellectual vision, is revealed to it through a certain representation of the truth" (IC 7.1.6). She continues in this dwelling place to describe her experience of the three Persons of the Blessed Trinity: "Here all three Persons communicate themselves to it, speak to it, and explain those words of the Lord in the Gospel: that He and the Father and the Holy Spirit will come to dwell with the soul that loves Him and keeps His commandments" (IC 7.1.6).

The two components in this supreme happening are the human and the Trinitarian. From the perspective of the human being, a spiritual center emerges in the deepest part of the soul that only now reveals itself for the first time as destined or reserved for union with God. This center is characterized by its capacity for transcendence. Inspired by St. Paul, Teresa distinguishes between the soul and the human spirit. The soul has the biological function of animating the body. The spirit has a transcendent dimension. The sanctifying element does not flow from the spirit but from God, who becomes present and operative from this depth of the created spirit. Teresa knows that God alone is holy, and that all possible human holiness is derived from communion in Christ's sanctity. For the Christian, this communion carries the Trinitarian seal. From the moment of baptism, the believer is sealed with the grace of the Trinity. As for the fullness of this grace, Jesus makes the supreme promise of the indwelling: if anyone is faithful to me in life, "we will come to them and make our home in them" (Jn 14:23).

What is special about Teresa, and other mystics, is that they not only hear and believe these words, but also experience them: "Oh, God help me! How different is hearing and believing these words from understanding their truth in this way! Each day this soul becomes more amazed, for these Persons never seem to leave it anymore, but it clearly beholds . . . that they are within it. In the extreme interior, in some place very deep within itself, the nature of which it doesn't know how to explain, because of a lack of learning, it perceives this divine company" (IC 7.1.7).

In her *Spiritual Testimonies*, Teresa speaks of other experiences of the indwelling of the Blessed Trinity in her soul:

> On the Tuesday following Ascension Thursday, having remained a while in prayer after Communion, I was grieved because I was so distracted I couldn't concentrate. So I complained to the Lord about our miserable nature. My soul began to enkindle, and it seemed to me I knew clearly in an intellectual vision that the entire Blessed Trinity was present. In this state my soul understood by a certain kind of representation (like an illustration of the truth), in such a way that my dullness could perceive, how God is three and one. And so it seemed that all three Persons were represented distinctly in my soul and that they spoke to me, telling me that from this day I would see an improvement in myself. . . . I understood those words the Lord spoke, that the three divine Persons would be with the soul in grace; for I saw them within myself in the way described. (ST 13.1)

This presence was still with her a month later, as we read in *Spiritual Testimony* 14. A year and a half later, she speaks of a vision of the Blessed Trinity which was not permanent but was beheld in an imaginative vision, which wore away after a few days (ST 29.1). But actually, this indwelling presence which she began to experience in the seventh dwelling place continued right up to her final *Spiritual Testimony* in 1581; she writes:

> The imaginative visions have ceased, but it seems this intellectual vision of these three Persons and of the humanity of Christ always continues. This intellectual vision, in my opinion, is something much more sublime. Now I understand, as it seems, that these imaginative visions I experienced were from God, for they disposed the soul for its present state. Since it was so miserable and had so little fortitude, God led it as He saw was necessary. In my opinion when visions are from God they should be greatly prized. (ST 65.3)

What Teresa explains about her experience in *The Interior Castle* did cause trouble for her text later on. The text reads thus:

> It knows in such a way that what we hold by faith, it understands, we can say, through sight—although the sight is not with the bodily eyes nor with the eyes of the soul, because we are not dealing with an imaginative vision. Here all three Persons communicate themselves to it, speak to it, and explain those words of the Lord in the Gospel: that He and the Father and the Holy Spirit will come to dwell with the soul that loves Him and keeps His commandments. (IC 7.1.6)

This passage seemed problematic for the theologians of Teresa's time. Didn't Jesus say that no one has seen God, but only the Son? Luis de León, in editing this page for the first time, thought that a marginal note was called for, which appeared beside the text in his edition. It began in this way: "Although a human person in this life, losing the use of the senses and elevated by God, can see in passing his essence, as it is said, probably is true in the cases of St. Paul and Moses . . . but Teresa is not speaking of this kind of vision." He is affirming that Teresa is not saying what she says but what, according to theologians, she ought to have said. But even before Luis de León, another theologian, a friend of Teresa's, the Carmelite Jerónimo Gracián, somewhat alarmed by the boldness of the author, imposed his own corrections on the text. He crossed it out and emended it in such a way that it reads: "What we hold by faith, the soul understands better there. We can say that it seems to be through sight, although it is not sight through the eyes of the body or of the spirit." He actually dilutes the pure wine of Teresa's testimony. Our question is: are the theologians faithful in their interpretations to the prophetic witness of Teresa?

In her role as a prophet, called to give testimony, Teresa does not make use of the terms used by the theologians of her times. She speaks directly of her experience with a realism we expect from a firsthand witness. She is caught in the abyss existing between her explanation and what cannot be explained, the ineffable mystical experience. And she finds the narrow confines of theological categories of no help. In fact, theologians did denounce her to the Inquisition for these pages of *The Interior Castle*, and this even reached Rome at the time of her cause for beatification.

The ultimate end of the whole divine economy is the entry of God's creatures into the perfect unity of the Blessed Trinity. But even now we are called to be a dwelling for the Most Holy Trinity: "Those who love me will keep my word, and my Father will love them, and we will come to them and make our home with them." (Jn 14:23)

Perhaps it is best to turn to one of St. Teresa's daughters for further elucidation on this matter:

> O my God, Trinity whom I adore, help me forget myself entirely so to establish myself in you, immovable and peaceful as if my soul were already in eternity. May nothing be able to trouble my peace or make me leave you, O my unchanging God, but may each minute bring me more deeply into your mystery! Grant my soul peace. Make it your heaven, your beloved dwelling and the place of your rest. May I never abandon you there, but may I be there, whole and entire, completely vigilant in my faith, entirely adoring and wholly given over to your creative action. (Prayer of St. Elizabeth of the Trinity, CCC 260)

Questions for Discussion

1. Why do we fail to understand the deep secrets that lie within souls?
2. What is required for God to take the soul as his spouse?
3. What are the very generous alms we can give a soul?
4. What does God do before he grants the grace of spiritual marriage?
5. What happens when the soul is brought into the center dwelling place?
6. What is the difference between the soul and the spirit?

CHAPTER 2

Continues on the same subject. Explains the difference between spiritual union and spiritual marriage. Describes this difference through some delicate comparisons.

Now then, let us deal with the divine and spiritual marriage, although this great favor does not come to its perfect fullness as long as we live; for if we were to withdraw from God, this remarkable blessing would be lost.

The first time the favor is granted, His Majesty desires to show Himself to the soul through an imaginative vision of His most sacred humanity so that the soul will understand and not be ignorant of receiving this sovereign gift. With other persons the favor will be received in another form. With regard to the one of whom we are speaking, the Lord represented Himself to her, just after she had received Communion, in the form of shining splendor, beauty, and majesty, as He was after His resurrection, and told her that now it was time that she consider as her own what belonged to Him and that He would take care of what was hers, and He spoke other words destined more to be heard than to be mentioned.[1]

2. It may seem that this experience was nothing new since at other times the Lord had represented Himself to the soul in such a way. The experience was so different that it left her indeed stupefied and frightened: first, because this vision came with great force; second, because of the words the Lord spoke to her; and also because in the interior of her

---

1. See her corresponding account in ST 31.

soul, where He represented Himself to her, she had not seen other visions except the former one.[2] You must understand that there is the greatest difference between all the previous visions and those of this dwelling place. Between the spiritual betrothal and the spiritual marriage the difference is as great as that which exists between two who are betrothed and two who can no longer be separated.[3]

3. I have already said[4] that even though these comparisons are used, because there are no others better suited to our purpose, it should be understood that in this state there is no more thought of the body than if the soul were not in it, but one's thought is only of the spirit. In the spiritual marriage, there is still much less remembrance of the body because this secret union takes place in the very interior center of the soul, which must be where God Himself is, and in my opinion there is no need of any door for Him to enter. I say there is no need of any door because everything that has been said up until now seems to take place by means of the senses and faculties, and this appearance of the humanity of the Lord must also.[5] But that which comes to pass in the union of the spiritual marriage is very different. The Lord appears in this center of the soul, not in an imaginative vision but in an intellectual one, although more delicate than those mentioned,[6] as He appeared to the apostles without entering through the door when He said to them *pax vobis*.[7] What

---

2. The one referred to in IC 7.1.6–7.

3. Teresa first wrote: "between two who have consummated marriage." She then changed it to the present reading.

4. In IC 5.4.3.

5. See IC 7.2.1; ST 31.

6. See IC 6.8.

7. Jn 20:19–21. See IC 5.1.12.

God communicates here to the soul in an instant is a secret so great and a favor so sublime—and the delight the soul experiences so extreme—that I don't know what to compare it to. I can say only that the Lord wishes to reveal for that moment, in a more sublime manner than through any spiritual vision or taste, the glory of heaven. One can say no more—insofar as can be understood—than that the soul, I mean the spirit, is made one with God. For since His Majesty is also spirit, He has wished to show His love for us by giving some persons understanding of the point to which this love reaches so that we might praise His grandeur. For He has desired to be so joined with the creature that, just as those who are married cannot be separated,[8] He doesn't want to be separated from the soul.

4. The spiritual betrothal is different, for the two often separate. And the union is also different because, even though it is the joining of two things into one, in the end the two can be separated and each remains by itself. We observe this ordinarily, for the favor of union with the Lord passes quickly, and afterward the soul remains without that company; I mean, without awareness of it. In this other favor from the Lord, no. The soul always remains with its God in that center. Let us say that the union is like the joining of two wax candles to such an extent that the flame coming from them is but one, or that the wick, the flame, and the wax are all one. But afterward one candle can be easily separated from the other and there are two candles; the same holds for the wick. In the spiritual marriage the union is like what we have when rain falls from the sky into a river or fount; all is water, for

---

8. Again she changed what she had previously written, "those who have consummated marriage," to the present reading.

the rain that fell from heaven cannot be divided or separated from the water of the river. Or it is like what we have when a little stream enters the sea; there is no means of separating the two. Or, like the bright light entering a room through two different windows; although the streams of light are separate when entering the room, they become one.

5. Perhaps this is what St. Paul means in saying *He that is joined or united to the Lord becomes one spirit with him,*[9] and is referring to this sovereign marriage, presupposing that His Majesty has brought the soul to it through union. And he also says: *For me to live is Christ, and to die is gain.*[10] The soul as well, I think, can say these words now because this state is the place where the little butterfly we mentioned[11] dies, and with the greatest joy because its life is now Christ.

6. And that its life is Christ is understood better, with the passing of time, by the effects this life has. Through some secret aspirations the soul understands clearly that it is God who gives life to our soul. These aspirations come very, very often in such a living way that they can in no way be doubted. The soul feels them very clearly even though they are indescribable. But the feeling is so powerful that sometimes the soul cannot avoid the loving expressions they cause, such as: O Life of my life! Sustenance that sustains me! and things of this sort. For from those divine breasts where it seems God is always sustaining the soul there flow streams of milk bringing comfort to all the people of the castle. It seems the Lord

9. 1 Cor 6:17. This text from St. Paul and the application were written between the lines. Teresa first wrote and then crossed out: ". . . we are made one spirit with God if we love Him; he doesn't say that we are joined with Him . . . but are made one spirit with Him."

10. Phil 1:21. Teresa cited the passage in her own form of Latin: *Mi bivere Cristus es mori lucrum.*

11. See IC 5.3, note 1.

desires that in some manner these others in the castle may enjoy the great deal the soul is enjoying and that from that full-flowing river, where this tiny fount is swallowed up, a spurt of that water will sometimes be directed toward the sustenance of those who in corporeal things must serve these two who are wed. Just as a distracted person would feel this water if he were suddenly bathed in it, and would be unable to avoid feeling it, so are these operations recognized, and even with greater certitude. For just as a great gush of water could not reach us if it didn't have a source, as I have said, so it is understood clearly that there is Someone in the interior depths who shoots these arrows and gives life to this life, and that there is a Sun in the interior of the soul from which a brilliant light proceeds and is sent to the faculties. The soul, as I have said,[12] does not move from that center nor is its peace lost; for the very One who gave peace to the apostles when they were together[13] can give it to the soul.

7. It has occurred to me that this greeting of the Lord must have amounted to much more than is apparent from its sound. So, too, with the Lord's words to the glorious Magdalene that she go in peace.[14] Since His words are effected in us as deeds, they must have worked in such a manner in those souls already disposed that everything corporeal in the soul was taken away and it was left in pure spirit. Thus the soul could be joined in this heavenly union with the uncreated Spirit. For it is very certain that in emptying ourselves of all that is creature and detaching ourselves from it for the love of God, the same Lord will fill us with

---

12. In IC 7.2.4.
13. Jn 20:19–21.
14. Lk 7:50.

Himself. And thus, while Jesus our Lord was once praying for His apostles—I don't remember where—He said that they were one with the Father and with Him, just as Jesus Christ our Lord is in the Father and the Father is in Him.[15] I don't know what greater love there can be than this. And all of us are included here, for His Majesty said: *I ask not only for them but for all those who also will believe in me*; and He says: *I am in them.*[16]

8. Oh, God help me, how true these words are! And how well they are understood by the soul who is in this prayer and sees for itself. How well we would all understand them if it were not for our own fault, since the words of Jesus Christ, our King and Lord, cannot fail.[17] But since we fail by not disposing ourselves and turning away from all that can hinder this light, we do not see ourselves in this mirror that we contemplate, where our image is engraved.

9. Well, to return to what we were saying.[18] The Lord puts the soul in this dwelling of His, which is the center of the soul itself. They say that the empyreal heaven where the Lord is does not move as do the other heavens; similarly, it seems, in the soul that enters here there are none of those movements that usually take place in the faculties and the imagination and do harm to the soul, nor do these stirrings take away its peace.

It seems I'm saying that when the soul reaches this state in which God grants it this favor, it is sure of its salvation and safe from falling again. I do not say such a thing, and

---

15. Jn 17:21.
16. Jn 17:20, 23.
17. Allusion to Lk 21:33.
18. In IC 7.2.3.

wherever I so speak that it seems the soul is secure, this should be taken to mean as long as the divine Majesty keeps it in His hand and it does not offend Him. At least I know certainly that the soul doesn't consider itself safe even though it sees itself in this state and the state has lasted for some years. But it goes about with much greater fear than before, guarding itself from any small offense against God and with the strongest desires to serve Him, as will be said further on,[19] and with habitual pain and confusion at seeing the little it can do and the great deal to which it is obliged. This pain is no small cross but a very great penance. For when this soul does penance, the delight will be greater in the measure that the penance is greater. The true penance comes when God takes away the soul's health and strength for doing penance. Even though I have mentioned elsewhere[20] the great pain this lack causes, the pain is much more intense here. All these things must come to the soul from its roots, from where it is planted. The tree that is beside the running water is fresher and gives more fruit. What is there, then, to marvel at in the desires this soul has since its true spirit has become one with the heavenly water we mentioned?[21]

10. Now then, to return to what I was saying,[22] it should not be thought that the faculties, senses, and passions are always in this peace; the soul is, yes. But in those other dwelling places, times of war, trial, and fatigue are never lacking; however, they are such that they do not take the soul from its place and its peace; that is, as a rule.

---

19. In IC 7.3.3, 6; 7.4.2.
20. Probably in IC 5.2.7–11.
21. In IC 7.2.4; see also 4.2.2–4.
22. In IC 7.2.9.

This center of our soul, or this spirit, is something so difficult to explain, and even believe in, that I think, sisters, I'll not give you the temptation to disbelieve what I say, for I do not know how to explain this center. That there are trials and sufferings and that at the same time the soul is in peace is a difficult thing to explain. I want to make one or more comparisons for you. Please God, I may be saying something through them; but if not, I know that I'm speaking the truth in what I say.

11. The King is in His palace and there are many wars in His kingdom and many painful things going on, but not on that account does he fail to be at his post. So here, even though in those other dwelling places there is much tumult and there are many poisonous creatures and the noise is heard, no one enters that center dwelling place and makes the soul leave. Nor do the things the soul hears make it leave; even though they cause it some pain, the suffering is not such as to disturb it and take away its peace. The passions are now conquered and have a fear of entering the center because they would go away from there more subdued.

Our entire body may ache; but if the head is sound, the head will not ache just because the body aches.

I am laughing to myself over these comparisons for they do not satisfy me, but I don't know any others. You may think what you want; what I have said is true.

THE DIFFERENCE BETWEEN SPIRITUAL
UNION AND SPIRITUAL MARRIAGE:
HERE THE BUTTERFLY DIES

7.2.1–3 Teresa begins explaining the difference between spiritual union and spiritual marriage, emphasizing that the effects of the two are very different. She notes that the favor of spiritual marriage, as great as it is, does not come to its perfect fullness in this life; the blessing can be lost if we withdraw from God.

7.2.4 Teresa uses some comparisons to help her readers understand that the union of spiritual marriage is so complete that the soul becomes one with God, while the union of spiritual betrothal passes quickly. Spiritual betrothal is like the joining of two candles; the flame becomes one but becomes two again when the candles are separated. Spiritual marriage is like rain that falls into a river or a stream that flows into the sea; the waters are then one, and inseparable.

7.2.5 Teresa thinks that St. Paul must have experienced the same thing she experienced (union of spiritual marriage). She says, with St. Paul, that the soul's life is now Christ.

7.2.6–8 Teresa describes in more detail the experience and effects of the union of spiritual marriage. She proposes that her description of this union has a scriptural basis, or more specifically, a Christological basis. Jesus says of believers, "I am in them." She laments that we do not better dispose ourselves to receive God's favors.

7.2.9–11 Teresa tries to explain how, although the soul feels peace, the faculties, senses, and passions are not always in the same peace. Exterior disturbances, however, do not as a rule disturb the soul. She repeats, as in paragraph 1 of this chapter, that the soul who experiences the spiritual marriage does not feel sure of salvation, nor is it permanently safe from falling again. Instead the soul feels increased care in serving God and guarding against offending him. She concludes by repeating that the soul in the center dwelling place is well protected by God and remains in peace.

Interpretive Notes

Teresa continues to treat of sanctity, which is the theme of this section of the seventh dwelling places. She does this not so much from the viewpoint of the human virtues, but from a theological perspective: the mystery of God in the human being.

She has dealt with the mystery of the Trinity (the indwelling) in the first chapter. Now, in this second chapter, Teresa focuses on the mystery of Christ in this highest phase of her spiritual life in which she experiences manifestly that "Christ is living in her." The mystery of this experience is profound. Doesn't the Christian life consist merely in a relationship with or the following or imitation of Christ? But here we have a compenetration of two lives, that of Christ and that of our own. This comes about not through empathy, but through a mysterious union of the lives of both persons.

But what is really surprising here is that the autobiographical testimony of Paul becomes autobiographical for Teresa as well. She maintains this definition of her Christian existence from her first autobiographical writing to the last pages of her *Interior Castle*: "For in writing this it seems to me that with Your favor and through Your mercy I can say what St.

Paul said, although not with such perfection, that I no longer
live but that You, my Creator, live in me" (L 6.9). This early
experience of Teresa's and the manner in which she understood her own Christian life in Pauline terms comes to flower
again in the depths of the seventh dwelling places. But here
she brings together two planes: autobiographical and doctrinal. On the autobiographical plane, Teresa tells how in the
plenitude of her life (at age sixty-two), she experiences, but
now with greater penetration, what St. Paul says—that for
him, to live is Christ. On the doctrinal plane, she systematizes
the final stage of the Christian life as a union between two
lives, his and ours, to the point of their becoming one spirit
alone. These two Pauline expressions, "to live" and "one
spirit," summarize the content of this second chapter of the
seventh dwelling places.

    We must recall, before entering into the study of this
chapter, another chapter of Teresa's in this book (IC 6.7) in
which the humanity of Jesus Christ is strongly emphasized—
that is, his human history, his deeds and words as presented
in the gospels, including the bodily examples of his condition as human (suffering, humiliation, passion). These were
not something to be considered only by novices in the Christian life, as valuable only for the first stages of the way, but
are meant for all stages and extend to the entire Christian
life, for neophytes and the perfect. Jesus himself says that
he is the way. No one is dispensed from all reference to
the bodily condition of Christ, no matter how refined their
mystical experience may be. "We are not angels" (L 22.10),
Teresa used to insist. Nor are we dispensed from remembering the bodily existence of Jesus. This she affirms against
every temptation to understand Christianity in a Neoplatonic vein, as if the life of grace dealt only with our spirit.

She observes further: "Anyone whom the Lord places in the seventh dwelling place . . . walks continually in an admirable way with Christ, our Lord, in whom the divine and the human are joined and who is always that person's companion" (IC 6.7.9). In her dialogue with the theologians of her time, as must be the case in our present dialogues with secular philosophies or non-Christian religions, we must not place boundaries on the mediation of Christ in the Christian life. In fact, according to Teresa, the divine humanity of Jesus exercises his mediation in an admirable way when grace arrives at its fullness in the process of Christian growth.

Different from the everyday Christian who lives this incorporation into Christ in faith and hope with a limited experience of the mystery, Teresa gives witness to it through her own experience. She exercises her mission to be both a witness and a prophet. She begins this chapter giving testimony to how this came about as a culmination of her own biography. "With other persons the favor will be received in another form" (IC 7.2.1).

Teresa writes in her *Spiritual Testimonies*:

> While at the Incarnation in the second year that I was prioress, on the octave of the feast of St. Martin, when I was receiving Communion, Father John of the Cross who was giving me the Blessed Sacrament broke the host to provide for another sister. I thought . . . that he wanted to mortify me . . . His Majesty said to me: "Don't fear, daughter, for no one will be a party to separating you from Me," making me thereby understand that what just happened didn't matter. Then He appeared to me in an imaginative vision, as at other times, very interiorly, and He gave me His right hand and said: "Behold this nail; it is a sign you

will be My Bride from today on. Until now you have not merited this; from now on not only will you look after My honor as being the honor of your Creator, King, and God, but you will look after it as My true bride. My honor is yours, and yours Mine." This favor produced such an effect in me I couldn't contain myself, and I remained as though entranced. I asked the Lord either to raise me from my lowliness or not grant such a favor; for it didn't seem to me my nature could bear it. (ST 31)

Now writing five years later, after this powerful experience that continued with varying degrees of intensity, Teresa began to understand better how this new manner of life fit into her Christian life as a whole. There was the first mystical grace that allowed her to become aware objectively of Christ in his own person. And as life went on for Teresa, she began to be aware of a new, purely spiritual and permanent perception of his presence in the innermost center of her soul.

And that its life is Christ is understood better, with the passing of time, by the effects this life has. Through some secret aspirations the soul understands clearly that it is God who gives life to our soul . . . But the feeling is so powerful that sometimes the soul cannot avoid the loving expressions they cause, such as: "O Life of my life! Sustenance that sustains me!" and things of this sort. (IC 7.2.6)

For Teresa now, Christ is the life of her soul, as he was for Paul. She is secretly convinced that her experience of this mystery coincides with that of Paul's. Another statement by Paul also became a part of Teresa's experience. It comes from 1 Corinthians 6:17: "But whoever is joined to the Lord becomes one spirit with him." What Teresa experienced was a union between spirit and spirit until she became one spirit with Christ the Lord. She has recourse to the distinction between the soul and the spirit. There in the center of the soul, the seat of the spirit, at a most profound psychological level, the human spirit is united with the divine spirit.

Teresa also keeps in mind other symbols and images used to explain her experience. Above all she recalls the symbol of marriage, which she used to structure the three last dwelling places. The symbol has its origins in the Bible and expressed well for Teresa the union between the soul and Christ. In these seventh dwelling places, she speaks of the spiritual marriage between Christ and the soul. For her, Christian holiness does not consist in an ethical fact of personal perfection; rather, it has as its characteristic the trait of an intimate living together of two persons: Christ and the human person. It is the holiness of Christ that floods the soul, and "there is no more thought of the body than if the soul were not in it, but one's thought is only of the spirit. . . . this secret union takes place in the very interior center of the soul, which must be where God Himself is, and in my opinion there is no need of any door for Him to enter" (IC 7.2.3).

Two other biblical images that Teresa makes use of to explain this experience of union in which the two become one are fire and water. The spiritual betrothal is like the fire joining together into one flame from two lit wax candles. But the candles can be separated. When rain, however, falls from the sky into a sea, all is water and cannot be separated, but the rain becomes one with the water in the sea, as happens here between the soul and Christ.

In her *Life*, when Teresa begins to experience visions of Christ, she speaks of him as being beside her. "It seemed to me that Jesus Christ was always present at my side" (L 27.2).

Now, in this final stage, the experiences of Christ are not of him at her side but within her, in the deepest center of her being. It seems that she is saying that when one reaches this state, it is safe from falling again. But she doesn't say this. The soul "goes about with much greater fear than before . . . and with strongest desires to serve Him. . . . and with habitual pain and confusion at seeing the little it can do and the great deal to which it is obliged" (IC 7.2.9).

Questions for Discussion

1. Do all receive this favor of spiritual marriage in the same way as Teresa did?
2. Where does this spiritual marriage take place?
3. How does it differ from the spiritual betrothal?
4. Are there any scriptural texts that give support to this event?
5. Is the soul in the spiritual marriage sure of its salvation?

CHAPTER 3

Deals with the wonderful effects of this prayer that was mentioned. It is necessary to pay attention and heed to these effects, for the difference between them and the previous ones is remarkable.

N ow, then, we are saying that this little butterfly has already died, with supreme happiness for having found repose and because Christ lives in it. Let us see what life it lives, or how this life differs from the life it was living. For from the effects, we shall see if what was said is true. By what I can understand, these effects are the following.[1]

2. The first effect is a forgetfulness of self, for truly the soul, seemingly, no longer is, as was said.[2] Everything is such that this soul doesn't know or recall that there will be heaven or life or honor for it, because it employs all it has in procuring the honor of God. It seems the words His Majesty spoke to her produced the deed in her. They were that she look after what is His and that He would look after what is hers.[3] Thus, the soul doesn't worry about all that can happen. It experiences strange forgetfulness, for, as I say, seemingly the soul no longer is or would want to be anything in anything, except when it understands that there can come from itself something by which the

---

1. Teresa numbers only the first two effects; the others are present in the midst of a series of digressions and commentary. Here is a list of these effects: First, forgetfulness of self (in 7.3.2); Second, desire to suffer (in 7.3.4); Third, deep interior joy in persecution (in 7.3.5); Fourth, desire to serve (in 7.3.6); Fifth, great detachment (in 7.3.8); Sixth, no fear of the devil's deceits (in 7.3.10); and finally, a recapitulation of all the effects (in 7.3.13).

2. In IC 7.2.4–5.

3. An allusion to the grace of spiritual marriage. See IC 7.2.1; ST 31.

glory and honor of God may increase even one degree. For this purpose the soul would very willingly lay down its life.

3. Don't think by this, daughters, that a person fails to remember to eat and sleep—doing so is no small torment— and to do all that he is obliged to in conformity with his state in life. We are speaking of interior matters, for there is little to say about exterior works. Rather, the soul's pain lies in seeing that what it can now do by its own efforts amounts to nothing. For no earthly thing would it fail to do all it can and understands to be for the service of our Lord.

4. The second effect is that the soul has a great desire to suffer, but not the kind of desire that disturbs it as previously. For the desire left in these souls that the will of God be done in them reaches such an extreme that they think everything His Majesty does is good. If He desires the soul to suffer, well and good; if not, it doesn't kill itself as it used to.

5. These souls also have a deep interior joy when they are persecuted, with much more peace than that mentioned, and without any hostile feelings toward those who do, or desire to do, them evil. On the contrary, such a soul gains a particular love for its persecutors, in such a way that if it sees these latter in some trial it feels compassion and would take on any burden to free them from their trial, and eagerly recommends them to God and would rejoice to lose the favors His Majesty grants it if He would bestow these same gifts on those others so that they wouldn't offend our Lord.

6. You have already seen the trials and afflictions these souls have experienced in order to die so as to enjoy our Lord.[4] What surprises me most of all now is that they have

---

4. She is referring to the experiences spoken of in the sixth dwelling place; see particularly IC 6.11.

just as great a desire to serve Him and that through them He be praised and that they may benefit some soul if they can. For not only do they not desire to die but they desire to live very many years suffering the greatest trials if through these they can help that the Lord be praised, even though in something very small. If they knew for certain that in leaving the body the soul would enjoy God, they wouldn't pay attention to that; nor do they think of the glory of the saints. They do not desire at that time to be in glory. Their glory lies in being able in some way to help the Crucified, especially when they see He is so offended and that few there are who, detached from everything else, really look after His honor.

7. It is true that sometimes these things are forgotten, and the loving desires to enjoy God and leave this exile return, especially when the soul sees how little it serves Him. But soon it turns and looks within itself and at how continually it experiences His presence, and with that it is content and offers His Majesty the desire to live as the most costly offering it can give Him.

It has no more fear of death than it would of a gentle rapture. The fact is that He who gave those desires that were so excessive a torment, now gives these others. May He be always blessed and praised.

8. The desires these souls have are no longer for consolations or spiritual delights, since the Lord Himself is present with these souls and it is His Majesty who now lives. Clearly, His life was nothing but a continual torment, and He makes ours the same; at least with the desires, for in other things He leads us as the weak, although souls share much in His fortitude when He sees they have need of it.

There is great detachment from everything and a desire to be always either alone or occupied in something that will benefit some soul. There are no interior trials or feelings of dryness, but the soul lives with a remembrance and tender love of our Lord. It would never want to go without praising Him. When it becomes distracted the Lord Himself awakens it in the manner mentioned,[5] for one sees most clearly that that impulse, or I don't know what to call the feeling, proceeds from the interior depths of the soul, as was said of the impulses in the previous dwelling place.[6] Here, in this dwelling place, these impulses are experienced most gently, but they do not proceed from the mind or the memory, nor do they come from anything that would make one think the soul did something on its own. This experience is an ordinary and frequent one, for it has been observed carefully. Just as a fire does not shoot its flames downward but upward, however great a fire is enkindled, so one experiences here that this interior movement proceeds from the center of the soul and awakens the faculties.

9. Certainly, if there were no other gain in this way of prayer except to understand the particular care God has in communicating with us and beseeching us to remain with Him—for this experience doesn't seem to be anything else— it seems to me that all the trials endured for the sake of enjoying these touches of His love, so gentle and penetrating, would be well worthwhile.

This you will have experienced, sisters. For I think that when one has reached the prayer of union the Lord goes about with this concern if we do not grow negligent in keeping His commandments. When this impulse comes to you, remember that it comes from this interior dwelling place where God is in our soul, and praise Him very much. For certainly that note

5. In IC 6.2.
6. In IC 6.2.1; 6.11.2.

or letter is His, written with intense love and in such a way that He wants you alone to understand it and what He asks of you in it. By no means should you fail to respond to His Majesty, even though you may be externally occupied or in conversation with some persons. For it will often happen that our Lord will want to grant you this secret favor in public, and it is very easy—since the response is interior—to do what I'm saying and make an act of love, or say what St. Paul said: *Lord, what will You have me do?*[7] In many ways He will teach you there what will be pleasing to Him and the acceptable time. I think it is understood that He hears us, and this touch, which is so delicate, almost always disposes the soul to be able to do what was said with a resolute will.

10. The difference in this dwelling place is the one mentioned:[8] There are almost never any experiences of dryness or interior disturbance of the kind that were present at times in all the other dwelling places, but the soul is almost always in quiet. There is no fear that this sublime favor can be counterfeited by the devil, but the soul is wholly sure that the favor comes from God; for, as I have said,[9] the faculties and senses have nothing to do with what goes on in this dwelling place. His Majesty reveals Himself to the soul and brings it to Himself in that place where, in my opinion, the devil will not dare enter, nor will the Lord allow him to enter. Nor does the Lord in all the favors He grants the soul here, as I have said,[10] receive any assistance from the soul itself, except what it has already done in surrendering itself totally to God.

---

7. Acts 9:6.
8. In IC 7.3.8.
9. In IC 7.2.3, 10.
10. In IC 7.2.5–6, 9.

11. Every way in which the Lord helps the soul here, and all He teaches it, [takes place with such quiet and so noiselessly] that, seemingly to me, the work resembles the building of Solomon's temple where no sound was heard.[11] So in this temple of God, in this His dwelling place, He alone and the soul rejoice together in the deepest silence. There is no reason for the intellect to stir or seek anything, for the Lord who created it wishes to give it repose here and that through a small crevice it might observe what is taking place. At times this sight is lost and the other faculties do not allow the intellect to look, but this happens for only a very short time. In my opinion, the faculties are not lost here;[12] they do not work, but remain as though in amazement.

12. I am amazed as well to see that when the soul arrives here all raptures are taken away. Only once in a while are they experienced and then without those transports and that flight of the spirit. They happen very rarely and almost never in public as they very often did before. Nor do the great occasions of devotion cause the soul concern as previously. Nor, if souls in this dwelling place see a devout image or hear a sermon—previously it was almost as though they didn't hear it—or music, are they worried as was the poor little butterfly that went about so apprehensive that everything frightened it and made it fly. Now the reason could be that in this dwelling place either the soul has found its repose, or has seen so much that nothing frightens it, or that it doesn't feel that solitude it did before since it enjoys such company. In sum, sisters, I don't know what the cause may be. For when the Lord begins

---

11. 1 Kings 6:7.

12. In Teresa's terminology "not lost" is the equivalent of not being enraptured. In this dwelling place the faculties remain in amazement but not ecstatically suspended.

to show what there is in this dwelling place and to bring the soul there, this great weakness is taken away. The weakness was a severe trial for the soul and previously was not taken away. Perhaps the reason is that the Lord has now fortified, enlarged, and made the soul capable. Or it could be that His Majesty wished to make known publicly that which He did with these souls in secret for certain reasons He knows, for His judgments are beyond all that we can imagine here below.

13. These effects, along with all the other good ones from the degrees of prayer we mentioned, are given by God when He brings the soul to Himself with this kiss sought by the bride,[13] for I think this petition is here granted. Here an abundance of water is given to this deer that was wounded. Here one delights in God's tabernacle. Here the dove Noah sent out to see if the storm was over finds the olive branch as a sign of firm ground discovered amid the floods and tempests of this world. O Jesus! Who would know the many things there must be in Scripture to explain this peace of soul! My God, since You see how important it is for us, grant that Christians will seek it; and in Your mercy do not take it away from those to whom You have given it. For, in the end, people must always live with fear until You give them true peace and bring them there where that peace will be unending. I say "true peace," not because this peace is not true but because the first war could return if we were to withdraw from God.

14. But what will these souls feel on seeing that they could lack so great a blessing? Seeing this makes them proceed more carefully and seek to draw strength from their weakness so as not to abandon through their own fault any

---

13. Allusion to Song 1:2; there follows a series of biblical allusions to: Ps 42:2; Rev 21:3; Gen 8:8–12.

opportunity to please God more. The more favored they are by His Majesty the more they are afraid and fearful of themselves. And since through His grandeurs they have come to a greater knowledge of their own miseries, and their sins become more serious to them, they often go about like the publican[14] not daring to raise their eyes. At other times they go about desiring to die so as to be safe; although, with the love they have, soon they again want to live in order to serve Him, as we said.[15] And in everything concerning themselves they trust in His mercy. Sometimes the many favors make them feel more annihilated, for they fear that just as a ship too heavily laden sinks to the bottom they will go down too.

15. I tell you, sisters, that the cross is not wanting but it doesn't disquiet or make them lose peace. For the storms, like a wave, pass quickly. And the fair weather returns, because the presence of the Lord they experience makes them soon forget everything. May He be ever blessed and praised by all His creatures, amen.

---

14. Allusion to Lk 18:13.
15. In IC 7.3.6.

THE WONDERFUL EFFECTS
OF THIS PRAYER

7.3.1 Teresa introduces chapter 3 of the seventh dwelling places by saying it deals with the wonderful effects of this prayer (the prayer of spiritual marriage). She intends to demonstrate the truth of her assertion that the soul in the union of spiritual marriage lives a different life—a new life in Christ and of Christ in it. To do so, she will write about the effects of the union.

7.3.2–3 Teresa says that the first effect is forgetfulness of self, and gives examples. She emphasizes that the forgetfulness of self is not of a sort that would let a person forget to eat and sleep, or to meet all obligations. The soul suffers from seeing how little it can do by its own efforts.

7.3.4 The second effect of this prayer is that the soul has a great desire to suffer, but it has an even greater desire for the will of God to be done.

7.3.5–7 These souls experience joy when they are persecuted, and they are able to obey the gospel command to love their persecutors. The former desire to die (so as to enjoy our Lord) gives way to an equally great desire to serve him in every possible way, and without thought of any reward.

Teresa does amend this description of selfless desire for suffering, saying that there are times when loving desires to enjoy God and leave this exile return. When the soul looks within, however, and at how continually it experiences God's presence, the desires to live and serve him return.

7.3.8–9 Teresa continues to explain that these souls no longer desire consolations, since the Lord himself is present in them; it is Christ who now lives. Teresa characterizes these souls as detached, loving solitude (when not working to benefit others), and inspired from within to praise and love. Teresa cautions that it is very important to respond with love and gratitude to these secret, inner inspirations, and to take care in keeping the Lord's commandments.

7.3.10–11 Teresa returns to the description (begun in no. 8 of this chapter) of how the union in spiritual marriage in the seventh dwelling places differs from experiences in the other dwelling places. Here there are no experiences of dryness or inner disturbance. The soul is almost always in quiet, free of fears that this favor could be counterfeited by the devil. The soul is well protected. Its only role is to surrender itself totally to God. God and the soul rejoice together in his dwelling place in deepest silence. The intellect isn't needed and can only glimpse, as through a small crevice, the way the Lord teaches and helps the soul.

7.3.12–15 The soul here seldom experiences raptures, but it is strengthened and experiences peace. Teresa uses words and examples from Scripture to try to convey the great blessings and delights of this dwelling place. She reminds us that even this deep peace cannot be considered permanent in this life. We must take care not to lose it through our own fault by withdrawing from God. Souls in this dwelling place have an increased awareness of their sins and failings, and fear their own weakness; but in everything they trust in God's mercy. Teresa says that here the cross is not lacking, but it doesn't make souls lose peace. The presence of the Lord that they experience makes them soon forget their fears. This is the peace of Christ.

Interpretive Notes

"Now, then, we are saying that this little butterfly has already died . . . Christ lives in it." So Teresa begins this chapter of the seventh dwelling places. The butterfly, we recall, was the new self, freed from the restraints of the cocoon. The soul of this new self had flown gracefully and freely about in the fifth and sixth dwelling places. Now in these seventh dwelling places, the initial metamorphosis of the silkworm into the butterfly undergoes another radical change. Teresa refers to this with two key words: death (it dies with supreme happiness) and life (Christ lives in it). This final detail serves to connect with what was said in the previous chapter: that its life is now Christ.

The triptych is now completed in which Teresa analyzes the final situation of the Christian who has reached all fullness in Christ. The state of fullness began with the Trinitarian fact of the indwelling (7.1); it followed with the full insertion into the Christological mystery (7.2); and, lowering our sights, we come to the human element: how the interior life is lived and how the Christian lives who is blessed by the Trinity and by Christ in such fullness (7.3).

We know from other sources of the human drama taking place around Teresa while she is writing these pages. Yet there is not the slightest echo of this messy situation that she was involved in at the time in what she describes in these final pages of her book. She writes not of the exterior world in which she is entangled but of the interior world in which she now lives. She is writing these final chapters of her *Interior Castle* in the winter of 1577 in her cell at St. Joseph's in Ávila. At the other side of the city, St. John of the Cross, who serves as confessor to the nuns at the monastery of the

Incarnation, is taken prisoner. Many of the nuns there, going against orders, had elected Teresa prioress, for which they were immediately excommunicated. St. Teresa lives their experience intensely. Many of the excommunicated nuns had proceeded with recourse to the court in Madrid. These very disturbing events culminated in the arrest of St. John of the Cross, who was thought to have been backing the "disobedient" nuns who voted for Teresa.

But all these events which oppress Teresa on the outside receive not even the slightest reference in this book she is now composing. It seems as though a great wall has gone up, separating what is happening outside her from what is happening within in these seventh dwelling places. Interiorly she experiences much peace and a particular love for her persecutors and, in fact, she eagerly recommends them to God. She has just as great a desire now to live and serve him as she did before to die, and even to suffer many years and even the greatest trials if through them she can be helped to praise the Lord. She has no more fear of death than of a gentle rapture.

If a theologian of her time, such as Báñez or Gracián, had taken up this question Teresa deals with in this chapter, they would probably have formulated the question in this way: in what does perfection consist, and how does the Christian in this state behave? They would no doubt have answered according to the three traditional stages of the spiritual life: beginners, proficients, and the perfect. Teresa is familiar with these categories, but she does not follow them. For her, the talent of a soul who has reached this stage of the Christian life is the result of the work of the Blessed Trinity who dwells within, as well as of the Humanity of Christ that sanctifies it. The final stage consists of the highest stage of relationship of a human being with God in Christ.

To explain, she divides the text of her chapter in two: first, the new manner of life lived by the Christian who has arrived here (the psychological and ethical aspect); second, the special care God takes in communicating with the soul (the theological aspect). In the first half of the text (7.3.1–8), she deals with the first aspect, and in the second half of the text (7.3.9–15), she deals with the second. She does so with her typical freedom of exposition to which she is accustomed, not adhering rigidly to any pattern.

First of all, there is a forgetfulness of self, "for truly the soul, seemingly, no longer is" (7.3.2). There is no longer any touch of egoism. All it cares about is the honor and glory of God. As for its desires, it longs to suffer so as to be more like Christ. But this desire is held in check and surpassed by the desire that God's will be done in its own life. All the past afflictions and trials it suffered so as to die and enjoy God are now transformed into desires just as great to serve him.

In its theological life, it experiences the particular care God has in communicating with it and beseeching it to remain with him. This communication comes about through touches of love, so gentle and penetrating that all the trials suffered are made well worthwhile. This concern of God, if we do not grow negligent in keeping his commandments, begins when the sisters have reached the prayer of union, which, Teresa says in her *Foundations*, most of the nuns reach (F 4.8). This impulse of love comes from the interior dwelling place, where God is, in our soul. It's like a letter written by him with intense love and in such a way that he wants the receivers alone to understand it and what he asks them in it. It is not only in the quiet of prayer that the Lord communes with the soul in this way, but in the midst of its external activities. And it is very easy for the soul to respond with an act of love or by saying with St. Paul, "Lord what will you have me to do?" (Acts 9:6).

Finally, in this dwelling place there are almost no experiences of dryness or loss of peace, but the soul is almost always in quiet. God reveals himself to the soul and brings it into this dwelling place, where the devil, in Teresa's opinion, "will not dare enter." "Who would know," Teresa asks, "the many things there must be in Scripture to explain this peace of the soul?" (7.3.13). But in the end people must always fear until the Lord gives them the "true peace" of heaven, because the first war could return if we were to withdraw from God. So we must always proceed carefully and seek to draw strength from our weakness so as not to abandon any opportunity to please God more. The more favored we are by God, the more we are fearful of ourselves, and go about like the publican, not daring to raise our eyes and ask for his mercy.

Questions for Discussion

1. What is the meaning of the symbolism of the butterfly that now dies?

2. What are some characteristics of the soul in this dwelling place?

3. What is God's concern after the soul has reached the prayer of union?

4. In what way do God and the soul rejoice together in this dwelling place?

5. Do they still experience raptures and do they feel like saints?

6. Are there any more trials or sufferings in its life once the soul has reached this stage?

CHAPTER 4

Concludes by explaining what she thinks our Lord's purpose is in granting such great favors to the soul and how it is necessary that Martha and Mary join together. This chapter is very beneficial.

You must not think, sisters, that the effects I mentioned[1] are always present in these souls. Hence where I remember, I say "ordinarily." For sometimes our Lord leaves these individuals in their natural state, and then it seems all the poisonous creatures from the outskirts and other dwelling places of this castle band together to take revenge for the time they were unable to have these souls under their control.

2. True, this natural state lasts only a short while, a day at most or a little more. And in this great disturbance, usually occasioned by some event, the soul's gain through the good company it is in becomes manifest. For the Lord gives the soul great stability and good resolutions not to deviate from His service in anything. But it seems this determination increases, and these souls do not deviate through even a very slight first movement. As I say this disturbance is rare, but our Lord does not want the soul to forget its being, so that, for one thing, it might always be humble; for another, that it might better understand the tremendous favor it receives, what it owes His Majesty, and that it might praise Him.

3. Nor should it pass through your minds that, since these souls have such determination and strong desires not to commit any imperfection for anything on earth, they fail to

---

1. In IC 7.3.2–10.

commit many imperfections, and even sins. Advertently, no; for the Lord must give souls such as these very particular help against such a thing. I mean venial sins, for from what these souls can understand they are free from mortal sins, although not immune. That they might have some sins they don't know about is no small torment to them. They also suffer torment in seeing souls go astray. Even though in some way they have great hope that they themselves will not be among these souls, they cannot help but fear when they recall some of those persons Scripture mentions who, it seems, were favored by the Lord, like Solomon, who communed so much with His Majesty, as I have said.[2] The one among you who feels safest should fear more, for *blessed is the man who fears the Lord*,[3] says David. May His Majesty protect us always. To beseech Him that we not offend Him is the greatest security we can have. May He be praised forever, amen.

4. It will be good, sisters, to tell you the reason the Lord grants so many favors in this world. Although, if you have paid attention, you will have understood this in learning of their effects, I want to tell you again here lest someone think that the reason is solely for the sake of giving delight to these souls; that thought would be a serious error. His Majesty couldn't grant us a greater favor than to give us a life that would be an imitation of the life His beloved Son lived. Thus I hold for certain that these favors are meant to fortify our weakness, as I have said here at times,[4] that we may be able to imitate Him in His great sufferings.

5. We have always seen that these who were closer to Christ our Lord were those with the greatest trials. Let us

---

2. 1 Kings 11 [3 Kings 11]. See IC 3.1.1–4.

3. Ps 112:1.

4. In IC 6.9.16–17; see also IC 7.1.7.

look at what His glorious mother suffered and the glorious apostles. How do you think St. Paul could have suffered such very great trials? Through him we can see the effects visions and contemplation produce when from our Lord, and not from the imagination or the devil's deceit. Did St. Paul by chance hide himself in the enjoyment of these delights and not engage in anything else? You already see that he didn't have a day of rest, from what we can understand, and neither did he have any rest at night since it was then that he earned his livelihood.[5] I like very much the account about St. Peter fleeing from prison and how our Lord appeared to him and told him, "I am on my way to Rome to be crucified again." We never recite the office of this feast, where this account is, that I don't find particular consolation.[6] How did this favor from the Lord impress St. Peter or what did he do? He went straight to his death. And it was no small mercy from the Lord that Peter found someone to provide him with death.

6. O my sisters! How forgetful this soul, in which the Lord dwells in so particular a way, should be of its own rest, how little it should care for its honor, and how far it should be from wanting esteem in anything! For if it is with Him very much, as is right, it should think little about itself. All its concern is taken up with how to please Him more and how or where it will show Him the love it bears Him. This is the reason for prayer, my daughters, the purpose of this spiritual marriage: the birth always of good works, good works.

7. This is the true sign of a thing, or favor, being from God, as I have already told you.[7] It benefits me little to be

---

5. Allusion to 1 Thess 2:9.

6. This *quo vadis* legend appeared in the Carmelite breviary, used in the time of St. Teresa, on the feast of St. Peter (June 29).

7. In IC 5.3.11.

alone making acts of devotion to our Lord, proposing and promising to do wonders in His service, if I then go away and when the occasion offers itself do everything the opposite. I was wrong in saying it profits little, for everything having to do with God profits a great deal. And even though we are weak and do not carry out these resolutions afterward, sometimes His Majesty will give us the power to do so, even though, perhaps, doing so is burdensome to us, as is often true. Since He sees that a soul is very fainthearted, He gives it a severe trial, truly against its will, and brings this soul out of the trial with profit. Afterward, since the soul understands this, the fear lessens and one can offer oneself more willingly to Him. I meant "it benefits me little" in comparison with how much greater the benefit is when our deeds conform with what we say in prayer; what cannot be done all at once can be done little by little. Let the soul bend its will if it wishes that prayer be beneficial to it, for within the corners of these little monasteries there will not be lacking many occasions for you to do so.[8]

8. Keep in mind that I could not exaggerate the importance of this. Fix your eyes on the Crucified and everything will become small for you. If His Majesty showed us His love by means of such works and frightful torments, how is it you want to please Him only with words? Do you know what it means to be truly spiritual? It means becoming the slaves of God. Marked with His brand, which is that of the cross, spiritual persons, because now they have given Him their liberty, can be sold by Him as slaves of everyone, as He

---

8. There is a Teresian proverb that reads in Spanish: *La virtud se ha de ver no en los rincones sino en medio de las ocasiones*. It might go like this in English: "Look for virtue not in corners away from the din but right amidst the occasions of sin." See F 5.15.

was. He doesn't thereby do them any harm or grant them a small favor. And if souls aren't determined about becoming His slaves, let them be convinced that they are not making much progress, for this whole building, as I have said,[9] has humility as its foundation. If humility is not genuinely present, for your own sake the Lord will not construct a high building lest that building fall to the ground. Thus, sisters, that you might build on good foundations, strive to be the least and the slaves of all, looking at how or where you can please and serve them. What you do in this matter you do more for yourself than for them and lay stones so firmly that the castle will not fall.

9. I repeat, it is necessary that your foundation consist of more than prayer and contemplation. If you do not strive for the virtues and practice them, you will always be dwarfs. And, please God, it will be only a matter of not growing, for you already know that whoever does not increase decreases. I hold that love, where present, cannot possibly be content with remaining always the same.

10. It will seem to you that I am speaking with those who are beginning and that after this beginner's stage souls can rest. I have already told you[10] that the calm these souls have interiorly is for the sake of their having much less calm exteriorly and much less desire to have exterior calm. What, do you think, is the reason for those inspirations (or to put it better, aspirations) I mentioned, and those messages the soul sends from the interior center to the people at the top of the castle and to the dwelling places outside the center where it is? Is it so that those outside might fall asleep? No, absolutely not!

---

9. In IC 1.2.8–9, 11, 13.

10. In IC 7.3.3, 5–8.

That the faculties, senses, and all the corporeal will not be idle, the soul wages more war from the center than it did when it was outside suffering with them, for then it didn't understand the tremendous gain trials bring. Perhaps they were the means by which God brought it to the center, and the company it has gives it much greater strength than ever. For if here below, as David says, in the company of the saints we will become saints,[11] there is no reason to doubt that, being united with the Strong One through so sovereign a union of spirit with spirit, fortitude will cling to such a soul; and so we shall understand what fortitude the saints had for suffering and dying.

11. It is very certain that from that fortitude which clings to it there the soul assists all those who are in the castle, and even the body itself which often, seemingly, does not feel the strength. But the soul is fortified by the strength it has from drinking wine in this wine cellar, where its Spouse has brought it[12] and from where He doesn't allow it to leave; and strength flows back to the weak body, just as food placed in the stomach strengthens the head and the whole body. Thus the soul has its share of misfortune while it lives. However much it does, the interior strength increases and this, too, the war that it waged; for everything seems like a trifle to it. The great penances that many saints—especially the glorious Magdalene, who had always been surrounded by so much luxury—performed must have come from this center. Also that hunger which our Father Elijah had for the honor of his God[13] and which St. Dominic and St. Francis had so as to

---

11. Ps 18:26.

12. Allusion to Song 2:4.

13. Allusion to 1 Kings 19:10 [3 Kings 19:10]. The shield of the Carmelite order takes as its motto the prophet Elijah's words: *Zelo zelatus sum pro Domino Deo exercituum* [With zeal have I been zealous for the Lord God of hosts].

draw souls to praise God. I tell you, though they were forgetful of themselves, their suffering must have been great.

12. This is what I want us to strive for, my sisters; and
let us desire and be occupied in prayer not for the sake of
our enjoyment but so as to have this strength to serve. Let's
refuse to take an unfamiliar path, for we shall get lost at the
most opportune time. It would indeed be novel to think of
having these favors from God through a path other than the
one He took and the one followed by all His saints. May
the thought never enter our minds. Believe me, Martha and
Mary must join together in order to show hospitality to the
Lord and have Him always present and not host Him badly
by failing to give Him something to eat. How would Mary,
always seated at His feet, provide Him with food if her sister
did not help her? His food is that in every way possible we
draw souls that they may be saved and praise Him always.[14]

13. You will make two objections: one, that He said that
Mary had chosen the better part. The answer is that she had
already performed the task of Martha, pleasing the Lord by
washing His feet and drying them them her hair.[15] Do you
think it would be a small mortification for a woman of nobility
like her to wander through these streets (and perhaps alone
because her fervent love made her unaware of what she was
doing) and enter a house she had never entered before and
afterward suffer the criticism of the Pharisee and the very many
other things she must have suffered? The people saw a woman
like her change so much—and, as we know, she was among
such malicious people—and they saw her friendship with the
Lord whom they vehemently abhorred, and that she wanted

---

14. Lk 10:38–42.
15. Allusion to Lk 7:37–38.

to become a saint since obviously she would have changed her manner of dress and everything else. All of that was enough to cause them to comment on the life she had formerly lived. If nowadays there is so much gossip against persons who are not so notorious, what would have been said then? I tell you, sisters, the better part came after many trials and much mortification, for even if there were no other trial than to see His Majesty abhorred, that would be an intolerable one. Moreover, the many trials that afterward she suffered at the death of the Lord and in the years that she subsequently lived in His absence must have been a terrible torment. You see she wasn't always in the delight of contemplation at the feet of the Lord.

14. The other objection you will make is that you are unable to bring souls to God, that you do not have the means; that you would do it willingly but that not being teachers or preachers, as were the apostles, you do not know how. This objection I have answered at times in writing, but I don't know if I did so in this *Castle*.[16] Yet since the matter is something I believe is passing through your minds on account of the desires God gives you I will not fail to respond here. I already told you elsewhere[17] that sometimes the devil gives us great desires so that we will avoid setting ourselves to the task at hand, serving our Lord in possible things, and instead be content with having desired the impossible. Apart from the fact that by prayer you will be helping greatly, you need not be desiring to benefit the whole world but must concentrate on those who are in your company, and thus your deed will be greater since you are more obliged toward them. Do you think such deep humility, your mortification, service of

16. See W 1–3; SS 7.
17. In IC 3.2.13.

all and great charity toward them, and love of the Lord is of little benefit? [This fire of love in you enkindles their souls, and with every other virtue you will be always awakening them] Such service will not be small but very great and very pleasing to the Lord. By what you do in deed—that which you can—His Majesty will understand that you would do much more. Thus He will give you the reward He would if you had gained many souls for Him.

15. You will say that such service does not convert souls because all the sisters you deal with are already good. Who has appointed you judge in this matter? The better they are the more pleasing their praises will be to our Lord and the more their prayer will profit their neighbor.

In sum, sisters, what I conclude with is that we shouldn't build castles in the air. [The Lord doesn't look so much at the greatness of our works as at the love with which they are done.] And if we do what we can, His Majesty will enable us each day to do more and more, provided that we do not quickly tire. But during the little while this life lasts—and [perhaps it will last a shorter time than each one thinks]—let us offer the Lord interiorly and exteriorly the sacrifice we can. His Majesty will join it with that which He offered on the cross to the Father for us. Thus even though our works are small they will have the value our love for Him would have merited had they been great.

16. May it please His Majesty, my sisters and daughters, that we all reach that place where we may ever praise Him. Through the merits of His Son who lives and reigns forever and ever, may He give me the grace to carry out something of what I tell you, amen. For I tell you that my confusion is great, and thus I ask you through the same Lord that in your prayers you do not forget this poor wretch.

OUR LORD'S PURPOSE
IN GRANTING FAVORS

7.4.1–2 Teresa explains that the effects of the union of spiritual marriage mentioned earlier are not continuously present in these souls, although ordinarily they are present. Sometimes the Lord leaves these individuals in their natural state for a day or so, and they experience disturbance. When this disturbance happens, the soul appreciates how much it gains from the Lord's presence because the soul has great stability and great determination not to deviate from the Lord's service in any way. Although such disturbance is rare, the Lord does not want the soul to forget what it is of itself so that it might always be humble; and also understand the tremendous favor it receives, what it owes His Majesty, and that it might praise him.

7.4.3 Teresa wants us to understand that these souls are not free from imperfections and venial sins, but she emphasizes that these sins and imperfections are not deliberate. From what they can understand, because of the Lord's help, they are free from mortal sins, though not immune. These souls suffer torment at the thought that they may have some sins that they don't know about and also at seeing other souls go astray. We should never be complacent; our greatest security is to pray always that we do not offend the Lord.

7.4.4–6 Teresa believes that God's greatest favor is to give us a life that would be an imitation of Christ's life. She writes that God's favors and delights are meant to fortify our weakness so that we might imitate Christ in his great sufferings. She points out that those closest to Christ were those with the greatest trials. The willingness to suffer is evidence that visions and contemplation are genuinely from God and not from the imagination or the devil's deceit. The reason for prayer and the purpose of the spiritual marriage are the birth of good works.

7.4.7–8 Here Teresa seems to be thinking through the topic as she writes. At first, she says there is little benefit in making acts of devotion and proposing to do wonders in God's service if we do not carry out our resolutions. But on second thought, she does see some benefit, for everything having to do with God profits a great deal. God may assist the fainthearted by giving them trials against their will and bringing them out with profit. Teresa concludes her musings with the thought that resolutions not acted on, though not worthless, benefit little in comparison to the instances when our deeds conform with what we say in prayer. She offers encouragement—what cannot be done all at once can be done little by little. Continuing to stress the importance of deeds, Teresa uses a metaphor from her cultural period. She says to be truly spiritual means to become slaves of God, marked with his brand, which is that of the cross. Continuing with this metaphor, she says that God can then sell such souls to be slaves of everyone, as he was. She urges the sisters to be slaves of all, seeking to please and serve others. The foundation of the spiritual life must consist of more than prayer and contemplation. We must strive for and practice the virtues; otherwise, instead of gaining in the spiritual life, we will decrease.

7.4.10–13 Teresa continues the theme of service. Interior calm inspires the soul to less calm exteriorly. The soul now wages war from the center, and the faculties, senses, and all the corporeal will not be idle. She thinks it may be that earlier trials, even though less understood then as being beneficial in the spiritual life, were the means by which God brought the soul to the center. Here the company it has within (the Holy Trinity) gives it greater strength than ever. She tells the sisters to pray, not for their own enjoyment, but so as to have the strength to serve. Returning to her earlier example of Mary and Martha, Teresa argues strongly that both prayer and service are essential.

7.4.14–16 Teresa answers objections that apparently at times have been made by the sisters, who said that they had the desire, but not the means, to bring souls to God. First, she cautions that sometimes the devil gives us great desires so that we will neglect the tasks at hand. Instead of doing the possible, we will be content with desiring the impossible. By prayer we can help greatly. We should not think that we have to help the whole world; instead we should concentrate on those around us. By practicing humility, mortification, service, and charity to all, along with love of the Lord, we can please the Lord and enkindle the fire of love in the souls of others. The Lord does not look so much at the greatness of our works as at the love with which they are done. Even though our works are small, they will have the value our love for him would have merited had they been great.

Interpretive Notes

At times the Lord may leave the soul in its natural state and it seems that all the poisonous creatures from the other dwelling places attack it and take revenge on it. But this does not last long, a day at most. For the Lord has given the soul great stability and good resolutions not to deviate from his service in anything. These souls would not deviate so much as by an imperfection for anything on earth, although they are never secure against sinning. They may commit many imperfections and even venial sins, but not advertently. And now that the soul is a saint in the Church, it exists so as to serve its neighbor, like Jesus Christ, who was the servant *par excellence* of God and of his brothers and sisters. This fourth and last chapter completes Teresa's picture of Christian holiness marked by the indwelling of the Trinity, the full incorporation into Christ, human fullness and maturity, and now, ecclesiologically, the charism granted to a person, in union with God, for the building up the mystical body of Christ here on earth in the service of humankind.

When Teresa had finished writing her work and was reading it over, she divided it into chapters and summed up in chapter headings what was contained in each one. This reading was done quickly, just to get the idea of where a good place to break a chapter would be. She wrote the chapter headings on separate paper, which was quickly lost. Fortunately, before this happened, one of Teresa's great admirers, Father Gracián, had made a copy of these chapter headings, which have thus reached us. She introduces this last chapter with the words: "Concludes by explaining what she thinks our Lord's purpose is in granting such great favors to the soul and how it is necessary that Martha and Mary join together. This chapter is very beneficial" (7.4 chapter heading).

What happened to Teresa did not come about just at random; there is a silent aim of God. At the end of the journey, amidst all the great favors (graces of God) received by a human soul, the result is patently what God was aiming after in giving it life, inserting his own life. We are not dealing with a planned course of action, but with a mysterious, guiding presence of the divine in the depths of the human being.

In the end, in the last dwelling place of the *Interior Castle*, Martha and Mary work together. The two sisters in Bethany are two symbols of human life. Martha stands for action, Mary for contemplation. It is necessary that the two work together because in the first through the sixth dwelling places there is a disassociation between the two. To reach a union between these two, Martha and Mary, action and contemplation, the two levels have to be united in the same person.

"This chapter is very beneficial" is what Teresa says about this chapter. Teresa is convinced of the realism and practicality of what she writes. This sense of the practicality of what she is saying extends through her entire work. "What does it mean to be truly spiritual?" This is a question Teresa asks in the middle of the chapter. And she gives us an excellent answer, especially for anyone who thinks it consists in being filled with delightful favors from God:

> It means becoming the slaves of God. Marked with His brand, which is that of the cross, spiritual persons, because now they have given Him their liberty, can be sold by Him as slaves of everyone, as He was. . . . And if souls aren't determined about becoming His slaves, let them be convinced that they are not making much progress. (7.4.8)

The calm they have interiorly, she says, is for the sake of their having much less calm exteriorly. Thus, at the end of these dwelling places, Teresa gives two important counsels: "Fix your eyes on the Crucified" (7.4.8), so as to be totally configured with him. The second counsel follows: having fortitude in bearing your daily cross and unconditional service of your brothers and sisters.

Why did God lead us through these six dwelling places to this seventh? Why did he gradually open the doors to these dwelling places which contained so many graces, purifications, trials, and favors? Why does God intervene in this way in the affairs of humans, even bringing them to the final dwelling place of the castle? Is it for the sake of just giving delight to our souls? No. "His Majesty couldn't grant us a greater favor than to give us a life that would be an imitation of the life His beloved Son lived. Thus I hold for certain that these favors are meant to fortify our weakness . . . that we may be able to imitate Him in His great sufferings" (7.4.4).

What is the reason for prayer, the purpose of the spiritual marriage? Teresa gives us a surprising answer now at the end of her book. "This is the reason for prayer, my daughters, the purpose of this spiritual marriage: the birth always of good works, good works." But Teresa also knows the complaints of her sisters. How could they engage in good works? They were women living a strictly cloistered life as she had established it for them. How could they bring souls to God? They didn't preach; they didn't teach or work in hospitals. Teresa's answer is plain and encouraging: first of all, your prayer will be doing a great deal; you need not take on the whole world, but concentrate on those who are in your company, and your deed will be greater because you are more obliged to them. And the fire of love in you will enkindle their souls, and you will be always awakening them with all your virtues. Such service will not be small but very pleasing to the Lord. By what you do in deed—that which you can— His Majesty will give you the reward he would if you had gained many souls for him. The Lord doesn't look so much at the greatness of our works as at the love with which they are done (7.4.14–15).

Three hundred years after Teresa wrote these words, another Carmelite nun in a convent in Lisieux, France, experienced great desires for God and wrote in her *Story of a Soul* a similar message:

You know, Mother, I have always wanted to be a saint. Alas! I have always noticed that when I compared myself to the saints, there is between them and me the same difference that exists between a mountain whose summit is lost in the clouds and the obscure grain of sand trampled underfoot by passersby. Instead of becoming discouraged, I said to myself: God cannot inspire unrealizable desires. I can, then, in spite of my littleness aspire to holiness. It is impossible for me to grow up, and so I must bear with myself such as I am with all my imperfections. But I want to seek out a means of going to heaven by a little way, a way that is very straight, very short, and totally new.

We are living now in an age of inventions, and we no longer have to take the trouble of climbing stairs, for, in the homes of the rich, an elevator has replaced these very successfully. I wanted to find an elevator which would raise me to Jesus, for I am too small to climb the rough stairway of perfection. I searched, then, in the Scriptures for some sign of this elevator, the object of my desires, and I read these words coming from the mouth of Eternal Wisdom: '*Whoever is a LITTLE ONE, let him come to me.*' And so I succeeded. I felt I had found what I was looking for. But wanting to know, O my God, what You would do to *the very little one* who answered Your call, I continued my search and this is what I discovered: '*As one whom a mother caresses, so will I comfort you; you shall be carried at the breasts, and upon the knees they shall caress you.*'

Ah! Never did words more tender and more melodious come to give joy to my soul. The elevator which must raise me to heaven is Your arms, O Jesus! I had to remain *little* and become this more and more. (Thérèse of Lisieux, *Story of a Soul*, Manuscript C, Chapter 10)

And in another place in this same book we read:

What this child asks for is Love. She knows only one thing: to love You, O Jesus. Astounding works are forbidden to her; she cannot preach the Gospel, shed her blood; but what does it matter since her brothers work in her stead and she, a little child, stays very close to the throne of the king and queen. She loves in her brothers' place while they do the fighting. But how will she prove her love since love is proved by works? Well, the little child *will strew flowers,* she will perfume the royal throne with their *sweet scents,* and she will sing in her silvery tones the canticle of *Love. . . .* O Jesus, of what use will my flowers be to You? Ah! know very well that this fragrant shower, these fragile, worthless petals, these songs of love from the littlest of hearts will charm You. Yes, these nothings will please You. They will bring a smile to the Church Triumphant. She will gather up my flowers unpetalled *through love* and have them pass through Your own divine hands, O Jesus. And this Church in heaven, desirous of playing with her little child, will cast these flowers, which are now infinitely valuable because of your divine touch, upon the Church Suffering in order to extinguish its flames and upon the Church Militant in order to gain the victory for it! (St. Thérèse of Lisieux, *Story of a Soul*, Manuscript B, Chapter 9)

Questions for Discussion

1. Do souls in the seventh dwelling places commit sins or imperfections?

2. Do they fear sin?

3. Why does God give us favors?

4. Why should we persevere in prayer?

5. What is Jesus's food?

6. How will His Majesty understand that you would do much more?

7. Does he look for the greatness of our works? What does he look for?

Epilogue[1]

Although when I began writing this book I am sending you I did so with the aversion I mentioned in the beginning,[2] now that I am finished I admit the work has brought me much happiness, and I consider the labor, though I confess it was small, well spent. Considering the strict enclosure and the few things you have for your entertainment, my sisters, and that your buildings are not always as large as would be fitting for your monasteries, I think it will be a consolation for you to delight in this interior castle since without permission from the prioress you can enter and take a walk through it at any time.

2. True, you will not be able to enter all the dwelling places through your own efforts, even though these efforts may seem to you great, unless the Lord of the castle Himself brings you there. Hence I advise you to use no force if you meet with any resistance, for you will thereby anger Him in such a way that He will never allow you to enter them. He is very fond of humility. By considering that you do not deserve even to enter the third you will more quickly win the favor to reach the fifth. And you will be able to serve Him from there in such a way, continuing to walk through them often,

---

1. This epilogue was sent in the form of a letter along with the original manuscript to the Discalced Carmelite nuns in Seville.

2. In IC Prol 1.

that He will bring you into the very dwelling place He has for Himself. You need never leave this latter dwelling place unless called by the prioress, whose will this great Lord desires that you comply with as much as if it were His own. Even though you are frequently outside through her command, you will always find the door open when you return. Once you get used to enjoying this castle, you will find rest in all things, even those involving much labor, for you will have the hope of returning to the castle which no one can take from you.

3. Although no more than seven dwelling places were discussed, in each of these there are many others, below and above and to the sides, with lovely gardens and fountains and labyrinths, such delightful things that you would want to be dissolved in praises of the great God who created the soul in His own image and likeness.[3] If you find something good in the way I have explained this to you, believe that indeed His Majesty said it so as to make you happy; the bad that you might find is said by me.

4. Through the strong desire I have to play some part in helping you serve my God and Lord, I ask that each time you read this work you, in my name, praise His Majesty fervently and ask for the increase of His Church and for light for the Lutherans. As for me, ask Him to pardon my sins and deliver me from purgatory, for perhaps by the mercy of God I will be there when this is given you to read—if it may be seen by you after having been examined by learned men. If anything is erroneous it is so because I didn't know otherwise; and I submit in everything to what the holy Roman Catholic Church holds, for in this Church I live, declare my faith, and promise to live and die.

---

3. Allusion to Gen 1:26. See IC 1.1.1.

May God our Lord be forever praised and blessed, amen, amen.

5. This writing was finished in the monastery of St. Joseph of Ávila in the year 1577, the eve before the feast of St. Andrew,[4] for the glory of God who lives and reigns forever and ever, amen.

---

4. That is, November 29, 1577, close to six months after she had begun writing on June 2nd of that same year. See IC Prol 3.

IN EACH DWELLING PLACE
THERE ARE MANY OTHER
DELIGHTFUL THINGS

Epil 1 Here Teresa herself seems to be writing from the innermost of the dwelling places of the castle. She says that the work has brought her much happiness. She says, "I think it will be a consolation for you to delight in this interior castle since without permission from the prioress you can enter and take a walk through it at any time."

Epil 2 She conveys a deep peace, clearly writing from her own intimate experience of God. She repeats a frequent theme that humility is of great importance to growth in prayer. She repeats also that some rooms of the castle cannot be entered through one's own efforts. Instead the Lord of the castle himself must bring us there. She holds out to her readers a great hope, the hope that we also may draw ever nearer to the Lord in the castle, which she says no one can take from us.

Epil 3 Teresa adds that even though she has discussed only seven dwelling places, in each of these there are many other delightful things such that in experiencing them we would always be praising God, who created the soul in his own image and likeness.

Epil 4–5 Teresa concludes by expressing the strong desire that she can play some part in helping those who read her words to serve the Lord. She asks her readers to pray for her and again expresses her submission to the church. Her final words are a prayer that God may be praised and blessed forever and a statement that she has completed her task for the glory of God.

Interpretive Notes

When Teresa finished her work, she composed a separate letter for readers. Gracián and other initial readers of the book placed it at the beginning of the book, but it has become the epilogue of the book. It served, in the beginning, as a letter of introduction for the Carmelite nuns of St. Joseph's in Ávila, Medina del Campo, Toledo, and so on. In open dialogue with them and their daily lives, the manuscript has come down to all of us, readers of today, spiritual readers, literary, secular readers, or even those dialoging with Teresa from other religions, in all languages, including Arabic, Korean, and Japanese.

What is this interior space, open to each one of us, so mysterious and promising? In the end what interests us is not that we have knowledge of it, but that we enter it: "it will be a consolation for you to delight in this interior castle" (Epil 1).

In the life of the soul there are the dwelling places that it can enter through its own effort; but the other and better ones are a pure gift of God, which he gives us freely and out of love. Without regard to these, he is a great friend of humility. Love does not buy; it receives.

The interior life is an adventure in rock climbing, with a route that is secret and one that is always going further and further with no other goal than God himself, who created us in his own image and likeness. But entering deeper into the castle does not necessarily mean going further away from the outside world, nor withdrawing one's hands from the service of our neighbor.

Before placing the date on this letter and before submitting everything to what the holy Roman Catholic Church holds, she asks her readers for three things:

1. To praise His Majesty very much.
2. To pray for the increase of his church and light for the Lutherans (whom she mistakenly identified with all Protestants of her day; see below.)
3. To pray that God might pardon her sins and free her from purgatory.

The work was finished on the vigil of St. Andrew, November 29, 1577. Teresa was sixty-three years old and had four more years to live.

In asking for prayers for the Lutherans, Teresa shows her lack of knowledge of the facts. Some harsh rumors had reached Teresa about what were actually the religious wars between Catholics and the Huguenots in France. "Lutherans" was a general term in Teresa's vocabulary for Protestants in general. In Teresa's mind the Roman Catholic Church and Christianity were identical. Any attack against the church by "Lutherans" was like an attack against Christ. But Teresa's solution was not war but prayer. Today we must pray and work for unity within the Christian Church. The decree on Christian unity of the Second Vatican Council (*Unitatis Redintegratio*) writes this:

> For although the Catholic Church has been endowed with all divinely revealed truth and with all means of grace, yet its members fail to live by them with all the fervor that they should. As a result the radiance of the Church's face shines less brightly in the eyes of our separated brothers and sisters and of the world at large, and the growth of

God's kingdom is retarded. Every Catholic must therefore aim at Christian perfection and each according to his station play his part, that the Church, which bears in her own body the humility and dying of Jesus, may daily be purified and renewed, against the day when Christ will present her to himself in all her glory without spot or wrinkle. . . . On the other hand, Catholics must acknowledge and esteem the truly Christian endowments for our common heritage which are to be found among separated brethren. (UR 1.4)

Questions for Discussion

1. Was Teresa inspired in the writing of this book?
2. Can we enjoy this castle about which Teresa wrote?
3. What must we do each time we read this book?
4. Who are the "Lutherans" for whom we should pray?
5. How has Teresa's writing inspired you in your spiritual life?

Glossary

Castle The *interior castle* is the image most developed by Teresa. It forms the basis of all her teaching in this book. She uses it to picture the entire spiritual process, serving as a means of explaining the structure of human persons (body, soul, and spirit), and their relationship with God, who is both transcendent and immanent. It serves as well to comment on the biblical text of the indwelling of God in the soul (Jn 14:23). Standing for the soul, or for the human person, the castle is separated from the world by a ditch and wall around it, with a vast interior and a vocation to transcendence because of its being ultimately a dwelling place for God.

Other Important Images in the Castle

The two water troughs filled with water in different ways
The water in one trough comes from a source far away. Great ingenuity is required to transport the water to fill this trough. The second trough, however, is situated at the water's source. The water wells up and spills into the trough, filling it effortlessly. The two ways of filling the troughs image the ascetical and mystical life. The ascetical requires work and effort along with God's grace. The mystical comes in a mysterious and gratuitous way from God.

The transformation of the silkworm into the butterfly
Teresa draws a comparison using the experience of being transformed from an ugly and fat silkworm into a beautiful

427

butterfly, flying about freely, capable of living now without touching the earth. Teresa thinks the life cycle of the silkworm provides a helpful parallel to spiritual transformation. The soul then works to do God's will by keeping his commandments, making use of the sacraments, reading good books, and prayer. It makes use of these means to overcome its sins and to live a true life in Christ until it is grown. While doing this, it is building the house wherein it will die. All of this we can do with the help of God's grace, like weaving the cocoon. The prayer of union is like the cocoon in which the silkworm is placed. Through this prayer the soul dies to itself and comes out of the "cocoon" transformed, like a little white butterfly. It is amazed by the effects of this prayer. Even though it has never been quieter or calmer in its life, it is now restless with love and flies about above the earth, for what it sees on earth displeases it.

Spousal and bridal love This image underlines and defines the relational character of the life of grace in which the soul enters a process of union with the Divine Persons, that union in which Christian holiness consists.

Leading to this holiness in the castle are seven dwelling places which represent the entire process of sanctification.

The first three dwelling places are ascetical. This means that through our own efforts we must turn gradually away from a worldly life and all its distractions outside the castle. We have to enter the castle through a personal relationship with God in prayer.

The fourth dwelling places are a mixture of the ascetical and the mystical life. The interior fountain springs up, the action of grace, through a sense of God's presence.

Quiet and peace in prayer is experienced passively, although intermittently. But during this quiet, love, and peace, one can also suffer from distractions and disturbances. So some effort is required to keep the attention fixed on God during this initial infused prayer.

The last three dwelling places are the dwelling places of mystical union. In the prayer of union, unlike the prayer of quiet, there are no distractions while the union lasts. During this time the soul neither sees, nor hears, nor understands, because "God so places Himself in the interior of that soul that when it returns to itself it can in no way doubt that it was in God and God was in it" (IC 5.1.9). The silkworm dies; the soul, like the butterfly, is reborn in Christ ("our life is Christ" [IC 5.2.4]). It is also a state of conformity with the will of God, manifested especially in the love of neighbor.

In the bridal imagery, this prayer of union is like the meetings in which the two get to know each other and find out if they are suited for marriage with each other. Their love can grow in intensity so that it has its repercussion on the body, and hence there are the experiences of ecstasy. Now the bridal image of betrothal comes into play. These experiences of ecstasy are accompanied by locutions and visions in which further loving knowledge of God's presence and mysteries are given. The butterfly restlessly flies about in love. A new manner of feeling and measuring past sins occurs. And Christ is present, "in whom the divine and the human are joined and who is always that person's companion" (IC 6.7.9).

Finally, the restless butterfly dies. In the prayer of union and ecstasy, the soul was brought into its deepest center, but it wasn't conscious during the union of where it was; now the scales fall from its eyes and it sees the mystery of God present in its deepest center. This mystery is that in God are three Persons—Father, Son, and Holy Spirit—who communicate with each other and with this soul. In the bridal image, "the mystical marriage" with Christ takes place in this deep center. We have in these seventh and final dwelling places a soul that is fully calm and at peace, always experiencing God's presence in its deepest center, fully inserted into the Christological and Trinitarian mysteries. It is, as well, fully inserted into the action of good works, experiencing "a hunger for the honor of God," "the hunger to bring souls to him," as did St. Dominic or St. Francis (IC 7.4.11).

Contemplation Teresa understands contemplation to be a form of prayer consisting of the experience of the presence and love of God. This prayer cannot be obtained through our own efforts. Contemplation is superior to types of prayer that we can obtain through our own efforts, such as discursive meditation or active recollection.

Faith Faith is a gift God pours into the intellect, by which we know and give assent to all that God revealed to us about himself and about the means by which we can reach him. Through trials that test and perfect it, faith brings the soul into an ever-deeper likeness to Christ.

Imagination The power to picture things to ourselves from the sense or material world around us. It is of special use in discursive meditation, in which a person pictures scenes from the life of Christ to help draw out some knowledge and love of the Lord. Teresa, when she wrote her *Life* and *The Way of Perfection*, was not clear on the difference between the imagination and the intellect, and often confuses their activities. For example, in her descriptions of the prayer of quiet in *The Way of Perfection*, she speaks of the bother the wandering of the intellect caused her during the time of this prayer. She later understood that it was not the intellect but the imagination that was causing the trouble.

Intellect A spiritual power by which we come to know truths, either by the gift of faith or by drawing them out from other truths we already know from our experience of the senses. For Teresa the intellect is the thinking power; it is also called "reason" because it is the power by which we draw conclusions from other judgments. It is the power by which we ask questions about the what, the why, and the wherefore of things. "God didn't give me talent for discursive thought or for a profitable use of the imagination" (L 4.7). Teresa did not think she had good reasoning powers or a good imagination by which she could practice discursive meditation.

Locutions Along with visions, they are the extraordinary mystical forms most frequent in Teresa's life. In a locution one hears or listens to what another says; there is, then, one who speaks and one who listens or hears. God speaks; Teresa listens or hears. Locutions are divided, according to Teresa, into bodily (formed in the external sense, as in the case of a person who hears with his ears); imaginative (formed in the internal sense of imagination, as in the case of a person who gradually composes); intellectual locutions, or purely spiritual (the words take place in the most intimate depths). The intellectual ones are the clearest of the locutions, so clear that the soul remembers every syllable. With these words there is often given much more to understand than is ever dreamed possible without words. But no matter where they are experienced, when they come from God, they first of all bear a great power and authority, for they then effect what they say. Secondly, when from God they also leave an effect of quiet and peace and the readiness to engage in the praises of God. Third, when from God they remain in the memory for a long time, and some are not forgotten.

In the beginning Teresa showed herself very fearful of these experiences but, with much caution, as time went on, she became more favorable toward this whole range of experiences, and thankful to God for them, recognizing in them their concrete sanctifying power, although they should never be desired.

Memory The power to recall past events and keep before our minds the things we have come to know in the past. With our memory we must therefore strive to keep before us the mysteries of the life of Jesus Christ. In the prayer of quiet, the memory would not want to be occupied with anything else than God. In the prayer of union, the memory and intellect seem to be asleep to the things of the world and to ourselves, or like one who has died to the things of the world so as to live more completely in God.

Powers or Faculties Teresa speaks often of the powers or faculties of the soul, but she is not at all clear on what they are. She learned about them vaguely through the books she read and through the confessors and learned men she consulted. These terms originated with the ancient and medieval philosophers. Observing the different forms of life activity, these philosophers deduced that since we can do certain things, we have distinguishable powers for such activities. The external and internal senses are means by which we function at the level of both sensory and material creation. We can easily conclude that since we are able to see, hear, smell, touch, and taste things from the world around us, we have the external sense powers for doing so. And since we can picture to ourselves things, such as a tree or a cat, from the world around us, we have internal sense powers or faculties for doing such things. We also have other faculties in order to deal with objects imperceptible to the senses, objects like animal, human, truth, goodness, beauty. For this work we have the spiritual faculty of intellect. Thus, we have external, internal, and spiritual faculties or powers by which we come to know in different ways the world around us.

Prayer For Teresa it was a loving personal relationship with the Lord. "Speak with Him as with a father, or a brother, or a lord, or as with a spouse; sometimes in one way, at other times in another" (W 28.3). A human-divine relationship within the mystery of faith, hope, and love. This leads to her famous definition: "For mental prayer in my opinion is nothing else than an intimate sharing between friends; it means taking time frequently to be alone with Him who we know loves us" (L 8.5). The definition is based on faith, on the conviction that God loves us, and this conviction is founded on the idea that God proposes himself to the one praying as a friend. This supposes the lowering of God in Christ to make this friendship possible—thus the importance of the humanity of Christ in our prayer. There are different kinds of prayer, and for Teresa they are as follows:

Ascetical prayer This is the prayer found in the first three dwelling places; it depends on human effort along with God's grace.

Mystical prayer This is the prayer found in the last four dwelling places. It is called by Teresa "supernatural prayer" because it is a gift of God and cannot be acquired through our own efforts.

Painful Prayer The soul is in total dryness; no consolation is admitted into its interior. It seems to it that God is far away and that it has never been mindful of him and never will be. Its prayer becomes a torment to it. It feels rejected by God and an unbearable interior oppression. Its intellect is so darkened that it becomes incapable of seeing the truth and believes whatever foolish things the imagination represents to it. Books are of no help because it doesn't understand what it reads; the intellect is incapable of understanding. The only remedy is to wait for the mercy of God.

Soul The spiritual component in the human person, the body being the material component. Supported by Pauline texts and the liturgy, Teresa speaks of the body as the prison of the soul and of the soul imprisoned in the body as long as this earthly condition endures: "our poor little imprisoned soul shares in the miseries of the body" (L 11.15). In her mystical life, Teresa experiences her own soul as the subject of all her experiences of Christ, of God, of the Trinity, of the church, as the container receiving all of these experiences, their carrier. In her openness to transcendence she experienced her soul as God's garden, a symbolism she developed in her *Life*. The soul is fertile land in hopes of water (or of grace or of prayer).

The idea that Teresa has of the soul does not proceed from a psychological approach but from a religious and metaphysical one. Only obliquely does she allude to its biological function of animating the body.

Spirit In the chapter heading of the first chapter of the seventh dwelling places, Teresa differentiates the spirit from the soul: "Interior things are seen in such a way that one understands with certitude that there is some kind of difference, a difference clearly recognized, between the soul and the spirit, even though they are both one." She has recourse to the biblical account of Martha and Mary. Martha, the soul, is occupied in living and doing. Mary, the spirit, is totally absorbed by the presence of God and orientated toward transcendence. Also in this context the image of the center reappears. The center of the soul, or the spirit, or the depth, or the very interior part, always coincide with the last dwelling places (the seventh) of the castle. The soul "is called to enter into its center as it is here in this dwelling place" (IC 7.1.5). "In the spiritual marriage, there is still much less remembrance of the body because this secret union takes place in the very interior center of the soul, which must be where God Himself is" (IC 7.2.3). Thus, the depth of the human soul, the spirit, and the relation between soul and spirit has a religious sense.

Supernatural Teresa uses this term rather than "mystical" to explain what God does in the soul or what we cannot achieve through our own efforts. She begins to explain supernatural experiences in the fourth dwelling places, and these experiences are very difficult for her to explain. Nonetheless Teresa does so very well, pointing out the different ways in which God works in the soul as it continues advancing through the remaining dwelling places. These experiences grow deeper and more varied, always increasing one's desire for God and to serve him through the love and service of others.

Visions Seeing is proper to the vision as hearing is proper to the locution. Visions are supernatural perceptions of objects naturally invisible, or not visible by human beings through any natural means. Teresa divides mystical visions into three general kinds: bodily, imaginative, and intellectual. These are according to the different levels of the human faculties: external sense faculties, internal sense faculties, and spiritual faculties. These three classes of mystical visions can be pure or mixed.

Bodily Visions Bodily visions are visions seen with the bodily eyes. Teresa says she never experienced any. But she did at times wish that she would have them so that she could tell her confessors that what she saw was with her bodily eyes.

Imaginative Visions They are seen with the eyes of the soul; that is, with the internal sense of imagination. In them there are present very concrete images.

Intellectual Visions In these we have the absence of any image, without seeing anything with the eyes of the body or with those of the soul. Thus they cannot be described, and Teresa tries hard to share with us something of the admirable reality of what she contemplates.

Mixed Visions Both the imaginative and the intellectual elements are present.

Visions of the Seventh Dwelling Place His Majesty communicates himself in other ways that are more sublime. In this seventh dwelling place, the soul sees and understands, although in a strange way. It sees through an admirable knowledge the Holy Trinity, all three Persons, in an intellectual vision, and these Persons never seem to leave it. It clearly perceives that they are within it, in the extreme interior, in some place very deep within itself. Why does God give these visions and other mystical favors? Teresa answers that God couldn't give us a greater favor than a life that would be an imitation of the life his beloved Son lived. "Thus I hold for certain that these favors are meant to fortify our weakness . . . that we may be able to imitate Him in His great sufferings" (IC 7.4.4).

Will The power to make choices, good or bad. The whole aim of the persons who are beginning prayer should be that they work with determination and with every possible effort to bring their will into conformity with God's will. What cannot be done all at once can be done little by little. The soul should bend its will if it wishes that prayer be beneficial to it.

Index

Note: page numbers in **bold** indicate study guide material

S

Sacrosanctum Concilium
(Constitution on the
Sacred Liturgy), **95**
sanctity, **366, 381**
second dwelling places
 biblical comparisons, **51**
 hearing the word of the
  Lord, 38–40, **47**
 need for conformity to
  God's will, 43–44, **48**
 overview, xxvii–xxviii
 prayer for souls facing
  temptation, 42
 tension between reason
  and faith, 40–42, **47–48**
 as a time of struggle,
  49–51, 64
 trust in God in the midst
  of failures, 44–45,
  48–49
Sega, Felipe, xx, **185**
self-knowledge, 23–27, **32,
 36, 64,** 161, **337**
Seneca, **173**
service, 200, 202, 401–409,
 410–417
seventh dwelling places
 overview, xxv–xxxviii
 peace of souls in, 392–
  394, **396, 400**
 revelation of the Trin-
  ity, 360–363, **365,
  367–371**
 spiritual marriage, 358–
  360, **364,** 372–379,

380–381, 385, 391–
392, **396**
spiritual marriage effects,
387–394, **395–400,**
401, **410**
suffering as preparation
 for entering, 346–347,
 352
visions of, 437
works as the purpose
 of spiritual marriage,
 401–409, **410–417**
shepherd's whistle, 111–112,
121
silkworm metaphor, xxxi–
xxxii, 146–152, **155–156,
158–159,** 161, 164, **185,**
397, 427–428
sin(s)
 battling against the evils
  of, **50–53**
 consequences of mortal,
  19–21, **31,** 33–35
 praying for those in mortal, 359, **364**
 suffering over one's, 281–
  283, **291, 294–296**
 torment of, 196–198,
  201–202
 venial, 401–402, **410,
  413**
 vigilance against, 55–56,
  62
sixth dwelling places
 awakening of the soul in,
  207–212, **213–214**

Biblical Index

About Us

ICS Publications, based in Washington, D.C., is the publishing house of the Institute of Carmelite Studies (ICS) and a ministry of the Discalced Carmelite Friars of the Washington Province (U.S.A.). The Institute of Carmelite Studies promotes research and publication in the field of Carmelite spirituality, especially about Carmelite saints and related topics. Its members are friars of the Washington Province.

Discalced Carmelites are a worldwide Roman Catholic religious order comprised of friars, nuns, and laity—men and women who are heirs to the teaching and way of life of Teresa of Ávila and John of the Cross, dedicated to contemplation and to ministry in the church and the world.

Information about their way of life is available through local diocesan vocation offices, or from the Discalced Carmelite Friars vocation directors at the following addresses:

Washington Province:
1525 Carmel Road, Hubertus, WI 53033

California-Arizona Province:
P.O. Box 3420, San Jose, CA 95156

Oklahoma Province:
5151 Marylake Drive, Little Rock, AR 72206

Visit our websites at:
www.icspublications.org   and   *http://ocdfriarsvocation.org*